Reinventing Bradford City

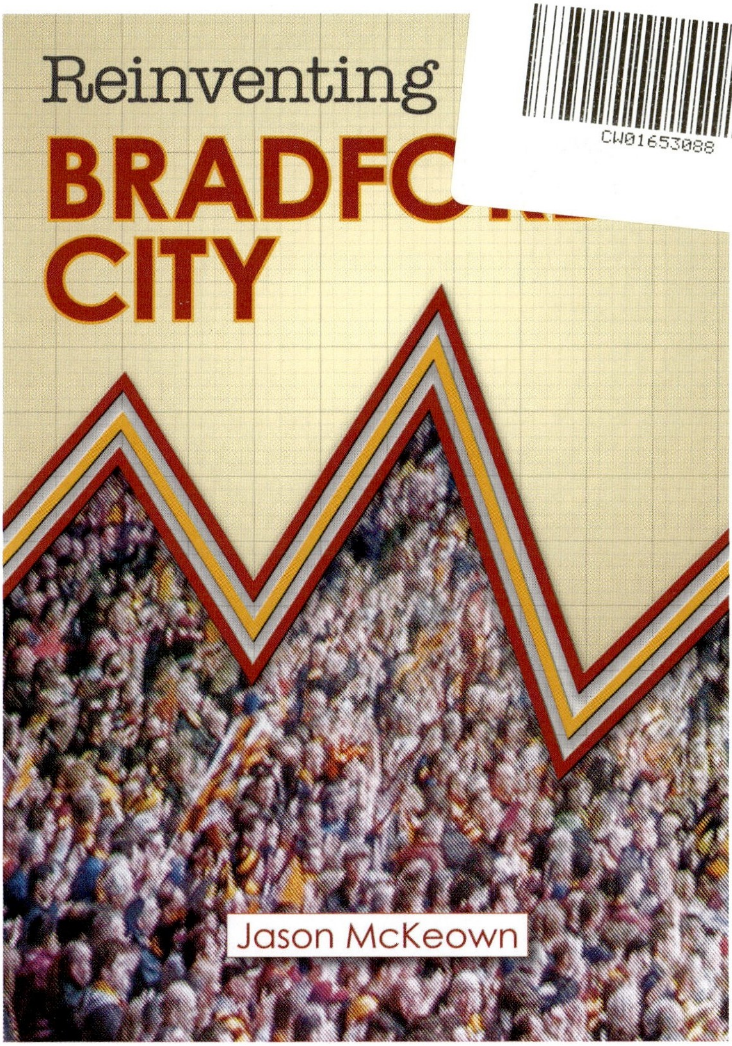

The extraordinary story of Bradford City's modern history
(1985-2016)

Jason McKeown

Cover design by John Ashton

Printed by Hart and Clough Limited, Cleckheaton West Yorkshire BD19 4TQ

A bantamspast publication

PO Box 307, Shipley BD18 9BT

www.bantamspast.co.uk

email: glorious1911@paraders.co.uk

ISBN 978-0-9566984-6-9

First printed 2016

We are grateful to BCAFC for permission to use the club crest in the design of the cover and for the co-operation in the production of this publication.

About the author

Jason McKeown is a content manager for a financial services company - a role that primarily involves working as a copywriter and includes writing for national newspapers.

After emerging from university in 2003 clutching a journalism degree, but with what he considers to have been a mediocre grade, Jason realised he needed to build up some genuine writing experience and so began contributing to the popular Bradford City website, Boyfrombrazil.co.uk (BfB). It helped him get a writing job in 2005, and he continued contributing to BfB until 2011, spending the last four years as co-editor.

In December 2011 Jason set up his own Bradford City website - widthofapost.com (WOAP). Through this he was able to report on Bradford City's incredible cup adventures in 2012/13 and 2014/15, as well as cover all angles of the club's re-emergence from the League Two doldrums. More than 50 people have also contributed articles for the site, and the daily readership has grown to between six and seven thousand people, with more than two million hits since launch. In 2013, WOAP beat heavy competition to win 'Best Established Blog' at the Football Blogging Awards and was a finalist again the year after. In 2015 WOAP was named amongst the top 50 UK football blogs by Futbol50.

Jason first attended a Bradford City match in November 1997 and has been a season ticket holder for the majority of the subsequent years. In 2011 he had a book published about his time following the club, titled "Paying on the Gate".

Jason lives in Skipton, North Yorkshire with his wife Rachel and daughter Georgina.

With thanks to...

First of all I have to thank John Dewhirst. John originally approached me with the idea of writing this book as part of his excellent new history revisited series on both Bradford City and football in Bradford. We spent the best part of a year bouncing ideas back and forth, and John has continued to provide support and feedback throughout the writing of the book. He is always honest, challenging and helpful – and I feel the quality of the book is a million times better for his input. Thank you also, John, for publishing it.

A massive thanks to all my family for their support and especially my wife Rachel and my daughter Georgina, who are both such huge inspirations every day. Rachel has been hugely supportive and patient with the hours I have spent writing the book. An especially memorable moment was when she entertained Georgina in a soft play centre for more than three hours, so that I could pop up the road and interview Stuart McCall. Sorry again that I took so long!

A big thanks to the photographers who have kindly let me use their work in the book free of charge. It is hugely appreciated that Paul Thompson, Charles Hague, Alex Dodd, Mike Holdsworth and Kieran Wilkinson have been so helpful, and I hope you enjoy their images as much as I do.

Thanks to Rick Cowling, Kieran Wilkinson, John Dewhirst and Adam Pickles for their assistance with the research. I'm also grateful to the staff at Bradford Library for letting me use their microfilm facilities to go through old editions of the Telegraph & Argus – their patience over my clumsy use of their equipment was especially appreciated.

I am hugely in debt to Nick Beanland for proof reading this book on my behalf. I owe you many pints of beer mate; just let me know when and where.

Thank you to the Width of a Post writing team, and especially Katie Whyatt, for manning the website whilst my focus was on this book. Thank you also to regular WOAP readers for their ongoing support which has helped me to grow as a writer

With extra special thanks to Ian Dennis, for writing the excellent foreword for this book.

Interviewees

Listed in alphabetical order, the following players, managers, directors, journalists and supporters were interviewed for this book and their views and opinions feature throughout.

This is their story, and I am very grateful to each and every one of them for allowing me to tell it.

Alex Scott, Andrew Davies, David Baldwin, David Markham, Dominic Newton-Collinge, Gareth Walker, James Hanson, James Mason, James Pieslak, Jamie Lawrence, Joanne Golton, John Dewhirst, Julian Rhodes, Katie Whyatt, Kieran Wilkinson, Lee Duxbury, Mark Bower, Mark Douglas, Mark Ellis, Michael Flynn, Michael Wood, Mike Harrison, Richard Wardell, Phil Parkinson, Simon Parker, Stuart McCall, Terry Dolan and Tom Fletcher.

About the photos in this book

The following photographers have very kindly allowed me to use some of their work within this book.

Paul Thompson

westyorkshireimages.photoshelter.com

paul@westyorkshireimages.co.uk

07791316627

Charles Hague

@cjhague24

07713274815

Alex Dodd

@alsdodd

07811606061

Mike Holdsworth

Kieran Wilkinson

Wembley, Sunday 24 February, 2013. *Image by Paul Thompson.*

Reinventing Bradford City

Written by Jason McKeown

Foreword by Ian Dennis

Image by Paul Thompson.

To Rachel and Georgina, and to our families – you mean everything to me.

Foreword

By Ian Dennis

I've experienced every emotion at Valley Parade. Laughter, tears, elation, despair and sadly, sheer horror.

Anybody who was present on the 11 May, 1985 will agree that is a day that will live with them forever.

A football stadium is always seen as "home" to its supporters, but Valley Parade will always carry extra spiritual significance.

Brought up in West Yorkshire, as a young boy it was only natural to watch your local club.

1981 was my first visit to Valley Parade for a "derby" against Doncaster Rovers. I think Bobby Campbell scored the only goal, but the game is a hazy memory. Instead, my recollections are of the aroma and atmosphere – the smell of tobacco and Bovril; a fight that broke out in the wooden stand behind two timid, 10 year old twins, watching two talented brothers for the opposition by the name of Snodin.

Aside from the visit of Oxford United in the early 80s I never physically sat in the old stand again.

Instead, the crumbling open ended Kop on the right of the divide, looking at the pitch, towards the front was my spot. The decaying terrace sank so low for such a small boy (pre puberty) that I was left with a ground level view.

I recall as the terrace bent round to join the Main Stand there was a gap in the mesh that enabled those small enough to "enter" the Paddock.

The frenzied activity always seemed a daunting place – I never did dare to venture, although on that fateful day in May I did break through the gap.

My family couldn't attend, so as a 13 year old boy I went alone with some lads from the village where I grew up. I remember the day vividly and with instructions to meet up after the match, I was left to my own devices.

I perched myself on top of the tea bar in the corner to witness the title presentation. I, along with a few others, would have stayed there for the match, until we were told to move because we were an obstruction.

There is no need to dwell what happened next – although, needless to say, nobody will ever forget those who perished.

Aside from witnessing that horrific event, Valley Parade is also where I gained valuable grounding.

As a teenager I had aspirations to become a football commentator, but it felt like a pipe dream – so imagine my delight when I was asked on "trial" to report for City Chat Line in 1989. Little did I realise it was the start of a life-changing experience.

What prompted it was a letter from John Motson, in 1988, which provided the inspiration.

Determination and enthusiasm were the two key attributes to succeed, and I've never forgotten it.

I also firmly believe that, regardless of what you want to achieve, they are qualities you require in abundance.

I bombarded every station in Yorkshire, desperate to gain work experience. Derm Tanner, a future Bradford City commentator, was Sports Editor at BBC Radio York, who was the exception of the many reject replies.

Little did I realise how much influence Derm was to have on my career, something for which I will always be grateful.

Derm had recommended me for a job at BBC Newcastle, where I later became Sports Editor. And he then enticed me to Leeds, which was a crucial step before I moved to BBC 5 Live in 2002.

I now travel and follow the fortunes of England, as well as Premier League matches each week for BBC 5 Live and, sometimes, Match of the Day. I'm privileged, I have my dream job – but I'm also aware there is life outside the top flight in England.

I'm fortunate to travel the world watching football and visiting some of the best stadiums, but nothing stirs the emotions like Valley Parade.

Ian Dennis is a commentator and Senior Football Reporter at BBC Radio 5 Live. He also commentates on Premier League games for BBC Match of the Day.

He has worked for the BBC full time since 1996 at BBC Radio Cleveland, former Sports Editor at BBC Radio Newcastle, then BBC Leeds before joining BBC Radio 5 Live in 2002. In addition to commentating and reporting on the Premier League and the England team, Ian has covered several World Cups, European Championship Finals and African Cup of Nations.

Contents

Reinventing Bradford City

At Valley Parade there is always a sense of perspective. Whilst Bradford City supporters would reject the old brush off that football is "only a game", everyone who walks through the turnstiles at Valley Parade knows that this sport is not a matter of life and death. When things go wrong on the pitch, such as a home defeat, a terrible goal is conceded or when a striker misses a sitter, it's never labelled a "disaster". At Bradford City there is a much deeper understanding of what the term "disaster" truly means.

On May 11, 1985, 11,076 people went to Valley Parade to watch the home team lift the Third Division championship trophy, prior to a home game against Lincoln City. 56 never returned. They lost their lives after a fire engulfed the main stand just before half time. More than 250 people were injured. Thousands of others took home with them mental scars that have influenced their lives for years to come. No one who was there that day will ever forget the terrible events they bore witness to. And no one connected with Bradford City will ever allow the tragedy to be forgotten.

The fire was caused by a build up of rubbish underneath a main stand that, with cruel irony, was due to be bulldozed over and rebuilt following the completion of this game. A cigarette was lit and accidentally dropped through a hole within the stand's wooden floorboards, igniting the fire below. It spread devastatingly quickly, and not everyone could get out of the stand fast enough to avoid its deadly effects. Access was difficult at both the back and the front of the stand. And fire doesn't wait around for people to orderly queue and get out of its path. There was no escape for many people. The scenes of chaos and tragedy were devastating. This was supposed to be one of the greatest days in the club's history. Instead, it proved to be its darkest.

The Valley Parade fire was an event that sent shockwaves not only around Bradford but across the country. The then-Prime Minister Margaret Thatcher made a visit to the site a few days later, before going to see many of the injured and burned, as they were treated at the Bradford Royal Infirmary. Stafford Heginbotham, the club's chairman, ensured that he and others attended every single funeral. It was of a little consolation, of course, but what happened at Valley Parade that day could just have easily occurred at any number of lower league grounds. In those days, football clubs were allowed to host matches in neglected and dilapidated stadiums. In truth, no one really saw them as a danger. The Valley Parade fire began to change that apathy; and when the Hillsborough disaster occurred four years later, football stadiums throughout the land would be transformed into safe environments.

Hillsborough was as much about human failings – most notably from the police – rather than an unfortunate accident. It was immediately followed by the unforgiveable cover up attempts and false newspaper headlines, which triggered a 23-year battle from the victims' families to uncover the truth and bring people to justice. In contrast, at Valley Parade there was only limited blame attributed, by some, towards the football club. Instead, the Bradford City community rallied around the families of the victims, and supported the physically and mentally injured. Football – only a game, of course – became a beacon of positivity to drag people through bleak times.

The Bradford City footballer Stuart McCall – whose own father was injured in the fire and spent weeks recovering at Pinderfields Hospital in Wakefield – recalled to me, "The aftermath was difficult for everybody. The supporters, the players, the staff, and the chairman. It was just horrendous for everyone. My dad was seriously burned and was at Pinderfields. I used to go and visit him every day and I got close to a few people who were also recovering with him. I used to go and take the trophy down and our medals. Even though football should be irrelevant, to a lot of people it wasn't. They just wanted to get back to watching City and especially watching them in the Second Division, as it was the first time we'd been in that league for a long time."

May 11, 1985 could conceivably have led to the extinction of Bradford City Football Club itself. The Bantams were, after all, left homeless due to the wreckage of the fire. But the club regrouped. The bond between the club and its public grew stronger following this incredibly difficult experience. Somehow, City and its community rebuilt. Newly promoted to the Second Division, the team continued to play football matches. McCall added, "I remember the first game after the fire, Carlisle away. We won 2-1. We stopped at a town on the way up pre-match, and it was just full of City tops everywhere. To win that game – that was for everyone who had been there that day. The first game back after the last game, to win at Carlisle how we did was really special."

Eighteen months were spent in exile at Odsal, before an emotional return to Valley Parade in December 1986. Life goes on, as the saying goes, although the loss of 54 Bradford City supporters and two Lincoln City fans has continued to be remembered. Every year, the final home game of the season includes a minute's silence to remember the 56. And at Bradford's Centenary Square, the date of May 11 is marked by an annual memorial service that is always well attended by people connected with the club, past and present. Always remember.

The terrible events of May 11, 1985 have left a major imprint on Bradford City. Things were and could never be the same again. And as the club and its fanbase attempted to put that awful afternoon behind them and recover, the beginnings of the modern history of Bradford City Football Club were formed.

And what a modern history it has been. For a club which had spent so much time, pre-1985, nestling in the bottom two divisions with very little happening season on season, the 30 years that followed the Valley Parade fire have been filled with drama. Incredible highs, and some dreadful lows. In modern times City have tasted the glamour of the top and the desolation of the bottom. It has rarely proven dull, that's for sure.

Three short years after the Valley Parade fire, City were on the brink of promotion to the top flight for the first time in 66 years. They couldn't take the opportunity, and fell into a decline of mediocrity that threatened to wipe away the spirit of the 80s. But then a chap named Geoffrey Richmond rocked up with big ambitions for the club, and within five years City had fulfilled his grand plan of making it to the top flight. The Premier League, as it had become, with a now-global audience, took the battling Bantams to their hearts, as they improbably avoided an instant relegation. Sadly, Richmond over-stretched the club with dire consequences, and within six years of losing their Premier League status the Bantams had fallen all the way to the bottom tier. During that bumpy decline, City endured the considerable headache of administration twice – prompting the very real possibility of the club folding. On the field it threatened to get worse as City diced with the prospect of yet another relegation and, with it, non-league football. But then a man named Phil Parkinson took charge of the playing side, revitalised the club and amazingly took the team all the way to a major cup final. He also got them promoted and engineered some more cup heroics two years later. Did you hear the one about a Premier League team that cost £200 million to construct, losing at home to the lowly Bantams – despite having a two-goal head start?

It has been an incredible ride, the three decades that followed May 11, 1985. So many great victories, great players, great goals, great occasions. They were punctured by awful defeats, dismal players, woeful City own goals, and dreadful moments. But even though there is a lot we supporters would change about the club's post-May 1985 modern history, if such a possibility existed, we'd probably leave them as they were if it meant trading in the amazing experiences we have enjoyed along the way. Bradford City is a special club. Every football club in the land would argue that they are special too, but the spirit fostered from 1985 has, in a positive way, given the Bantams' a level of courage that has taken them to incredible highs. Too often City are under-achievers for sure, but at other times they go and punch well above their weight, and further strengthen the hearts and minds of their passionate supporters. When success occurs, it means even more for having experienced the rough.

But the 30 years that have followed May 11, 1985 are also about the reinvention of Bradford City. Back in 1981, barely one thousand fans turned up for a Fourth Division game against Hereford United. In 2012, the same fixture in the same division attracted a crowd of 17,000. Over this 30-year period, football in general has been completely transformed, with the advent of the Premier League and the explosion of interest in the game which now sees an amazing level of media coverage and fan engagement. At times, Bradford City have clearly grappled with an identity crisis over its place in the new football world. The amazing climb up the ladder under Richmond was all about securing a permanent place at the top table, perhaps best characterised by the chairman's desperate attempts to engineer a Premier League 2 after City's relegation from the top flight in 2001 (it was a doomed attempt). During City's six-year stay in League Two (2007-2013), there was a widely held belief that the club were too big to be in the bottom division – such a feeling wasn't there in the 60s, 70s and early 80s, when City were a seemingly permanent member of the bottom tier.

Fittingly given May 1985, and the way people stuck with the club during such traumatic times, the reinvention of Bradford City has supporters at the heart of it. In 2007 chairman Julian Rhodes implemented a cheap season ticket initiative that has transformed the club's support base and proven sustainable despite the initial lack of success on the field. A new generation of Bradford City supporters have been formed, and numbers have grown further on the back of the success achieved by Parkinson. City may never reach the heights of Premier League football again, but they arguably have a bigger fanbase now than at any time since the 1910s. Certainly relative to the club's fortunes on the field.

For the 2015/16 season, Bradford City attracted a record number of season ticket holders – more than 18,000. This was for third tier football, and the attendances that the Bantams subsequently enjoyed are considerably better than the majority of their division rivals. In fact, their 2015/16 average attendance is on course to double 21 of the other 23 teams – and is three times higher than fourteen of those clubs. They are also on track to better more than half of the average attendances in the division above (the Championship).

In a way it is becoming wrong to label Bradford City's cheap season tickets an initiative or an offer – given it is almost a decade since they were launched. It has become the norm at Valley Parade, and it has worked well in a city that has endured economic hardship for decades and is widely quoted as being one of the poorest parts of the country. Bradford as a city has a dreadful national reputation and frequently appears close to the top of the "worst city for..." lists that crop up in the media every now and then. Much of it might be unkind, but statistically Bradford has a higher unemployment rate than the national average. It also has some of the lowest gross disposable household incomes in the country at £13,654 a year. Alongside Hull, it is said to have the worst quality of life in the UK. Throw in the global credit crunch and subsequent recession, and there have been many reasons why Bradford City might have struggled to attract supporters to pay hundreds of pounds for a season ticket; when for many people in the region, such a luxury would have proven beyond their means.

Bradford City has priced season tickets majorly out of synch with the rest of English football – they are by far the cheapest of the 92 clubs, and there are many non-league sides who charge more. Such a pricing point has been criticised by some observers for artificially raising attendances, and making them less comparable to other clubs. But then at the top end of English football there has been a sharp increase in supporter protests over extortionate ticket prices. Frankly it bemuses me why we don't see every football supporter in the land shouting loudly about what Bradford City are doing, and how successful it has proven. Other clubs should be pressured into considering following suit.

Commercially cheap season tickets work with Bradford City. And commerciality has never been far away from its history. This is a club that in 1903 was elected into the Football League without ever kicking a ball, as the Football League sought to make sure the region of West Yorkshire had a football club to compete against the growing popularity of rugby league in the North. Bradford City had evolved from the rugby club Manningham FC; when at the turn of the century the members elected to change sports and swap an egg-shaped ball for a round one. Association football first came to Bradford in the shape of a City game against Gainsborough Trinity at Valley Parade, in the Second Division. Five years later, Bradford City won promotion to the top tier. In 1911, they won the FA Cup after defeating Newcastle United in a replay at Old Trafford, whilst finishing fifth in the First Division. It was their best-ever league performance, and the Paraders were firmly amongst the best teams in the country. The Football League's decision, eight years earlier, to elect the club before it had played so much as a competitive game of football had paid off.

The First World War of 1914-1918 saw the Football League put on hold, and the break was not kind to City. They lost their FA Cup Final scoring hero and captain, Jimmy Speirs, who was killed in action. Four years after football resumed, in 1922 the club was relegated alongside Manchester United. One team would recover quickly from the set back, and enjoy a glittering history of European and domestic triumph. It wouldn't be Bradford City. They were relegated again before the 1920s were out; and although they bounced back to win the Third Division (North) in 1928/29, a lifetime of mediocrity was beginning. Bradford City were never to be the force in English football that they had been, and they weren't even top dogs in West Yorkshire. Leeds United had formed in 1919 following the demise of Leeds City, whilst the legendary manager Herbert Chapman was inspiring Huddersfield Town to three successive First Division titles in the late 1920s. Within Bradford, there was now a local rival in the shape of Bradford Park Avenue. Oh, and despite the attempts to freeze out rugby league, Bradford Northern were establishing themselves on the other side of the city. Both these sporting clubs were competing with Bradford City for the local public's affections, and that level of choice hurt the Paraders.

It wasn't all bad at Valley Parade; but the middle part of their history was largely colourless and filled with underachievement. Promotion from the Fourth Division in 1969 – the first promotion in 40 years – was a highlight, but they fell back down again. As future Bradford City chairman Mark Lawn told me when I interviewed him for boyfrombrazil.co.uk in 2011 – "Then we had the bleak years didn't we? I think everyone forgets that." Indeed it got so bad that, in the 1974/75 season, the Valley Parade average crowd was a pathetic 2,916. They only just avoided the ignominy of finishing in the re-election places – the teams who finished here had to apply to the rest of the Football League to be kept in the league – and the club's board talked of going part-time, due to the excessive pressure on the finances. Only two years earlier (1974), Bradford Park Avenue had been liquidated and there was every possibility that the same fate would befall City. The 1975/76 season changed that, as Bradford City went on an extraordinary FA Cup run that included defeating one of the country's then-top sides – Norwich City – on their own Carrow Road patch. They welcomed Southampton to Valley Parade in the quarter finals, narrowly losing 1-0 in front of 14,195 people. The cup run recaptured the Bradford public's interest in their only surviving football club. It was a crucial moment in Bradford City's history.

Six years later City were promoted from the Fourth Division, and then in 1984/85 came that long-awaited first return to second tier since the 1920s. To win the league that season had been largely unexpected and was a stunning achievement – it is one of only three occasions that City have been champions of a division – and for supporters young and old, going to the Lincoln City match on May 11, 1985 must have felt so exciting and should have gone down as a memorable day, because of football. Alas, it was unforgettable for all the wrong reasons. Tragedy struck. A community had to come to terms with losing loved ones in such a public and horrific way. The world of football stood side by side with Bradford, bowing their heads in respect. Recovering was not easy, but the experiences and lessons learned from that day have acted as an inspiration for modern successes. It admittedly wasn't to everybody's taste – but when in 2013 Bradford City reached a major cup final at Wembley stadium, before the match a giant flag was passed around the sell out Bantams end in memory of the 56 people who lost their lives.

This book is the story of Bradford City's modern history. It takes the format of looking at twelve key matches from the 30 years that followed 1985, with the story of the events in and around each game. I have not picked City's best twelve matches, as doing so would be an unfair reflection of those 30 years, which have featured plenty of struggle. Instead, the great matches are included alongside more unpleasant days at the office. The highs and the lows are both presented side by side. This book is not an attempt to tell the full story of these 30 years. Other people have already done that sort of thing. In contrast, I wanted to focus on the really big moments – good and bad – that characterise these three decades. So, apologises in advance, but you won't find the story of Chris Waddle at Bradford City here. Nor will you read much about Colin Todd's time in charge (nothing personal against Colin, who I happened to like, but three years muddling in League One does not make a great story).

That said, you will read and hear from other players and managers. When writing this book I have interviewed a number of key people from this 30-year period in Bradford City, to get their accounts of the games and events I cover. In addition to players and managers I've spoken to board members past and present, local journalists and supporters. I think the last group are equally as important as the others. Whilst not taking anything away from players and managers involved, Bradford City results can often mean more to us supporters – and our own individual experiences of being at Bloomfield Road or Molineux or Stamford Bridge matter just as much.

The purpose of retelling the stories of these games is to show how Bradford City has reinvented itself in modern times. How it has gone from a club elected into the Football League in 1903 for commercial reasons, to one that has sought to remain relevant not only to its local community but in terms of finding its place in the modern game. Pick up the paper and turn on the news, and it is easy to believe that football is all about the few. The top players, the best managers, the biggest clubs, the major games. Manchester United vs Liverpool, Arsenal vs Chelsea, Van Gaal vs Wenger, Rooney vs Terry. The soap opera of the Premier League can be riveting but also frustrating. Much of it has removed itself a long way from reality. In contrast to Bradford City's £149 season tickets, at Arsenal you would have to part with just short of two thousand pounds for a season-long seat at the Emirates.

Yet the soul of football can truly be found at places like Valley Parade. Where instead of superstar players and eye-watering ticket prices, there is a close bond between the community and the footballers decked out in claret and amber. Phil Parkinson often refers to a "Bradford City way" of doing things, and when he does he is talking about honest values and a hardworking, team-based ethic. Many Bradford City players present and past talk about how the teams they were part of didn't have stars and that is true to an extent. We fans know that we are not supporting the world's best players, but those who exhibit our values of commitment and passion were deeply loved and are remembered fondly in spite of their failings.

Bradford City are an amazing club to support. We are big, but not so big that as a supporter you feel that you don't matter. We are admired and respected by many football fans around the country (but also disliked by others – often without realising). Valley Parade wouldn't ever be in the reckoning for the best stadium in the land, but the atmosphere and intensity that it can produce, when full, rivals anywhere else in the country. When City played Arsenal in the League Cup quarter finals in 2012, BBC Radio 5 Live Commentator Alan Green recalled of the experience, "I'd finished my commentary stint and had to leave to answer a call of nature. I heard a roar from the Bradford end and rushed back. 'Surely Bradford haven't scored?' I asked. 'No' came the reply – 'they've won a corner'. I had a tear in my eye!"

Most of all, Bradford City are an amazing club to support because of the extremes we go through. In my time as a supporter I have watched them at Wembley for a major cup final, and at Barnet whilst the team were second bottom of the entire Football League. I've watched us beat Arsenal in the Premier League and get thrashed by Accrington Stanley in League Two. I've seen Benito Carbone in claret and amber, and I've seen Barry Conlon. It is rarely dull, for long anyway. We like to think of ourselves as a club with the potential to be bigger and more successful than we are, and yet we are never more comfortable in our own skin than when we have to assume the role of the underdog.

This is the story of how Bradford City emerged from the dark shadows of May 11, 1985, and how they have evolved in these modern times. How they have continued to re-invent themselves, in both good ways and bad.

A quick statistical summary of Bradford City's modern history (1985-2015)

In both 1992 and 2007, the top four divisions in England were renamed. Throughout the book, when referring to the division that Bradford City are in, I have used the titles as they were at the time.

In 1985, the Football League was made up of the top 92 clubs in England, with the leagues named First Division, Second Division, Third Division and Fourth Division.

Season	League	Position	Position on 92	Manager
1985/86	Second Division	13	35	Trevor Cherry
1986/87	Second Division	10	32	Trevor Cherry/Terry Dolan
1987/88	Second Division	4	25	Terry Dolan
1988/89	Second Division	14	34	Terry Dolan/Terry Yorath
1989/90	Second Division	23	43	Terry Yorath/John Docherty

City relegated to the Third Division

1990/91	Third Division	8	52	John Docherty
1991/92	Third Division	16	60	John Docherty/Frank Stapleton

In the summer of 1992 the Premier League was formed after the top division voted to break away from the Football League. Beneath them, the three remaining divisions became the Division One, Division Two and Division Three

1992/93	Division Two	10	54	Frank Stapleton
1993/94	Division Two	7	51	Frank Stapleton
1994/95	Division Two	14	58	Lennie Lawrence
1995/96	Division Two	6	50	Lennie Lawrence/Chris Kamara

City promoted to Division One

1996/97	Division One	21	41	Chris Kamara
1997/98	Division One	13	33	Chris Kamara/Paul Jewell
1998/99	Division One	2	22	Paul Jewell

City promoted to the Premier League

1999/00	Premier League	17	17	Paul Jewell
2000/01	Premier League	20	20	Chris Hutchings/Jim Jefferies

City relegated to Division One

2001/02	Division One	15	35	Jim Jefferies/Nicky Law
2002/03	Division One	19	39	Nicky Law
2003/04	Division One	23	43	Nicky Law/Bryan Robson

Football League rebrands its three divisions The Championship, League One and League Two
City relegated to League One

Season	League	Position	Position on 92	Manager
2004/05	League One	11	55	Colin Todd
2005/06	League One	11	55	Colin Todd
2006/07	League One	23	67	Colin Todd/David Wetherall

City relegated to League Two

2007/08	League Two	10	78	Stuart McCall
2008/09	League Two	9	77	Stuart McCall
2009/10	League Two	14	82	Stuart McCall/Peter Taylor
2010/11	League Two	18	86	Peter Taylor/Peter Jackson
2011/12	League Two	18	86	Peter Jackson/Phil Parkinson
2012/13	League Two	7	75	Phil Parkinson

City promoted to League One

2013/14	League One	11	55	Phil Parkinson
2014/15	League One	7	51	Phil Parkinson

Average Attendances

1985/86	5,816	2000/01	18,511
1986/87	8,246	2001/02	15,488
1987/88	12,906	2002/03	12,500
1988/89	10,524	2003/04	11,377
1989/90	8,777	2004/05	8,572
1990/91	6,644	2005/06	8,264
1991/92	6,115	2006/07	8,694
1992/93	6,581	2007/08	13,756
1993/94	6,395	2008/09	12,704
1994/95	6,152	2009/10	11,422
1995/96	5,708	2010/11	11,127
1996/97	12,925	2011/12	10,171
1997/98	15,564	2012/13	10,323
1998/99	14,299	2013/14	14,092
1999/00	18,030	2014/15	13,373

Bradford City Chairmen

1985-87: Stafford Heginbotham	2002-03: Gordon Gibb
1987-90: Jack Tordoff	2004-present: Julian Rhodes
1990-94: David Simpson	2007-present: Mark Lawn
1994-02: Geoffrey Richmond	

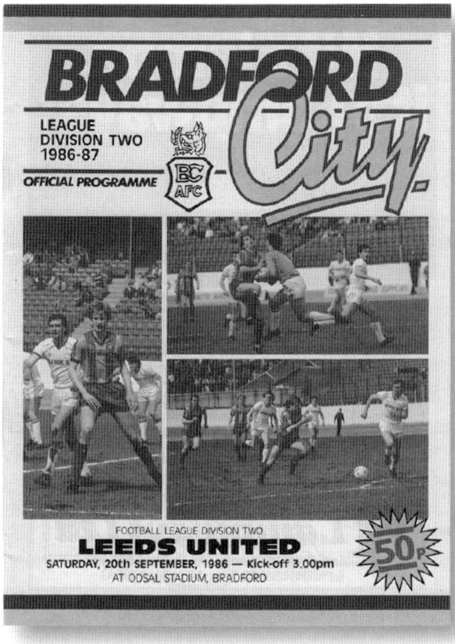

The alternative reality

Bradford City vs Leeds United

Second Division, Saturday 20 September, 1986

The suburb of Odsal towers above much of the city of Bradford. It stands tall at the end of Manchester Road, which takes you out of the city centre; and is located close to the junction for the M606 motorway that connects Bradford with major cities like Leeds, Sheffield and Manchester. Yet despite Osdal's high vantage point, you wouldn't realise that this part of Bradford was home to a huge, 27,000 capacity sports stadium unless you were standing inside it.

Odsal Stadium is an enormous bowl. A giant hole in the ground, which it is said was carved out during the Ice Age. In previous guises, Odsal was used as a quarry and latterly a rubbish tip by the council to serve the south side of Bradford. In 1932, a deal was struck to convert the crater into a stadium for the city's rugby league side, Bradford Northern (known in more modern times as the Bradford Bulls). 22 years later, Odsal set a world record rugby league attendance when more than 102,000 people attended a Challenge Cup replay between Halifax and Warrington – a record that still stands today and will, in all probability, never be broken.

The potential of Odsal stadium is huge. It has been granted the nickname the 'Wembley of the North' following grandiose claims from various developers over the years, who talked of upgrading the ground so that it could host the country's biggest sporting events. But such fanciful plans have never being realised. These days, Odsal is home only to Bradford Northern (now Bradford Bulls), having for many years also hosted speedway and, on occasions, show jumping and kabaddi.

And, for a brief eighteen-month period, Odsal was also the home to association football and to Bradford City. A short-lived relationship that prompted dissatisfaction from supporters from both of Bradford's major sporting clubs; and which despite the occasional modern day threat seems highly unlikely to ever be repeated. Whilst there could be some value in City and the Bulls sharing a stadium in the way that different sporting teams of other UK towns and cities successfully manage; strong geographical ties, allegiances and history mean it seems unlikely to occur in Bradford – at least not at Odsal. There might be many people in Bradford who support both clubs, and there are only 3.1 miles between the two stadiums. But the closer you get to the issue, the bigger it appears – a bit like the walk through the Odsal turnstiles, and into the large bowl that is otherwise hidden from the outside.

Life out of a suitcase

Yet for Bradford City, the summer of 1985 was no time for being choosy or holding back – pragmatism was the only way forwards. With Valley Parade in a state of wreckage following the fire disaster, Bradford City had to find an alternative venue to play home matches in – at least for the short-term. There was, understandably, great uncertainty over when – or, indeed, if – City would return to Valley Parade. Initially it was claimed that the club could go back as soon as January, 1986 – seven months after the Fire. By October this promise had been postponed to the start of the following season, and it would later be pushed back again. Eventually, at the end of 1986, City made a much-desired return to their Manningham home; but only after enduring a period living out of a suitcase and playing home games at the home of other clubs.

Both Leeds United and Huddersfield Town offered the services of their Elland Road and Leeds Road grounds, which were taken up on a handful of occasions. But there was an obvious desire to keep Bradford's only surviving professional football club within the city itself. That meant Odsal or nothing. And so it was that City spent a season and a half primarily playing at the 'Wembley of the North'/great hole in the ground.

John Dewhirst – a supporter of many years, author of several Bradford City books, and co-founder of the-then recently launched City Gent fanzine – remembers with a grimace the dilemma over where City should play after the Valley Parade fire. "The positives of Odsal were that it meant the club continued to exist and were playing within the city of Bradford itself, but that was about it. The list of negatives was much lengthier. There was the inconvenience of the change of routine, the awful pitch, poor atmosphere and horrible weather that seemed unique in Odsal. Right from the start, there was also a nagging fear that it could become a permanent move."

The Telegraph & Argus' Bradford City reporter, David Markham, had been in the Valley Parade press box on the fateful day of the fire. Having moved into journalism straight from school in 1957, Markham was offered the chance to cover City for the T&A in 1974 – a job he continued to hold into the new millennium. Reflecting on the 1985 move across to Odsal, he explained to me, "The Bradford City directors had some difficult decisions to make – where to play when much of your ground lay in ruins following the fire. And, remember, City had gained promotion to the second tier of English football after winning the Third Division championship. Huddersfield Town and Leeds United offered their ground for the early matches, but the club were looking for somewhere to play in Bradford and that meant Odsal.

"Although not made public at the time, it was known that manager Trevor Cherry would have preferred to have continued to play at Elland Road and Leeds Road because they were 'proper' football grounds and crucially provided better pitches. However, the directors and Bradford Council thought it was important for City to continue to play in Bradford, albeit at a Rugby League ground where the playing surface was far from ideal. In fact, the council would have liked City to abandon Valley Parade and share Odsal with Bradford Northern; and I am sure they would have been willing to invest more money into the stadium, if they could have been assured that it was going to be used in both winter and summer by the city's two professional clubs."

To play at Odsal required alterations to be made to the stadium, in order for it to be fit for Football League requirements. In the hooligan-fuelled 1980s, this meant the installation of segregation fences to Odsal's main stand – to keep visiting fans separate from home supporters. One thousand seats were also bolted onto the terracing, and there was a plan to add another seven thousand at a later point. With Rugby League having no such need to keep fans segregated, the new fences were unwelcomed by Bradford Northern supporters. If Bradford City were down-on-their-luck house guests that you dutifully took in, this was the equivalent of discovering they had rearranged your living room and redecorated the bathroom.

The Football League, doing what it could to help City, arranged for only four of the club's first thirteen games to be at 'home', so Odsal could be brought up to code. In the meantime, City mainly played at Huddersfield Town's Leeds Road – a stadium they would remain unbeaten at during this period – before the first Odsal-hosted home match took place on 8 October 1985: a 2-0 League Cup loss to Brighton.

It was a rude awakening for City supporters, as the downsides of Odsal became abundantly clear. With only one of the four sides having a roof, fans were open to the elements and an October downpour, coupled with the Brighton defeat, cast a gloomy mood over the majority of fans within the 5,368 crowd. The attendance was below the typical average of that era – over this troubled 1985/86 campaign, the average home crowd was 5,816 compared to 6,639 for the championship-winning season a year before. But even on days when the number of spectators was higher, they would never come close to filling this vast bowl and the atmosphere suffered badly. City's record Odsal crowd was just over 14,000 for a League Cup tie with Brian Clough's Nottingham Forest – a game they lost 5-0. Good times were few and far between.

Adding to the emptiness was the relatively huge distance that the crowd were situated away from the pitch – especially compared to Valley Parade. At the time, Odsal was home to the popular Bradford Dukes speedway team, and there was a circular racing track in-between the pitch and the stands. This even impacted on the playing surface, with the track overlapping the pitch on the four corners; which meant turfs of grass were artificially added to the pitch before games, so they could be easily removed again for speedway meetings. Players had to take corners on lumps of turf that were added a few hours before the match and then taken away at full time.

And of course, we were heading to winter. Odsal's high vantage point over much of Bradford was a huge disadvantage in this respect, as it meant the area – and stadium – was more exposed to bad weather compared to Valley Parade. With no roof for cover, City fans spent the winter months acquiring frost bite on their knuckles and enduring regular soakings. The weather was so bad that some home games had to be postponed and rearranged at either Elland Road or Leeds Road. This was a really unhappy state of affairs for the club, supporters and players, who were all still coming to terms with the tragic events of 11 May, 1985.

Mark Ellis was one of many City players from the team who especially had the club at heart. A Bradfordian, Ellis had been spotted as fifteen-year-old and emerged through the youth ranks to make his debut in 1981. A left winger who would eventually make more than 200 appearances for the Bantams, Ellis explained to me the players' perspective of the Odsal experience. "All the lads thought Odsal lacked noise and we all really missed playing at Valley Parade. It wasn't the same. It was just so big and it didn't have the same atmosphere. But at least we were still in Bradford. We had several games there and we did alright. We played some games at Huddersfield Town, we enjoyed playing there. We also played some at Elland Road. It was just great really that those clubs let us play there. We just wanted to carry on playing and to take the name Bradford City forward. But obviously they were hard times."

Not that Ellis found the entire Odsal experience unappealing – nor, indeed, was he a stranger to the stadium. "For me it was funny," he admitted. "My dad used to take me to the rugby everywhere, even though I only wanted to go to the football. So I had been to every rugby ground going and I used to regularly go to games at Odsal. It was quite good for me playing there, because I'd been to Odsal to watch games more often than I had Valley Parade. But actually playing there was difficult because there was just no atmosphere. Odsal was just so massive. I guess the rugby players get used to it; but compared to Valley Parade, it was just so quiet. Even when visiting teams brought lots of fans, it didn't seem to add much to the atmosphere because they were so far away from the pitch."

Alongside Ellis, Stuart McCall was another player who had emerged through the Bradford City youth ranks and established himself as a first team regular during the first half of the 1980s. The flame-haired midfielder made his debut as an eighteen-year-old on the opening day of the 1982/83 season, quickly became a regular, and established himself as one of the star players of the 1984/85 championship-winning side. McCall would become arguably the most popular player in Bradford City's history, making 395 appearances over two separate spells that together totalled ten years. He also returned as manager in 2007, where he oversaw more than 130 matches.

McCall recalled his breakthrough to me, "I played for Leeds Boys and then I played for Farsley Celtic. There were only two of us who had not been taken on by clubs. Four lads had gone to Leeds, one at Huddersfield, two at Forest and one at Arsenal. I was very small at the time. We played against Bradford City juniors, and I don't think I particularly played very well. I think Bryan Edwards was there at the time, watching the game. And he asked our Farsley coach if there were any young lads who had not been taken on, and they said 'oh yeah the little ginger lad in midfield'. And he said, 'well do you mind if we take him on for another couple of games?'

"I played four or six trial games and then they offered me an apprenticeship, when at the time I was writing away to banks and building societies looking for a job. I wanted to be a footballer but I just thought it had passed me by. So I was lucky. I signed a two-year deal. The night I signed was Peter Downsborough's testimonial [a Bradford City goalkeeper who played 225 times for the club]. It was my 16th birthday. And my signing on fee was that George Mulhall [the Bradford City manager of the time] gave my mum a whisky and that was it! My mum got on well with George because they were both Scottish.

"I started work 10 June during the close season. Half way through my first season George got sacked and Roy McFarland came in as manager. Mick Jones also came in and had a big influence on me. In those days there were only three apprentices. I used to do all the boots, the pitch, we just did everything."

Prior to May 11, 1985, Bradford City were a club on the up – gaining promotion from the Fourth Division in 1982, and surviving the threat of receivership the year afterwards. 1984/85 was a Championship-winning season of course, before the fire overshadowed that achievement. McCall grew in prominence over this period, building a reputation as one of the brightest young midfielders in the lower leagues. "I think when Roy and Mick came in, the club was on the rise. I remember Mick and Roy left for Derby on not the happiest of terms. I'm sure they wish they'd have done things differently, because they'd got City promoted and they'd got the crowds coming back to what they were. And then who comes in, Trevor Cherry and Terry Yorath [as assistant manager]. They both really helped me and brought me on. They just picked up the club and took it further.

"1984/85 football-wise was fantastic. We played brilliant football and we had so many derbies. I remember going to Rotherham on New Years Day where we won 2-1, and there were City fans everywhere. It was a great time. We were a social bunch too and I think in those days the fans and the players mixed much more than they do nowadays. It was just a great atmosphere. I ended up living in Farsley between Leeds and Bradford. Back then, people from Leeds would come for a night out in Bradford – you can't imagine that now. I think the football helped the city, and Bradford was thriving at that time. It was a good place to be. A great place to play football. Crowds had come back."

The fire disaster put paid to that feel-good factor, particularly with the club forced to play away from Valley Parade in the aftermath. Despite the dislike for Odsal, John Dewhirst recalls that crowds held up reasonably well. "I don't think that attendances suffered unduly, but tended to be five or six thousand. Once mid-season security was guaranteed, the final games of that first season were a bit meaningless and

I recall that the season just drifted away. That said, whenever it was wet, the attendances plummeted as there was no covered terrace."

David Markham added, "The council did their best to prepare the ground for City with various safety measures installed to comply with Football League requirements, but the pitch wasn't good enough and was regularly criticised by visiting managers, notably Brian Clough despite the fact that his Nottingham Forest team beat City 5-0 in a League Cup match [in November 1985], while there was not enough covered accommodation for standing spectators at an often cold and windswept ground. That said, it was right for City to play at Odsal, even though the pitches at Elland Road and Leeds Road were clearly better suited for League football. They had to keep faith with their supporters to play in Bradford rather have them travel to Leeds or Huddersfield, and they could not afford to snub the council – nor was it right to do so after the local authority had done so much to provide for the club to play at Odsal."

Speaking on a 'History of Bradford City' video that was produced in 1991, the-then City manager Trevor Cherry said, "Odsal was a horrible place. I can't understand why anyone plays any sport there. It should be filled in and used as a rubbish tip as far as I am concerned, I just don't see it as a sporting centre. But to play football on the pitches we had to was just a joke really. We managed it for a spell. The first season we got away with it, but going back the second season was a real slog, just the thought of it."

Fostered team spirit

Yet because of such adversity, the achievements of the Bradford City team during this era seem even more impressive. The 1980s Bradford City side has gone down in folklore as having one of the best team spirits the club has ever seen, and that spirit was tested in ways that simply do not usually happen in football. Even years on, it is obvious just how much affection many of the players from that era retain for the club, which is in contrast to many of the players who have followed them over the subsequent decades. Stuart McCall, Greg Abbott, John Hendrie, Peter Jackson and Ian Ormondroyd were just five of the most celebrated names, who evidently still care deeply for City decades later.

Mark Ellis revealed, "The squads were a lot smaller back then. But when we got promotion we had a good team spirit and anybody who came to the club afterwards would find that it was a tight bond. Nobody wanted to forget what happened. It was always at the back of everybody's mind, but we just wanted to do our best and carry the club forward no matter where we were playing."

There was the emotion of the Valley Parade fire – where many of the players' own families were present and some, such as Stuart McCall's father, suffered injuries. Then there was the challenge of playing at other stadiums away from Valley Parade. Finally, there were the increased demands of playing in a higher division. These were incredibly testing times for the players, and they performed wonders in continuing to move the club forwards through adversity. This was City's first return to the second tier of English football since 1937, and meant they welcomed big names such as Middlesbrough, Crystal Palace, Norwich City, Stoke City and, of course, Leeds United. This group of players – many of whom had been playing for the club in the Fourth Division four years earlier – kept their high professional standards to finish in a respectable mid-table position during 1985/86. But it was a strange season and a strange existence, not knowing how long the exile at Odsal would last for. Or, indeed, if it would last forever.

David Markham reflected on the campaign, "For a time, City did well at Odsal with victories over Portsmouth, Carlisle and Brighton before Christmas and a four match winning run – they beat Carlisle, Brighton, Oldham [away on Boxing Day] and Sunderland [at Huddersfield on New Year's Day] – put them into a safe mid-table position. It was after Christmas that City encountered another handicap affecting Odsal. The ground's exposed position made it vulnerable to frost and snow and City were forced to play away from Odsal until mid March.

"So, after beating Sunderland, they played only two more League matches in January – away defeats at Hull and Stoke – plus an FA Cup third round tie against Ipswich where they lost 1-0 in a replay at Elland Road after a dramatic 4-4 draw at Portman Road. Remarkably, City didn't play a match of any description in February because none of the three grounds they were using was fit or available, which meant a huge backlog of fixtures which saw them play eighteen matches – nearly half their League programme – in March, April and May. Overall, though, City could look back on a satisfactory season, playing in the second tier for the first time for 48 years. To finish thirteenth was a creditable performance given the huge problems that few other clubs could have faced in the history of the Football League."

A month to the day after City's first game at the other side of the city, Bradford Council announced big plans to redevelop Odsal and belatedly realise the 'Wembley of the North' dream. It included two new, 14,000 capacity cantilever stands, terracing behind each goal and – ultimately – a 61,000 capacity ground by 1990. They talked of Odsal hosting rugby league Challenge Cup Finals and football FA Cup Semi Finals. All of which sounded fantastic, but to City fans shivering inside an Odsal stadium that was far too big for their needs, it wasn't home. These big plans never came to fruition, and City's desire to return to Valley Parade meant they held little interest in supporting them.

David Markham explained, "For years, there had been talk of making Odsal the so-called 'Wembley of the North'. However, then as now, no one was able to provide the millions required to bring this dream into a reality and, although money has been spent on improvements over the years, the stadium is still far from complete.

"To the outsider, the council's plans made sense. Why couldn't the two professional clubs share the same stadium? Why re-develop Valley Parade, an old sub standard ground at an unsuitable inner city location with extremely limited car parking and access? Wasn't this the opportunity to make a fresh start in another part of the city? What these people didn't take into account was the sentiment towards Valley Parade, the emotional attachment that football supporters have to their own ground and this feeling was even stronger following the fire. The fire tragedy made City supporters determined to return to Valley Parade despite the obvious difficulties in obtaining the finance required to re-build the ground and once the ground was re-developed it was seen by many as a fitting memorial to those who died in the fire."

Terry Yorath, then assistant manager to Trevor Cherry, summed up the mood at the time when interviewed for a Yorkshire TV documentary. He was asked whether a new stand should be built at Valley Parade, on top of the site of the old main stand which had housed the fire. "Certainly yeah. It is the best thing that could happen for the people who died, for their families, for those who have been burned. This is where they came. This is where they enjoyed coming. It's part of their life, it's part of their family's lives. Some of the families will never, ever want to come here, will never ever want to remember. But I think we owe it to them. We've got to keep playing here, keep doing our stuff here and keep winning for them." Reflecting back to me, Stuart McCall added, "I remember afterwards the big decision was whether football should ever take place again at Valley Parade. And I remember the poll was over 90% that supporters wanted us to go back, it was almost unanimous. They wanted to go back to watch the club at Valley Parade."

By the end of the season, funding was secured to rebuild Valley Parade from West Yorkshire council, the Football Trust, insurance payments and the club itself. The Main Stand was obviously going to be reconstructed, whilst the Bradford End was re-roofed and re-terraced, and the Kop modernised. The Midland Road side of the ground also benefited from structural improvements. In all, the capacity of the redeveloped ground would be around 16,000. During the summer of 1986 it was announced that Valley Parade would be ready to re-open before the end of the year, meaning City just had to get through the first few months of the 1986/87 season playing at Odsal before they could return home.

At least winter won't have fully kicked in before the move back...

Bragging rights

The rivalry between Bradford City and Leeds United had been building up. This was, after all, the peak years of hooliganism between factions of certain supporters up and down the land, and West Yorkshire was certainly no exception. Yet for decades Bradford City and Leeds had moved in very different circles. Leeds were one of the country's biggest teams during the 60s and 70s, finishing in the old First Division's top two for five successive seasons and winning the FA Cup in 1972. Meanwhile Bradford City were slumming it in the fourth tier, with little glory to be had save for the occasional promotion or cup run. It meant that many Bradfordians turned their back on their home city and headed to Elland Road instead. The Telegraph & Argus even favoured covering Leeds United over City. The glamour was all in Beeston, not Manningham.

The rivalry between Bradford City and Leeds United had been building up. In 1983, Bradford City went into receivership after their bigger and more prosperous neighbours, Leeds United, issued a winding up petition against them over the unpaid transfer fee of Trevor Cherry. City's very existence went right to the wire, with supporters' collection buckets wheeled out and the club's hero Bobby Campbell sold to raise the money needed. City survived, but not without retaining resentment to Leeds United over their part in the saga.

The rivalry between Bradford City and Leeds United had been building up. In 1985, City's promotion to the old Second Division meant that they would get to face Leeds for the first time in more than 50 years. After the success of Don Revie, Leeds' fortunes had floundered in the eighties and they were relegated from the top flight in 1982. They struggled in the wilderness of the second tier, and it would take them eight seasons to earn promotion back to the First Division.

A rivalry between Bradford City and Leeds United that had been building up was about to really take off.

John Dewhirst reflected back on the glamour of facing Leeds and the old second division. "There was a massive buzz in anticipation of the Leeds fixture. During the 60s, 70s, and 80s, City had played only a limited number of higher league teams. Given we'd been in the bottom two divisions, there was always massive excitement prior to a game against a club that we hadn't played in years."

During City's first season in the second division – playing at Odsal – Leeds narrowly won the home and away derby fixtures. Yet they finished one place in the league below City, demonstrating just how closely matched the two clubs had become. Everyone connected with Bradford City wanted to beat Leeds United, even the players, and so the following season's September 1986 meeting at Odsal offered a chance to put that right.

Dewhirst added, "Prior to games with the likes of Huddersfield there were always stories about the yobs pre-arranging where to meet for a scrap. For weeks on end, the talk of the Leeds game at Odsal in September 1986 was more to do with the probable terrace aggro than the game. Everyone expected some sort of trouble, and I think that much of it was instigated by people from Bradford who understood the significance of the game. I cannot remember what happened the previous season, but I seem to think that the Bradford gangs had plotted revenge – the game in September 1986 was a kind of showdown. With Leeds hovering near the top of the table that season it gave added intensity."

In contrast to a promising opening month for Leeds, it had been a very poor start to the season for City. The first five games saw no victories, two draws and three defeats – with the Odsal record reading one point from three games and seven goals conceded. The Saturday before Leeds came to town, a first victory of the campaign was finally achieved at Millwall. Yet City were struggling near the bottom of the league, winless at Odsal, and the desire to get back to the home comforts of Valley Parade was strong. Mark Ellis recalled of the match, "I was really up for the game. I was a bit of a Leeds fan in my youth; because Leeds had a fantastic team back then with the likes of Billy Bremner. But as soon as I started playing for Bradford, all I wanted to do was beat Leeds."

This could – and should – have been the club's best afternoon at Odsal. It was a match City had to approach without their injured McCall, but just four minutes into the encounter Leeds United endured a similarly crucial blow. Ian Snodin – an England Under 21 international of immense promise – went down injured. And although he attempted to carry on, by the 19th minute he had to be substituted and with it Leeds' control of the middle of the park suffered. With the home side beginning the game in an edgy manner, the visitors dominated the first half hour of the contest, with Andy Ritchie latching onto a weak back pass but shooting into the side netting from an angle; whilst John Buckley, Keith Edwards, John Stiles and Snodin all came close. City hung on during these stages, and eventually began to find their rhythm.

Just before half time, they struck the all-important first goal. John Hendrie picked up the ball out wide, and sent over a perfect cross to allow Bobby Campbell to plant a header past Ronnie Sinclair. It was a goal that sparked scenes of delirium in the City sections, and it ultimately went down in history for its own reasons. For it was club record goalscorer Campbell's 121st for Bradford City and – to everyone's surprise – his last. At the time it was a third goal in seven matches for the striker, but shortly afterwards Cherry made the shock decision to sell Campbell to Wigan Athletic for £25,000. The Northern Ireland international fared well at Springfield Park, and he was much missed. He remains hugely popular at Valley Parade and across the city itself, and he even opened a bar in Bradford in 2015. Over two spells at Valley Parade, Campbell's endeavours and adventures have gone down into folklore. Perhaps it was fitting that his final City goal was such a memorable one.

Leeds came roaring back after the interval and put City under pressure. In the 54th minute Peter Swan – who had replaced Snodin – hit a rasping 25-yard shot that had the beating of goalkeeper Peter Litchfield but not, crucially, the frame of the goal. The ball bounced back off the upright, and less than 60 seconds later Bradford City made it 2-0. A flowing four-man move, initially involving Hendrie and the outstanding Martin Singleton, ended up with Greg Abbott playing Don Goodman through, and he finished clinically from ten yards out.

For Goodman the goal also had special significance. Born in Leeds and a former ball boy at Elland Road, Goodman played for Hunslet Club and Leeds City Boys as a kid and was watched by his hometown club, who eventually ruled out signing him due to fears that he was too small. Goodman ended up at Valley Parade instead, and at the end of this season would move to West Brom and later onto Sunderland and Wolves, enjoying an excellent career. Scoring for Bradford City at Odsal against his boyhood club, after they had written him off, evidently meant a lot. After the game he told the Telegraph & Argus, "It was a special goal for me. I scored with my left foot as well, I don't get many with my left, but I just swung my foot and the ball went in…It was special for the lads. I think we wanted to win more than they did and it showed." Goodman's goal ensured there was no way back for Leeds, indeed City were unfortunate not to cap off a fine team performance with a third goal.

A proud Trevor Cherry – who spent ten years at Elland Road as a player – would later tell the Telegraph & Argus that the victory was a landmark moment for City, "It was a tremendous achievement to beat Leeds and I am delighted with the win and the way we played after the first quarter on an hour…We played with a lot of confidence in the second half and I just wish I could convince our players what a good side they are. Certain players don't believe in themselves enough."

Sour ending

After Goodman's goal, that should have been that. City were seeing out the match comfortably, and the home supporters who made up the majority of a healthy crowd of 13,521 were ready to claim long-awaited bragging rights over a neighbouring city, and over a football team that they had for too long lived in the shadow of. But instead, there was to be a horrible and cruel late twist to the afternoon – one that for many brought back the most traumatic recent memories.

For Goodman's strike was cue for a section of Leeds fans to begin rioting. A mixture of the opponents – local rivals Bradford City – and Odsal's vastness would have serious consequences. Leeds United's hooliganism problem was no secret in the eighties, and had led to the Football Association (FA) imposing an all-ticket ruling on the club's away games. In other words, Leeds fans could only attend away games if they purchased tickets beforehand. An arrangement that meant not just anybody could turn up, namely known trouble makers and those with a National Front allegiance. However, the FA had relaxed these conditions – and this game at Bradford City was to be the first away match with the lenient rules in place. After all, there was plenty of room at Odsal, so why limit the amount of visiting supporters who could attend?

Yet the whole day was played out to a backdrop of fighting and clashes between both sets of supporters, with rioting breaking out at 1pm in the Forster Square, Manchester Road and Ivegate parts of the city. Witnesses reported of bricks being thrown at passing cars and buses, and dozens of shop windows were smashed. Pubs were also targeted and some had to close their doors. Inside Odsal, fighting broke out between both sets of supporters in the 25th minute of the game, causing some frightened supporters to spill onto the pitch to avoid getting involved. The game carried on at that point at least, but after Goodman's goal the trouble really began to escalate.

Those present for the game witnessed Leeds fans taunting home fans about the Valley Parade fire. According to a national TV news story about the events – uploaded on YouTube – some Leeds fans set fire to some of the grass on the Odsal hill. As the Fire Brigade raced to the scene and the Police tried to restore order, both emergency services' crews were hit by stones hurled by Leeds fans. And then, with three minutes left on the clock, a chip van parked on the away terrace was somehow turned onto its side and set on fire.

Fire, once again at a Bradford City match. The sights, the smell and the fear. Painful and disturbing flashbacks. This, after all, was just sixteen months on from the Valley Parade fire.

David Markham was a witness to these distressing events, "City were cruising to victory when we saw what appeared to be Leeds fans trying to push chip van on the top of the large terrace at Odsal opposite the main stand. The van was swaying alarmingly and one hoped the spectators would see sense and not continue to push it, because it would topple over. Unfortunately, they continued to push and the van crashed on to the terracing and burst into flames, reminding some people of the tragic events at Valley Parade sixteen months earlier. Fortunately, the other spectators had got out of the way so no one was hurt, but the referee was understandably alarmed and wisely took the players off the field with just over two minutes of the match remaining. Just why those spectators pushed over the van no one knows, but it was a dangerous act of football hooliganism and could have resulted in serious injury."

The injured McCall also had a close-up view of the dreadful scenes, "I was sat in the stand as I was injured. It was a good day in one way, and a sad one in another. The game itself was a great one for us as it was the first time we had beaten Leeds for a long, long time. But it was a sad day in the main because of what happened off the park.

"I was in the stand opposite where the chip van was set on fire. And the panic that was felt when it happened is something I can't forget. There was the noise, the smoke and fumes, and it caused panic. It brought it all back for everyone. It was like it was being revisited again for so many people. We were a full pitch away from it, but the smoke in the air and the smell brought it all back. I think everybody was sickened. It was just horrendous and it left a really sour taste. Months later, I found out that the lad who started the chip van fire used to go to the same school I went to in Leeds."

Indeed for Stuart McCall, who had grown up as a Leeds United supporter, the disappointment at what he had seen from his hometown team caused him to lose his boyhood affection for the Elland Road outfit. "I was born 200 yards away from Elland Road. Leeds was my team and I had followed them home and away. But that day took a lot away of that love away from me; it took a lot of my feelings for Leeds away – because of what they had done. It was only a few people who caused the trouble, but even so. In years to come I had four opportunities to join Leeds, but out of loyalty I just couldn't do it."

Two days after the rioting, the Telegraph & Argus published an interview with the two men who ran the mobile chip shop, Steve Dewhirst and Mike Reynolds, under the headline "A pack of animals!" Steve was quoted as saying, "We were inside the van when people began stoning the crowd. Some hid behind the van. That's what caused it. They began shaking the van to try and turn it over. We opened the door and jumped out. As we did that, someone snatched the takings. I saw someone overturn the generator. He then threw a match onto the petrol and up it went. When they were shaking the van it caused the fat to boil over. We scrambled out just in time. They are not football fans. They are bastards."

John Dewhirst, who was stood on the Rooley Avenue terrace opposite to the Leeds fans, reflected, "The pre-match violence and the raw atmosphere was not a surprise, the chip van fire was. There had been disturbances building up with police ejecting Leeds fans – and then all of a sudden the chip van set alight. There are conflicting versions on how the fire began, ranging from being deliberately set alight to being a consequence of the chip van being turned over. On the face of it, the police did a good job and I don't recall that fans had got into the opposing ends, which was the usual fear at these games."

The turning over of the chip van was cue for the referee to take both sets of players off the pitch. The Telegraph & Argus also interviewed the match referee, Neville Ashley, who said, "My reaction was one of horror. It was a very sad day for football…at no time did anything that happened on the terraces emanate from the field. That is important. I cannot give enough credit to all 23 players who took part. There was not a nasty incident in the game. If they had misbehaved, they could have started a riot. But they behaved impeccably." With the players back in the dressing rooms, at this point the TV news story states that the pitch was "promptly invaded by hundreds of youths heading for rival supporters on the other side of the ground". The footage shows Leeds fans climbing over advertising hoardings and the parameter fence, whilst in the home stand City supporters fled out of the stadium in fear and panic.

That was how the afternoon ended for home fans. The joy that was supposed to be theirs was snatched away in traumatic fashion. The gloss was firmly taken off City's first victory over their rivals in more than half a century. After the police finally cleared the ground of Leeds United supporters, the referee brought both sets of players back onto the field. The game was restarted, with the two remaining minutes played out in front of an empty Odsal stadium. City held on for a victory, but the achievement was undoubtedly overshadowed by the trouble in the stands.

David Markham said, "There was no indication as to whether the match would resume or be abandoned. Most of them assumed that it would be abandoned and there was hardly anyone of the crowd left in the ground when, half an hour later, the referee surprisingly brought players back on to the field to complete the match. Perhaps he hoped that any possible trouble makers would have left so the match could move to its conclusion without any further problems. And in that, he was right. Also, what neither he nor anyone else, certainly in the Bradford City camp, wanted was for the match to be replayed with so little time left to play. Nonetheless, it was a strange experience, watching the players go through the motions to play out the remaining last two minutes or so at a near deserted stadium."

The joy of the victory was undoubtedly tarnished by the off the field troubles. Yet Mark Ellis himself has over the years tried to retain the happiness of such a big victory, rather than dwell on the unsavoury scenes. "I try not to relate the trouble to that game or to think about it being related to the Valley Parade fire, to be honest," he admitted. "A chip van got set on fire; we were taken off the pitch. Everyone got thrown out of the ground and we came back and finished the final two or three minutes of the game. Whether it was an accident or it was on purpose, I try not to relate to what had happened. I try to blank it from my mind."

For a generation of Bradford City supporters, the trauma of the afternoon firmly sowed the seeds of a lasting hatred of Leeds United. John Dewhirst summed up the feelings of many by stating, "The events served only to reinforce what everyone thought about Leeds United. In the 70s and 80s their supporters had always sought to be the most extreme, and I think that in the 80s they assumed that title – whereas in the 70s it had been Man United. There was genuine contempt for Leeds supporters. The reality is that there it was six of one and half a dozen of the other, but the Leeds supporters had appeared to celebrate the chip fire incident. There had also been taunting about the fire."

Justice was swift. 64 people were arrested on the day and within 48 hours the first thug was jailed for 28 days – guilty of throwing a lump of concrete at people fleeing from the blazing chip van. Plenty of others – both Leeds and City fans – were handed similar punishments. In the wake of the trouble, the FA immediately opened up an inquiry and its chairman Bert Millichip told the Telegraph & Argus, "My feeling is one of utter frustration and despair. I really don't know how we are going to control law and order in this country." Meanwhile Bradford councillor Barry Thorne revealed that a complete ban on visiting supporters was being considered by the council, following the example of Luton Town, who at the time had such a ban in place. The idea would be that you had to have a membership card to get into the ground, proving you are a home supporter. "I am totally in favour in making entry to Bradford City games dependant on membership," Thorne told the Telegraph & Argus. "We want to leave football for the majority of decent fans who want to watch the game rather than making Odsal a meeting place for all the scum of Bradford." Reader letters in the Telegraph & Argus suggested some City fans supported the idea, but it was never enforced. At the time, Luton were facing a ban from the FA Cup unless they lifted their no-away-fans rule.

Although Bradford City and Leeds United would continue to lock horns in the Second Division for three further seasons, in 1990 Leeds were promoted and City relegated – and subsequent meetings have been few and far between. It wasn't until August 2014 that City finally recorded another victory over their neighbours. In a pulsating second round League Cup tie at Valley Parade, two goals in two minutes from Billy Knott and James Hanson saw City overturn a 1-0 deficit. In response to Hanson's header – which came with just four minutes left on the clock – many Leeds fans in the Midland Road stand began causing disturbances and throwing their seats onto the pitch. The match had to be delayed by more than six minutes; suggesting that even in these modern times where football hooliganism is all but stamped out in this country, some old habits die hard amongst a minority.

Still, back in 1986, at least the Bradford City players were still able to toast their achievement. Mark Ellis revealed, "Me and Stuart McCall actually went out to Morecambe to celebrate. I remember celebrating with these big steins of beer in a pub somewhere.

"Even though it got spoiled with what happened at the end of the game, we were just so happy that we had won."

Into the valley

Less than two months after the battle of Odsal, City finally played their last game at the 'Wembley of the North'. Fittingly, it was dismal home defeat, as David Markham recalled, "It was a windy evening when Odsal was at its most inhospitable. The team lost 3-1 against West Bromwich Albion with one of the goals being blown into the net by the high wind, leaving on-loan goalkeeper Eric Nixon, playing his third and final match for the club, with no chance to save. The small crowd of 4,580 on a cold Friday night, a fortnight before Christmas, reflected the low key nature of the match and the fact that City supporters had seen enough of their hill top temporary home."

A week later, Valley Parade was officially reopened by Sir Oliver Popplewell – who had led the enquiry into the disaster – and an England XI featuring the star names of the time, and led by England manager Bobby Robson, provided the opposition for City's first game back. Don Goodman and Mark Leonard – the man with the unenviable and impossible task of filling Bobby Campbell's shoes – got the City goals in a 2-1 win. A capacity crowd was present. It was, to say the least, an emotional afternoon.

Mark Ellis recalled playing at Valley Parade before it was fully redeveloped, "I actually played in a reserve game, which was the first time anyone had ever played back there. I can't remember who it was against and we won 6-0 I think, but it was all so insignificant because it was like a ghost town. It was just horrible." However the day of the England XI match was a much happier affair for Ellis. "It was fantastic" he smiled. "I think I played second half in it because we had a bigger squad. There was a brilliant atmosphere and a brilliant day. Even though, obviously the memory of what happened will never be forgotten. It was great to go back."

John Dewhirst also remembers feeling emotional about the return home. "There was massive pride and relief, not only to be back but to have a self-respecting ground. The team had performed miracles in 1985/86 and I suspect that the adrenalin and momentum of the summer of 1985 had much to do with it. By around October 1986 it was becoming clear that the team was not only exhausted but probably not at the right standard, and we'd had a few disappointing results. Odsal was part of the problem, and it was difficult for players and supporters alike to be motivated to go there."

With City struggling near the bottom of the league, drastic action was taken and Cherry was surprisingly sacked in January 1987. Whilst form wasn't great – they hadn't won for eight matches – Cherry's achievements in guiding City to promotion in 1985, and through the traumatic events of May 11, surely warranted better treatment. Terry Dolan was named his successor, and form eventually picked up with a tenth-place finish. Stuart McCall said, "We had struggled at Odsal and we weren't going great. I think that Trevor as much as anyone was looking forward to going back to normality at Valley Parade, and so it must have been quite disappointing for him that not long after he lost his job."

John Dewhirst added, "The mentality on the terraces was focused on returning to Valley Parade as the cure-all, but by January 1987 it really felt like we were doomed and the sacrifices of the previous eighteen months had been in vain. Then came Terry Dolan and miracles which kept the dream alive. I am unsure what his secret was, but a big part of it must have been motivation and team spirit. To finish tenth was a massive achievement that restored self-belief and confidence, which carried the club forward over the following two seasons."

Huge credit to Dolan for the improvement, but the emotion and positivity of returning home evidently played a huge part too. After losing the first league fixture back at Valley Parade, City's home league record for the rest of the campaign read: W8 D3 L1. Up at Odsal, it had been W3 D2 L5.

The wilderness of Odsal was over for Bradford City. They were home; in their own surroundings; in their own part of the city. There have subsequently been threats issued by future owners of a return to the great hole in the ground – most notably in 2011 when the club's board talked openly of abandoning Valley Parade in protest over the high rent they were forced to pay to play there – but since 2012, a relocation to Odsal has never looked more unlikely.

For in January 2012 – and with Bradford Northern (now the Bulls) having fallen into deep financial trouble – Rugby League's governing body, the Rugby Football League (RFL) stepped in to buy Odsal to avoid "predatory approaches". The RFL's ownership of the ground means it is likely to firmly remain a stadium suited to Rugby League. A good job then, given Odsal's biting cold, that rugby league is a summer sport.

Valley Parade was almost completely rebuilt following the fire. But it is testament to the speed of change that would follow 1986 that – only fifteen years later – the ground had been completely transformed again, with new stands built on all four sides. The only remaining stand, from 1986, is fittingly the Main Stand itself. It now has a second tier – unnecessarily added in 2000, during what seemed to be more prosperous financial times – but the lower section itself is almost completely unaltered from the stand that rose from the ashes of one of the UK's worst sporting tragedies.

A fitting and lasting tribute to the 54 Bradford City supporters and two Lincoln City fans, who unjustly lost their lives for merely attending a football match.

City (vs Leeds): Peter Litchfield, Gavin Oliver, Chris Withe, Greg Abbott, Peter Jackson, Dave Evans, John Hendrie, Don Goodman, Bobby Campbell, Martin Singleton

Not used: Aidey Thorpe

So nearly

Bradford City vs Ipswich Town

Second Division, Saturday 7 May, 1988

It all sounded so simple: just win the game. And yet as Bradford City walked out onto the Valley Parade pitch against Ipswich Town, for the final match of the 1987/88 season, the burden and expectation weighed heavily on their shoulders. The pressure was intense, the fear of losing overwhelming, the stakes were incredibly high.

Just win the game. For if the Bantams could defeat a mid-table Ipswich side that had nothing to play for, and if results elsewhere went their way, a huge prize would be theirs: promotion. And not only that, promotion to the top flight; and, with it, the rewards that included the opportunity to pit their wits against the country's elite players, and to play at some of the English football's most famous stadiums. This was a chance to go down in history as Bradford City legends; to grasp immortality, and to bring First Division football back to a club that had not seen it for more than half a century.

You had to go back to 1908 – exactly 80 years – for the last time that Bradford City had been promoted to the top division. Back then the club was only five years old, and there were only two Football League divisions. Football's greater equality meant that City's early year feats, such as winning the FA Cup in 1911, were unremarkable at the time – yet to future generations of City supporters, it seemed incredible that the club was once one of the best teams in the country. In 1922, City were relegated from the First Division and they spent the majority of the next six decades nestled in the bottom divisions. This, it seemed, was their permanent place on football's food chain.

But here they were, on the brink of an amazing return to the top flight. Just win the game. Listen out intently for other results and hope for the best.

Succeed and it would be one hell of a story.

Bantams' progressivism

On Friday 11 May, 1979, Crystal Palace earned promotion to the First Division after beating Burnley in front of more than fifty-thousand fans at Selhurst Park. The impressive manner in which the team had performed, and their relatively young age, led to the former Tottenham striker-turned-TV-pundit, Jimmy Greaves, famously predicting that Crystal Palace would be the "Team of the Eighties".

It didn't really work out that way. Palace looked dominant in the First Division for all of eight games, before slumping to finish mid-table and getting relegated the season after. And though they came back and experienced some heady moments, such as an FA Cup Final appearance in 1989/90, English football was once again dominated by Liverpool during the eighties, as they won six of the ten league titles that were contested over the decade. But arguably the really amazing football stories of the eighties came from the tales of the underdogs. In what was to prove to be the last full decade before the Premier League was formed in 1992, which caused the gulf between the rich and poor to grow disproportionately, so many so-called unfashionable clubs enjoyed a day or two in the sun.

There was, of course, Wimbledon's incredible FA Cup Final victory over the seemingly unconquerable Liverpool in 1988, a year after little-old Coventry City lifted the same trophy in their one and only major domestic triumph. Wimbledon had famously only reached the Football League in 1977, before a four-year surge up the divisions, between 1982-1986, saw them take on the cream of English football and routinely upset the odds. They weren't the only small club punching above their weight during the decade. Oxford United – another outfit with a relatively short Football League history – were promoted from the Third to First Division in two years, and won the League Cup in 1986. And there was also Swansea City, who at the end of the 70s/early 80s rose up all four divisions in consecutive seasons, only to slide back down to the bottom tier equally as fast. Watford, Luton Town and Brighton & Hove Albion were other small clubs who soared high in the eighties. It would be wrong to say that the advent of the Premier League has killed off such dramatic rises – witness the post-millennium achievements of Bournemouth, Hull City and, again, Swansea – but football in the eighties was full of tales of the underdog triumphing; and of small club accomplishments that now happen only rarely.

And yet, on that May afternoon at Valley Parade, Bradford City were on the verge of making a strong – and credible – claim to be the true "Team of the Eighties". Like Swansea and Wimbledon, during the eighties, City had climbed from the fourth tier and up the pyramid swiftly, and yet they had also done it with the added distraction of considerable off-the-field turmoil. In 1981/82, City were promoted from the Fourth Division under the management of Roy McFarland, but lost his services just six months later, as he took over at Second Division Derby County, with the Bantams ultimately only narrowly avoiding an instant relegation from the Third Division. This was just the beginning of the problems though. During the summer of 1983, City chairman Bob Martin had to call in the receivers, as the club had received a winding up order from Leeds United over an unpaid transfer fee for buying defender Trevor Cherry (who by now had become the City manager). They were saved from going out of business by two local businessmen, Stafford Heginbotham and Jack Tordoff, but still had to sell star striker Bobby Campbell to McFarland's Derby in order to raise funds.

Yet despite this turmoil, City very quickly found their feet in the Third Division, aided by Campbell swiftly returning after the Northern Ireland striker struggled to settle in the East Midlands. In 1984/85, two seasons after nearly going out of business, City romped to the Third Division title. They received, and paraded, the trophy on May 11, 1985, at home to Lincoln City – the day of the devastating Valley Parade fire. And so, as they faced the on-the-field challenge of adapting to a higher division next season, they did so with the considerable off-the-field turmoil of grieving for the 54 City supporters, and two Lincoln fans, who had lost their lives that day, and the hundreds of others who were injured. They had to cope with playing away from Valley Parade, within the Odsal bowl. And yet, just like post-1983, the club and the players dug in, and they prospered. Just eighteen months after the emotional return home to Valley Parade at the end of 1986, they now stood on the brink of a third promotion in five years.

When you consider this ongoing adverse backdrop, where the emotions of those at the club were tested in unprecedented ways, the achievements of Bradford City during the 1980s are all the more commendable. This truly was a special team; who rather than allowing hardship and upheaval to become an excuse, used these issues as an inspiration. The Bradford City team of the eighties is fondly remembered for its amazing team spirit, and that cannot have been easy to foster against emotions that would test any human being to the full.

Mark Ellis, who had been a regular since his debut in 1981, told me of the loyalty he and his team mates felt for the club, "It was a special team. It's more about money these days. I remember my first two years at Bradford, and I would have played for nowt – I nearly did anyway! It wasn't about money then, it was all about playing for the club." Stuart McCall added, "We didn't have a lot of money. We got free transfers in like Greg Abbott, John Hendrie, Ian Evans and Bobby Campbell came back. We had John Hawley, we had Eric McManus. We had some young players but we also had that little bit of experience."

At the time the City Gent magazine, which was formed in October 1984, coined the phrase 'Bantam Progressivism' to reflect the club's rise and rise. There was momentum and there was ambition. Although City hadn't played in the First Division since before World War II – and there would have been very few people in the crowd, if any, who were old enough to have seen those days – the belief grew in the summer of 1987 that the club could take another giant step forwards and reach the top flight. After all, they'd gone through so much to get this far.

Dolan's big impact

Terry Dolan had some mightily big shoes to fill. After Trevor Cherry was controversially sacked as Bradford City manager in January 1987, the club ultimately turned to the Bradford-born midfielder, who had hung up his boots in 1981, and spent a year working as youth coach at Valley Parade, before being promoted to Cherry's assistant, following Terry Yorath's decision to take up the Swansea managerial post in 1986. Just as Roy McFarland had been a success, Cherry had taken the Bantams forward; guiding the club to the Third Division Championship in 1985, and leading them through the trauma of the fire and the difficult existence at Odsal. His sacking was highly controversial and sparked outrage amongst the wider football community. After everything Cherry had done for City, and with the emotion of human tragedy still so raw, his dismissal appeared to be cold and cruel.

Dolan was initially made caretaker manager and did well. A team that was struggling to avoid relegation under Cherry, despite the return to Valley Parade mid-season, were transformed; and Dolan was handed the job on a full time basis. Dolan told me, "Everything happened fairly quickly. I came back to the club in 1985 as youth team coach. I was youth team coach for twelve months. The fire happened in-between as well. Terry Yorath, who was assistant, went to Swansea. And then I moved up to assistant and Stan Ternent came in as youth team coach. And then when Trevor got sacked, I was made caretaker manager. And I think I was caretaker manager for about five to six games. Then I actually got the job. You could say I was in the right place at the right time. Having said that, I had during my later years been player-coaching a Sunday league team, for six or seven seasons, which was good experience for me.

"We were down near the bottom when I took over as City manager, I'd nothing to lose! The key was we changed the formation and started playing with a sweeper. That made a big difference. We managed to survive the rest of that season, and then the following season was the nearly season, as people keep saying."

City eventually finished the 1986/87 campaign in the top half of the table, paving the way for a push for the First Division in 1987/88. The-then Telegraph & Argus journalist David Markham told me, "Terry Dolan guided City to tenth place after a remarkable end of season run – seven wins and only one defeat in their last nine matches. That provided the springboard for the following season as Terry Dolan strengthened his team with two major signings – goalkeeper Paul Tomlinson from Sheffield United and young central defender, a pacy defender, a feature of the modern game, Lee Sinnott, a £147,000 signing from Watford." Another addition was defender Brian Mitchell.

Dolan explained of the summer activity, "It was vital, because we had a fairly small squad. We needed to strengthen. I think it was fair to say that my first few signings were good signings: Paul Tomlinson, Brian Mitchell, and Lee Sinnott, who were all regulars in the team the following season."

But arguably even more important was the re-signing of the team's two star players, Stuart McCall and John Hendrie, who were both the seemingly never-ending target of tabloid speculation about big money moves. Both went into the summer of 1987 with their contracts having expired and with serious interest from top flight clubs. Stuart McCall said, "We had all gone to Magaluf on a holiday at the end of the 86/87 season. Stafford Heginbotham had come along with us, and he got me and John together after a couple of beers and said 'I want you to sign for another year'. Everyone else was saying to us 'it's time for you to move now'. But I wanted to give it another year. I was getting towards 23/24 and I had been linked with lots of other clubs. I had opportunities to go, but my dream was to get to the top flight with Bradford City. I never regretted it for a second and signed another year. People outside the club couldn't understand it, but they didn't know about the bond we had as players and as a club."

The pre-season hype proved justified. City raced out of the blocks with back-to-back 2-0 victories over Swindon and Oldham. Amazingly, they won ten of their first thirteen matches. This included a thumping 3-1 victory over the eventual champions, Millwall, at Valley Parade, and further home wins over promotion rivals Blackburn and Middlesbrough. By the end of October, City had lost only two games. They topped the league in mid-September, and excitement grew around the city that this was going to be their season. Dolan stated, "Everybody talks about McCall and Hendrie, but we had a great team spirit which I have always felt is important. We very rarely changed our system, and we always had good balance."

It was a great season to be a Bradford City supporter, as long-standing fan James Pieslak, Width of a Post and Bantams Banter writer, and who was then just nine-years-old, recalled to me, "It was my fourth season supporting City. At that age I was City mad and the success of the 87/88 season just strengthened that bond. It was the most exciting and optimistic season I remember watching, until over a decade later when we were promoted to the Premiership [see chapter five]. In the 1987/88 season my Dad and I would watch games from the old 'Rabbit Hutch' or Midland Road stand. I'd sit on a barrier separating the crowd from the pitch so my feet could kick the advertising hoardings. Occasionally a police officer would ask me to move, but other than that I managed to get incredibly up close to the action. I was literally within touching distance of the players, which made it all the more magical for a young whipper-snapper."

On the success of the team, James Pieslak added, "Dolan had a very small squad that season but the mix was right, and there seemed to be a spirit and camaraderie amongst the players. That combination meant we had a small bunch of talented pals who knew each other inside out and would run their socks off for one another. When that comes together you have a very potent mix and it worked a treat for Dolan, for the most part."

Success wasn't limited to the league either. In the League Cup, City eased past Fulham, Charlton and Reading to reach the quarter finals of the League Cup, only to lose to the eventual winners, Luton Town. They reached the fifth round of the FA Cup, after wins over Wolves and Oxford, going down 3-0 at First Division Portsmouth. They also reached the semi finals of the Football League Trophy, bowing out against Reading after victories over Aston Villa, Newcastle and Southampton. For a small squad, this fixture congestion might have posed a real challenge, but Dolan emphasised that his team largely coped okay, "I don't think it was a case of a fixture pile up. If you think about football now compared to then we didn't rotate. We didn't have that big of a squad anyway."

After some poor results over Christmas, City continued to prosper in the league over January and February. They completed the double over Millwall, and were victorious for a second time against Middlesbrough. This was a City team packed with quality and a strong, resilient streak. As James Pieslak reflected, "You could tell they just hated losing". Tomlinson was thriving in goal; Sinnott was marshalling the defence superbly alongside Gavin Oliver and Brian Mitchell. Up front Ron Futcher led the line well with nineteen goals in all competitions, supported by Ian "Big Stix" Ormondroyd (twelve goals) and Mark Leonard (ten). On the wing, Mark Ellis was another important player.

But the two star names were clearly McCall and Hendrie. The pair continued to be linked with other clubs on an almost weekly basis, but were playing their hearts out for City. McCall got twelve goals from midfield, whilst Dolan felt that Hendrie benefited from being pushed further up the pitch, with seventeen goals his reward. "John Hendrie had previously just been a right winger, and we gave him a lot more licence to float around up front. And he came into his own then. Stuart was getting better all the time, but I think one of the keys during that season was signing Micky Kennedy in January [for £250,000], with his experience."

James Pieslak felt that Futcher was an important player too, "Futcher made a big difference. With the iconic Bobby Campbell gone, the previous season we'd relied on John Hendrie's goals, but as is often the case, a prolific striker helped propel us to even loftier heights." He added that McCall and Hendrie were the two star players, "Without those two, we had a good side but with them we were on a different level. The flame-haired prince McCall dragged the players around him onto a different level, through his cajoling, leadership, grit and talent. He's a once-in-a-generation player, and I feel honoured to have grown up watching him develop into a top class footballer.

"Hendrie meanwhile was a constant menace down the flanks and in front of opposition defenders, providing ammunition for Futcher, Leonard and Stix to get onto. I've no doubt that opposition team talks were focused around stopping Hendrie; but talking about it, and actually doing it, were two very different concepts when the stocky winger was on song – which was very often that season. Hendrie ran riot in City colours, and every time he got the ball the atmosphere in the ground would change. He was exceptional." David Markham added, "In my time, City had two outstanding teams – this team, and the team that won promotion in 1999 and went on to survive in their first season in the Premier League. The 1987/88 team was the result of careful, steady planning – much the same methods that Phil Parkinson uses in the current era. The team was remarkably consistent."

It was all coming together superbly. In a division frequented by such big names as Aston Villa, West Bromwich Albion, Middlesbrough, Blackburn Rovers, Leeds United, Stoke City, Birmingham City, Crystal Palace and Leicester City, the Bantams were not only holding their own but out-performing the majority of their peers. James Pieslak said, "After the good start we had a tricky winter, losing a few games, but we got back on track and I remember us thumping West Brom at home 4-1 in the spring. We were simply unplayable against the Baggies. Everything we touched turned to gold. Walking away on a high after that game, promotion seemed a real possibility and 'Going Up' was sang with real conviction by the fans." On Tuesday 1 March, they welcomed local rivals, and bottom club, Huddersfield Town with just thirteen games to go. They had only lost three times at home all season, so another City victory seemed a formality.

Yet Huddersfield won the game 1-0; and then an almighty argument broke out that, to this day, remains unresolved.

The transfer fall out

Jack Tordoff's positive influence on Bradford City's history is undisputable. When the club fell into receivership in 1983, and the supporters did their bit by raising funds, he and Stafford Heginbotham were the only people who came forward with enough wealth to pay off the remaining debts and to save the club. Tordoff remained at the helm until the early 1990s before stepping down; but he has subsequently, and over different periods, provided important financial support to the club, in the shape of shirt sponsorship through his Bradford-based motor retail company, JCT 600. Tordoff remains life president at Bradford City, in recognition of his support and dedication to the club. It's simple really: no Jack Tordoff, no Bradford City.

Yet Tordoff has always struggled to shake off one highly controversial moment – the failure of Bradford City to strengthen during the run-in of the 1987/88 season. To some supporters, it will forever taint his association with Bradford City. To others, there is forgiveness in view of the bigger picture of what he gave to, and how he continues to financially support, the club. Nevertheless, Tordoff took a heck of a lot of stick in the aftermath of 1987/88, and the emotion in the argument lingers on to this day.

During the previous summer, Heginbotham – who was the chairman – endured two heart attacks. He was advised by his doctor to give up his role at Valley Parade, and midway through the 1987/88 campaign finally agreed to step down, selling his shares to Tordoff, who became the chairman. City were performing well on the pitch at the time, but Dolan was keen to ensure there was enough player cover going into the run-in, and that he had sufficient strength in depth. His two transfer targets were Keith Curle – a Reading centre back – and Andy Townsend – a young midfielder, languishing in Southampton's reserves. Neither signing ultimately happened, and the finger of blame was pointed squarely towards Tordoff.

Terry Dolan explained, "We felt that the time to sign the players was while we were on a good run, not when we were having a bad run. We were always going to score goals, but we probably conceded too many. We'd spent some time trying to identify the correct type of players, and most people know that the two players that we really wanted to sign were Keith Curle and Andy Townsend. We wanted Keith Curle to strengthen our backline. To be fair to the back three of Evans, Oliver and Sinnott, they played most of the season and fortunately they didn't get any injuries, but we needed someone else there as well.

"With Andy Townsend, although we were a largely balanced side we didn't have a left footed player in midfield and he was the perfect fit for that. We knew what it was going to cost us. Both players were going to cost us £300k each. But it didn't happen. As everybody realises, we weren't allowed to sign anybody."

Dolan's sense of frustration clearly lingers, even decades on. To him, there was no risk in committing to paying £600,000 on two additional players; because even if promotion wasn't achieved, the club could recoup this outlay by selling McCall and Hendrie. He continued, "What myself and Stan Ternant couldn't understand was we knew that if things didn't work out at the end of the season, Stuart McCall was going to go and John Hendrie was going to go. We knew what we'd get for them. So, for an outlay of £600,000, we knew that we would get somewhere between £1 million to £1.5 million for those two players. From our point of view, and from a business point of view, it was a no-brainer. But it didn't happen, and you have to accept that. The board decided no, and we had to get on with it."

Nevertheless, Dolan was unable to keep his feelings private at the time, and he elected to go public two days after the home defeat to Huddersfield Town. Via the Telegraph & Argus, Dolan stated, "We are on the verge of bringing First Division football back to Bradford for the first time for 66 years. This is something people have dreamed about for years and we want to give ourselves the best possible chance of achieving that objective...We know the squad needs strengthening and we were hoping we would have been given the facility to strengthen before the deadline. Now it appears that is not going to be the case. Although the board don't see the need for signings we, as a management team do. The directors' policy means we are not being given the chance to continue the work we have done in the past fourteen months...We feel the policy the board are pursuing is the wrong one if they are ambitious to get into the First Division."

It was striking stuff from someone who was in his first managerial job, but demonstrated just how strongly Dolan felt about the need to make signings. "From a business point of view, never mind from a football point of view, the club were going to make money", he continued to me, looking back on these events from the present day. "That's why I was so upset. And I knew that we needed extra players." Tordoff, unsurprisingly, was unimpressed by what he read in the T&A at the time. Only a day earlier, the City chairman had been quoted in the paper saying that City would need to sell before they could buy anyone else. "We have managed to hang on to our better players and we have also spent just short of £½m in excess of what we have received in transfer money. Unfortunately we don't have any more available money to strengthen the squad unless the manager is able to sell before the transfer deadline…I feel the squad we have, although it is a small squad, is good enough to get us out of the Second Division barring injuries and suspensions." Tordoff's words would prove prophetic, but for all the wrong reasons.

Whilst there is no doubt harsh words were exchanged between Tordoff and Dolan behind the scenes, following the latter's public criticism of the board, there were other victims too – namely David Markham. The T&A reporter was the subject of an angry letter from Tordoff, and was banned from travelling on the team coach to away matches – an arrangement that had been in place for years. Markham recalled of the transfer fall out, "There is little doubt that the squad needed strengthening in the run-up to transfer deadline day. The team were doing exceptionally well, but needed strengthening for the final push and, although the first choice team was good, it was a small squad and there was little quality cover for injuries and suspensions. Terry Dolan, it was reported, wanted to sign defender Keith Curle and midfield player Andy Townsend, both quality players, but neither signing materialised. Dolan went public about the need for new signings and all the players agreed with him – they too wanted the team to be strengthened.

"It was well known, of course, that Jack Tordoff was cautious about spending money and not one to waste it – that's why he has been a successful businessman – and it is also true that had he continued to be in charge of the club, Bradford City would not have gone into administration once, never mind twice."

Whilst Tordoff is on record at the time saying there was no money for signings, and that players needed to be sold first, nine years later he shared his own version of the events around the transfer fallout in an interview for the City Gent. "Two players keep getting brought up, One was Keith Curle…we approached Reading and offered £350,000 – an awful lot of money for a second division side in 1988 – we spoke to Curle and he was ready to come to Bradford…Terry Dolan rang me and said "we've missed him. Bobby Gould [then at Wimbledon] has offered £500,000". I asked whether the door was closed. Terry Dolan said "Jack I don't rate him at £500,000, so if that's the price they're wanting then count us out.""

Then there was Andy Townsend. Tordoff continued, "We offered £250,000. Southampton were interested and would have taken it…but he didn't want to come to Yorkshire. We upped the bid to £275,000 to try and put pressure on Southampton to push through the deal, but the player wouldn't come to Yorkshire and within a few weeks he'd gone to Norwich."

Dolan, however, correctly points out that the eventual moves of Curle to Wimbledon, and Townsend to Norwich City, took place during the summer, not in those March weeks when he was desperate to bring them to West Yorkshire. "We knew that we wouldn't be able to get them in the summer. Keith Curle went to Wimbledon in the First Division and Andy Townsend – who funnily enough at the time was in Southampton's reserves, which is why we felt we could get him – he ended up going to Norwich."

As David Markham pointed out, the City players too were unhappy. Mark Ellis reflected, "I think Stuart [McCall] and Jack had a bit of a fall out about it. Stuart was Bradford City crazy. I kept out of it. I was a bit of a follower at the time not a leader. I just got on with it. But probably if they'd gotten a couple of players it would have helped." In the City Gent nine years later, Brian Mitchell recalled the sense of disappointment about the lack of signings, "Within the dressing room, amongst the payers [sic] and management, morale was certainly affected. We all felt that Jack could have taken a chance and loosened the purse strings on the aforementioned players. We felt that the signings, if anything, would have had a positive mental effect and provided the lift necessary for the final push."

Stuart McCall added to me, "We didn't have a big squad and we were picking up a few injuries, and we apparently had the chance to sign Andy Townsend and Keith Curle in March. We were in need of an injection of freshness in the team, and they would have provided that. I remember people saying that you've got to speculate to accumulate. I don't know if Jack will look back with regret. I know that Stafford would have gone for it and signed them, because he was a gambler. I remember that Stafford's arch nemesis was Oldham, and whenever we played them he would come into the dressing room and offer us a bigger bonus if we won!

"There was no guarantees that we would have been promoted with those two players, but I think there was a sense of speculate to accumulate was needed. That said, Bradford City will go down in history now for the gamble in 2000 that backfired [see chapter six] and it shows there are no guarantees. But signing those two players would have definitely given us a better chance of promotion. The comfort blanket was they were always going to recuperate the money if we hadn't have gone up, as they could sell me and John."

The lack of team strengthening was immediately felt in a negative way, as in the next game – away at Birmingham City – Mark Ellis suffered a bad injury that would end his season. Ellis explained, "I missed the last ten games because I got injured at Birmingham. I had to have this massive operation on my knee. Looking back, I was so immature and daft at the time, and played with injuries. I'd get half my knee taken out and think 'I'll be fine'. For me it was a nightmare. Before it happened we were flying." Andy Townsend would have proven a good replacement for the injured Ellis, and without him form began to stutter, with a succession of draws over March and April. "That was the time when we needed the extra players," rued Dolan.

The second part of Tordoff's fears – suspensions – came to fruition during the final fortnight. With four games to go, City travelled to Man City and drew 2-2, but the result was overshadowed by a red card to John Hendrie of all people, and a controversial one at that. Dolan said, "John Hendrie getting sent off at Man City was a massive blow to us, because he was flying at that time. And as most people will tell you at the game, it was an unjust red card. He has supposedly gone into the Man City keeper [Mike Stowell] in a dangerous manner. He was going onto a through ball, stuck his foot out, and the referee deemed it to be violent conduct." Stuart McCall added with a grimace, "The John Hendrie sending off robbed us. It was an absolute travesty. He went in on the keeper and it was an absolutely shocking decision."

Back then, a suspension for a red card didn't commence until two weeks later, meaning Hendrie was ruled out of the final game of the season – at home to Ipswich. It would be the first time in four seasons that the always-available Hendrie would miss a game for City. Dolan added, "We'd picked up again. We beat Hull City, we beat Reading. But then we drew with Man City when John was sent off. And the blow with that was that we knew John was going to miss the last game, because back then you were suspended two weeks after you were sent off, which unfortunately proved to be the Ipswich game."

With three games to go it was very much in City's hands – win two of the final three, and they would achieve automatic promotion. They started off in the best possible way by defeating Leicester City 4-1 at Valley Parade, in impressive style, setting up a May bank holiday Monday trip to promotion rivals, Aston Villa. On the day, 36,423 people were present at Villa Park, including 6,000 City supporters; but alas there was no victory to seal promotion. Stuart McCall admitted, "David Platt scored and I had the role to look after him. We did okay but then he scored with a header from a free kick." David Markham reflected of the day, "Unfortunately, virtually the whole team had an off day at Villa Park, failing to rise to the big occasion in front a 36,000 crowd and lost 1-0 with the only goal being scored by David Platt, a future England international whom Villa had signed fairly recently from Crewe."

James Pieslak was also there that day and commented, "My entire family drove down and we arrived with hours to spare. There were so many City fans there that day, and everybody was very excited but nervous. Villa Park seemed huge, but the amount of City fans in Birmingham was astonishing. Sadly, it was a bad day at the office. Whether it was nerves, an off-day, or a good Villa side I cannot put my finger on, but we never really got going. Hendrie had a decent chance at 0-0 but unfortunately David Platt buried a header in the first half and we never really looked like getting back into it. Two years later Platt would be striking home a superb volley for England in the knockout stages of a World Cup, so Villa were clearly a decent side.

"It's a long way back to Bradford when you've lost, and we trooped back to the car to find the battery had gone flat so we had to sit glumly and wait for Dad to sort that, as smug Villa fans filed past us. Then, finally driving home, a Villa fan mooned us out of his car window."

Suddenly it was no longer in City's hands. They had fallen to fourth, and went into the final game against Ipswich Town needing to win, and then hoping that other results would go their way if they were to clinch the second automatic promotion place. Middlesbrough beat Barnsley 3-0 on the same afternoon as Villa defeated City, meaning they moved into the second promotion spot behind the champions, and already promoted, Millwall. Middlesbrough were at home to Leicester on the final day, and City had to pray they lost – even a Boro draw would mean they couldn't be caught by the Bantams. Meanwhile Aston Villa – who were now third – travelled to Swindon Town, needing to better Middlesbrough's result. As long as Villa didn't win, the Bantams could overtake them if they were victorious themselves. So the ideal scenario was that Middlesbrough would lose and Aston Villa would lose or draw. "City must win…and hope" stated the headline in the Telegraph & Argus on the Friday edition before the Ipswich game, with the piece quoting Mark Leonard as saying, "The worst thing that can happen is for the other teams to slip up and for us not to have done our job by beating Ipswich."

The worst thing happened.

A day of heartache

And so to Ipswich, a sell out crowd of 16,017 – the highest since the club's return to Valley Parade, and a season's hard work on the line. After seven years of amazing progress on the field, City were on the brink of reaching the summit. Just win the game and hope for the best. The Suffolk club were sat in the top half of the table, but were a long way behind the play off places. They had won only four away matches all season and had nothing to play for. Ipswich manager John Duncan's pre-match comments that City "can expect a very tough challenge from us and we are confident of getting a good result" felt more like bravado than a serious threat. Surely City would at least do their own job? Surely it was more a case of clinging onto the hope of miracles taking place elsewhere?

It certainly began that way. After just eleven minutes, Greg Abbott eased home nerves by steering City into the lead. Ron Futcher had delivered an incisive through ball for Abbott to run onto, which he slipped past the Ipswich goalkeeper, Ron Fearon. It got even better a few minutes later, as news filtered through that Middlesbrough had surprisingly gone a goal behind at home to Leicester. A highly charged home crowd, which included several fans clutching transistor radios, who relayed the good news to others, loudly cheered the Leicester City goal. As things stood, City would be promoted, rather than Middlesbrough or Aston Villa.

But then, very quickly, it started to go wrong for the Bantams. Firstly, Mich D'Avray equalised for Ipswich with a close range strike after great work by Dalian Atkinson. In his T&A match report David Markham wrote that "City struggled to contain the talented Dalian Atkinson, whose pace, power and skill make him a tremendous prospect." Atkinson indeed went onto have a good career with Aston Villa in the early Premier League era. In the opening stages of this game, City had suffered another major injury problem as Brian Mitchell had to leave the field following a bad challenge by midfielder Jason Dozzell. The clumsy tackle by Dozzell would not be the last piece of damage that he would inflict upon City, as in the 25th minute he was left free to head Ipswich Town into a 2-1 lead. An afternoon that was set to be full of joy for the home faithful was going badly wrong. Dolan ruefully told me, "We'd done our homework on Ipswich and Jason Dozzell, one of their midfield players, who went on to play at Tottenham, was a very talented player. On the research we had done, he'd not scored a goal for thirteen months, and yet he ended up getting one." City were spurred into life and Leonard went close to an equaliser, but his header was off target. Eight minutes before half time, the inspirational McCall drilled home for 2-2 to give City renewed hope. Futcher again was the architect, playing McCall through on goal. With other results going exactly the way that City wanted, the half time talk would have been strikingly similar to the pre-match one: just win the game.

The minutes ticked by painfully slowly, with City's attempts to get a third and decisive goal thwarted by a resolute Ipswich defence. The home side were laying siege to the Ipswich goal, with Fearon in fine form and saving impressively from Lee Sinnott, Futcher and Leonard. And then, with 19 minutes to go, came the knock-out blow at the other end. Sinnott attempted a back pass to Tomlinson, but he misjudged the power that was required and David Lowe was able to intercept. The Ipswich midfielder rounded Tomlinson, before laying the ball back for Simon Milton to score what would be the winner, Bradford City 2 Ipswich Town 3. There was no way back, and the pain of defeat was made worse by the fact that other results ultimately went the right way for City. Middlesbrough lost 1-2 to Leicester, whilst Aston Villa drew 0-0 at Swindon. Both sides finished on 78 points, but City's loss left them on 77. Villa and Boro had the same goal difference, but the former had scored five more goals than the latter over the season, which meant the Birmingham side were celebrating promotion at the County Ground. Middlesbrough would play against Bradford City in a two-legged play off semi final. Blackburn – who finished fifth, and in the final play off place – would face Chelsea of the First Division in the other play off semi final (back then, the third from bottom top flight team would also go into the play offs, in a bid to retain their First Division status). It was a dreadfully disappointing day. David Markham recalled, "They couldn't handle the big occasion and went down 3-2. No Bradford City supporter who saw that match will ever forget it."

Dolan recalled of the defeat, "We were confident. The only thing was Ipswich had nothing to play for so were probably a bit more relaxed than our players. To concede three at home was very disappointing. Everything just seemed to go against us that day." If only Dolan could have called upon Ellis and Hendrie, but instead the pair were sat next to him on the bench. "I was in the dugout with John Hendrie and I couldn't believe we lost the game," added Ellis. "I had gone to Villa as well and we only needed one win from our last two games to get promoted, and we lost both of them. But it didn't happen, and that's football. It's just so unfortunate. Then you think 'oh well, we will win in the play offs as we're the best team'. But sadly it doesn't work that way."

For Stuart McCall the regret lingers on, "You always look at games you'd want to play again. If I could turn back the clock, certainly the last game at home to Ipswich is one I would have loved to have played again. It was as if we had let everyone down. If we had have won we would have gone up. The expectation level was so high. John Hendrie was a big miss. We still went into the game confident, but during the game we were edgy. It was a sore one to come off to." James Pieslak added of the day, "I remember pure desperation from the crowd, from my Dad and from my friend who came with us. I imagine that seeped into the players. The mood was shrill panic – 'get it forward', 'attack', 'come on' – but, sadly, desperate pleas aren't enough in football, or in life, and we came away with nothing. A 2-3 reverse tells you a lot; we were wide open at the back as we put everything into scoring goals."

The play offs – which had only been introduced by the Football League the season before – did at least guarantee the club around £100,000 in extra gate receipts, and Tordoff told the T&A after the Ipswich game that this windfall would be used for new signings. "I believe we can still get promotion and the extra money from the play offs is going towards new players for the First Division. That is my pledge." Dolan was similarly bullish at the time, stating, "It's been a great season and it's not over yet. Our players are upset, but imagine how Middlesbrough must feel. They probably feel worse than we do because they have thrown their chance away."

But despite the confidence – and the return of Hendrie from suspension – playing resources were stretched to the limit. Mitchell joined Ellis on the sidelines, after having to undergo a cartilage operation, whilst Ron Futcher hurt his hip against Ipswich and was a major doubt. In the T&A on the eve of the first leg against Middlesbrough, Markham wrote, "City start a momentous three weeks with only 12 fit senior players." Stuart McCall nevertheless recalls feeling upbeat, in view of the fact City had beaten Middlesbrough home and away during the regular league campaign, "We came off disappointed against Ipswich, but knowing we still had a chance. We knew we were playing Middlesbrough, who we had beaten twice, we beat Middlesbrough at home 2-0 and we beat them away 2-1 over the season, so we went into the play offs feeling confident."

The dream dies

At lunchtime on the Saturday that followed the Ipswich defeat, another sell out crowd convened at Valley Parade, for the first leg of the play offs, against Middlesbrough. The Bantams played really well and struck the opening goal of the tie in the 67th minute through defender Karl Goddard. Trevor Senior equalised less than a minute later, but McCall struck the winner to ensure that City went into the second leg with a slender advantage. James Pieslak added, "Arriving at Valley Parade in a positive mood, I remember experiencing a coming-of-age when suddenly the confidence drained out of me as we took our spot in the Midland Road rabbit hutch. Memories of Villa and Ipswich came rushing back, and I remember experiencing a feeling, for the first time at Valley Parade, that I'm all too used to now – dread. Still we played fairly well, and it was fantastic to get back to winning ways on a wonderfully sunny day."

But in truth it should have been a healthier lead as City spurned numerous chances. It would unfortunately come back to bite, as Stuart McCall reflected, "We went 1-0 up. Trevor Senior equalised at the Kop end which was a sickener. I scored to make it 2-1, but we came off the pitch feeling that we should have won by four or five. There was a sense that we should have finished them off. Yet we'd now played them three times and won all three of them. If it would have been an award, we would have kept it on top of our mantelpiece." David Markham agreed, "City played exceptionally well in the first leg, dominating the game but went into the second leg with only a 2-1 margin, when 4-1 would have been a fair reflection of the play. Many of us suspected that 2-1 would not be enough and that proved to be the case."

Three days later at Ayresome Park, Bernie Slaven levelled the tie on aggregate for Middlesbrough in front of 25,868 fans; and, with no away goals rule, the game went into extra time. But as Dolan reflected, the cost of the high number of league and cup fixtures, and a small squad, was taking its toll, and an ever-tiring City went 2-0 down on the night, thanks to an extra time goal from Gary Hamilton. There was no way back. City had lost 3-2 at home to Ipswich to miss out on automatic promotion, and in the play offs they lost 3-2 on aggregate to Middlesbrough. Dolan explained, "We didn't need to lift the players after Ipswich. For the league game against Middlesbrough we had played ever so well. In the first play off game we played very well again, but Trevor Senior scoring for Middlesbrough gave them a bit of hope for the second leg. Even with the second leg, we were 1-0 down after 90 minutes and then it went to extra time. I think by then, with the extra games we had played and with a smallish squad, it did take its toll." David Markham stated, "For me, there was an irony in the Middlesbrough defeat was that City had beaten them twice in the regular season with two of the best footballing displays of what was successful campaign, until it ended in disappointment. It was one of the saddest nights I experienced in covering Bradford City, not just because they team had missed the chance to win promotion to the top division – that was the most important factor – but also because we knew that the two best players, Stuart McCall and John Hendrie would leave the club if the team failed to gain promotion."

Stuart McCall said of the second leg, "There were City fans everywhere. The support was incredible. It was sickening to lose the way that we did. I remember there been a lot of tears in the dressing room afterwards, and a lot of tears on the bus journey home too." Mark Ellis watched events from afar as he received treatment for his injury. "We were so unfortunate not to get promotion," he reflected. "I remember being at Lilleshall, with Peter Beardsley and a couple of other players, when Bradford played Middlesbrough. That's where I watched it from. And I remember the other players saying to me 'you'll beat Middlesbrough' and of course we didn't. I just shrugged it off and thought 'oh well, there's always next year'. But unfortunately it doesn't work like that.

"Looking back now I realise that I had a great chance to play in all four divisions for my hometown club, and those opportunities don't come along too often. But I can't complain, I played from my hometown club and they were great times."

James Pieslak also has mixed memories of that season, "We missed out on promotion so you have to say it was a missed opportunity. The table doesn't lie. We lost three out of four games at the end of the season when it really mattered, including the play offs, which is disappointing. But still, it was a fantastic season. Even though it ended so painfully, on the whole I look back on it with happy memories instead of sad ones. It was an early lesson in how emotional it can be supporting a football team, one which I'm still learning."

Promotion truly was a now-or-never-moment. As expected, Hendrie and McCall departed Valley Parade during the summer, in order to satisfy their understandable career aspirations of playing at the highest level. Hendrie moved to Newcastle United for £500,000, whilst McCall made a tearful exit to Everton for £850,000. He explained to me, "I knew that Colin Harvey [then-Everton manager] had been up at Ayresome Park to watch me. Someone on the bus home from Middlesbrough turned around and said to me 'you shouldn't be upset, you're moving on' and I remember snapping back at them. As much as I was confident I was going to play for Everton, I wanted to get promoted with Bradford City.

"I always said that if Bradford City had have won promotion, I'd have signed a ten-year deal. It wasn't a lack of ambition; it's sometimes where your heart wanted to be. It was quite ironic that the first game of next season, City were down South somewhere and so a bus load of City fans came to Goodison Park for my debut, as I was playing against John, who had signed for Newcastle. We won the game 4-0 in front of 40,000 people and it was an incredible atmosphere. But if you'd have given me and John the opportunity to be running out for City against Everton or Newcastle, that's what we would have wanted."

The £1.35 million profit made on McCall and Hendrie was of little consolation to Dolan and supporters. These were two of the club's most popular modern day players – the fact that Valley Parade's two function suites are now named after each player says it all – and they would prove impossible to replace. David Markham said, "Both players had agreed to stay for another year to see if the club could gain promotion. If they failed – which they did – both would leave to fulfil their ambitions of playing in the top flight elsewhere. The only consolation for the club was that they received big fees for both players. I am not sure they could have received more. And, to be fair to Jack Tordoff, he allocated the whole of the combined fee £1.35 million to Terry Dolan to rebuild the team. And, of course, when Ian Ormondroyd was sold the following January for £650,000, that money was also allocated for team strengthening making £2 million in all. A lot of money then, and a lot of money now." Dolan added, "There was no hope of keeping them. John Hendrie's contract was up so we knew he was going to go. Stuart had a clause in his contract that if we didn't get into the First Division he could go. We knew they were going to go."

Amazingly, Dolan would leave Valley Parade shortly afterwards too. In January 1989 he was sacked. He was able to use the Hendrie/McCall windfall to bring in new players during the summer of 1988, but the new arrivals were not of the same of ilk. Dolan was a victim of the heightened expectations, but City struggled to match their feats of 1987/88 and the team were lumbered in mid-table for most of the season. Despite more cup heroics – Dolan's City beat McCall's Everton 3-1 in the League Cup and Tottenham 1-0 in the FA Cup – Tordoff swung the axe. Dolan stated, "The following season, we got to the quarter finals of the League Cup, beat Tottenham in the FA Cup, but then three weeks after that I was gone. It was hard to take. I'd played for the club and I'd supported the club, so it hurt even more. But you have to get over that. From there I went to Rochdale and started over again."

Dolan's replacement was Terry Yorath – lured back from Swansea City – but despite having money to spend, the tide had shifted and City were looking downwards rather than up. Mark Ellis never fully recovered from his injury, and played only a handful more times for City, before moving to Halifax and then retiring. Ellis has retained close links with the club, and was partly responsible for City signing James Hanson (2009) and Nahki Wells (2011) after he mentored and recommended the pair. Ellis said, "To be honest I didn't realise how bad my knee was. I think I played about five or six games after that. I remember playing against Man City on the last day of the season and scoring [1988/89], but it took four days for my knee's swelling to go down. And we played in Malta and my knee was massive. Terry Yorath just told me to get out and play, without any understanding of what I was going through. That was him all over – not that I don't like the guy, I do! I never recovered from that injury. It was horrible and I didn't realise what I was getting myself in for.

"I knew a lot of the fans and I grew up with them on Holme Wood – they're the ones who used to shout at me! You used to recognise certain fans at away grounds. I'm not sure if it's like that anymore, I'm sure the players recognise certain fans. I knew a lot of the fans and I still know them now. I love going down to Bradford City because I still see the same faces."

The play off defeat was a bitter pill to swallow for everyone. 1987/88 has forever been nicknamed "the nearly season" and it haunted the club for a decade. James Pieslak sums up the scale of the missed opportunity, "If we had been promoted we may well have kept McCall and Hendrie and then bolstered the squad with some good signings and who knows after that. The gap between the rich and the poor was much smaller in 1988 than it is today, so we probably stood a better chance of establishing ourselves as a decent top flight side back then." It was also a career-defining moment for Terry Dolan, who despite a good managerial career in the lower leagues with clubs like Rochdale and Hull City would never touch the same heights as he did at Bradford City. Dolan has more recently worked as a Premier League referee's assessor, and despite the nagging feeling of regret he remembers the nearly season fondly. "It's at the top," he revealed when I asked him how 1987/88 ranks in his career. "If you talk to most supporters, who watched that team for those two years, they will tell you that they really enjoyed it, because we played good football.

"Looking at my career as both player and manager, there are two things I regret. As a player I left Bradford City and then went to Bradford Park Avenue, and then I went to Arsenal. Arsenal wanted to sign me, but I just couldn't stand London! I should have stayed at Arsenal. The other regret is that I wish we could have beaten or drawn with Ipswich that day and got us into the First Division, because that might have changed my pathway as a manager."

As for the Bantams, it took them another eleven years to fully recover and get back to the position of challenging for a place in the top flight – and in the run-in for that 1998/99 season; the memories came flooding back to those who were still healing from the pain of 1988. Ironically, in 1999, Ipswich Town were City's main rival for the second automatic promotion spot, and towards the end of the season the Bantams endured a shock home loss to Huddersfield. But unlike in 1988, this time City strengthened the team in March, to ensure there was cover for injuries, suspensions and loss of form.

They had the insurance policy that was so badly lacking in 1988.

City: Paul Tomlinson, Brian Mitchell (Greg Abbott 8), Karl Goddard, Stuart McCall, Gavin Oliver, David Evans, Mark Leonard, Lee Sinnott, Ian Ormondroyd, Mick Kennedy, Ron Futcher
Not used: Leigh Palin

We want football

Bradford City vs Swansea City

Third Division, Saturday 23 November, 1991

The true level of character, and the depth of history, that resides inside the modern day Valley Parade stadium can be evidenced in the uneven structure of the four stands that surrounds the pitch. There aren't too many other Premier League and Football League grounds – especially the modern ones – which have such an unusual look as Valley Parade; but to those of us who love it and call it our home, the stadium's imperfections are part of its charm. And nowhere is this better illustrated that the Bradford End of the ground.

Whereas the towering, modern day Kop stand, located behind the goal at the opposite end of the pitch, is testament to the strength of Bradford City's late century rise to the Premier League – and the Main Stand has become a permanent reminder of the folly of over-ambition – the Bradford End is a basic, two-tiered stand. One that is so small in comparison to the Kop that it provides the ground with a lop-sided feel. Commonly referred to as the TL Dallas Stand, due to a long-standing sponsorship agreement, the Bradford End is usually used for visiting supporters, and has a succession of pillars that obstruct the view. It's said that if you are sat at the very back of the top tier, you can't properly see the pitch immediately below you. To call the toilets basic is probably over generous – a succession of visiting supporters have labelled them an embarrassment to Bradford City. The entire 1,800 capacity stand has just one snack bar available, and it doesn't even serve beer.

When Saturday Comes magazine published a scathing review of the stand in January 1997, with author and Barnsley fan Richard Darn stating that it offers, "A magnificent blend of restricted views, two-dimensional toilets and external piping that makes the Pompidou Centre look banal…It's called a stand but otherwise has no other connection with sport or spectator comfort." That review might be harsh, yet there is no question that the Bradford End is an economical, no-frills stand. But beyond everything, it is a reflection of a more modest, make-do era for the club. Built as it was in 1991, when Bradford City were in decline and were badly lacking in foresight, vision and ambition. The Bradford End is a mediocre football stand, constructed at a time when Bradford City seemed perfectly happy to become a mediocre football club.

The big football shake-up

If you were to plot a graph measuring Bradford City's fortunes, and the popularity of English football itself, between 1986 and 1994, you would have two lines that moved upwards and downwards in very different directions.

After the nearly season of 1987/88, the decline of the Bantams was swift and brutal. Just two years after almost making it to the top flight, City were relegated from the Second Division and consigned to the doldrums of the bottom two divisions. After Terry Dolan's sacking mid-way through the 1988/89 season, the former assistant manager to Trevor Cherry, Terry Yorath, was lured away from managing Swansea City. Yorath combined his role in the dugout at Valley Parade with taking charge of the Wales national team, on a part-time basis. The decline was setting in and, in the 1989/90 season, it was clear, very early on, that City were fighting for their Second Division lives. Jack Tordoff sold his shareholding in the club, to a consortium that included Bradford-based businessman David Simpson (a successful travel agent), for a reported £700,000, and the new owners quickly removed Yorath from the hot seat. But still, relegation couldn't be avoided. They finished second bottom of the table, nine points short of safety. At home they were decent, but a failure to win a single away game all campaign was costly. The pain was compounded by the fact local rivals Leeds United won the Second Division title that season, and were promoted to the First Division, just two years after City had come so desperately close to doing so.

Kieran Wilkinson has supported Bradford City since the nearly season of 1987/88, when as a seven-year-old he was taken to a home game against Blackburn Rovers. He writes for Widthofapost.com and told me of how the club struggled to recover in the aftermath of failing to get promoted in 1988, and losing their two star players, Stuart McCall and John Hendrie, culminating in 1990's relegation, "With the catalysts of that nearly season gone, things soon fell away. Whilst there were some promising moments in the year after – the cup wins against Everton and Spurs – the years, post-nearly season, were ones of hype that failed to be lived up to. There were disappointing returning heroes, namely Peter Jackson and Terry Yorath, and disappointing "big" signings like Andy Thomas and Tony Adcock. It quickly became apparent that the nearly season had probably been our one big shot at the big time. Bearing in mind that City had spent the majority of the previous 50 years in the bottom two tiers, there was probably less of a sense of entitlement compared to that which some fans have now, and there would have been some sense that the 1990 relegation took us back to more of our natural level. It's a typically Bradfordian trait to look on the dark side of life! I don't recall there being any great feeling that we were too big to be in the Third Division."

Indeed, rather than push for a quick return to the Second Division, the decline continued and City became stuck in the middle of the third tier. Results were mixed, the football was desperate. The strong affinity shared between the crowd and players, which had been fostered during the club's eighties' rise up the divisions, and strengthened by the fire disaster, was suddenly lost.

And what was happening elsewhere, in the wider landscape of English football, only brought home the gravity of just what a missed opportunity 1988 had become for Bradford City. Whilst on the field City had a largely brilliant time during the eighties, it was a truly dismal decade for the sport itself, one that was headlined by human tragedy. There was, of course, the Valley Parade fire which should have given the authorities a wake-up call about the dilapidated state of football grounds up and down the country. Then a few weeks later came Heysel – when, an hour before the European cup final between Liverpool and Juventus was due to kick off, a group of Liverpool fans charged at their Italian counterparts, prompting panic and for a wall to collapse, crushing people and resulting in 39 fatalities.

This tragedy underlined the seriousness of British football's hooligan problem. English clubs were banned from European competition for five years as punishment. In April 1989 came the Hillsborough tragedy, when 96 innocent Liverpool fans lost their lives due to shocking negligence, during the first few minutes of an FA Cup semi final with Nottingham Forest. The families of the victims were about to begin a 23-year long battle to uncover the truth over what really happened. Meanwhile football hooliganism was rampant across the land, and a disapproving Government, led by Margret Thatcher, attempted to implement an ID scheme upon all football supporters. Attendances were in decline up and down the country. In 1985/86 – the season after the Valley Parade and Heysel disasters – the average Football League attendance fell to 8,130. This was its lowest average since 1902, and it would barely improve up until 1992.

In the wake of Hillsborough, the highly respected magazine, The Economist, ran a cover story about the future of football under the headline "The game that died" it predicted a grim future for the sport, unless radical change occurred. Writing in the Guardian in December 1989, the legendary football journalist David Lacey stated, "Football will remember the Eighties as the decade when the fans died. The last ten years have seen fundamental changes in the way the English game is run and watched, if not the manner in which most of it is played, but the fact that so many spectators have been killed in such avoidable circumstances makes this the most sorrowful, shameful period in soccer history.

"A lot of the old assumptions have evaporated. The game has fallen so low in public esteem that the Government can force spectators to carry identity cards without considering the scheme a political risk, the very opposite in fact."

Yet the turning of the decade from the eighties to the nineties would herald the biggest revolution to English football since it was created, more than 100 years earlier. The Taylor Report, which looked into the reasons for the Hillsborough disaster, delivered a conclusion that standing sections in football grounds was unsafe, and that public money should be used so that clubs in the top two divisions could convert their stadiums into all-seater venues. England's heroic 1990 World Cup campaign helped to reverse the public's declining opinion of football. From becoming a sport notorious for hooliganism, blighted by tribal males acting in brutal, violent ways, we suddenly had Paul Gascoigne crying during the World Cup semi final, over a yellow card that would mean he would miss the final, should England have won the game. Suddenly football had an iconic, and very different, hero that captured the public's imagination. Gascoigne was an astonishingly talented footballer, with a cheeky persona and who evidently had a sensitive side to him. Significantly for the future of football, he struck a chord with middle class people who had turned away from the sport.

Most importantly of all, football club owners at the top of the game had now firmly shaken off their previous mistrust of TV, and realised that – with the birth of Satellite TV – there was serious money to be made. And crucially, they wanted to keep it themselves, rather than share it around. Thus, in the summer of 1991 – and, amazingly, with the backing of the FA – a new blueprint for the game was unveiled which included a breakaway top division.

Prior to 1983, all TV money was distributed amongst the four divisions, and gate receipts from matches were shared 50-50 between the home and visiting team. Such a principled, even-handed approach ensured that smaller clubs could still prosper. Brian Clough's Nottingham Forest won back-to-back European cups at the start of the 1980s, which was a remarkable achievement for a club whose previously mediocre history could match Bradford City. Yet the gate sharing was done away with that summer, so that away teams no longer received 50% of league match gate receipts. This instantly gave the bigger clubs – who had the larger gates – a big financial advantage. The terms of the collective TV deals of the time were also renegotiated in the mid-80s, to give the top flight clubs greater amounts of the pot. But this wasn't enough for them. Attitudes had changed, and the old worry that the presence of TV cameras would put people off attending matches was fading, as people realised that there was a big financial windfall available from TV. And, ultimately, the bigger clubs wanted to keep all of the television money for themselves.

Thus the top division breakaway – known today as the Premier League – was eventually agreed. From 1992 onwards, the clubs in the top flight have by and large kept all the money generated from increasingly huge TV deals. Sky TV won the exclusive rights, smashing the BBC and ITV monopoly that had succeeded in keeping the price down. Suddenly football fans had to pay a subscription to watch top flight football live on TV. The product of football became glamorous and ticket prices rose to eye-watering levels. Rather than the cost putting people off, the glitz of the Premier League led to a rise in attendances. People were willing to pay inflated ticket prices, although others were being priced out. Gascoigne's tears had won over middle class people, and football was more than willing to rebrand itself, sweep away working class people (and hooligans) and take the money of the new punters. The TV money, and the rising ticket charges, guaranteed the elite unprecedented levels of wealth.

The other 70 clubs (as it was back in 1992, with the top division having 22 teams until 1995) were left to fend for themselves. They have also benefited from the love affair between football and television, with TV deals of their own, but nowhere near in the same league as the Premier League. Suddenly, just to be a low-achieving top flight club, finishing mid-table each year, gave you a colossal advantage over teams in the divisions below, battling gamely to take their place in the Premier League. The divide between the rich and the poor, the haves and the have nots, began.

And, crucially for Bradford City, they were on the wrong end of that divide. If, in 1988, they had only beaten Ipswich on the final day of the season, a place at this new exclusive millionaires club could have feasibly been achieved. With football's greater equality back then, it would not have been unreasonable to believe that a promoted Bradford City could have comfortably established themselves in the First Division, and remained there for years to come, growing their financial strength and fanbase along the way, and being ideally placed to benefit from the Premier League and the ever-increasing Sky Sports TV deals. After all, teams of comparable size like Oldham Athletic, Southampton and Coventry City managed to do just that. In the 1980s Chelsea were in the Second Division with City, a million miles away from their Roman Abramovich-fuelled future. It was like a grown up game of musical chairs. Wherever you happened to be, when the music stopped in 1992, would go a long way towards defining your future.

But in this brave new world, where the Premier League would launch to glitz and glamour, going on from strength to strength to become the world's most popular and watched league by a country mile, Bradford City faced being left behind. They had slumped into the third tier two years before the Premier League launched, and they were going nowhere fast. It was as though the agony of missing out in 1988 had given them a lasting hangover that they just couldn't shake off. The City Gent had coined the club's rise during the 1980s 'Bantams Progressivism', and the fanzine had a suitable nickname to sum up City's fortunes during the first half of the nineties: 'The Doldrums'.

The tale of two McCalls and of City's relegation

A real sense of frustration and loathing built up around Valley Parade following 1988, with a feeling that the fall of the club was largely self-inflicted, and the result of mis-management. It is a story that has occurred at football clubs up and down the land before and after the Bantams' fall, as the consequences of selling your best players – even for really good money – are that they are almost impossible to replace to the same level, and so then the decline sets in. Players can be club heroes in front of your eyes. But if, and when, they leave, and they aren't adequately replaced, their legendary status grows even further, because of how badly they are missed.

There is no doubt that the sales of Stuart McCall and John Hendrie, after 1988, fall into this category. Despite having a sizeable transfer kitty, born from the sales of these two heroes, Terry Dolan was unable to spend this money wisely. He brought in inferior replacements, who struggled not only to live up to the high standards of McCall and Hendrie, but also failed to cope with the rising demands of a crowd, who understandably now had much bigger expectations of their club. McCall was sold to Everton for £850,000. John Hendrie joined Newcastle United for £500,000. The 1987/88 top scorer, Ron

Futcher, was sold to Port Vale for a knock-down fee of £35,000. Ian Ormondroyd was another high profile departure a year later, moving to Oldham Athletic for £625,000. £2 million was raised from selling just four players; but whilst much of this money was reinvested back into the team, Terry Dolan couldn't find the same quality. Ian Banks and Paul Jewell came in, and a then-club record £350,000 was spent on bringing Peter Jackson back to Valley Parade, after he had left City in the summer after the fire disaster. Whereas Jackson was a hero during his first spell, his second coming proved to be a huge disappointment and he didn't stick around for long, handed a free transfer by the club to save money on his considerable wages. Ian Banks – who later returned to City as Nicky Law's assistant, in 2002 – lasted just one season. Paul Jewell stayed on for more than a decade as a player, and later became manager, which worked out famously. Jewell proved a good player over the years, but wasn't in the McCall or Hendrie class.

The club struggled badly over the first half of the 1988/89 campaign; with Terry Dolan claiming he was trying to further strengthen the side, but that other clubs knew he had money and were unrealistically inflating asking prices for players who he enquired about. In January – and just eight months after the Ipswich game that could have put City in the top flight – Dolan was sacked following a cup defeat to Hull. Terry Yorath came in but lasted only thirteen months, by which point City were heading towards relegation back to the bottom two divisions. Given it had taken almost 50 years to regain Second Division status the last time, the despondency felt by supporters over City's impending fall was understandable. Even a change of regime – Jack Tordoff leaving and David Simpson taking control – was met with cautious optimism at best.

The McCall/Hendrie/Futcher/Ormondroyd money was not spent wisely by either Dolan or Yorath. If there was a singular transfer that summed up the sheer wastefulness of City's riches, it lied in the name 'McCall'. At the start of the 1989/90 season that ended in relegation, Terry Yorath caused a stir by announcing he'd signed McCall. Alas, it wasn't Stuart, but Ian. A journeyman Scottish midfielder, who had failed to make an impression at Rangers, Ian McCall was utterly woeful at Valley Parade, and made just twelve appearances all season. He cost the Bantams £200,000. Somehow the word disappointment doesn't do it justice.

There was, however, still the odd chink of light. Lee Duxbury was one such bright hope, having emerged through the youth ranks at Valley Parade in 1988/89 and becoming a regular the season after. He captained the side in the 2-1 loss at Hull that confirmed relegation to the Third Division, in April 1990. He had been sat in the Main Stand right where the fire broke out on that fateful day of 11 May, 1985, vacating his seat five minutes before the stand ignited, to go for a drink.

Duxbury told me about the beginnings of his career, "I was looking after people's boots, and kits. This, that and the other. I was captain of the intermediate team, which was the under 19s at the time. For the first time we won the league. In those days that was big for the club. We were playing against Leeds, the two Sheffields, Newcastle and Sunderland. So that was a big step for Bradford City. It was the first time that Bradford City won that league. You get put into the first team and then dragged back out. You're training with the first team, and sometimes you'd feel like you were out of your depth. Then other times you think you've done something good, and you feel like a million dollars and that you should be there. It was an up and down time.

"I went on loan for three months to Rochdale. Terry Dolan was in charge of Rochdale at the time [his next manager job after leaving Valley Parade]. I had a good three months there. We got a good draw in the FA Cup, losing to Crystal Palace away 1-0, with Geoff Thomas getting the winner. That was a great experience. You come back a different player, more experienced. People at the club who knew me were watching me at Rochdale and told everybody how well I was playing. I came back and more or less got straight into the first team."

But whilst Duxbury was beginning to firmly find his feet in the side, those around him where either failing miserably or being sold. Jimmy Quinn was a rare good signing by Yorath, but was transferred to West Ham in January 1990. He was the only player regularly scoring, and so his departure all but doomed the team to the drop. A 2-7 thrashing at Watford over Christmas pushed City into the bottom three, and they would never recover.

Yorath was dismissed in March, with relegation looking inevitable. It was vital that the club brought in the right man to revive the club; someone who could plot a quick recovery back up the divisions.

Send in the Doc

The man who Simpson and the new board turned to was John Docherty. It would be fair to say that the Doc has made a strong and lasting impression amongst City supporters of that era – but not in a positive way. Poll long-standing fans on the worst manager they have ever seen at Valley Parade, and John Docherty would win the vote by a landslide. If, after watching City fail to grasp the opportunity of promotion in 1988, and then be relegated to the Third Division within two years, people thought that things couldn't possibly get any worse, they were about to be proven wrong.

John Docherty's history prior to joining Bradford City was impressive. For a City board who wanted someone to deliver promotion and who looked for a strong track record in the candidates for the vacancy, Docherty would have ticked all the right boxes. An unremarkable player mainly with Reading and Brentford, Docherty cut his teeth in management at Brentford in 1975, before spending nearly six years at Cambridge United – a period where he guided the U's into the Second Division and almost took them into the top flight. Docherty's next stop was Millwall, where he had the seemingly unenviable task of succeeding George Graham, who had just moved to Arsenal. Yet he took the Lions up to the First Division for the first time in their history, in 1988, aided by the prolific strike partnership of Teddy Sheringham and Tony Cascarino. Docherty certainly had a notable CV, which helped him secure the position of the Bradford City manager. Big things were expected.

The-then Telegraph & Argus journalist, David Markham, had a close up view on events and explained to me, "John Docherty was appointed in March 1990 as successor to Terry Yorath with Bradford City facing relegation, despite a huge investment in new players over the previous two years after the club failed to gain promotion in 1988.

"Yorath favoured a close passing game which was pleasing to the eye, but the team struggled to create chances and score goals. So, the directors decided to make a change – as directors do – and they appointed a manager with a different philosophy on football, but also a manager who gained success with Millwall leading them to the old Second Division Championship in 1988 when Bradford City lost in the play offs to Middlesbrough. So, he had a track record of success at that level of the Football League, but first he had to save City from relegation. He made a good start with a 3-2 home win over Newcastle United, but after that City just slid away and went down to the Third Division – five years after being promoted as Division Three champions. John Docherty was confident he could lead the team back to the Second Division, but as we all know it is easier to be relegated than to gain promotion."

There was one, huge issue that ultimately doomed Docherty at Valley Parade – his style of football. Docherty was a long ball man, and for a crowd still pining for the midfield skills of Stuart McCall and John Hendrie, watching long ball football tactics, which seemingly didn't even require a Bradford City midfield, very quickly alienated many fans. Docherty was only ever going to succeed at Valley Parade if his kick and rush ways delivered results. Time would tell that it wouldn't.

Within the City Gents of the 1990/91 season – City's first back in the third tier – the primitive nature of Docherty's tactics was relayed by increasingly disgruntled contributors, and City Gent readers who sent in letters of complaint. These were the days before the back pass rule came into being, meaning that rather than goalkeepers not being allowed to handle the ball if a team-mate plays it to them, they could pick up the ball and boot it up the pitch, from out of their hands. That, in essence, was

Docherty's masterplan. Players were instructed to work the ball back to goalkeeper Paul Tomlinson, and then push up the pitch as they awaited his long punt. Try to win possession from Tomlinson's clearance, or at the very least put pressure on the opposition, so they concede a throw in or a corner. Get the ball into the final third, and up to the strikers, as quickly and as aerially as possible.

This was not for the purists. This was not a copy of Holland's Total Football philosophy of the 1970s. And in most of the crowd's eyes, this was not football. David Markham added, "Along with most other people I didn't like his style of football – long ball, direct – a complete contrast to Terry Yorath's short passing style. John Docherty defended his style of football by saying it had been successful at Millwall – and, to his critics, he would say well. Terry Yorath's methods did not succeed so it was time to try something different. The problem was that his methods didn't succeed either so supporters had the worst of both worlds – an ugly style of football, that also did not bring success either."

Lee Duxbury told me of Docherty, "He wasn't a man-manager. He wasn't a coach. I don't like judging people, because he was successful at Millwall beforehand, so there must have been something there. But it didn't happen at Valley Parade. His strengths, I can't put my finger on them. I didn't see it really! There were a lot of factors, such as the style of play. It just wasn't right. I don't know who brought him in and why, other than that he was a success at Millwall."

Before the 1990/91 season had reached its half way point, and with City's results back in the Third Division largely indifferent, the first dissenting chants from the Valley Parade crowd could be heard. "We want football" was sung around the ground during a dismal 4-2 loss to bottom-three side Shrewsbury. It wasn't that City were losing every week – they were making a decent fist of, at the very least, pushing for a play off position – but it was appalling to watch. At times, it seemed as though Docherty was listening to his public and slowly evolving the playing style into something more appealing, but all too quickly he reverted to bad habits. Kieran Wilkinson added, "John Docherty came with a reputation of paying unattractive, direct football and did nothing to change that reputation! It had paid dividends at Millwall and presumably the Bradford City board thought it worth the gamble – that we fans would accept less entertainment, if the results were positive. His first full season in charge saw us hovering around 11th/12th/13th spot for most of the season – not really palatable, when the fayre on offer wasn't too easy on the eye."

January of that season was a particular flash point. After the Shrewsbury debacle, a five-game unbeaten run was achieved that included an improved style of play. And then City lost 2-1 away to a high-flying Tranmere side, but pushed the home team all the way. Yet rather than keep faith in this new, more refined approach, Docherty went back to "kick and hope" for the next league game, at home to second-place Grimsby. And then three days later they were knocked out of the Football League Trophy at home to Fourth Division Burnley. The only goal was scored by Ron Futcher, of all people.

"Don't give up on us yet" was the message from defender Brian Tinnon in the Telegraph & Argus, "I know everyone is disappointed at recent results, but we have got to put them behind us. The manager will make sure we keep our heads up." But even more worrying than City's fading play off hopes was the disengagement of supporters to these events. City won their next game, at home to Bournemouth (3-0), but only 4,914 people were there to see it. This was the second lowest league attendance since City's return to Valley Parade in 1986 – and it was less than half the average crowds of 12,000+ that were achieved during the 1987/88 season.

After the Bournemouth victory, David Markham reported in the Telegraph & Argus that the dwindling crowds were hurting the club's finances. He wrote, "City who showed a record loss of £643,000 last year are heading for another big deficit this time. With crowds running 20 per cent down on last season, gate income is set to fall by about £130,000 following City's relegation to the Third Division." In the following City Gent, editor Mick Dickinson strongly queried how the club's finances were so poor. "The most damning indictment of the Valley Parade situation is the squandering of such large amounts of money. What happened to the fees for McCall, Hendrie, Ormondroyd and Quinn? How

CAN the club be over £600,000 in the red; with no possibility of recouping the money through saleable assets and with attendances beginning to plunge?...The club has betrayed its fans and we have been left with a legacy which favours the long ball kick-and-rush game and a club which is going nowhere except, perhaps, Div 4 in two or three years." The Telegraph & Argus journalist Jim Greenhalf wrote on a similar theme, "An interesting question for young economics students would be this: How did a club with a new £2.6 million stadium (rebuilt after the 1985 fire), players worth £3m, and more than £400,000 on deposit at Lloyds Bank in 1988, get into such a mess? Quite a few Bradford City fans would like to know the answer...What is so galling to fans, however, is that City should now be a struggling small club when not so long ago they were on the verge of the big time."

In the Telegraph & Argus piece penned by Markham, chairman David Simpson was quoted as saying, "We need 9,000 to break even, but we are not getting it for whatever reason. The figure is needed because of the long standing contracts we still have at the club bases on Second Division status which we don't have. We are struggling financially and always will be with gates like Saturday's, but the public will say that's all we deserve."

The public was indeed having their say, and their message was loud and clear. We want football.

The Millwall connection

If strikes one and two against Docherty were the lousy football and underwhelming results, the third, and the clincher, was his poor signings. More specifically, his regular choice of club from which to buy players: his old stomping ground Millwall.

In total, Docherty made nine signings over his time in charge – and six of them were his former players from the London club. Steve Torpey, Phil Babb, Wesley Reid, Darren Morgan, Alan Dowson and Darren Treacy moved North over this period. They were, to put it bluntly, not in the same league as Teddy Sheringham and Tony Cascarino – in fact, they weren't even players who had been getting near to Millwall's first team. They were youth or reserve players. Another club's cast offs. Only Phil Babb could be justifiably held up as a successful signing. A free transfer, who played in defence or attack, Babb eventually established himself as a cultured centre half and was sold to Premier League Coventry City for £300,000, after which he moved to Liverpool. Docherty also made the successful signings of Sean McCarthy and Robbie James; but it was the Millwall contingent which caused the most gripes, from both the stands and amongst other players.

Lee Duxbury recalled, "There was Steven Torpey and Phil Babb that came up from London, out of the six. There was a lad called Wes Reid who was half decent. But apart from that they struggled. I don't think he [Docherty] had the right players. He tried to bring in players that he trusted. But it's hard enough settling when you move from Bradford to Huddersfield – which I know – it takes a while. You're talking about London to Bradford. It was a massive step, and they were only young lads." Indeed for Reid and Treacy in particular, the move away from their South London home soon brought problems, as stories of their off-the-field behaviour around Bradford began to circulate. Treacy eventually walked out of the club and was never seen again, with rumours the police were chasing after him for allegedly smashing shop windows in the centre of Bradford.

Steve Torpey was another player who struggled. A 6ft 3 inch centre forward, Torpey's game should have been ideally suited to City's long ball approach, but he fared badly over three seasons at Valley Parade, netting just 22 goals in 96 appearances. Torpey eventually moved to Swansea, and had a decent career in the lower leagues that lasted until 2008. At Valley Parade, he was often singled out by the increasing number of boo-boys in the stand. The pint-sized Darren Morgan, signed at the end of Docherty's first full season, has gone down in infamy as one of the worst right backs the club has ever had. We will get to his worst afternoon shortly, but the fact that Morgan made just eleven appearances at Valley Parade, before dropping into non-league wilderness, said everything about his ability.

Kieran Wilkinson recalled of the Millwall players brought in, "They weren't all bad is probably the best that I could say! Phil Babb was a decent player who made good money for City when he was sold. Steve Torpey was regarded as somewhat of a donkey, but I suppose the fact that he went on to make nearly 500 more league appearances after leaving City points perhaps more to the shortcomings in Docherty's management and style of football than it does Torpey himself. However, the likes of Darrens Treacy and Morgan, along with Alan Dowson, were a long way short of what was needed to get City anywhere near the top of the table."

Of course it was significant that these players came from Millwall, Docherty's former home. It was another stick to beat the manager with. Docherty's assistant manager was also recruited from the Den – their chief scout Bob Pearson. Yet it became a running joke that Pearson was never actually spotted inside Valley Parade. The City Gent even ran a spoof competition where the first fan to spot Pearson inside the ground would win a free season ticket from the man himself.

Writing for Widthofapost.com in 2013, long-standing City supporter Ian Hemmens told a story about Docherty's judgement of talent which, to many supporters of that era, summed the manager up. "During this period we took a Belgian defender on loan at the transfer window period of 1991. He was from Royal Antwerp in the Belgian First League and had played over 100 games for them. His name was Rudi Taeymans. He played two reserve games before Docherty sent him packing saying his style of continental play wasn't conducive to the English game. Fair enough, but he then ripped into the player for not being good enough to be a pro at any level in any country. Rudi returned to Belgium.

"In 1993, Antwerp reached the European Cup Winners Cup Final at Wembley against Italian side Parma. An ever present that year, and in the final, at centre back was one Rudi Taeymans."

Being fair to Docherty, the club was clearly undergoing drastic cost-saving measures that severely limited the resources at the manager's disposal. He had to get rid of high earners, and saleable assets, in a bid to counter City's growing debts. David Markham agreed that the quality of the new signings left something to be desired, but argued the difficult financial situation was a big factor in how, and where, Docherty shopped, "There were obvious financial consequences to relegation, with the club having to cut costs as they tried to adjust to life at a lower level. So, at the end of the season, Docherty was instructed to sell most of Terry Yorath's expensive signings to raise money and cut the wage bill. This he did, albeit he had to sell the players at cut price. The problem was the generally poor quality of some of the players that John Docherty brought in, mainly young players from his old club Millwall. Morgan and Darren Tracey spring to mind. Supporters also did not like Steve Torpey, but he enjoyed a long career as a typical lower division centre forward, not all that skilful, but fairly tall, useful in the air and difficult to mark.

"Docherty's two best signings were central defender Phil Babb, also used as a centre forward, who joined City in August 1990 as a free agent after being released by Millwall and went on to join Coventry and then on to Liverpool. His other big signing was Sean McCarthy, a natural goal scorer, who cost £250,000 from Plymouth, scoring 60 goals in 131 League appearances and was then sold for £350,000 to Oldham and played for them in the Premier League."

The success of McCarthy and Babb aside, it was a vicious circle. Good players sold, inferior replacements brought in – poor results, falling crowds, more financial headaches. As the boos and grumbles got louder, and the abuse got personal, Docherty made little attempt to placate this growing section of unhappy supporters, telling the Yorkshire Post – following a desperately poor 0-0 draw at home to relegation-bound Fulham – "Spectators pay their money and are entitled to have their say – I'm not against that at all. But I would prefer it if they waited until time is up to show their feelings. It was not very nice for my players to be booed back on to the field for the second half, especially as they had taken sixteen points from the previous six home games, and had scored sixteen goals against two."

Yet the Yorkshire Post match report of that Fulham draw was scathing of Docherty's tactics. "Slow hand-clapping and chants of 'what a load of rubbish' were perhaps not as helpful as they were accurate but the fans were bang on the mark in shouting 'we want football'. They simply did not get what they paid for. Bradford produced a horrible mutation of the game, whirling round in a maelstrom of mistakes, and after an appalling first half defied hope and logic by getting marginally worse after the break."

City ultimately ended the 1990/91 season in eighth – just one place short of the play offs – but in truth they never looked likely to crash into the top seven, let alone achieve an instant return to Division Two. And during that summer, there had to be yet more player sales. Lee Sinnott was sold to Crystal Palace for £350,000, and long-serving midfielder Greg Abbott was moved on to Halifax for £25,000. Docherty was only able to bring in two new faces: the aforementioned Morgan, and Alan Dowson. Both on free transfers. Both from Millwall. Dowson managed a grand total of eighteen games in claret and amber.

Kieran Wilkinson stated that the relationship between fans and the manager got worse and worse over the 1990/91 season, and this ever-darkening mood continued into the next one too. "Although some were before my time, I think that previous managers were ones which the fans could identify with or respect to a certain extent – Roy McFarland and Trevor Cherry had been top players, Terry Dolan an ex-player and a Bradfordian and Terry Yorath someone who was associated with previous success. The Doc wasn't a warm, charismatic personality and had the added disadvantages of an industrial style of football and only ever having managed down South. An assistant manager who no-one ever saw [Bob Pearson] didn't help either. To the best of my knowledge, the Doc has the ignominy of being the only City manager to have a pie thrown at him by a City fan [during an away game at Wigan]. That tells you all you need to know."

Yet to David Markham, for whom part of the job was to build a good working relationship with Docherty, there was a marked difference between the City boss' dour public persona and what he was really like when you got to know him, "I spent hours and hours listening to his ideas on football while he smoked his Hamlet cigars and found him an engaging character, who was convinced that his methods were right for the club."

The bitter end

Despite a promising start to the 1991/92 season, which included an entertaining opening day victory over Stoke City, all too quickly City reverted back to their kick and rush type of football. They failed to win any of the next seven league matches. They remained stuck in lower mid-table. Crowds fell further. Away at Preston in September, Docherty raced out of his dug out to remonstrate over a decision and fell over the advertising hording. The visiting City supporters cheered and laughed. This was such an unhappy marriage. A happy ending looked impossible. Writing in the City Gent that October, editor Mick Dickinson reflected the mood of the fans, "Of course we want the team to do well, we want them to win. But not, I believe, at the expense of entertainment. I feel the success of the 80s has spoilt us, to a great extent. Now we have a situation where we are not prepared to see a return to a drab, mediocre game against drab, mediocre opposition."

After a run of seven defeats in nine matches, the game was finally up for Docherty. A November 1991 2-1 loss at Peterborough was very quickly followed by David Simpson and the board calling time on his miserable 20-month tenure, with the manager paid £122,000 in compensation. Simpson told the Telegraph & Argus, "We brought in John Docherty to bring in some much needed stability to the club bearing in mind Bradford City have had nine managers in 16 years...The reason we brought him in was because of his good track record and I am very disappointed it has worked out like this." He added that with gates down 16% on the season before, the club had acted for financial reasons. His fellow director, Terry Goddard, reiterated this point in the Telegraph & Argus a few days later, "It was not the so-called boo boys who cost John Docherty his job, it was the people who didn't come through the turnstiles. The three or four hundred people who don't come – perhaps because they've read a negative report in the T&A – can represent £2,000 or so a week which, with a limited number of games, can't be got back."

Whether the barracking of those fans who did continue to attend games had no influence on the Board's decision is a matter of debate, but David Markham was in doubt it had caused huge problems, when writing in the Telegraph & Argus, the Saturday after Docherty's sacking. "The mere sight of him emerging from the dug-out to make a substitution was enough to send some into howls of rage." In Lee Duxbury's opinion, Docherty's failure was as much about geography than poor football. "I've been in coaching and managing myself now, and I think there is a North/South divide with managers and coaches. You don't get a lot of Southern coaches coming up and doing well up here, and vice-versa. And I think there was an element of that with John."

First team coach Leighton James was made caretaker manager, as out-of-work managers rushed in their applications for the vacant role. They included future City manager Colin Todd – who for now would ultimately get the role of assistant manager. Don McKay, Mick Buxton and John Bird were also linked, but James – who began his caretaker spell with a win over Bury and draw against Hartlepool in the FA Cup and Football League Trophy respectively – was firmly in the driving seat. James told the Telegraph & Argus, "My application will be on the field in the form of results. If we can win every game while I am in charge the directors will find it difficult to appoint someone else."

His first league match in charge? At home to bottom of the table Swansea City.

Ten goal thriller

The strange irony about John Docherty's desperately disappointing spell in charge of Bradford City is that the most famous game associated with his time took place when he wasn't anywhere near the stadium. It is one that has become a modern day standard bearer for ineptitude, and the blame for it continues to be pinned on Docherty, even though Leighton James was now in charge. It is a game that has gone down in folklore. Did you hear about the time Bradford City welcomed a Swansea City team to Valley Parade in November, with the Swans bottom of the table, having failed to score a SINGLE goal away from home all season? The final score: Bradford City 4 Swansea City 6 (Six!)

In less than half an hour, Leighton James' hopes of securing the job on a permanent basis were pretty much dashed, as Swansea raced into a three-goal lead. Attacking the Kop end of Valley Parade, they struck early doors when a scramble in the box enabled John Williams to prod the ball past City goalkeeper Paul Tomlinson. Williams – a summer signing from West Midlands' non-league outfit Cradley Town – laid on the second goal for Joey Beauchamp to tap home, with Darren Morgan badly out of position. After Beauchamp's through ball caught out the whole back four, and Alan Dowson lost his runner, Andy Legg raced through to score the third. That increasingly familiar sound at Valley Parade – loud booing – returned.

James had attempted to change the team's style, throwing out Docherty's Stone Age tactics in favour of a passing, attacking style of football. But the gaps between midfield and defence were alarming, and Swansea – buoyed by a midweek victory over their fierce local rivals, Cardiff City – were in clinical mood. There was hope offered just before half time, when Brian Tinnon's shot from distance was palmed out by Swans keeper Roger Freestone, and Sean McCarthy buried the rebound. But before the half time whistle sounded, John Williams broke clear of the defence and slotted home his second. 4-1 to Swansea. The City players went into the dressing room with boos ringing in their ears.

The goal rush continued in the second half, with the Bantams pulling another back – this time a 30-yarder from Lee Duxbury – but the leaks at the other end were to continue. Indeed, Duxbury was to find to his personal cost that, what he could do, John Williams could better. "This lad called Williams played for Swansea, he was 100 metres champion or something," Duxbury told me. "I played in that game and all I can remember in that game was I knew he was fast, but that he wasn't a good footballer. I was chasing him, he was about 30 yards out, and I was joking with him, 'go on, shoot, shoot' thinking he was never going to score from that far out. And I think he put it in the top corner. That's a game that I can remember just by that."

Indeed Williams' goal from the edge of the area flew past the helpless Tomlinson and into the far corner, even prompting sporting applause from home supporters. Williams went onto score eleven goals for the Swans that season and earned a summer move to Coventry City, which meant he ended up playing in the inaugural Premier League season. Back at Valley Parade, he had stolen the headlines but not ended the game's scoring, as with the game at 2-5 there were still more goals to be had. The first offered another flicker of hope, as a slip up by Freestone enabled Steve Torpey to make it 3-5. But once again Swansea got the next goal, after a free kick that was swung into the box evaded everybody, and the ball was steered home by Jimmy Gilligan at the far post. From no away goals all season, Swansea had achieved six of the best. Home fans had already begun filing out at 2-5, and by now there was a significant exodus. They missed a late consolation goal from Torpey that made it 4-6. An afternoon of non-stop goal action, but this was not the type of entertainment that City fans had been craving.

"My application will be on the field in the form of results" – those words had come back to haunt Leighton James, his chances of getting the job in tatters. But in truth, the supporter blame for this debacle was still pinned on Docherty, and the fact it was his misfiring team. Seven of the starting XI against Swansea had been signed by Docherty – five of them came from Millwall. Indeed, the game has become associated with the defensive shambles of the two summer signings from London, Darren Morgan and Alan Dowson, who endured a nightmare afternoon in the two full back slots. Morgan was certainly no match for John Williams, and he soon moved from City to London non-league club Erith & Belvedere, where he faded into obscurity. Dowson went to Darlington the following summer, before a career in non-league circles.

By the time of City's next home match – West Bromwich Albion – a new man was in charge, and a coup at that. Rather than employ any of the people who had applied for the vacancy, Simpson and the Board turned to Frank Stapleton, a Republic of Ireland international striker who more than 100 goals for Arsenal and Manchester United. Stapleton was recruited as player manager, with Simpson telling the Telegraph & Argus, "The board were unanimous in their choice of Frank Stapleton. His playing record is of the highest order and the board were impressed by his obvious knowledge of the game coupled with his youthful enthusiasm to continue his playing career…He will bring a young outlook to the club."

Kieran Wilkinson has fond memories of Frank Stapleton's time as manager, "To start off with, it was a breath of fresh air. Frank was a famous name and perhaps anyone after the Doc would have been welcomed. Ultimately, it was still an era of falling short, flirting with the edge of the play offs but not quite getting there. In Stapleton's first full season in charge, we did manage to hit the top of the table in November, but still only finished tenth. The next season we finished three points and one place off the play off positions. If nothing else, the football was infinitely more enjoyable than it was under Docherty."

Bottoming out

Whilst there was no magic wand to revive Bradford City's fortunes, and they remained stuck in the third tier for another four seasons after 1991/92, this campaign carries a sense of rock bottom, and an application of the brakes was subsequently applied, following the slide that had begun in 1988. City's average 1991/92 crowd of 6,115 was their worst since 1983/84's 4,203 – but they have never since reached such a low, and with the modern day spike in crowds it seems unlikely they ever will do so again. Kieran Wilkinson reflected on the disillusionment felt at the time, "We were a mid-table Third Division club who had had a five-year dalliance with the second tier. We were typical of many clubs –

not much money, local businessmen running the club trying to do their best. The McCall/Hendrie era seemed a distant memory already at that stage. If you'd have said that on the equivalent weekend eight years on from the Swansea game, we would be playing Leeds United in the top flight, I think you'd be getting funny looks and visits from men in white coats."

With the Doc gone, a line was drawn in the sand, and slow and steady building blocks were put in place. The removal of Docherty had a uniting effect, after a period where divisions ran high. David Markham summarised, "John Docherty was probably the most unpopular manager the club have had in most of our lifetimes – towards the end of his time at Valley Parade he was booed before the game – on his way from the dressing room to the dug out. I can't remember that sort of resentment towards any other City manager." In another City Gent piece penned by Mick Dickinson after Docherty left, he wrote on similar lines, "I cannot remember a more hated manager at the club. He was not just disliked, he was hated. The team were even getting booed off after winning and the atmosphere at the ground on matchdays was unhealthy in the extreme. If it had been allowed to continue, there would have been no fans, other than the hard-core diehards, left. More than anything else, Docherty represents the final betrayal of the dream of First Division soccer."

Indeed, Stapleton was able to benefit from a lower expectation level, compared to the one Docherty faced. But that is largely because of the extent that the unpopular manager had extinguished hope from Valley Parade in the first place. And though some of Docherty's managerial successors over the coming years would be able to identify with the problems that he experienced regarding the limited patience amongst City fans, and the crowd has turned on the likes of Colin Todd and Peter Taylor, no one has ever endured as much abuse as the Doc. Tellingly, whatever future woes there were to be had at Valley Parade, any supporter who dubbed it to the worst of times would be quickly corrected by a long-standing fan. "You think this is bad, you should have seen the days of Docherty."

As Swansea rattled in their fifth and sixth goals during what was a humiliating November afternoon for the Bantams, the visiting players celebrated in front of an empty stand that was more or less complete, and which would be opened in a few short weeks. It was the new Bradford End, the creation of the mini two-tier stand, which is to this day still a part of Valley Parade. It reportedly cost the club £700,000 to build, with £500,000 of that payment coming via a Football Trust grant.

The Bradford End looks strange in the glare of the modern era, especially with two of the other Valley Parade stands towering high above it. And yet its humble construction leaves a lasting legacy that no one should ever forget. The basic, no-frills Bradford End stand is a constant reminder that, no matter how bleak things might be on the pitch, it is so important to always retain ambition and hope – from a time when, at Valley Parade, there was neither.

City (vs Swansea): Paul Tomlinson, Darren Morgan, Steve Gardner, Phil Babb, Alan Dowson, Sean McCarthy, Robbie James, Lee Duxbury, Wesley Reid, Stephen Torpey, Brian Tinnion
Not used: Paul Jewell, Mark Stuart

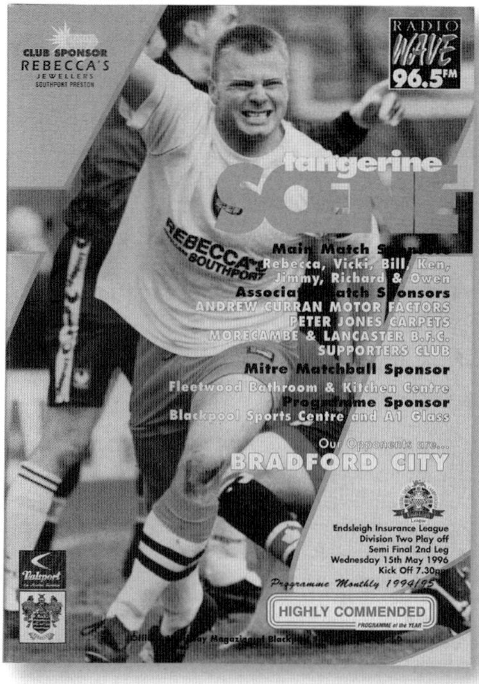

Comic book stuff

Blackpool vs Bradford City

Division Two play off semi final second leg, Wednesday 15 May, 1996

He bought the club in the same way that kids swap football stickers in the playground. He talked about the future with a ludicrous level of optimism, akin to a five-year-old matter-of-factly telling their teacher that, when they grow up, they will play football for England. But if he wanted his grand vision to have any hope of coming to life, he desperately needed his team to deliver a comic book, Roy of the Rovers moment on a warm May evening at Bloomfield Road.

Bradford City were in the popular seaside town of Blackpool, looking for a miracle. It was the second leg of the Division Two play offs; but after a calamitous first leg at Valley Parade, they trailed the tie 2-0. To reach the play off final, they would have to achieve something that no club had ever managed in the history of the play offs – overturn a two-goal, first leg deficit. And they had to do it at the home of a team who had been beaten only four times on their own patch all season, and who had finished nine points better off than the Bantams over the regular campaign. As outcomes go, it seemed so far-fetched, that it would have been rejected out of hand as a possibility, even for a Roy Race comic story. To everyone else, the second leg match on Wednesday 15 May, 1996 was a foregone conclusion.

But if the new leader of Bradford City was going to have any chance of convincing the Bradford public that he could deliver on his grandiose promises, he had to prove to them that miracles were indeed possible. That the mountain he wanted Bradford City to climb was scalable. This was only the first step in the journey, after all. And if they fell here, it would be very difficult to get back up and go again. It had to be tonight.

Geoffrey Richmond needed this.

"Let them laugh"

Rewind back just over two years, to January 1994, and Geoffrey Richmond made his whirlwind entrance into Valley Parade. In total he would be at the club for eight years, during which he would transform the outlook, status and set up of Bradford City. He repositioned the ceiling above the club's head, and the floor beneath it. He changed the perception of Bradford City; within the club, amongst its fanbase, and to the outside world. His influence at Valley Parade would prove to be colossal – although not always in a good way.

Before 1994, Richmond had started to make his name in football at Scarborough Football Club. He became chairman of The Seasiders in 1988, the year after they had been promoted into the Football League, but with the club saddled with debts and requiring a buyer. Neil Warnock had been the manager who oversaw the historic Scarborough promotion, before leaving for bigger and better things. Under Richmond's tenure, Scarborough once made the Fourth Division play offs, and achieved several cup giant killings over the years, such as knocking Chelsea out of the League Cup in 1989. But for a town with a population of only 61,000, in what is a remote location in the country, the struggles near the foot of the Football League were Scarborough's ceiling. This was as good as it would ever get for the club. Richmond was said to have done a good job in balancing the books, but had his run-ins with supporters from time-to-time. In 1991, for example, there were supporter protests demanding that he leave, believing Richmond wasn't putting enough money into the transfer kitty, and was instead diverting vital funds to the rugby league side that he had recently set up, the Scarborough Pirates. The Pirates were a short-lived venture, with Richmond quitting as director seventeen months after its creation, the club already saddled with unmanageable debt and folding shortly afterwards. Richmond rode through that storm, and continued to give the football club a steady hand, but his own personal ambitions were too big to match Scarborough's potential. He wanted more than this.

So the Leeds-born entrepreneur began to look elsewhere for a football club that could match his vision, one that was closer to his roots. Having started out his career as a door-to-door children's encyclopaedia salesman in Leeds, Richmond subsequently made his fortune from buying Ronson cigarette lighters in 1983, when the company was in administration. The £250,000 he paid to buy the company proved to be a bargain, as a further injection of £3 million capital helped him to turn around Ronson's fortunes. In December 1993, Richmond was able to sell the North East-based business for a whopping £10 million. Rather than pump some of this new-found wealth into Scarborough, with its limitations, Richmond eyed up the greater potential of Bradford City, closer to his Yorkshire home. He had been linked with the Bantams for more than a year, although the eventual buying of the club proved to be a quick transition. Less than a week after meeting up with current City chairman David Simpson, a deal – and a highly unusual one at that – was agreed.

The Bantams were still in the third tier of English football, recovering from the mediocrity of the John Docherty era. David Simpson was struggling to keep the club afloat, and had put it up for sale ten months earlier, placing an advert in the Financial Times, to no success. There was also the threat of a winding up petition hovering over Valley Parade due to City's sizeable debts, so Simpson was more than willing to talk to Richmond when he was approached by his counterpart, telling the Telegraph & Argus, "I've always said that if someone comes of the right calibre then the club should be sold to that person." Only Simpson wasn't just selling, he was trading places with Richmond. Like a children's game of swaps in the playground, Richmond proposed that the two owners exchanged clubs – Richmond taking over at Valley Parade and taking on the debts, whilst Simpson would become the chairman of Scarborough.

The-then Telegraph & Argus journalist, David Markham, explained, "Geoffrey Richmond arrived at the club as the result of an unusual swap deal. He was chairman of Scarborough, but wanted to be in charge of a bigger club with more potential. So he and the Bradford City chairman, David Simpson swapped places with some of the City board moving to Scarborough. I think it is fair to say that David Simpson – a lifelong City supporter – and his board had no more money to invest in the club and were keen to get out and let someone else take over, so quickly came to an agreement with Geoffrey

Richmond." The deal was agreed in January 1994 – barely a month after Richmond's Ronson sale, and £10 million windfall. Richmond and Simpson swapped shares in each club, with the new City chairman loaning the club £1.5 million to wipe out its bank overdrafts and money owed to creditors. This left Richmond taking "a 58% controlling of the issued share capital", as the Telegraph & Argus put it, when they announced the amazing deal on the 27 January, 1994. That day's front page of the paper featured a large picture of a smiling, 52-year-old Richmond, under the headline "My dream for a new City".

And that first interview with the local media makes for interesting reading, more than 20 years on. Unsurprisingly, Richmond was full of confidence, and talked big about the future. "There is no limit as to what we can achieve at Valley Parade if we can get things right," he told the T&A reporter, Robert Irvine. "I see Bradford City as a sleeping giant. I hope we can realise that potential by getting things right on and off the field." In a further piece in the same edition of the Bradford paper, David Markham quoted more grounded comments from the new chairman. "I am no Santa Claus," was Richmond's declaration. "I see myself as a person who is determined to run the club on strict business principles, and the first business principle is that income and expenditure must be in equilibrium... My first priority is to create more income and look to decrease expenditure, so we can create a situation where income and expenditure are pretty well in line. That creates a situation where the club does not have to sell to survive and it also means we can go out into the transfer market and we don't have to sell our players at less than they are worth." Such words would have been hugely encouraging to a City fanbase, still disgruntled by the club's decline post-1988, and in particular the way the previous board had continued to sell off City's best players in a forlorn attempt to balance the books. Indeed, only a few weeks before Richmond had joined, City had sold their top scorer and crowd favourite, Sean McCarthy, to fend off their creditors. The prolific McCarthy, a John Docherty signing, moved to Premier League Oldham Athletic, and the £500,000 deal (which included young forward Neil Tolson moving the other way) was scant consolation to fans, thoroughly fed up by the club's lack of ambition.

Although Simpson stepped aside, the other City directors, David Thompson and Terry Goddard, remained on board for the time being. Richmond's wife, Elizabeth, also joined the City board. This development ended an antiquated Valley Parade tradition that women were not allowed in the Valley Parade boardroom on match days – Bradford City were finally moving out of the dark ages and catching up with modern times. The first game of the Richmond era was a 1-1 draw away to York City, with Paul Showler netting for the play off-chasing Bantams. Richmond watched in the stands; and after the game, he declared how impressed he was by the fact the 5,985 Bootham Crescent crowd included 2,147 City supporters. "It was tremendous support. This is exactly what motivated me to buy the club. When supporters are prepared to go away from home at that level there is no limit to what can be achieved." On Saturday 5 February, 1994, the week after the York City game, Richmond presented himself to his new audience with a lap around the Valley Parade pitch, before a home game with Hartlepool United. It was immediately evident that Richmond liked the publicity and the limelight. The showman was in town.

And he really was a headline-grabber, talking big about the future, sharing a vision for the club that its own supporters could scarcely imagine could ever come to fruition. In the Telegraph & Argus, shortly after the swap deal with Simpson was completed, Richmond revealed his ambition to get third tier Bradford City – habitual underachievers and who seemingly sold any decent player they stumbled upon – up to mixing with the big boys, in the top flight, "I look at the teams in the Premiership and lots of them come from towns with similar potential to Bradford – Norwich, Ipswich, Oldham and Coventry – so why shouldn't Bradford aspire to reach the Premiership?" And shortly after that, he set a timescale for when the Premier League would be reached. At a packed supporters club meeting at the Fountain Inn pub – which gave supporters a first chance to meet and quiz Richmond, and his intentions – he memorably stated, "Let them laugh, but in five years' time we will be in the Premier League". It's not clear who "them" was referring to, but it's fair to say that supporters left that meeting laughing themselves, over the sheer ridiculousness of such a claim.

Bradford City in the Premier League? Sure, they had come close to the top flight in 1988, but the subsequent decline – coupled with the breakaway of top clubs in 1992, who formed the Premier League to keep all of the rising TV money to themselves – meant the door had seemingly been closed on that dream a long time ago. Football had moved on, leaving City firmly behind. In February 1994, as Richmond was making this outlandish promise, Manchester United were closing in on a second straight Premier League title, with a side packed full of the talents of Eric Cantona, Mark Hughes and Ryan Giggs, and playing to crowds of more than forty thousand. The TV money was building up, and top flight clubs were about to start using that windfall to buy the best overseas talent, making the Premier League even more glamorous and appealing. It was already starting to look like a very different world, or as Sky TV put it in their inaugural marketing campaign "A whole new ball game".

Bradford City were playing in a very different world. English football's elite had locked themselves in a castle, built a moat around themselves, and pulled up the drawbridge. Bradford City would surely never be part of the elite for as long as they existed – never mind making it in five years' time.

Untapped potential

Richmond's external perspective of Bradford City, and the city itself, gave him the foresight of being confident that his plan could work. At the time the Bantams were playing to crowds of around six thousand, yet the Bradford district was one of the biggest populations in the country, equating to just over half a million. Even allowing for the size of near neighbours Leeds United – who in 1992 had become English football champions and who, in 1994, were very much part of the Premier League elite – Richmond believed that the Bradford public would back a top flight football club. That he had a catchment area which he would really tap into. It took an outsider, someone not worn down by decades of the city of Bradford's decline, to understand the vast potential. He told the Telegraph & Argus early doors, "I am absolutely certain that the Bradford public will respond to a successful team and considering the years of disappointment that followed the good years of the 1980s, I think the fans have been absolutely terrific. These fans have supported the club through thick and thin, but there are others, who I feel sure would come along if they felt the club were going places."

Whilst Richmond's record at Scarborough was commendable, it had evidently proved a topsy-turvy time, and he had threatened to walk away more than once; whilst others found his overbearing style difficult. In his terrific 2013 book 'The Gaffer', Neil Warnock admitted that he had found Richmond "impossible to work with" at Scarborough, although conceded that he later realised his chairman was only doing what he thought was best for the club. At City, it wasn't long before Richmond was sacking non-playing staff, including the chief executive David Clayton. He later reflected that he felt he had inherited a club that was rotten to the core, with selfishness and self-interest prevailing at the top. He was clearly not afraid of upsetting people. And, as the Telegraph & Argus' Jim Greenhalf summarised rather wonderfully, "I don't think City's fans will object to a benevolent despot at Valley Parade – providing they are convinced the club is going places."

Indeed supporters, whilst guarded, warmly welcomed Richmond, and the way that he talked up the future. This was a fanbase that had grown increasingly disillusioned by Bradford City owners past and present, following the fall out of the nearly season and Jack Tordoff's supposed conservatism in the transfer market, plus the fact the Simpson era had seen several player sales that undermined progress on the pitch.

Joanne Golton is a long-time Bradford City supporter who saw her first match in March 1986 – a 1-0 home defeat to Grimsby, played at Leeds United's Elland Road. A particularly passionate fan, who habitually travels to most away games, Joanne is one of those people who you always see on a cold, Tuesday evening in winter, at an away ground miles from home, where usually only a few hundred City supporters will be in attendance. She does the miles, she has seen the worst of times, and was well-placed to judge the glory moments when they finally came. Joanne recalled to me of Richmond's arrival, "He was just a bit different. He was somebody new, and he wasn't the usual old-fashioned chairman – you know, someone local with a bit of an interest in keeping the club going. He was someone who had ambition, and someone who also wasn't afraid to sack managers, which was new to us really. It was an exciting time, because he was a bit different. He was a bit of a louder character and I think people bought into that."

Early doors at Valley Parade, Richmond declared "I have not come here to preside over mediocrity" and he was true to his word. He brought along a hands-on approach that meant he worked tirelessly all hours to turn around the club, and he expected those who he employed to match that ethic. He would make significant sums of money available for his managers to buy players, but he also prioritised marketing the club to the Bradford public and driving up the fanbase. This included freezing season ticket prices for five seasons – something that was out of synch with the rest of the country, as the explosion of interest in the Premier League resulted in the cost of watching football flying through the roof. He also set to work on a plan to rebuild three sides of Valley Parade, so that the capacity of the stadium could increase, to meet his crowd projections. The phrase "if you build it, they will come" rang true here. Valley Parade would be transformed as a ground, and the affordability of watching games would, over the next few seasons, result in crowds tripling.

Nowhere was the vision and long-term thinking of Richmond better illustrated than the conversion of the Midland Road stand that runs along the length of the pitch. With Valley Parade residing halfway up a steep hill, and with the busy Midland Road right behind the stand, building something grander than the plain 'shed' stand, which existed on that side of the pitch, was a considerable challenge. The solution was a £1.4 million, cantilever stand where the back hung up in the air, above the pavement outside. The construction of the stand was announced in February 1996, on a Tuesday evening where City defeated Wrexham 2-0. The attendance was just 3,804 – which was less than the proposed capacity of the new Midland Road stand. To have proposed such an ambitious project, whilst City sat slumped mid-table in the third tier, with less than four thousand people bothering to attend some games, was an incredible piece of foresight.

Yet despite all of these big plans, and the greater playing resources, shaking the Bantams out of their slumber proved to be the toughest of challenges for Richmond. When he took over mid-season in 1994, City were in the hunt for a play off spot. One of Richmond's first acts was to hand the manager, Frank Stapleton, £200,000 to bring in another forward, Lee Power, from Norwich City, to replace McCarthy. Sadly, the move didn't work out, as Power failed to impress. Richmond – who seemingly never took to Stapleton – sacked his manager when play off hopes were finally ended with two games left to play. It was the first illustration of Richmond's ruthless streak with his managers, and of how hard he expected everybody to work for him. Several years later (in November 2000) Stapleton and his City assistant, Stuart Pearson, were heavily involved in media work and slated Richmond on national radio. Richmond retorted in the next City matchday programme, "If I was so wrong in 1994 dismissing them, why is it nobody else has picked up their great talents on the Management side?...For the record the true reason I sacked them in 1994 was because they considered management to be a part-time profession. Four hours a day, four days week, commuting in from Manchester is not what I would call commitment! Second division mid-table mediocrity was the limit of their ambition." City ended up winning both their final games of the 1993/94 season to finish seventh, one place outside the play offs; and there was confidence that with Richmond's financial backing and know-how they would be pushing harder the following season.

Yet despite recruiting Lennie Lawrence – a manager of some lower league distinction, after a hugely successful nine years at Charlton – to replace Stapleton, City's bumbling ways continued. Despite spending some £800,000 – a small fortune for a lower league club back then – many of Lawrence's buys didn't work out, and the club remained stuck in the mid-table mud for 1994/95. It just wasn't to be for Lawrence at Valley Parade, who was given a chance again next season. But when a bright start to the 1995/96 campaign faded once again into middle-of-the-road nothingness, Richmond sacked his man and turned to one of the club's most experienced players to take on the job – a person who he admitted in private that he had earmarked to take over as manager, even before Lawrence was given his P45. His name was Chris Kamara.

Unbelievable

Long before Chris Kamara's incredibly successful TV career with Sky Sports, he had been a journeymen lower league footballer with a string of former clubs. In 1994, Lawrence had brought Kamara to Bradford City, after the tough-tackling midfielder had fallen out of favour at Sheffield United. Kamara didn't play too often at Valley Parade, but was promoted to Lawrence's coaching staff and began to learn the ropes. Having had no success with the tried and trusted hand of Lawrence as manager, Richmond went to the opposite end of the spectrum, by looking inwards and promoting the inexperienced Kamara, to replace his sacked mentor. It worked out so well that Richmond's next two managerial appointments were also internal ones.

Joanne Golton was studying for a degree in Southampton during the 1995/96 campaign, and would travel to City's Southern-based games, as well as time her visits home with weekends when the Bantams were playing at Valley Parade. She was present for Lawrence's final game in charge, a 2-1 loss at Brentford on 25 November, 1995, and was encouraged by the change of manager. "I was at the Brentford away game where it was a farewell to Lennie Lawrence," she stated. "I took a couple of mates with me; we lost and Lawrence was gone after that. I wasn't sad at all to see the back of Lennie Lawrence, I was quite pleased that he'd gone. Kamara came in and I remember thinking 'he will be alright'. Kamara was a great character and he was a good player for us really. I always thought he would do a good job, because he was a player's manager. He was someone who would get them all working hard. Kamara proved to be a good manager and I really liked him."

Other than being allowed to sign Derby County reserve forward, Mark Stallard, Kamara was left to work with the same group of players that he had inherited from Lawrence. And for most of the second half of the 1995/96 season, it didn't look like the managerial shake of the dice would achieve anything different. With sixteen games to go, City were still lumbered in their oh-so-familiar mid-table spot. It just so happened that they would finally find the missing spark on the same night of the announcement of the Midland Road stand construction – that 2-0 victory over Wrexham would be the first of ten wins and two draws, which would enable the Bantams to crash the play off party. Joanne added, "Chris quickly added more spirit to the team. We were quite far away from the play offs, but they never gave up. I'm always a positive person, and I remember remaining confident that we could do it. I never thought that we wouldn't. Something clicked and they went on this amazing run. We just kept getting nearer and nearer. We had some good players that season."

Yet right up until the end of the campaign, the sudden surge in form still looked like it was a case of too little too late. There was simply far too little margin for error. When City lost 1-2 to Walsall on April 13, 1996, there were only four games to go and the gap to the top six was still considerable. The Telegraph & Argus ran with the headline "Mission Impossible!" in relation to the club's top six hopes. An enraged Kamara cut the article out, photocopied it several times and plastered it all over the dressing room. City picked up ten points from their final four games. It would not be the last time that Kamara successfully used a cutting to motivate his players that season.

A key member of the 1995/96 team was Lee Duxbury, who had left Bradford City for Huddersfield in December 1994 in a part exchange deal with Graham Mitchell. Later that season, Duxbury and Town won promotion at Wembley in the play offs, before he ended up re-signing for the Bantams midway through the 1995/96 season. As City made their late push for the play offs, Duxbury was fuelled by the motivation of achieving two Wembley promotions in two seasons. "I came back a much better player, a much more experienced player," Duxbury told me, as he revealed the change of perspective gained from moving away for a year, and how it aided his career development. "I had been at Bradford since I was eleven. I had been through a lot. I was training down there as a kid when Bobby Campbell,

Ces Podd and Joe Cooke. I went through the fire situation, because I was literally sat next to where it started. I left and then came back from Huddersfield a much better person, and a much better player."

On the 1995/96 play of surge Duxbury added, "With the players we had at the time, it just gelled together. We got a good run at the end of the season. We had 70 points before the last match of the season and the team underneath of us [Chesterfield] had 69."

Indeed, they sealed a sixth-place spot on the final day of the season, following a bad-tempered and highly charged affair with Hull City. The Tigers had endured a dreadful campaign and had already been relegated, when – prior to the game with the Bantams – the Hull police forced them to move their own fans out of the South stand behind the goal, where traditionally their most vocal supporters were housed, and instead hand that part of the ground to Bradford City fans. The Bantams were expected to take more than six thousand supporters to this must-win game, and Hull didn't want to miss out on this pay day by restricting City's allocation to just the regular away stand. The decision to swap the home and away stands went down dreadfully with Hull supporters, and the ill-feeling spilled over during the game. Joanne Golton was there that day, and recalled of the ugly atmosphere, "We were all lined up down a street with City fans on one side and Hull the other, and it was a bit daunting." The Hull City manager of the time had strong City connections – the manager of the nearly season team, Terry Dolan. He reflected to me, "I wasn't very popular as manager of Hull City with the fans at the time. The police decided that, because there were that many supporters coming from Bradford, to give the South stand end to Bradford fans. The Hull supporters weren't happy to start with. They blamed the chairman, and because I had a good relationship with the chairman I got the stick as well. We were at a fairly low ebb at that stage at Hull."

Just before kick off, a number of Hull fans invaded the pitch and charged at the City fans, delaying proceedings. They also invaded the pitch after taking the lead, and again when the visitors' equalised through Mark Stallard, each time causing the referee to take the players back to the dressing rooms for their own safety. Dolan added, "There was lots of trouble. The crowd got on and there were police horses on the pitch. It was very unsavoury, from a Hull point of view anyway." These continual delays meant the Bantams game was running a long way behind their rivals for the final play off spot, Chesterfield. The Spireities won their game against Notts County 1-0, thanks to a penalty by future City manager Nicky Law. With the Chesterfield result confirmed, City knew they had to beat Hull in order to ensure the sixth spot. Having got back to 1-1, they again fell behind, but eventually goals from Duxbury and Carl Shutt sparked gleeful celebrations from the 6,882 City fans who had made it to Boothferry Park. Back at Saltergate, and with their game having finished some time before, Chesterfield fans stayed behind to listen to radio commentary of the closing stages in Hull, which was pumped out over the PA system. There was no happy ending to the season for the Derbyshire club; and for the Bantams, there was to be an extended end to their campaign. From going nowhere, to going to the play offs.

Duxbury recalled of the Hull encounter, "It was a crazy game. I think we came off the pitch twice (due to the crowd trouble). We were coming back onto the pitch and finding credit cards and cash on the floor where spectators were before. There was police everywhere. There might be a pause in the game for an injury or a throw in or something, and you'd look on floor and see a tenner! It was a very strange experience. You'd be running off and there'd be a police horse running the other way at 20 miles an hour. And you'd be thinking 'bloody hell I was lucky not to get hit there!' At the end of the day though we came to win the game, and that's exactly what we did."

At last, City had made the play offs and now had the opportunity to climb back into the second tier, following five seasons of nothingness. For Geoffrey Richmond, it was a chance to take that first major step towards his top flight dream. Thanks to Kamara, the club were finally moving in the right direction. The stakes were huge. A defeat in the play offs would ultimately leave the club back where they were in the first place; and the heartache could leave a hangover that extended into the following season, undermining hopes of bouncing back.

No, this was City's big moment, and it had to be taken. First up, a two-legged semi final with Blackpool – a side they had already beaten three times in four league and cup meetings, over the course of the season. There was nothing to fear.

Finding answers at the bottom of a glass

Chris Kamara sunk into yet another pint, as he sat slumped in the corner of a Wakefield pub with his chief scout Andy Smith, the weight of the world upon his shoulders.

Earlier that day, Bradford City's first leg play off game with Blackpool had proven majorly disappointing. With eighteen minutes left to play, the wily veteran striker Tony Ellis had given the Tangerines a crucial lead in a game the visitors were dominating. Ellis had managed to get on the wrong side of Nicky Mohan, before finding room on the edge of the box to curl home an effort that flew into the bottom corner. Just two minutes later, Mark Bonner popped up at the back post to easily head a second goal for Blackpool. It meant they had a colossal 2-0 advantage to take back for the return leg at Bloomfield Road. The manager, Sam Allardyce, had out-thought Kamara, by playing Andy Morrison in front of his back four in order to cut out the service to City's target man, Ian Ormondroyd. But more painful than that was the knowledge that his players had frozen on the big occasion and not turned up, going down to a first home defeat in ten matches. The walls around the Valley Parade fortress had crumbled. "A towering task" was the Blackpool-inspired headline of the Telegraph & Argus match report, with David Markham declaring, "The truth was they were beaten by a better team on the day…The effort was there – there can be no complaints on that score – but no one player will be happy about his performance as City failed to produce the form that has taken from mid-table into the play-offs." Reflecting back on events now, David Markham added, "After seeing Bradford City under-perform in the first leg of the play-off semi-final at Valley Parade, and go down 2-0, I don't think many supporters gave them much chance of over-turning that deficit in the second leg at Bloomfield Road."

Kamara was full of bluster to the press after the game, stating that "the tie is far from over…don't write us off just yet". But he admitted in his brilliant autobiography, 'Mr. Unbelievable', that privately he took the result very badly, stating, "I just couldn't understand how and why it had gone so wrong. Mam and Dad were at the game, but afterwards I couldn't talk to them. I was inconsolable, and I knew I had made mistakes." Eventually he had to tell his parents to go home because he was no company, and ended up going for a few drinks with Andy Smith, in an attempt to come to terms with what had happened. "Boy, did we sink a few beers, but all we could talk about was football," Kamara wrote. "I dissected and analysed the entire game, but Andy and John Allott, an old pal, helpfully steered me away from the previous 90 minutes and we started to plot for the next 90."

Sentiments shared by Richmond, who in the 2006 book 'The Pain and the Glory' stated, "Chris came into the boardroom close to tears, and told me 'I'm sorry, I've made a mess of it, we've blown it'. I told him that in the second leg our tactics were easy. We need three goals. We've nothing to lose. Go for it." Back in the O'Donohue's pub in Wakefield, an epiphany occurred at around 9pm. As Kamara bemoaned how predictable his team had been in knocking the ball long towards Ormondroyd, he realised that the best way to beat Blackpool was to ensure that his players only crossed the ball from the last third of the pitch, rather than deep – and so would remove the temptation to target Ormondroyd, by leaving him out of the side.

A team meeting was called for the following morning, where the new plan was announced. Kamara recalled in his autobiography that Ormondroyd took the decision well. The gameplan agreed, City used the gap between Sunday's defeat and the second leg on the Wednesday to practice the tactics. Part of the execution was to draw up an imaginary line, 20 yards into the opposition half of the pitch, that only after going past were the players allowed to cross the ball. Another key part was making sure the players believed they still had a chance. Duxbury recalled, "I definitely thought it was all over after the first leg. They had a strong team and they had a really good home record. For the second leg, you were thinking we had nowt to lose. Let's just go there and at least compete this time."

City were ready. And far from being downhearted after Sunday's potentially terminal set back, they made the short journey to Blackpool with renewed confidence and quiet steel that, this time, they would demonstrate their true potential. Kamara had pledged to the Telegraph & Argus, on the day of the match, "Blackpool will see a different Bradford City tonight."

And after arriving at Bloomfield Road, Kamara was able to detect signs that their hosts already believed they had booked their place at Wembley, and that the second leg was nothing more than a formality. The story has gone into folklore. Leafing through the programme whilst killing time before the team talk, Kamara found a page advertising the Wembley play off final ticket prices for Blackpool fans, complete with a phone number to book travel to the game. Kamara raced out and found a programme seller in order to buy another ten copies, and pinned them up all over the visitors' dressing room. In his autobiography Kamara states, "I wanted them to see the booking form. My team talk was virtually done for me. 'This lot think they've reached Wembley already,' I said...It did the trick. They were like wild animals waiting to be unleashed on the Blackpool public."

Duxbury added, "Those promotions about coaches going down to Wembley – that was more or less the team talk. Kammy said 'look at that guys, they already think they are at Wembley. Just get out there'. Kammy is a great man-manager. He had a good technical coach in Martin Hunter, and Paul Jewell was also there ticking things over. I think Jewell had a big say in a lot of things. I think getting the best out of you was Kammy's strength, because he was that type of player himself on the pitch when you were playing with him. He did that as a manager too." David Markham stated, "Blackpool as a club, interestingly managed by Sam Allardyce, were guilty of over confidence in that they famously advertised trips to Wembley for the final even before they completed the semi-final second leg. Chris Kamara made this the basis of his team talk and the rest, as they say, is history."

On the night City were backed by a reasonably decent support of 1,482 fans – but many others had opted not to make the journey to the coast, as they believed the tie was over. Even those who did go surely travelled in hope rather than with expectation. The away following included Joanne Golton who, amazingly, made the 331-mile journey up from Southampton for this midweek game. She explained, "I didn't go to the home game. I couldn't get up from Southampton for some reason. And so when we lost, I thought to myself 'I need to be there for the away leg, my team needs me!' I drove up from Southampton to get to the away leg in a Morris Minor! I got back to Bradford and got a lift over to Blackpool with my dad.

"There was about 1,700 of us there, perhaps a bit less than that. I always go with my friend Fiona, and her dad and my dad. And Fiona's dad wouldn't come, because he thought after the first leg that was it. And he was so nervous he stayed out in his garden all night, pretending to do the gardening, just so he didn't have to listen to it on the radio. We were on the away terrace, which wasn't covered, and there was a great atmosphere. I remember looking to the left and seeing that the players [unused that night] were in with the crowd as well, people like Richard Liburd. I still believed we could do it. The team had been all about not giving up and I believed in them."

That faith looked well-judged when City started the game on the front foot. An early shot from Duxbury trickled wide, but set the tone. Carl Shutt and 20-year-old midfielder Des Hamilton both passed up good opportunities to open the scoring, as Blackpool seemed to be caught in a dilemma of whether to defend their considerable advantage, or go out to attack once more. The first goal was always going to be vital, and it came six minutes before half time – for the visitors. A long throw in from Duxbury was flicked on by Mohan, and there was Shutt with an opportunity on the edge of the six-yard box that he gleefully buried. Blackpool 0 Bradford City 1. Game on.

It could have proven only a token resistance, had City not benefited from a huge slice of luck just a minute later. Blackpool finally roared into life, and Tony Ellis found himself up against his rival Mohan, with an opportunity to shoot from a position strikingly similar to the one that he had scored from at Valley Parade, in the first leg. This time Nicky Mohan got tighter, but nevertheless Ellis still

(*Above*) The Odsal experience, Bradford City in action at their temporary home. They spent almost 18 months playing at the home of Bradford Northern, and the council were said to be keen to make it a permanent move.

(*Below*) An emotional return to Valley Parade in December 1986, as Bradford City host an England XI to mark the re-opening of their home.

(*Above*) A heart-breaking afternoon for Bradford City, as Ipswich Town prepare to kick off the final match of the 1987/88 'nearly season'. A City victory would have sealed promotion to the First Division, but they were defeated 3-2 and would go onto lose in the play offs. Image by Kieran Wilkinson.

(*Below*) Mick Kennedy warms up before the Ipswich game. Nearby (in blue and black) is John Hendrie, who was suspended. This would be the first game Hendrie missed in four seasons, and his absence was a key reason for the defeat. Image by Kieran Wilkinson.

(*Above*) A break in play during the Ipswich Town defeat. Lee Sinnott is down injured and Stuart McCall is in conversation with the referee. Image by Kieran Wilkinson.

(*Below left*) The decline begins. City march out for a home game against Walsall on 8 April, 1989, nearly a year after coming so close to promotion, McCall and Hendrie have departed and Terry Dolan has been sacked. Image by Kieran Wilkinson.

(*Below right*) The players warming up in front of the Kop prior to the same Walsall match. Peter Jackson is in the centre after he made an unsuccessful return as player that summer. He was unfortunately an example of how the McCall/Hendrie money was badly spent. Image by Kieran Wilkinson.

(*Above left and right*) Unlike Peter Jackson's return to Valley Parade, the second coming of Stuart McCall proved to be a resounding success. He captained the Bantams to promotion to the Premier League in 1999, and continued to be an inspirational figure during the club's top flight adventure. Images by Charles Hague.

(*Below*) Heading towards the peak. Andrew O'Brien shields the ball away from Liverpool's Michael Owen on the final day of the 1999/00 season. The Bantams went onto win the game 1-0, confirming Premier League survival only four years after playing in the third tier. Image by Charles Hague.

(*Above*) The Great Escape. The players celebrate Premier League survival after the final whistle of the Liverpool game. They had looked dead and buried, but won three and drew one of their final five games. Image by Charles Hague.

(*Right*) Paul Jewell salutes the crowd after keeping Bradford City in the Premier League. The victory over Liverpool would prove to be his last match in charge, as a fall out with Geoffrey Richmond led to his departure during the summer. Image by Charles Hague.

(*Above*) Mixing it with the big guns. Stuart McCall brings the ball forward, with Manchester United's Paul Scholes and Teddy Sheringham looking on. Image by Charles Hague.

(*Below*) Fans' favourite Jamie Lawrence in action for the Bantams during the Premier League days – the image on the left sees him up against Dean Windass, who had recently been sold to Middlesbrough but would return in 2003. Images by Charles Hague.

got a shot in. It cannoned off the City defender's back, changing the direction of the ball. Goalkeeper Jonathan Gould was beaten, but amazingly the deflected shot bounced back off the crossbar. Such thin margins were crucial, and meant the Bantams could go in at half time a goal to the good, and with Blackpool's nerves fraying. Joanne added, "We went for Blackpool, especially just before half time. We came out and we had nothing to lose. It was just a really good game."

In the second half City continued to knock loudly on the door. They had the momentum, they smelt blood. Kamara's gameplan was working, with wingers Andy Kiwomya and Des Hamilton stretching the play, and central midfielders Duxbury and Graham Mitchell dominating the middle of the park. Following the instructions beautifully, Kiwomya went on a jinking run midway through the second half that resulted in him getting free of his full back, Marvin Bryan, and into the area, with team mates charging into the box. Kiwomya timed it all wonderfully, sending a low pass into the path of Hamilton in the middle of the box. Hamilton showed the composure of a veteran to steer the ball into the bottom corner. 2-0 to Bradford City, 2-2 on aggregate. At the opposite end of Bloomfield Road, the City fans went wild on the uncovered terrace.

Writing in the City Gent in the following issue, future editor David Pendleton stated, "The scenes on the visiting terrace were utterly insane: arms and legs everywhere; strangers were hugged and kissed; fences swung on; bodies rolled past in bear hugs – total, joyful, mayhem. The home terraces were a complete contrast; stunned silence. Fans who had earlier taunted us with their gloating Wembley songs couldn't even bear to look in our direction."

Amazingly Blackpool hit the woodwork for a second time just after. Andy Preece was played through one-on-one with Gould and dinked the ball over the City goalkeeper, only for it to bounce down onto the top of the crossbar and out for a goal kick. Blackpool were falling to pieces, and the fine margins kept going against them. Sam Allardyce must have been praying for the full time whistle and a chance to calm his players down prior to extra time. City were in no mood to left their hosts off the hook quite so easily. With eleven minutes to go, they completed the job.

After the home side gifted the Bantams possession all too easily, Mark Stallard brought the ball forwards just inside the Blackpool half, before spraying it out wide to the flying Kiwomya. Bryan cleared for a throw in, which enabled Wayne Jacobs to get forward in support of the attack. The ball was worked to the City left back, who sent over a hanging cross from just past Kamara's imaginary line. Hamilton tried to head it towards goal, as keeper Eric Nixon rushed out to try and claim it, and the ball rolled untidily into the path of an unmarked Mark Stallard, who fired a low shot past a sea of defenders and beyond the scrambling Nixon, and into the bottom corner. Blackpool 0 Bradford City 3. On the pitch, the City players all piled on top of Stallard – who would later tell the Telegraph & Argus, "This is easily the proudest moment of my career." On the City bench, Kamara and his coaching staff punched the air and hugged each other. On the away terrace, absolute pandemonium. The impossible had been achieved. The miracle was about to happen. Eat your heart out, Roy of the Rovers.

David Pendleton described the moment, "Scenes of utter madness ensued, groups of fans huddled together in almost unbelieving, bouncing, screaming, joy. One or two just stood there rooted to the spot, staring motionless at the pitch, their senses overwhelmed. The celebrations just went on and on, a continuous roar, wild eyed fans went from one to another, hugging and leaping, all of the while continuing a mad primeval scream."

The final few minutes ticked by slowly as Blackpool poured forward in desperation. Gaps were left at the back, and Stallard should have capped off an incredible night for City with a fourth goal. Instead, he blasted the ball into the home crowd behind the goal, with just Nixon to beat. It didn't matter one jot. Within 30 seconds, the final whistle was sounded. The City coaching staff raced onto the field and, along with their players, charged over to the away end, where a mini pitch invasion began. The Blackpool fans loudly booed their team, who were slumped on the floor in disbelief. They'd done the hard bit by winning at Valley Parade, but they'd been punished in devastating fashion for believing they had reached Wembley, when it was only half time in the tie. Bradford City had been priced at 40-1 to win 3-0. If anyone had taken on that bet, they'd have ended that night considerably richer. David Markham enthused, "I cannot recall many better constructed performances by a City side. To have a hope of winning the tie they had to get a goal back before half time which they did and then scored twice in the second half to go through to the final 3-2 on aggregate."

It was the first time in Bradford City's history that the club would be playing at Wembley stadium. The moment has been immortalised by the local radio commentator for Pennine Radio (later renamed Pulse), Chris Cooper, screaming over the airwaves "The Blackpool tower is a mile down the road, but the Twin Towers beckon for City now". Joanne Golton recalled of a night that she ranks as her favourite supporting the Bantams, "When the final whistle went some chap picked me up. Everyone was hugging everybody else. There were loads of cheering and shouting. It was incredible.

"The reason why it's my favourite ever game is because I had never been to Wembley before, and a month or two before this game my dad had said 'if you like we can go to watch Bradford Northern [who that year had reached the Challenge Cup Final] at Wembley' and I turned it down. I remember saying to him that I never want to go to Wembley unless it's to see my own team. And that night, when that final whistle went, everyone was looking at each other and going 'oh my god we're going to Wembley'. It was amazing! City had never been before, and back then people didn't even go down to London that often – when you did, it was a treat. It was just an amazing feeling to think that we were going to go to Wembley for the first ever time. It hadn't happened to City fans before, and so the whole feeling in that away end was incredible. Everyone was so excited, not so much at the thought of promotion, but the simple fact we were going to Wembley. It was such a big thing."

Inside the dressing room, Kamara and his players celebrated one of the most amazing results in the history of the club. Unbeknown to them, in the home dressing room, Blackpool manager Sam Allardyce had forced his players to sit in silence and listen to the jubilant noises next door. Outside Bloomfield Road, angry Blackpool fans gathered to call for Allardyce's head. They got their way, as he was sacked shortly after the game. A tough lesson, but one that Allardyce clearly used to good effect, as he has subsequently gone on to achieve notable success as a Premier League manager.

Lee Duxbury reflected of the way he approached the game, "I remember the last game of the season at Hull, that Blackpool game and the final – they were massive games. I just wanted to be a seven out of ten player in them. To do my job, stop my player and to help our players; not do anything flash, just play to my strengths. I think the atmosphere inside the dressing room after we beat Blackpool was electric. And then we stopped over at a hotel after, and I remember playing pool all night. There were supporters who found out where we were stopping and joined us. It was just a really good night."

City fans celebrated on the Bloomfield Road pitch for a long time, before making their way back to Bradford, slowly, to keep the party going. Joanne Golton recalled how even this moment was memorable, "For some reason there was a queue on the M55, I don't know what it was, and all these City fans were leaning out of windows and honking the horns. It was just brilliant. There wasn't that many of us who went, but for the ones who were there it was fantastic."

The Telegraph & Argus journalist and City fan, Sarah Calvert, was another who was present, writing about the night for the paper, "The traffic jam on the M6 could have been tedious, but instead, with traffic at a standstill and City fans hanging out of sunroofs and windows, the motorway just echoed with choruses of "There's only one Chris Kamara" and "Wem-ber-ley". A small pub on the A59 was descended on by a few hundred City fans in search of a well-deserved pint after a night of exhausting support. With everyone on a high, the pub buzzed with songs, chants, and shouts of "See you at Wembley"."

The front page of the Telegraph & Argus, on the following morning, featured a photo of a bare-chested and smiling Chris Kamara, surrounded by gleeful fans. "Brilliant!" was the headline. Geoffrey

Richmond, the catalyst for the reverse in City's fortunes, told the paper, "What a wonderful occasion tonight has been for those supporters who have stood by the club for many years. For most of that time, they've not had a lot to cheer about." Kamara beamed, "I have had 22 years in the game but this was the best moment of my footballing life...Even after Sunday's disappointment I knew we were a better team than Blackpool and all we had to do was to play."

The Independent newspaper also carried a match report of the game the following day, stating, "Blackpool is the home of the outlandish and the fantastic, but it has seen few sporting turnarounds to rival the way City pursued the unlikely vision of a place in the Second Division final."

Wembley beckons

On Thursday 16 May, 1996, many people in Bradford woke up to a hangover and disbelief at what had been achieved the night before. Valley Parade was a hive of activity, as City fans, and the people of Bradford, descended on the club shop, seeking answers about when Wembley tickets would go on sale, and to buy Wembley merchandise, which amazingly was already on sale by the afternoon. David Markham said, "I think we saw the best of Geoffrey Richmond immediately after the Blackpool win, when he set up a temporary club shops selling every possible piece of memorabilia ahead of the play off final at Wembley – the work of a salesman, entrepreneur whatever you like to call it, but a businessman, who seized the opportunity that the success of the team had given him to make money for the club – I think City raised £70,000 from the sale of memorabilia in the ten days leading up to the final."

On the Saturday after the Blackpool win, tickets went on sale, with fans queuing from 3.30am to get hold of one. Seventeen thousand were sold in the first day, and the long queues continued for days to come. Richmond told the Telegraph & Argus, "It has been absolutely brilliant, I have never seen anything like it in my life." The City Gent was able to report on stories of fans from all over the world travelling back to the UK for this historic chance to see their team at Wembley. This included Alan Smith, who hitch-hiked back from India where he lived up a tree! The Telegraph & Argus ran a story about City supporter Steve Unwin, who flew over to the game from his South Africa home – despite the fact he was booked in for a serious brain tumour operation in Cape Town a few weeks after the game.

Duxbury, with his Wembley experience of just a year earlier, was a very important person in the dressing room in helping everyone prepare. He was determined to make the most of the day, explaining, "The year before [for Huddersfield] was just a dream. The chance to play at Wembley – that might never happen again. I had regrets about things I didn't do on the day, and I was determined not to repeat them this time. It was things like just getting a big black bin liner and getting as much stuff as I could, before and after the match, for memories. I took shirts, shorts, anything to remember that time, in case we won. It was a time where I thought, if we won – take it in more."

This huge interest in the game contributed to City taking more than thirty thousand fans to Wembley. In contrast their opponents, Notts County, sold fewer than ten thousand tickets. The first battle had been won in terms of support, and on Sunday 26 May, 1996 – the day of the play off final – the M1 was awash with claret and amber, as supporters coach after supporters coach made the journey South. Richmond – in typically shrewd fashion – arranged for all the coaches to stop off at Leicester Forest services, where he just happened to set up a temporary Bradford City shop selling scarves and flags. Needless to say, it was a good day for business.

Joanne Golton reflected, "It was just a big day out. It was a day where your whole family had to come along with you, not just the football fans. People like my sister and my mum came. We all went down and it was a special ride to London. Old Wembley was brilliant. I know it was a bit tired in 1996, but it was a proper football ground. Going down Wembley Way was brilliant. I was near the half way line, and I remember us all getting in there and realising how few fans Notts County had brought compared to us. It was a bit of a surprise, and left you thinking 'this day is definitely ours'. We stood up for most of the game, and I remember just enjoying it."

The game itself proved to be strangely routine. After everything Kamara's City had gone through to get to this point – the late charge for the play offs, the astonishing win at Blackpool – perhaps they had simply put supporters through enough nerve-jangling moments, so instead won the game as conventionally as possible. Early doors, Des Hamilton strode through the Notts County defence before unleashing a ferocious shot, whilst slightly off balance, that whizzed into the top corner. 1-0, and lift off for City. And apart from tipping over one long range shot that was more opportunistic than skilful, Jonathan Gould had nothing to do all afternoon. Not a great deal happened at the other end either, in truth, although Shutt had a great chance to make it 2-0 that was thwarted by the County keeper.

With only fifteen minutes to go, the game – and promotion – was clinched through that inspired Kamara signing, Mark Stallard. But there was an extra romance about the goal, given who it was assisted by. Ian Ormondroyd, the fall guy of the first leg; the man who graciously stepped back and ended up watching his team mates run riot at Bloomfield Road, whilst he remained on the bench. For this game Ormondroyd was once again a substitute, only this time he got to come on. Three minutes later, a long ball was typically sent his way, by Richard Huxford, and Ormondroyd headed it down and into the path of Stallard to volley home. A hard-working City player over two spells, and part of the 1988 team that lost in the play offs, Ormondroyd deserved to have this moment. And he and his team mates deserved to be celebrating promotion at the final whistle. Joanne Golton recalled, "It was a bit of a walkover really, it wasn't much of a contest. We were just better than them, and it was a super day with a carnival atmosphere."

They had most certainly done everything the hard way, and now they could walk up to the Royal Box and lift the play off final trophy. Not too many teams could claim to have a 100% record at the Old Wembley…

The Telegraph & Argus match report ran with the headline "Dream come true", with David Markham writing, "The players did themselves, the club, the fans and the city proud, but the name on everyone's lips was that of manager Chris Kamara. For it is Kamara who has transformed City from mid-table mediocrity when he took over six months ago into a promotion winning team that graced one of the world's most famous stadiums with the quality of their football." Kamara himself was modest over the praise showered upon him from all quarters, stating, "I have received plenty of credit but I believe in the players and if you treat them well they will perform for you and they have done that all the time I have been in charge." David Markham added, looking back, "Beating Blackpool in the semi final proved to be more difficult than beating Notts County in the final. That proved to be a fairly straightforward affair. Notts were poor and City won quite comfortably."

A civic reception and open top bus parade took place in Bradford the following day, a Bank Holiday Monday. It began at Valley Parade and the route took in Manningham Lane, Cheapside, Petergate and Hall Ings before arriving at City Hall, with people lining the route to cheer the players. It was the first time since 1985 that the club had picked up a piece of silverware, and for obvious reasons that particular triumph wasn't celebrated for long, given the tragic events of May 11. This time, the Bradford public came out to celebrate the achievement. The feel-good factor would last for a lot longer; throughout the summer months and beyond. In the Telegraph & Argus Jim Greenhalf summarised the achievement, "Bradford has known some bad times in the past. I doubt it has known, since the war, good times such as these." Blackpool was the catalyst for those good times, and would continue to be a source of inspiration. Joanne Golton explained, "I loved Blackpool, it's my favourite ever game. There have been some close ones since, but Blackpool is really special because it was the first time that we got that feeling. We've since gone into big games with expectation, but back then we had nothing. So to have something like that happen to us was just amazing."

And on that May Bank Holiday, and in front of thousands of people who had packed out Centenary Square, Richmond took to the microphone on the City Hall balcony. The ultimate showman was in his pomp, and was getting carried away, "We will never forget Sunday, we will never forget Blackpool – but that was, I promise you, only the start. We have already extracted a promise from the Lord Mayor that we will have another civic reception to celebrate getting into the Premier League next season."

That was to prove a wildly optimistic proclamation, even by Richmond's standards, as the demands of playing in the higher league of Division One proved greater than expected, in 1996/97, and City were left fighting relegation. The ongoing rebuilding of the Midland Road stand diverted vital funds away from team strengthening. Richmond and Kamara sought to fully capitalise on the recently-introduced Bosman ruling, by signing foreign players on free transfers. Some were successes, but others came and left quickly. England international Chris Waddle rocked up for five months, most notably starring in an FA Cup giant-killing of Everton. The high turnover of players meant that many of the promotion heroes departed the club before the season was out.

Lee Duxbury was one such player, transferred to relegation rivals Oldham for £350,000, much to his own dismay. "I'd been at Bradford for a long, long time, since I was eleven. I left, I came back and then I thought that was it. I'm going to stay here for the rest of my career. I was captain, top scorer and playing the best football of my career. So for the chairman to turn around and say to Kamara 'I've been offered decent money for Lee Duxbury', it was a real kick in the teeth. Loyalty just flies out of the window. Because why would they do that? People talk about loyalty in football, but there's only one loyal fraction of a football club, and that's the supporters. Directors, chairmen, managers, players, they come and go. But the only one true loyal person is the fan."

The Midland Road stand was eventually opened in December 1996, and it was needed too as crowds continued to grow. Eventually Kamara was handed more substantial transfer funds, and City narrowly avoided relegation by winning their final two games. This was so important, given an instant return to the third tier would have been a huge set back to Richmond's masterplan. City had made huge strides on the climb up the mountain to the Premier League, and now they had set up base camp, within touching distance of the final peak. And though talk of rubbing shoulders with Manchester United and the like still seemed highly fanciful to some, no one connected with the club was dismissing such a possibility out of hand anymore. Supporters began to believe that the Premier League was something that could, in fact, be achieved.

After all, that balmy night in Blackpool had redefined the impossible.

City (vs Blackpool): Jonathan Gould; Richard Huxford, Nicky Mohan, David Brightwell, Wayne Jacobs, Des Hamilton, Lee Duxbury, Graham Mitchell, Andy Kiwomya; Carl Shutt, Mark Stallard
Subs not used: Ian Ormondroyd, Paul Jewell, Neil Tolson

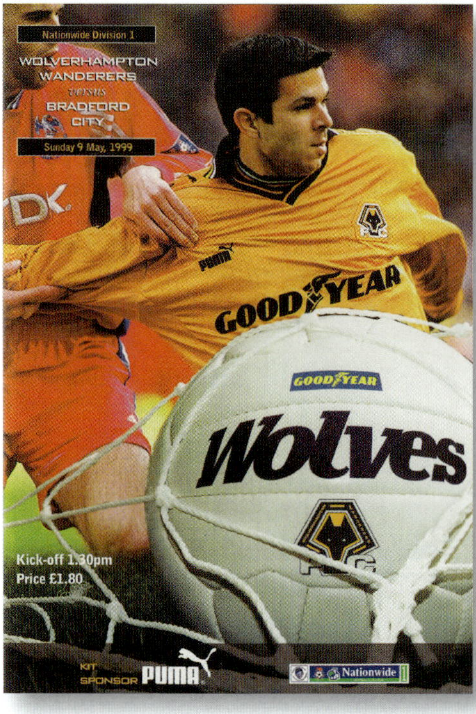

The promised land
Wolverhampton Wanderers vs Bradford City
Division One, Sunday 9 May, 1999

Above the players' entrance to the tunnel at Molineux stadium, home of Wolves, a simple Latin phrase is displayed – "Out of the darkness cometh light". It is the town of Wolverhampton's motto, but its meaning and significance translated perfectly to Bradford City, as they lined up in the players' tunnel, for the final Division One match of the 1998/99 season.

77 years had passed since Bradford City last graced the top tier of English football. Back in 1922, they had been relegated from the old Division One alongside Manchester United. Whilst for United, it would prove a temporary blip before their glory days of the 1950s, 60s and beyond, City would never return to the elite. The 1910s – when they were FA Cup winners and finished in the top five – were seemingly destined never to be repeated. They spent the majority of those 77 years languishing in the bottom two divisions, only once coming close to a return to the top flight, in 1988, when they blew their big opportunity by losing at home to Ipswich Town on the final day of the season.

Yet here they were, on the brink of the big time. A place at the top table. A home in the promised land. All they had to do was beat Wolves, and promotion to the top division would be theirs. And, of course, with this being the nineties, the top division meant the Premier League. After the breakaway of the top clubs in 1992, the Premier League had brought glamour, the world's best players and untold riches. The chance to mix it with Manchester United, Arsenal, Chelsea and Liverpool, with games beamed around the world, was an intoxicating prospect. Win this one final match, and all of this, and more, would be City's.

Ironically, their direct rivals for the final automatic promotion place were Ipswich Town themselves.

This was a real chance to put the ghosts of 1988 to rest, to wipe out away the lingering sense of bitterness and regret over how the club lost out on promotion, and to end 77 years of lower league darkness.

Light cometh.

The big plan

How Bradford City had found themselves going to Molineux on the brink of promotion to the Premier League was a masterstroke in tactical planning. Exactly on schedule to fulfil Geoffrey Richmond's 1994 grandiose promise of reaching the Premier League in five years' time. The final part of the chairman's ambitious plan was undoubtedly his finest hour.

It was all about timing, as could be illustrated by rewinding back twelve months to the final day of the 1997/98 Division One season. It had been a remarkable year for English football's second tier, as some big names battled over both promotion and avoiding relegation. Nottingham Forest – the double-European champions of the 1980s – were the championship front runners. With the might of Holland international striker Pierre van Hoojidonk, and the wily former Arsenal hotshot Kevin Campbell up front, the intelligent Steve Stone in midfield, and crafty Colin Cooper at the back, Forest marched their way to the title under the experienced manager Dave Bassett. Behind them were two North East giants, Middlesbrough and Sunderland, who went into the final day of the campaign fighting over the final automatic promotion spot. The Teesiders pipped the Wearsiders in finishing second by thrashing Oxford United 4-0. They had spent a fortune on the likes of Paul Merson, Paul Gascoigne, Franco Branca, Hamilton Ricard and Alun Armstrong, to ensure their quick-fire return to the Premier League. Sunderland – with the deadly strike duo of Kevin Phillips and Niall Quinn – would go on and lose to Charlton on penalties in the play off final. They had that season moved from their poky Roker Park home to the astonishing Stadium of Light, and were transformed as a football club because of it.

Meanwhile at the other end, hovering inside the bottom three on the final day of the campaign were Manchester City. Relegated from the Premier League in 1996, and at that stage something of a basket case, the Manchester club threw lots of money in a bid to reverse their dramatic fall from grace, but horrendous mismanagement meant they faced falling into the third tier for the first time in their proud history. To stay up on the final day of the 1997/98 season, Man City had to beat another big club who were down on their luck, Stoke City, who themselves faced relegation. Man City also had to hope that Bradford City or Huddersfield could do them a massive favour by defeating their relegation rivals Portsmouth and Port Vale respectively. In the event, a 5-2 Man City win sent Stoke down, and victories for Pompey and Vale in West Yorkshire meant the Maine Road outfit were relegated too.

After all of this drama, the strength of Division One, for the 1998/99 season, was drastically lowered. Replacing the promoted Nottingham Forest, Middlesbrough and Charlton were Bolton, Barnsley and Crystal Palace – the trio relegated from the Premier League after just one season, and from whom only Bolton looked strong financially. In place of the relegated Man City, Stoke and Reading were Watford, Bristol City and Grimsby – no great shakes, even though Watford would perform well over the 1998/99 campaign, and end up earning a second straight promotion via the play offs.

Speaking to the Telegraph & Argus in June 1999, Richmond revealed that the obvious weakening of Division One in the summer of 1998 persuaded him that the time was right for the Bantams to have a real go at promotion. That if the club were to spend significant sums of money improving the squad, they stood a real chance of making it to the Premier League. This wasn't a time for slow and steady progress, as who knows what fallen giants might drop into Division One over the coming years. Strike while the iron is hot was Richmond's mantra. "I sat down last summer and went through the First Division table and put a red line through all the teams that I felt were not capable of realistically challenging for a place in the top six," he told the Telegraph & Argus. "It became clear that there was definitely a chance of forcing our way into the promotion race if we were to spend money...The club had been quite careful the previous five years, but we felt the time had come to act…There are times at a football club where it is right to have a go when you think the time is right."

To fund the promotion push, Richmond turned to a couple of board members who had joined the club during the summer before. A father and son act, who were enjoying significant success in the business world, this family had made a small investment into the club in 1997, purely as a hobby. They had no desire to be anything beyond silent partners, and for the time being at least they could remain so.

That father and son act were Professor David and Julian Rhodes, who owned Bradford-based design electronics company Filtronic. Julian Rhodes told me, "I worked for my dad [at Filtronic] after University in 1992. Then in 1994 we floated the business. Over the next couple of years we sold a few shares which meant we had a bit of money. We started looking around for things to invest in, and decided 'well we love Bradford City, why don't we have a word with Mr Richmond?' We first spoke to him in January 1997, and we ended up finalising the deal that July. There was a lot going on at the club around that time. We had just survived in Division One on the last day of the season. It was very much a backseat role. Geoffrey Richmond was the man in charge."

Sensing the time was right to have a go for promotion, in May 1998, Richmond persuaded David and Julian to inject further capital that would be used for significant team strengthening. Julian continued, "We did have to borrow £5 million to fund the 1998/99 promotion push. It was the right thing to do because at the time Division One was a relatively weak league. It was the right time to have a go." The money was raised in a way that at the time was an unusual and innovative move, with a merchant bank providing the money to the Rhodes family, and the cost of the subsequent summer signings spread over the length of each player's contract. Certain securities were required by the bank, which were provided by the Rhodes family. Should City have been unable to meet their debts, the bank would have the legal right to sell these securities in order to repay the debts. In other words, the Rhodes family took on the risk of the club's lavish summer spending spree, and would face the consequences should City have later experienced financial problems (which, this time at least, they didn't).

Yet that was only part one of Richmond's masterplan – the second bit was one that was unobvious to everybody else, especially us supporters: the man with whom to entrust with the largest transfer budget in the club's history; the next permanent manager of Bradford City. Richmond's choice left many people flummoxed.

Midway during the 1997/98 season, Richmond had made the shock decision to sack Chris Kamara following a run of poor form. Yet City were eleventh in the division at the time of his dismissal – having narrowly survived relegation on the final day of the previous campaign. The club made a strong start to the 1997/98 season and even topped the division in the middle of September, but very soon a bright start turned into an indifferent one. The initial prospect of City pushing for promotion had raised expectations, and decent money was spent by Kamara, not least a club record £650,000 on transfer flop John McGinlay. Richmond acted ruthlessly, sacking the man who had got City promoted to Division One eighteen months earlier, via that astonishing night at Blackpool, and play off final victory over Notts County. After City were knocked out of the FA Cup in January, Kamara was handed his P45.

There was no doubt that, by sacking Kamara, Richmond was significantly raising the stakes. Whereas a year earlier a mid-table placing in Division One would have been seen as a big success, the chairman's drive to reach the Premier League meant this was no longer good enough. To see out the remainder of the 1997/98 season, Richmond turned to Kamara's assistant, Paul Jewell, who was appointed caretaker and then, after a promising start, confirmed as manager for the remainder of the campaign. A City striker of almost a decade, Jewell had remained on the coaching staff after his retirement. He spoke openly of his passion for the club, and his desire to get the job full time. The problem was that Jewell became increasingly unimpressive during the latter months of the season, not least after a dreadful ending that involved four defeats from the final five games. City finished the season thirteenth – two places lower than when Kamara had been fired – and Jewell had failed to convince supporters that he was worthy of filling the vacancy in the long-term.

It was assumed that Jewell was merely keeping the seat warm ahead of the arrival of a big name, but to everyone's surprise, at the end of the season, Richmond announced that Jewell was to be handed the role permanently, and the 33-year-old signed a two-year deal. Many supporters were underwhelmed by this move and suggested the club lacked ambition. Jewell was too young, and had no experience, they argued. As part of a Yorkshire TV documentary that was aired in May 1999, Richmond admitted that he received a lot of criticism for his decision, "A lot of people thought he would be on his way before the season even started, my mailbag last summer was horrendous…We lost a lot of season ticket holders, a couple of thousand season ticket holders didn't renew really. They thought the club had taken leave of its senses in the appointment. They were looking for a big name, and I understand why fans would look for a big name. But very often what a big name means is somebody who has failed elsewhere."

Richmond would later reveal that Jewell's lowest ebb in the caretaker role had been the moment he decided he was the right man for the job. It came on the penultimate weekend of the 1997/98 season, when City were thrashed 5-0 at Crewe in what still ranks as one of the worst performances in the modern history of the club. At half time and with City 4-0 down, Jewell banished his players from the dressing room, and forced them to spend the interval sat in the centre circle on the pitch, enduring stick from a sold out City away crowd and the laughter of home supporters.

Gareth Walker is a Bradford City supporter since the early 1990s, and contributes to Widthofapost.com. He recalled to me the negative supporter reaction to Jewell getting the job on a permanent basis, "We weren't jumping for joy put it that way. When Jewell got the job in the first place he was completely untried and inexperienced. He'd been given until the end of the season and he hadn't done particularly well, so there was an expectation that he'd be replaced with a bigger name, so to speak. Supporters really struggled to understand why he was given a two year contract. It didn't really smack of the ambition that Geoffrey Richmond had been talking about."

Big spending Bantams

Granted that two-year deal and armed with a huge transfer budget, Jewell set to work on rebuilding the team. In total he brought in seven players that summer, but no one was more important than his very first capture – a certain Stuart McCall. Since leaving City in 1988, after the club narrowly failed to get promoted to the top flight, McCall had enjoyed a glittering career at Everton and Glasgow Rangers – in Scotland he was a key part of the famous Rangers side that won nine titles in a row – and had appeared in a World Cup and two European Championships for the Scotland national team. But he'd always talked of unfinished business at Bradford City, and of his desire to come back. Ten years after his emotional departure from Valley Parade, McCall was ready to come home.

Stuart McCall told me of how he was hoping to return to West Yorkshire that summer, but that, for a time at least, it looked as though he was going to join Barnsley – recently relegated from the Premier League – instead, "I had a year left at Rangers. Dick Advocaat was coming in. I had a meeting with him and he wanted me to stay, because a lot of the old guard were departing. He was bringing in his own players like Gianni van Brockhurst, and there were some good young players coming through like Barry Ferguson. So he wanted me to stay to help the transition. But I looked at it and Walter Smith and Archie Knox had gone, all my pals had gone. It was the end of an era. So I went to see the chairman David Murray. He told me that Hearts had come in for me. He said that because of my service for the club, they would let me move South of the border for nothing, even though I still had a year on my contract. But if I went to another Scottish club they would want a fee of £200k.

"We had played Hearts in the cup final that year and Danny Wilson [then manager of Barnsley] came to watch me. I was travelling down to meet Danny at Barnsley, when I got a phone call out of the blue. Someone had tipped off Geoffrey Richmond that I was heading to Barnsley. I think they had said to him 'look McCall is coming back to Yorkshire; if you don't try to get him you'll regret it'. With no disrespect to Barnsley, or any of the other clubs interested in me at the time, I really wanted to come back to Bradford, but nothing had been mentioned. So I got this call out of the blue and diverted the car to Bradford instead. I rang Danny to tell him, and he understood.

"I met Paul and Chris Hutchings at the ground. Paul was actually a year younger than me and had recently had his testimonial year. He had taken over from Chris Kamara the season before. I wasn't sure if it was the chairman wanting to sign me or him, but we sat down and talked and he impressed me with what he had to say. Ultimately it could have been anyone who was manager, I just wanted to re-sign for Bradford City."

McCall's return caught the imagination of the Bradford public, and the club shop was quickly filled with Stuart merchandise. A new generation of supporters were about to fall in love with Stuart, in the same way those who followed the club during the 1980s had taken him to their hearts. Geoffrey Richmond told a Yorkshire TV documentary a year after McCall re-signed, "Stuart's special. A player coming back home, this is where it all started for him. Stuart will go down in this club's history and amongst supporters as a living legend, because that's exactly what he is. His attitude on the field and off the field is always absolutely fantastic."

Other new signings included spending £800,000 bringing in Ashley Westwood and Gareth Whalley from Crewe, and – most amazingly – the club's transfer record was broken twice in just six days. Firstly – on the Friday lunchtime before the 1998/99 season began – Port Vale striker Lee Mills became City's first-ever £1 million player. He was followed by fellow forward Isaiah Rankin – 20-years-old, and a £1.3 million signing from Arsenal. These moves shocked not only City fans but the rest of the division. Very quickly, the Bantams were re-christened "Big Spending Bradford City" in the national media. McCall added, "In fairness to the chairman, he had backed the manager, and put his money where his mouth was. Although I was a free transfer I was on good wages. We spent over a million each on Rankin and Mills. The manager bought wisely."

With such a flurry of transfer activity – and much of it carried out late in pre-season – it was perhaps no surprise that it didn't lead to instant results. Yet nevertheless, there were grave concerns early doors that Richmond's strategy was going to end painfully. It took City five matches to register a victory, and after a dreadful midweek 3-0 defeat at Ipswich Town in early September, the knives were out for Jewell. Early days they may have been, but rather than pushing for promotion, City were languishing in the bottom three. Dissent amongst supporters – who weren't convinced by Jewell in the first place – grew louder and louder. For Jewell and his players, the early-hours' journey home from Suffolk was a long and painful one.

Gareth Walker recalled, "Fans had their doubts about Jewell being appointed in the first place and then he'd been backed financially more than any other manager in City's history, so after the start we had there was a little bit of resentment growing. I heard a few boos and a couple of 'Jewell out' chants."

Stuart McCall added that the pressure on Jewell wasn't helped by some people suspecting – and loudly floating the idea – that McCall was waiting in line to take over as manager, should Jewell make a poor start. It was something that McCall himself was keen to shoot down at every opportunity, "One thing I did stress when I returned was that I didn't want to be the manager. I'd always said that one day I wanted to return, and I always thought it would be as a manager. And I think some people assumed that this was what was happening; that I was coming back to wind down my career. So I wanted to show Paul that I had as much hunger as before, probably even more, and wanted Paul to know that there was no way I wanted to be the manager, and that I still felt I had a few more years in me as a player."

Nevertheless McCall received an unexpected phone call that, in some ways, suggested the club were considering the possibility of dismissing Jewell, and making Stuart McCall the player Stuart McCall the manager, "A lot of people don't know this, but after the Ipswich game on a Tuesday night I got a phone call. We had been beaten 3-0 and got back really late, and I remember Jewell getting off the front of the bus and saying to the players 'I will see you all on Thursday, if I'm still here'. I got a call the next day, through a third party, asking me if I would consider becoming manager of the club, if the job arose. I categorically, 100% said I had no intention of taking over. I wanted to play and that was all that I was focused on. That there was plenty of time to turn the season around and I was focused on that. My answer got filtered back to whoever was originally asking the question."

Falling into place

The 1998/99 season would prove to be a special one for so many people – and that especially includes me. I had first stumbled upon, and instantly fallen in love with, Bradford City in November 1997. I was still at school, and held a morning paper round. One morning the papers were late arriving from the deliverers, and so me and other paperboys sat around outside, chatting to pass the time. A couple of friends told me they were going to watch Bradford City that afternoon. I felt instantly jealous and – with some prodding from my mum, later that morning – ended up joining them. I can still clearly remember surveying the Valley Parade pitch for the very first time. It was a life-changing moment, and I was completely smitten by this amazing football club that had been sat on my doorstep all this time.

After City had been promoted to Division One in 1996, I had harboured thoughts about going along to a couple of the more glamorous fixtures, like Middlesbrough and Manchester City. It never materialised, but here I now was, minutes before kick off of the Bantams' match with West Bromwich Albion. I was Bradford City's newest supporter, stood at the back of the terrace Kop with wide-eyed wonderment, amazed that it had only cost me £5 to get in.

Me and my friends went as often as possible over the rest of the 1997/98 season, including away games. I was at Maine Road for Kamara's final match in charge, the 2-0 FA Cup defeat to Man City. I was there also for the infamous 5-0 loss to Crewe. I remember the half time arguments from other fans over who should be the next manager, with everyone assuming Jewell would depart, and most wanting him to go. We bought season tickets that summer, and so 1998/99 has the personal distinction of being my first year owning a season ticket. Like Richmond and his grand strategy, my timing proved to be good.

During that dreadful start to the season, I can still remember sitting in my bedroom and listening to BBC Radio Leeds' commentary of the 0-3 Ipswich game. It sounded like a dismal night for the Bantams, and it was hard to know where the players and manager could go from there. As it happened, the answer lay in a man who was so far out of the first team picture at the time, he had been used by Radio Leeds as co-commentator for the evening: Robbie Blake.

A promising young striker signed from Darlington in 1997, Blake had endured a stuttering start to life at Valley Parade which included an arrest for drink driving just months after joining the club. Blake had shown flashes of what he could do over the 1997/98 season, but a needless sending off against Portsmouth on the final day meant he missed the first three games of 1998/99 due to suspension. And with Jewell having spent £2.3 million on a pair of strikers, it looked a long way back for him. In truth, you suspected he would leave the club at that point.

Yet four days after the Ipswich farce, Blake was brought in from the cold and given an opportunity on the right flank, in a home game against Sheffield United. Blake produced a dazzling display that included a well-taken goal. He was man of the match, and the 2-2 draw was by some distance City's best display of the season so far. Suddenly there was hope that this expensive new team was showing signs of gelling. And sure enough, the corner was turned very slowly. The draw with the Blades was the start of an eight-match unbeaten run, which lifted the club from the bottom three to the top half of the division. It was the beginning of something special.

If there was one moment where belief truly began to grow amongst wary supporters, it came at the end of September, when Barnsley came to Valley Parade. City produced a strong first half performance, only to go 1-0 behind early in the second half. Yet they never folded and accepted defeat. They continued to loudly bang on the Barnsley door, aided along the way by the visitors being reduced to ten men. With six minutes to go, striker Gordon Watson was summoned from the bench and City went 4-2-4. Three minutes later, Watson equalised in front of a jubilant Kop. And then two minutes after, Watson scored again to spark unbridled scenes of celebration that have gone down in folklore.

For Watson, it was an especially emotional moment. He'd been signed by City in February 1997, only to break his leg on just his third appearance, following a truly horrendous tackle by Huddersfield Town's Kevin Gray. He was out injured for eighteen months, and successfully sued Gray, via the courts, for the damage the crude challenge had done to his career. Those two goals against Barnsley were his first since returning to fitness. It was an incredible way to announce your comeback.

Whilst Watson deservedly grabbed the headlines, Stuart McCall recalled that Jewell's tactical changes had a big influence on City's astonishing late comeback, "They had Martin Bullock sent off. And Jewell made a substitution in taking the right back off and pushing me to right back. I couldn't believe it at the time, but in fairness to him it was a good spot as he had noticed the way that Barnsley had set up with ten men. The outlet for us was the right back, as there was no one near him. So I ended up playing right back and had more of the ball in those final ten minutes than I had had all game. I really enjoyed it, putting crosses in. And then we scored twice at the end through Watson. There was a big crowd there that day. It was a great day, and a huge result."

Gareth Walker added, "As confidence grew, the quality in the team started to shine through. One important game was Barnsley at home. From the moment we conceded we absolutely battered them, we really had them on the racks. You could just tell that something was building. It felt like something was going to happen. Watson ended up scoring two goals in the last five minutes for us to win the game 2-1. The noise and the crowd surge when that second goal went in were phenomenal. I think my feet were off the floor and I was moved half way across the Kop. It was an atmosphere the like of which I hadn't seen at Valley Parade before. That was when we realised that there wasn't just quality in that side, there was something special about it too. They were a really close knit group who would never give up."

Despite the odd setback here and there, City's form continued to soar. By the end of October they reached the play off positions. In December and January, their progress reached another level. After winning nine out of ten matches, City climbed into the top two. Sunderland were, unsurprisingly, racing away with the division, but the Bantams were very much in the hunt for the second automatic promotion spot, alongside Ipswich Town, Bolton Wanderers and Birmingham City. The latter two would eventually drop out of contention. It was all about City – the division's surprise package – and Ipswich.

These were really exciting times. Even the most optimistic of City supporters had felt the best the club could achieve was the play offs this season, not automatic promotion. The atmosphere around Valley Parade was fantastic. No one was complaining about Jewell – who earned himself an improved contract in autumn – anymore.

Point to prove

The 1998/99 Bradford City team has gone down in the club's history as one of the most affectionately remembered sides. From goalkeeper to the forward line, it oozed quality. And, at a time before squad rotation began to creep into football, there was a settled look to the team, and a familiarity about the players we watched week in week out over that campaign.

In goal was Gary Walsh, who had signed from Middlesbrough a year earlier, having a few years before that been understudy to the great Peter Schmeichel at Manchester United. The back four featured Stephen Wright at right back and the ever-green Wayne Jacobs at the opposite side – the only survivor from the 1996 promotion-winning side. Stuart McCall said of the full backs, "Wayne Jacobs has become a really good friend of mine. Stephen Wright had followed me from Rangers. I used to joke with that I'd brought him down as I needed someone to cut my grass!" In between them there was fierce competition for the centre back roles, between Darren Moore, Andrew O'Brien, John Dreyer and Ashley Westwood.

On the flanks were Jamie Lawrence, who we will come back to shortly, and a rejuvenated Peter Beagrie. The latter had enjoyed a fine top flight career with Everton and Man City, but was seemingly on his way downwards, yet over 1998/99 Beagrie was sensational for City and netted fifteen goals. Writing for the Two Unfortunates website in 2011, City fan Michael Wood recalled, "Everything Beagrie did seemed to have a point to it; every cross made to perfection, hanging impressively for Lee Mills to arrive onto." Stuart McCall had known Beagrie from their time together at Everton and, at City, the pair inadvertently became neighbours in Harrogate. McCall explained, "I remember I was staying in a hotel and we were looking for somewhere to live. We ended up looking at one in Harrogate; so after training we drove into Harrogate. I went to the bottom of the estate, which was a dead end, turned around using someone's drive and then went back up the road to look at the house. The next day Peter said to me 'that was a bit ignorant wasn't it?' And I said 'what do you mean?' He replied 'well you reversed into my driveway yesterday, I went to put the kettle on so we could have a cup of tea together, and when I came back you had gone!' I had no idea that he even lived in Harrogate! We ended up buying a house 200 yards away from him. I remember I was unsure whether to buy it, but then I thought 'well as soon as Beags moves to another club and sells his house, property prices on the street will rise'!"

McCall himself was made captain and played in the centre of the park – he was as brilliant and inspirational as the first time around, only with even more class to his game, gleaned from his ten years playing at the top for Everton and Rangers. McCall was the runaway winner of the player of the season award, and in June 1999 Telegraph & Argus journalist Richard Sutcliffe wrote about the inspirational skipper, "Whenever on the ball, McCall looked to have more time than any opponent while his ferocious tackling stopped many opposition attacks. It is also a huge testament to his character that he is also among the fittest players at the club, despite being in what is commonly known as the 'veteran' stage of his career." McCall was partnered by the cultured Gareth Whalley, whose passing and vision was a potent weapon all campaign. After a 2-0 victory over West Brom in September, Sutcliffe wrote of Whalley, "The most pleasing aspect of his play again being his willingness to find space after finding a team-mate with a pass rather than standing still admiring his own work."

And up front there was Lee Mills, who was partnered with Robbie Blake, after the latter's mid-season switch from right wing to striker. The pair developed an incredible understanding, collectively netting 42 goals between them. Mills was an old fashioned targetman with plenty of skill, whilst Blake's jinking runs and crafty forward play routinely bamboozled opposition defenders and prompted sizeable speculation that Premier League clubs were looking at signing him. Blake received so many votes, from his fellow professionals, for the PFA Division One team of the year that season, he should have joined Darren Moore in the final XI – alas, half of the votes cast were for him as a winger and the other half for him as a striker, which meant he missed out on this accolade.

Gareth Walker recalled of Mills and Blake, "It looked like the classic big man little man partnership, but it was a bit different really. Jewell kind of stumbled across the partnership as he probably intended to partner Mills with Isaiah Rankin, but once Blake got into the side and got his chance he was unstoppable. They were good friends off the pitch which obviously helps, but sometimes a strike partnership just seems to click and it's almost like telepathy. This, for that one season at least, was just like that."

Whilst Mills, Blake and Beagrie were netting the bulk of the goals and, with it, the headlines, Jamie Lawrence was another really key player. Signed by Chris Kamara around the same time as Beagrie, in the summer of 1997, Lawrence's name in the game was well-known after he spent time in prison for armed robbery, before earning an opportunity at Sunderland and later moving to Doncaster Rovers and Leicester City. He played in the Premier League for the Foxes although wasn't a regular, and manager Martin O'Neill eventually agreed to sell him to Bradford City. Lawrence had a good first season at Valley Parade and certainly built on it during the 1998/99 campaign. He was a whole-hearted player who gave everything on the field, and such a high level of work-rate helped to set the bar for others to follow.

Lawrence told me of the 1998/99 team, "We had some really resilient characters in the dressing room, and a lot of them felt like they had a point to prove because of experiences at other clubs before, where they'd had knockbacks. We all stuck together. To be part of that team was incredible. The way we tackled, and we played really good football too. I think when we went onto the field we would be prepared to battle, and would earn the right to play. What we also had in that team were really strong characters and a lot of honesty. If someone in the team wasn't doing their job, they would be told by the rest of the team, and the gaffer, and they would take it on board and try to recover."

Indeed, the work-rate from front to back was one of the key characteristics of that time. I have never seen a City side as well drilled and organised as the class of 99. Each and every player knew their job and they carried out Jewell's instructions perfectly. They played wonderful football, but they had resilience too. They evidently socialised as a group off the pitch too, which helped to strengthen the bond. Even the players' wives and girlfriends were a close-knit group, socialising together and organising mini bus trips to and from some away games. Paul Jewell stated on the May 1999 Yorkshire TV documentary, "Our strength has been our togetherness and our bond. We haven't got a massive squad, but when we go away from home we all travel together, and the lads who aren't playing are very disappointed, but they're supporters. Once that whistle goes, they are supporters too."

Stuart McCall is full of enthusiasm for the 1998/99 team, "When I looked back to that team we had a really good mix of players. We could play football and score goals, but we could also mix it physically when we needed to. The likes of Moore, Jamie, Jakes and Tumble – if there were any games where the opposition thought they could bully us, we proved that we could also battle when it was needed.

"The key was we had three forward type players who could score goals. Beagrie had an outstanding season, and Mills and Blake were terrific. I used to tell people that if you edited and put together a video of Blake's best bits of skill and goals of that year, you could have sold him to Real Madrid. He was fantastic. He was a little cheeky chappy, the banter use to fly around with him.

"We had lots of little partnerships, like Bruno [Darren Moore] and Tumble [John Dreyer] – Bruno would attack everything that came in the box and Tumble would sweep up behind him. Jakes [Wayne Jacobs] and Beags had a great understanding. Jakes would do the overlap whilst knowing that he wouldn't get the ball from Beags – he was just unselfish! Beags, for all his ability, was a team player. He would work hard and track back. On the other side you had Jamie who was so committed. He might not be the best player but he was full of pace, strength and could score. Gareth Whalley was just a really good footballer. Others played their part to. It was an all-round, well-balanced squad. Once we got on a roll, we were excellent."

As the season headed towards its conclusion, and with nothing to choose between City and Ipswich, Geoffrey Richmond sanctioned further team strengthening to provide the squad with extra insurance that – back in 1988 and with the failed top flight promotion push – had been lacking. Another £1 million was spent to secure the services of Oxford striker Dean Windass to back up Mills and Blake. Lee Sharpe also arrived, on loan from Leeds United, offering the versatility of being able to play on the left wing or at left back. Stuart McCall stated, "We brought in Dean Windass and Lee Sharpe on transfer deadline day. And when you compare it to 1987/88 when we didn't sign players on deadline day, the gamble was justified as they both made a difference."

Jamie Lawrence recalled, "Deano [Dean Windass] scored some important goals for us that season. He was a good player and good fit for the team. I think the squad needed to have a bit of competition. You can't have a team where everyone knows they will definitely be playing, because then they know they don't have to perform every week. But if you have someone looking over your shoulder and putting pressure on you, if you have anything about you it makes you perform better." During the run-in, Windass netted an important double during an Easter Monday victory over Bury, whilst Lee Sharpe scored vital goals in home wins over Grimsby and Portsmouth. With Beagrie experiencing some injury problems, and Blake hit by the devastating news that his father had passed away, the signings of Windass and Sharpe were indeed justified, despite some fears they might upset the obvious strong team spirit.

It looked increasingly like the promotion race would go right down to the wire, as both City and Ipswich surprisingly dropped points during the run-in. The final two games of the season at Valley Parade saw a painful 3-2 derby loss to Huddersfield Town, and a 0-0 draw at home to relegation-bound Oxford United. The Huddersfield Town defeat brought unwelcome flashbacks to 1988, given a shock home defeat to their near-neighbours that season proved so costly in the final shake up. On the 1999 sequel, Gareth Walker added with a shudder, "The Huddersfield game was awful. They were a horrible niggly side who should have been down to nine men. They beat us 3-2 and Peter Jackson [the former City hero and now the Huddersfield manager] celebrated by running down the touchline. I felt sick and cheated leaving that game. I don't think that I've ever been so angry leaving a game. It felt like we'd blown it against our nearest rivals, just like eleven years earlier.

"Then there was the Oxford home game. They were on the verge of being relegated and we didn't play well at all. We froze on the big occasion. McCall missed a glorious chance right in front of us at the end and it felt like we'd blown it again." Stuart McCall added, "We had played Oxford the week before Wolves, where I had missed that header after Windass crossed it. We had the player of the year awards on the Tuesday in-between the Oxford and Wolves games, and I won a couple of awards although it was all spread out evenly amongst the team. I remember that night, even thought it was joyous night, still feeling really low because of that miss. I was down for a couple of days, and the rest of the lads had to bring me up."

Despite City's stumbles, Ipswich were amazingly beaten at home by bottom club Crewe with three games to go, and on the penultimate weekend lost 0-1 at Birmingham City. It meant that with 45 of the 46 games completed, City were second in the league, with a one point advantage. All they had to do was match Ipswich's final day result, and they would be promoted to the Premier League. But the problem was Ipswich's last game was at home to a Sheffield United side that had nothing to play for. City, meanwhile, had to travel to Wolves and win to be sure of promotion. Not an easy proposition, given the hosts had only lost once at home all season, and were still fighting for a play off spot. Wolves had everything to play for, and would not make it easy for City.

The width of a post

And so the scene was set. At Sunday lunchtime, and with both games screened live on Sky Sports, City emerged from the darkness of the Molineux tunnel, with their destiny in their own hands, whilst 163 miles to the East, Ipswich welcomed Sheffield United to Portman Road, knowing they had to win and hope for a Wolverhampton favour. I was one of three thousand, very fortunate, Bradford City supporters to get a ticket for this game, and travelled to the Midlands on a very quiet supporters' coach that was riddled by nerves. It had been a long week waiting for this game, struggling to get to sleep at night, as you fretted over all the permutations. With City's form stuttering during the run-in – one win in four games – it was, in truth, difficult to see us defeating Wolves on their own patch. But could Sheffield United raise their game at Portman Road to do us a favour?

Molineux was sold out, and the noise generated by the home fans was both impressive and daunting. You felt very much in the minority being a City fan, and that it was going to be a challenge to make ourselves heard above the din. Stuart McCall recalled, "Wolves were still going for the play offs at the time and so had a lot to play for. Up front they had a young lad named Robbie Keane and they also had an old kid on the bench in Steve Bull! They had Mike Stowell in goal, who me and Peter Beagrie had played with at Everton. They had Dean Richards at the back. They had a good side. I remember coming out and the atmosphere was terrific. We had three thousand City fans there and I had all my family and friends in amongst them."

The City players started the game nervously, and Gary Walsh was called into action early doors to keep the score level. And then, only twelve minutes in, the worst possible thing happened. A Wolves corner prompted a scramble, City couldn't get the ball out of the area, and eventually Norwegian striker Harvard Flo was able to nod Wolves into a lead, despite huge suspicions that Walsh was fouled by Robbie Keane in the build up. 1-0 to Wolves, and a deafening roar. This was the stuff of nightmares, made doubly worse, within minutes, when news filtered through – via a man in front of me, listening to the radio on his Walkman – that Ipswich Town had taken the lead at Portman Road. The Premier League dream was dying in front of our eyes.

But the players were made of sterner stuff than this. In the 25th minute Kevin Muscat was caught dallying on the ball by Beagrie, who stole possession and set off on a jinking run. Beagrie typically left his defender flat footed, and falling over on his backside, and then the City winger caught sight of Stowell racing from his line, and coolly slotted the ball past him for the equaliser. We erupted in the away end, expressing feelings of relief rather than joy. "2-0 to Ipswich" said the man in front soon after – meaning that, as it stood, City would still miss out on promotion. We had to win this game, but at least that now seemed more possible. As the Yorkshire TV commentator John Helm stated, "The mood has changed."

Just before half time, Robbie Blake danced past a defender, just inside the opposition half, turned and assessed his options, before delivering an astonishingly weighted, and accurate, pass for his partner, Lee Mills. The ball took two defenders completely out of the game, freeing up Mills to take aim and pass the ball into the bottom corner beyond Stowell. It was a clinical finish by the former Wolves striker. 2-1 to Bradford City, and now we were bouncing. Before the half time whistle sounded, the man in front confirmed it was 3-0 to Ipswich. There was no doubt now that City had to do it themselves, if they were to book a place in the Premier League. Just 45 minutes to hold onto this slender lead, and the grandest of prizes was ours. The concourse at half time was carnage, as some fans celebrated, whilst others angrily warned them against jumping the gun. So close, but nothing was achieved just yet.

City could have made it more comfortable and, for fifteen minutes at least did so. In the 64th minute, Robbie Blake took advantage of a defensive slip, manoeuvred room for a shot and smashed the ball past Stowell for 3-1. Dreamland, and celebrations wilder than I had ever experienced before. John Helm exclaimed over TV pictures of City fans jumping up and down, "They are in heaven." Stuart McCall reflected, "We went 1-0 down, but we always believed that we could score goals. I had just come from Rangers, where we had Mark Hateley and Ally McCoist, and we always knew that, no matter what the score was, with those two we had goals in us. And it was the same for us that season. With Beagrie, Mills and Blake, we always knew that we had goals in us. We came back to 3-1, and scored three really good goals from those three players."

Incredibly it could have been 4-1 in the 78th minute, after Lawrence got free and was brought down in the box by former City defender Dean Richards. Beagrie stepped up to take the resultant penalty, but his side-footed effort was too telegraphed, and Stowell saved. Not only was the penalty drama between taker and keeper an extraordinary moment for the two former Everton team-mates to go through, Stowell was yet another ghost of the nearly season of 1987/88. Stowell was the young keeper, on loan at Man City, who John Hendrie has supposedly hurt and received a controversial red card for, during the run in, which caused the City man to miss the vital Ipswich game through suspension. Could Stowell be about to have a role in spoiling another Bantams' top flight bid?

Stuart McCall explained, "The key moment was the penalty. It was a really good save by Stowell. And then they grew in confidence. Then Robbie Keane comes off, and Steve Bull comes on in what is going to be his last game for Wolves. So the home crowd are now lifted and roaring them on. Our fans were quiet." Sure enough, within two minutes of passing up the chance to go 4-1 up, it was 3-2. Paul Simpson was played through on goal by the formidable Steve Bull, and he finished emphatically past Walsh, whilst City players claimed offside. "The complexion of the match turns again", stated John Helm. "What an incredible game this is." There were nine minutes still to play, and the Molineux roar had returned. Ipswich were now 4-1 up in their game – home and dry. City had to hold onto this advantage. A draw would consign them to the lottery of the play offs.

I have never known a more tortuous and long nine minutes as those that we endured that day. The clock ticked by painfully slowly, a whole season's efforts were on the line. With five minutes to go, Wolves won a free kick in a dangerous position, and I could hardly bear to watch (others, in fact, had left their seats and spent the closing stages in the concourse waiting for the full time whistle, because they were so nervous). Simpson stepped up, and, from my view – in the lower tier of the stand that ran the length of the pitch, my seat level with Gary Walsh's goal – it looked a certain goal all the way as it flew past the City goalkeeper. Incredibly, the ball smacked against the post, bounced back into the danger area, and was gleefully booted up the pitch by John Dreyer. Promotion was decided by the width of a post.

Stuart McCall had a close up view of this astonishing moment in Bradford City's modern history, "On the free kick, I was stood there in the wall praying that he didn't score, I can remember saying 'I'll do anything lord, I'll go to church, but please don't let them score'. Paul Simpson steps up and we knew what he was capable of. His shot hits the inside the post and we scrambled it away. My missus couldn't bear to watch the last ten minutes. She went down to the concourse and there must have been at least a hundred City fans who had done the same, as they couldn't watch the game. They sat on steps, biting their nails."

Gareth Walker was also in the away end that day and stated, "I spent a large part of the second half with my head in my hands unable to watch. I don't remember Blake's goal or the penalty that Beagrie missed. I do remember looking up just as Paul Simpson hit the post for Wolves late on which would have made it 3-3. I looked up again just as McCall was asking the referee how long was left to go, and the Wolves supporters were singing 'Bradford, are you shitting yourselves?' Everyone was fully aware throughout the game that Ipswich were comfortably beating Sheffield United, so we had to win."

Dreamland

Finally, the referee blew for full time and the celebrations could begin. It was incredible to be there in the away end that day, to be part of the scenes of joy. People were dancing up and down the aisles, strangers were hugging strangers, whilst others were in tears. In front of us the players and coaching staff were full of joy as they jumped on top of each other, and threw souvenir pieces of kit in the stand. Eyes were trained towards Stuart McCall. The man who was part of the team that came so close in 1988, only for the final day defeat to Ipswich to ultimately result in his departure. He had returned, talking about unfinished business, and delivered emphatically on that promise. "The best moment of my football career," was how he described the feeling to the Yorkshire TV interviewee.

McCall recalled to me, "It was a day for the fans. Football is about players but it's for supporters. As much as we were all elated the real joy was in watching the way our fans celebrated at full time. It was so special. I remember that I didn't want to give my shirt away and so I took my shorts off and threw them in the crowd. I saw people that I hadn't seen for many years – it was such a special day. You get what you deserve in football, most of the time, but there is no doubt that you always need a bit of luck. I go on these coaching courses and they always say 'what's the four key things you need as a manager?' You always forget that one of the four things you need is a bit of luck. On that day, with that ball hitting the post, I just felt someone up there was looking after us and knew that those fans deserved to be promoted to the Premier League. After all the things we had been through, to get there for the first time in 77 years was so special."

And with the drinks now flowing, McCall found that he was becoming increasingly merry. "We went back into the dressing room and it was buzzing. Some of the younger players went up to the players bar to get some drinks. In those days in the dressing room they still had single baths, and I remember six of us, experienced players all sitting in our single baths – myself, Beags, Jakes, Walshy, Tumble and Windass – with the champagne flowing. And we spent half an hour reminiscing about the season and the key moments – people like Windass joking how his two goals at Bury made all the difference. The media were waiting to speak to us, but we all wanted to enjoy every minute of the joy for as long as possible. The only problem for me was that, in that, time I had drank a full bottle of champagne without knowing! We then went back on the bus to Bradford with plenty of drinks, and when we got off the bus at Bradford the fresh air hit me a bit."

What happened next is remembered as much as the promotion – a moment captured on TV and watched thousands of times on YouTube. McCall climbed onto a car roof with a can of beer in hand to celebrate – and promptly fell off! "There were thousands of City fans there, and we started going on top of buses and cars to thank the fans. And then a Sky cameraman was there and – with an incredible piece of timing – actually started recording just as I fell off the car. To this day I argue that it wasn't the amount I had had to drink that made me fall off the car, but it was my trainer getting caught on the windscreen wiper causing me to trip! After I fell off, the wife came over to me and told me to get a grip of myself! That was about seven o'clock at night – I was still up at two in the morning, putting people to bed! I had calmed down and moved onto the coffee. I wanted to take everything in.

"The next morning we had the parade and reception, and Gareth Whalley and his wife came round to my house saying 'get Sky on, it shows you falling off a car'. I had no recollection of doing so, but my neck had been hurting all morning. Suddenly I realised why it was hurting!"

Jamie Lawrence added, "I will never beat that day! I've had promotions and won a cup at Leicester, but Wolves beats all of them because I felt like I'd played such a big part in getting to that point. We were so up against it that day. We went 1-0 down when Robbie Keane scored, although I think it was a foul on Walshy actually. Then I remember things like, at 3-1 up Bradford fans doing the 'oles', then we missed that penalty to go 4-1 up. It then came back to 3-2, they hit the post, had a penalty shout. It was just so nerve-wracking!

"But then celebrating with the fans after, who had been absolutely fantastic all day. And of course then when we got back to Bradford, Macca fell off the car! It was an absolutely tremendous day. I went out for about three days! I said to the Telegraph & Argus that, later that night, you'll probably find me drunk in a gutter somewhere. I was true to my words!" Speaking to the Telegraph & Argus immediately after the Wolves game, Jewell stated, "It's fantastic – we deserved it. People have worked ever so hard and I am delighted to be able to do it. It is the pinnacle of my career."

The following day, the city of Bradford once again played host to an open top bus parade and civic reception for the Bantams. In recognition of the way Richmond had built up the fanbase from across the area, rather than just the city – how he thought bigger than everyone else – the bus parade began in the nearby town of Keighley and took in Bingley, Saltaire and Shipley before reaching Centenary Square, where thousands were waiting. There was a memorable TV shot of Richmond surrounded by adoring City fans, hugging the charismatic chairman. Five years on from his "let them laugh" speech, Richmond had delivered his grand vision. An astonishing rise was complete. The Bradford City of 1999 was unrecognisable to the one he took charge of in 1994. He had remoulded the club on and off the field, shaping it from an underachieving third tier outfit, playing away games at Bootham Crescent and Victoria Park, to one that would soon be walking out at Old Trafford and Anfield. If you were one of the Scarborough fans who never took to Richmond, when he was in charge of the North Yorkshire club, that May weekend was an especially painful one. Not only was a beaming Richmond celebrating Bradford City's top flight promotion, amazingly, on that same weekend, Scarborough were relegated from the Football League.

For Richmond, for the Rhodes family, for Jewell and for the players, this was an emphatic reward for their hard work and vision in targeting promotion. 77 years the club had waited to return to the elite, and now Bradford City would be playing Premier League football. The newly erected Kop stand – which started to be rebuilt from terrace to a two-tier seated structure, midway through the campaign – would welcome the likes of David Beckham, Thierry Henry and Alan Shearer. The day after the Wolves game, all 14,000 season tickets that were available were snapped up. Money that was beginning to pour into the club and it should have set them up for life.

Promotion was all achieved in such memorable fashion. The strategy had paid off handsomely. The early adversity was managed with composure as everyone inside the club stuck together. The rise up the league over the course of the season was thrilling. The stylish football was a joy. The victories over Barnsley, Bristol City, Swindon, Tranmere, Stockport, Crewe, Watford and Norwich and – of course – Wolves would be talked about for years to come. What was so incredible, looking back, is just what an unprecedented achievement it was. The idea of our little club being in the Premier League was utterly mind-blowing, putting right the mistakes of 1988 was a redemption for a generation of supporters. Forget the 1910s and when City were a top team – most of us weren't alive to see it – this was a new height for the club. Decade upon decade of underachievement had been the Bradford City way of life. Not this, not ever.

In 2013, Wayne Jacobs arranged for a reunion of the 1998/99 team to raise money for his commendable One in a Million charity. The lure of once more seeing Peter Beagrie, Lee Mills, Stuart McCall, Darren Moore and others drew a healthy crowd, and when a piece of dazzling skill by Beagrie saw the winger cross the ball for Mills to steer home, you wanted to weep. 1998/99 was once of the most special seasons we will ever experience following Bradford City, one where the barriers and limitations of this football club were truly smashed. You can never go back to the Bradford City that was before Wolves 1999, it doesn't exist. That innocence we once had will never be reclaimed. Even if City were to somehow return to the Premier League it wouldn't be anywhere near as astonishing, unthinkable and jaw-dropping as it was then.

Gareth Walker added with a grin, "It was the best season for me. No contest. The team had everything – team spirit and quality. It's the only season that I've been going to City every week feeling that we were going to beat whoever we were playing. We were winning games without even getting out of second gear. It was a special, special time." The final word, fittingly, must go to Stuart McCall and that unforgettable final day of the season, "The Wolves game epitomised that season. We weren't going to go and carve out a 1-0 win. We didn't make it easy for ourselves but played some great football. It was a wonderful day and the celebrations were memorable – and it was all down to me, for missing that header against Oxford!"

Perhaps, ultimately, that Molineux tunnel motto didn't ring true for the Bantams. They did emerge from the darkness to find light; but even more darkness would ultimately follow. Going to the top table was a mixed blessing at best. The reality never quite lived up to the way we imagined it, and the hangover would be especially painful.

Yet still, the warm memories of 1998/99 would keep us supporters going through future lean times. It was a true privilege to be at Molineux in May 1999; but more than that it was a true privilege to watch this truly remarkable 1998/99 Bradford City team, week in week out, during that unforgettable campaign.

City (vs Wolves): Gary Walsh, Stephen Wright, Darren Moore, John Dreyer, Wayne Jacobs, Jamie Lawrence, Gareth Whalley, Stuart McCall, Peter Beagrie (Lee Sharpe 83), Robbie Blake (Dean Windass 83), Lee Mills

Not used: Gordon Watson

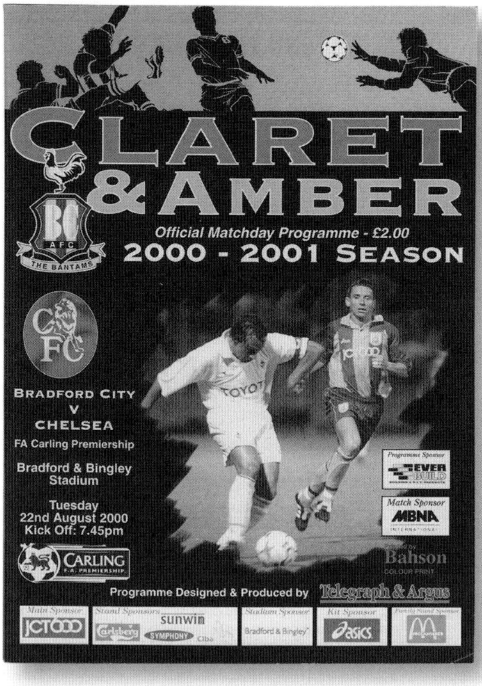

The (fleeting) view from the top

Bradford City vs Chelsea

Premier League, Tuesday 22 August, 2000

Every time that the East London under-achievers West Ham United sack a manager, whoever happens to be their owner will invariably talk of how the replacement must embody and play 'The West Ham Way'. There has never before been any attempt to define the equivalent Bradford City approach to football. But if you were to begin to do so, it's fair to assume that the best way of identifying the 'The Bradford City Way' would come from examining the last four promotion-winning sides, and what made them so popular.

The classes of 1985, 1996, 1999 and 2013 continue to be fondly remembered, and dearly loved, by the Bantams supporters who witnessed their heroics. And all of these successful teams shared certain traits and qualities. They were sides built upon strong team spirit, and who displayed dogged determination, desire and a willingness to battle. They were brave teams, who demonstrated their steel whenever its backbone was tested. There was certainly room for flair and excitement also – John Hendrie, Mark Ellis, Andy Kiwomya, Peter Beagrie, Robbie Blake, Nahki Wells and Kyel Reid were dearly loved by most supporters – but courage, endeavour and effort was applauded above all else. Stuart McCall (1985 and 1999), Lee Duxbury (1996), and Gary Jones (2013) were amongst each respective promotion-winning team's most popular players for a reason.

As Bradford City reached the top table of English football, in 1999, and threatened to establish themselves amongst the elite, the start of their subsequent downfall can be traced back to the moment the club decided to reject its own values and try to become something different. When they attempted to reinvent what the 'The Bradford City Way' was, with unsuccessful results and long-lasting consequences. When they started to think there was something wrong about the way they had been successful over the previous two seasons. When they naively began to imitate their illustrious Premier League friends, but choose the wrong things to copy.

In the 1999/00 season – Bradford City's first top flight campaign in 77 years – the club had confounded all expectations to win their desperate fight against relegation. Right up until the final minutes of the campaign, survival was in the balance. For a long time, it appeared that City were doomed to fall straight back into the Football League. On the final day of the season, they beat no less than the mighty Liverpool FC to avoid the drop, prompting wild celebrations that were laced with disbelief. Four years on from the 1996 promotion out of the third tier, Bradford City's incredible adventure up the ladder had reached another new high.

Yet by the time of City's next Premier League home game, against Chelsea – their first of the 2000/01 campaign – the speed of change had been dizzying. The Bantams may have finished seventeenth the season before – a long way short of the UEFA Cup and Champions League places – but they ended up spending the summer playing European football, after accepting an Intertoto Cup invitation that few other clubs wanted. The roof of the Main Stand was removed, as work began on building a second tier above it. Some fringe players departed from the building, and in their place came some of the most spectacular signings in the club's history. Oh and City changed managers too, with Paul Jewell walking out on the club to be replaced by his assistant, Chris Hutchings. This was not your average close season, but it also wasn't the best preparation for the campaign ahead.

And it was a summer period that ended with the chairman, Geoffrey Richmond, deriding past achievements. Believing that he was leading the club on another important step forward, he rubbished his own club, and the manager that he himself deserved so much credit for identifying and giving a chance to in the first place. Paul Jewell and Richmond had fallen out, just at a point where – looking in from the outside – they looked an invincible team. The football world was theirs to conquer; but it was all thrown away over an expensive lunch, during which harsh words were aired.

A few weeks later, Richmond and Hutchings were unveiling a number of expensive signings that were well known around the footballing world. They included Dan Petrescu, a Romanian international and classy full back, who enjoyed many successful years at Sheffield Wednesday and Chelsea. The transfer record was smashed with the arrival of David Hopkin from Leeds United, for £2.5 million. Ashley Ward was recruited from Barnsley for £1.5 million. And then there was Benito Carbone, the jewel in the crown.

Carbone agreed a contract with City worth an astonishing £40,000 per week, making him not only the best paid player in the club's history (a record you suspect may never be broken), but at the time one of the highest-earning footballers in the country. There were top Manchester United players earning less at the time, and they were the Premier League champions. Richmond would later describe this period of transfer activity as "six weeks of madness", but at the time he was full of bluster about how far the club was about to go, and why the revamped squad was so much better than the previous season's.

And this was where he derided the past, telling the Telegraph & Argus on the eve of the season, "We want not just to survive but to establish ourselves in the Premiership. Last season we were boring Bradford but this season we'll be entertaining Bradford and I hope we can make our mark." In what now reads as an astonishing piece of journalism, a Telegraph & Argus article on Monday 7 August, 2000 (writer unknown) took on board this mantra of rubbishing the previous season's achievements. "[Carbone] will be the orchestrator of the style which will see the 'boring Bradford' tag laid to rest as they plan to become the entertainers...Little Bradford have big ambitions and Carbone is the man they are looking at to become their star."

It doesn't really do it justice to say that the new-look Bradford City didn't work out. The Chelsea game in August 2000 would mark the beginnings of twelve years of misery and decline. Bradford City were heading for an almighty fall, and most of it was completely self-inflicted.

The end of an era

The idea that City were boring in 1999/00 seemed to reside outside of Bradford, rather than within the city and amongst supporters. After promotion to the Premier League was so memorably achieved at Wolves, everyone around the club assumed that their romantic back story, and the underdog spirit of the Bantams, would see them gleefully accepted into the elite. That we would become every football fan's adopted second team.

Yet instead there was a real hostility towards the club from the national media, summed up most provocatively by the Sunday Times, who on the eve of the 1999/00 season declared Bradford City to be "the unacceptable face of the Premier League". Whilst predictions of City being relegated were to be expected, there was a dismissive and patronising tone to the way that the club's fortunes were covered. On Sky Sports' ever-growing Soccer Saturday show, pundit Rodney Marsh began to belittle City on a weekly basis. Even opposition players got in on the act. When in September the Bantams were very fortunate to defeat Derby County on their own patch, the Rams' defender Spencer Prior labelled Bradford City "the worst Premier League team in history".

It was a rude awakening, and City's first few weeks in the Premier League were undoubtedly difficult. Jewell recruited sensibly during the summer, spending only £3 million in a division where the top clubs were routinely buying players for multiple times that amount. David Wetherall – captured for a then-club record £1.4 million – was the biggest buy. The Leeds defender brought valuable experience and composure to the backline; he was a grounded and sensible buy. He ended up playing every single minute of the campaign, and was in many people's eyes City's player of the season in 1999/00.

Although City won their opening game, at Middlesbrough, they struggled badly at first. A 2-0 midweek loss at Arsenal in August should really have been double figures; such was the gulf in class between the Gunners and Bantams. The likes of West Ham and Sunderland won early season games at Valley Parade at a canter. Finally, at the end of October, City got going and started to show what they were capable of. They beat Leicester, Newcastle, Watford and Arsenal at home over winter, and impressed in other games, but they were always there or thereabouts around the bottom three – completely in line with everyone's expectations. Whether they stayed up or went down was firmly in the balance.

In March it all started to go wrong. Eight consecutive defeats seemed to signal certain relegation. Some performances over that time merited more than zero points, others were completely inept. Jewell tried desperately to turn the tide, but after a 4-4 draw with relegation rivals Derby County on Good Friday it seemed that would be that. City were in the bottom three, with just four games to go, and running out of time. Amazingly they turned it around right at the end. A 1-0 Easter Monday win away to Sunderland resurrected hopes, and a 3-0 thumping over their now-only-rival to avoid the last relegation spot, Wimbledon, took them out of the bottom three. On the penultimate weekend City lost 3-0 at Leicester whilst Wimbledon picked up a draw that edged them ahead of the Bantams. It all went down to the very last game, where City had to better Wimbledon's result or they would be relegated.

Wetherall headed home an early goal on that final afternoon, against Liverpool, and Valley Parade roared the players onto a famous victory, against opponents who needed a win themselves, in order to make the Champions League spots. Wimbledon lost 2-0 to Southampton, meaning they would go down and City would stay up. At full time, a sell out Valley Parade home crowd invaded the pitch in celebration. It was a great story, and by that point a story that everybody else loved. With the Premier League title race having being wrapped up weeks earlier, the relegation battle became the big football story, and the country eventually took City to their hearts. Plucky underdogs, players who gave their all, cheered on by loud and passionate supporters. To this day, the last day victory over Liverpool remains one of the most memorable in the Premier League's history.

Jamie Lawrence told me, "Everyone expected us to go down that season. Rodney Marsh said we were going down. But as a group of lads in that changing room, along with the fans, we had the belief that we could stay up. Outside of that, I don't think there was anyone else who believed we could stay up. But we really enjoyed proving people wrong. We took it game by game, and we especially made Valley Parade a fortress. Teams didn't like coming here, especially in winter. Even Liverpool on the last game of the season weren't happy. Teams didn't like coming into such a small changing room, being cold, with only one toilet for both teams to share, nowhere to plug in your hairdryer, and all this stuff." Stuart McCall summarised the scale of the great escape, "We stayed up by beating Liverpool the last game, and at the back end of the season we won ten points in the final five games – almost a third of all the points we picked up that season."

Mark Douglas was at the time a young Bradford City supporter, who spent the 1999/00 campaign following his beloved Bantams around the country, whilst preparing to sit his A Levels. Mark was a columnist for the City Gent fanzine at the time, and has developed a very successful career in journalism. Today, he is the Newcastle United editor for the trio of North East regional titles: the Evening Chronicle, the Journal, and the Sunday Sun. He recalled to me, "Because I was a bit younger, I just thought that it was natural that Bradford City would be in the Premier League. I think my first season was 1993/94, and from then on City kept pushing up through the leagues. Now when I look back on it, the rise up the leagues was absolutely incredible. It hadn't happened to many clubs before or since really. We went from nothing. It was pretty amazing.

"What Paul Jewell did with building that team was absolutely phenomenal. The club felt vibrant during the first season in the Premier League, it felt like we were building something and that we were going places. When you're in the lower leagues, you look at the fixtures and the teams you're facing and almost shrug; but in the Premier League every fixture was a real occasion. It was good fun. At Valley Parade at least we gave everyone a game. We did get outplayed at times, but I remember Arsenal at home in particular, which was an incredible win – we played well and we beat a really good Arsenal team. That was my best memory of that season."

Despite the amazing escape from relegation and national acclaim, there were, of course, still critics out there. Yet if people really were still calling the club "boring Bradford" not many of us were listening – let alone caring. Jewell – who late on in the campaign came under pressure from some City fans – had proven a lot of doubters wrong. "The initial feelings are just of relief," Jewell told the Telegraph & Argus the day after the Liverpool win. "It has been a long season so it was good to do what we set out to achieve. We had been receiving so many negative vibes, both from outside Bradford and within the city, it was a very satisfying moment.

"This is an example of everyone pulling together because they all want to help the team."

The Bradford City Way, in fact.

"Boring Bradford"

As the celebrations finally faded post-Liverpool, there was no real hint of the drama that was about to unfold over the summer months. Indeed, the united front of Richmond and Jewell continued in public. Speaking to the Telegraph & Argus after the Liverpool victory, Richmond was full of praise for his manager. "We are talking about a young manager who at 35 years old has had all the pressure that comes with managing a Premiership club…I am absolutely delighted for him as the man who spotted his potential. I am very proud of how Paul has done. It is always pleasing to have your judgement vindicated and there is no doubt that whatever happens in the future, Paul will always be a manager. He has deservedly earned a lot of respect in the game for what he has achieved at Bradford City."

Telegraph & Argus journalised Richard Sutcliffe wrote, "No one should underestimate City's dream team of Richmond and Jewell who have beaten the odds before and I believe will do so again." Yet only a month after the Liverpool game, Jewell made the stunning announcement that he wanted to quit Bradford City. He was placed on gardening leave by Richmond, before rocking up at Sheffield Wednesday as their new manager, two days later. Unlike City, Sheffield Wednesday had been relegated from the Premier League that season, and were facing up to dealing with mounting debts. It was not an enticing job opportunity. Jewell – who had been at Valley Parade for more than twelve years – had always talked of his passion for Bradford City. That they were his club. Something didn't add up.

And it transpired that that something was an explosive lunch between Richmond and Jewell a few weeks after the Liverpool game. It was supposed to be a celebratory meeting, but months of private resentment towards each other was to spill over and leave an upset Jewell feeling that he had no choice but to walk away. The scene was a trendy Heaton restaurant called Clarks, which is no longer in business, where the two met alone. The story goes that Jewell presented Richmond with a list of his player targets for next season. After reading it, Richmond declared he had never disagreed with a list of players so much in his life, before whipping out his own list of transfer targets. Richmond went on to inform Jewell that the City manager had been lucky to keep the Bantams up, that he'd been shown up tactically in certain games, and that – were his contract be up for renewal – he would not be getting another one. A seething Jewell claimed in the 2006 book 'Bradford City: the pain and the glory' that upon leaving Clarks he got straight on the mobile to his agent and asked him to find out if there would be other clubs interested in his services. Wigan and Bristol City were thought to be keen on Jewell, alongside Sheffield Wednesday. Jewell went on holiday to Canada with his family, and upon his return handed in his resignation. Initially Richmond refused to accept it and instead placed Jewell on gardening leave; but the situation was clearly irreparable. In the end Jewell, moved to Hillsborough, with City receiving £300k compensation.

If there is a point at which the trigger for City's decline began, Jewell's walkout was that moment. It would later emerge that the pair were clashing for much of the 1999/00 season, and that the pressure of working for Richmond had become too much for Jewell to bear. After a 5-4 loss at West Ham United in February – City were 4-2 up midway through the second half – harsh words were spoken. At 4-2 up, Jewell opted to keep attacking the Hammers, rather than shoring up the game, with dire consequences. Yet Jewell – in a sign that Richmond, at least, was bothered by the 'boring Bradford' jibe, and had made adverse comments about the recent past – admitted he had not shut up shop for fear of upsetting his boss. A few weeks later, a 4-0 loss at Coventry triggered a similarly brutal inquest between Jewell and Richmond. Terry Yorath – back at Valley Parade to assist Jewell alongside Chris Hutchings – revealed in his autobiography that Richmond forced Jewell to select Jorge Cadete in the following game, at home to Manchester United. Cadete had been brought in on loan in February, but the Portuguese looked well short of match fitness and effort, and he was a flop. Against Manchester United, Cadete was virtually a bystander as the Bantams were rolled over 4-0 by the soon-to-be-Champions.

Despite this interference, Jewell was able to keep Richmond in check to a certain extent. Richmond may have forced Cadete onto him, but Jewell tried to dissuade his chairman from bringing in other luxury players, who he didn't believe fitted into the team ethos – tellingly, these luxury players were Benito Carbone and Stan Collymore. With Jewell no longer around that summer, Richmond was met with less resistance in overhauling the squad in the way that he believed would bring greater success. Chris Hutchings – a good club man – was given the manager's job, with Stuart McCall his assistant, but to everyone it was obvious who was calling the shots in the transfer market.

Mark Douglas commented, "Richmond thought he was getting so many things right, he thought he had the magic formula, and so he would keep doing what he was doing. He thought he knew everything because he'd had a bit of success, but in reality he didn't have a clue about the football side. He was a great businessman, but Jewell was the real reason we got into the Premier League and stayed up, because he had fostered such a great team spirit."

Whilst Hutchings guided City through the summer European Intertoto Cup adventure – another decision Jewell had been against – Richmond was making financial commitments that would hurt the club for more than a decade.

The summer of madness

So it was that Petrescu and Carbone signed up at Valley Parade. Carbone – a skilful Italian forward – had made his name in England with Sheffield Wednesday. But after bitter fall outs with his manager Danny Wilson, Carbone spent the majority of 1999/00 on loan at Aston Villa, where he impressed. Yet talks over a permanent deal went nowhere, due to Carbone's excessive wage demands. He retreated back to Italy, his adventure in English football seemingly over.

Richmond and Hutchings pounced. After failing to sign Costa Rican striker Paulo Wanchope, who chose newly promoted Man City over the Bantams, it was suddenly proclaimed, on the Bradford City website, that the Bantams were on the verge of making "the most exciting signing in the club's history". It quickly emerged that Carbone was the player who was in talks. The Italian already had offers in his home country, and also from Coventry City. Richmond and Hutchings flew over to Italy for talks that lasted seven hours, before finally returning with the 27-year-old's signature, the ink still drying on a four-year contract that would guarantee the Italian £40,000 a week. For good measure, City even bought Carbone a seven-bedroom, five-bathroom house in Leeds. Richmond argued, "We've had to look at the total financial package. Benito was available on a Bosman free, so we have worked out the total cost of the deal over four years without a transfer fee," before adding – in words that would come back to haunt the chairman and everyone connected with Bradford City – "We sit comfortably with the package we've negotiated."

Whilst Richmond went about making these colossal financial commitments, his co-owners, the Rhodes family, were watching on like everybody else. Their hands-off approach would not last for much longer, as they would soon have to get more involved and be forced to tackle the damage that had been done. Julian Rhodes told me of that summer, "We weren't involved at all. I remember finding out about the signing of Benito Carbone on Teletext! Geoffrey Richmond called it six weeks of madness but I actually think it was four, because he blitzed all of that money during a four-week period. The damage was done there and then. It was very apparent that, if we got relegated, we would be in big trouble. Once you have players on the kind of money they were on, if they're not doing the business, it's really hard to get rid of them."

Mark Douglas reflected, "It was a magical period. You couldn't believe that Benito Carbone had signed for Bradford City. It was a different time then. These days you get top players like Xherdan Shaqiri signing for Stoke and Yohan Cabaye going to Crystal Palace, who are mid-table Premier League teams; but Benito Carbone coming to Bradford City was bigger than that. He was one of the best players in the league. He was one of those players that you would have thought a top Premier League club would have taken on.

"On the face of it, we seemed to be adding real quality, but I think the problem was Chris Hutchings had not done anything before as manager. You had to have the right manager. That team had been one that Paul Jewell had dragged up from the Football League, and it had this fighting spirit. You can't change that overnight. More recently Stoke City have gradually changed into a more creative team than they were before, but the team that I cover now, Newcastle, have tried to change things quickly and only proven you can't change things overnight."

The national press reacted with incredulity to Carbone's arrival – stating that a small club like Bradford City should not be paying so much on a single player; that they had ideas about their station. It would all end in tears quickly, they stated. The Guardian described it as "a move that smacked as much of desperation as ambition". City's heroic battle against relegation won the club many admirers and national acclaim; but by throwing money at a troublesome foreigner, City were perceived to be abandoning the core principles behind their rise up the leagues.

The media's negative mood and attitude towards the Bantams was not helped when Richmond invited regular supporters to the press conference that introduced Carbone as a Bradford City player. Attempts by national journalists (sat in the front few rows) to question Carbone's dubious levels of loyalty were heckled by fans behind them. As the Mirror put it, Beni was "unveiled in front of 500 beer-swilling fans' who had gate-crashed the club's press conference". On Carbone's part, he quickly gave assurances over his commitment to City. "The money is important but most important was that Bradford showed how much they wanted me. They have big ambitions and that is why I came here. This is a big chance for me."

Understandably for a signing dubbed "the most exciting in history", a great deal of hope was placed upon Carbone's shoulders for Bradford City's continuing progress. Yet there were hints right from the start that expectations were unrealistic. Carbone was a truly gifted player. In his four previous years in England he had forged a reputation as a scorer of spectacular goals, and his speed of thought and admirable close control saw him out-wit defenders and create opportunities for team mates. All of these qualities would be displayed during his time at Valley Parade, yet Richmond and Hutchings seemed to be under the impression they were also getting a goalscorer. Despite having only netted 35 goals in four seasons in England, Hutchings stated, "I think he's a 20-goal striker. We've got a fantastic player who can score unbelievable goals. That has to be exciting."

After City defeated FK Atlantas 4-1 in the Intertoto Cup – their European run came to an end against Zenit St. Petersberg in the semi finals – Hutchings singled out players from the previous season who he felt had not performed, and who he declared needed to improve for this coming campaign. They included the promotion heroes of 1999: Lee Mills and Robbie Blake. As it was, Mills would depart before the Premier League season began. The new faces were taking residence at Valley Parade, and the old guard was making way for them. And as Jamie Lawrence told me, the spirit in the dressing room was being eroded too.

"When you were seeing those players come in, we were thinking 'we got the club into the Premier League and we kept them there, but now they are bringing people in on £40k a week, and weren't even from West Yorkshire'. We all loved the club, we loved the fans; we gave everything and didn't earn a lot. And then these players were just coming in for the money.

"I believe that we stayed up that first season because everyone gave 100%. We couldn't have carried anyone. We weren't good enough to carry anyone. Now we were carrying the likes of Benito Carbone and Dan Petrescu. I think that Chris Hutchings was out of his depth. If Paul Jewell had stayed, he would not have signed those players. The best thing would have been to not sign those players, and we could have stayed up that season. Our aim should have been to be like a Leicester; where what Martin O'Neill did was keep the core of the team, and keep adding grafters year on year, the likes of Neil Lennon and Muzzy Izzet. That's the way to do it, not go and sign these so-called football stars who had been at top clubs."

City began the Premier League campaign with a narrow 1-0 defeat to Liverpool at Anfield, but emerged with plenty of credit for their more attacking approach. Stuart McCall recalled, "We started away at Liverpool with Emile Heskey scoring late on. But we took so much from that, as we pushed them all the way in the game." Mark Douglas added, "I had a friend who supported Liverpool, and we both went to Anfield, and I remember him saying to me 'you've got a decent team this year'." Carbone – who had missed much of pre-season – came on as a second half substitute. He would make his full debut three days later, as City staged their first home league game of the season against Chelsea.

Hopes and expectations for the season ahead were neatly summed up by Hutchings in his programme notes that night, "We hope that we can play a little more attractively and pass the ball better now we all know about what the Premiership is about…I want to see us showing greater care when we are in possession and much of our work in pre-season has been aimed at improving our work with the ball. I hope that we will be able to play in a more attractive way and I am sure the acquisition of Benito Carbone is going to be a big help…I hope he can do for us what Gianfranco Zola has done so successfully for tonight's opponents Chelsea in recent years."

The peak of Bradford City

Everything went right that evening. It was a night where Richmond's grand vision was realised; where his new-look, more-skilful and entertaining team looked capable of beating the world. Of not only surviving in the Premier League, but pushing up to mid-table, if not better. It was a night where people talked of European football properly coming to Valley Parade – not through the Intertoto back door, but through finishing sufficiently high enough up the league.

They were up against a very strong and powerful Chelsea side. It might have been in the days before Roman Abramovich, but under manager Gianluca Vialli big money had been spent to add to an already stellar international roster. Ed de Goey was in goal that night at Valley Parade; World Cup winner Marcel Desailly at the back; a midfield of Gus Poyet, Roberto Di Matteo, Dennis Wise and Jody Morris; and up front, Jimmy Floyd Hasselbaink and the magical Italian, Gianfranco Zola. In 2004, Zola would be voted Chelsea's all-time greatest player by their fans. Chelsea had beaten West Ham United 4-2 on the opening day of the season, prompting much hype and acclaim. They were considered one of the favourites for the title, and the style of the West Ham victory was seen as a signal of intent. They would surely have too much for Bradford City.

Yet in a performance full of quality and sparkling football, the Bantams were magnificent in defeating their more illustrious opponents. After surviving the early scares of Poyet heading Wise's cross wide of the target and a sparkling Zola volley missing by a matter of inches, City seized control of the game in the middle of the park, with Stuart McCall and David Hopkin in superb form. Lee Sharpe, on the left, was enjoying one of his best nights for the club, and on 25 minutes he sent over a wonderful cross that was headed home at the back post by last season's top scorer, Dean Windass. Bradford City 1 Chelsea 0, and the bright new era had experienced take off. Mark Douglas said of Windass, "He was outstanding that night. He was a really good footballer and people almost forget that about him. He could really play, and he was adapting to what we were doing."

Chelsea were stunned to fall behind and reacted badly. Rather than continuing the fight, they retreated and allowed City to attack at will. Hopkin was played clean through on goal by Carbone, one-on-one with De Goey. His low effort beat the Dutch keeper, but rolled past the wrong side of the post. Then, in a sign of how rattled Chelsea had become, Brazilian defender Emerson Thome played a back header towards where he thought for De Goey would be stood, only to realise with horror that the Chelsea keeper had come out from his goal to catch the ball. The ball rolled past De Goey and towards the unguarded goal, but to the visitors' relief it just missed the target. Chelsea improved in the second half, especially after Tore Andre Flo replaced the disappointing Hasselbaink. The Norwegian striker forced City goalkeeper Matt Clarke into a smart save to maintain the home side's lead. Tellingly, it was Chelsea's first shot on target all night.

Mark Douglas recalled of the performance, "There was a confidence about City that day that you just don't normally associate with the club. We played a really good Chelsea team off the park. They never got a kick. We had gone away to Arsenal the year before and lost 2-0, but it could have been 20-0. They were in a different league to us. And then in little under a year we were beating a really talented Chelsea side, who were probably better than Arsenal that year. It was just madness really. It's probably the most complete league performance Bradford City have ever produced, certainly over my time supporting them, if not in the entire club's history. It was that good."

This famous Bradford City win was completed by the man who all eyes were trained upon. Benito Carbone had been magical all evening; pulling the strings between the midfield and attack, and running Emerson Thome ragged. After a flurry of good chances came and went, and with fifteen minutes left on the clock, Carbone was picked out in a deep position by Windass, and he charged forward with purpose before unleashed a stunning low finish past Ed de Goey, right in front of the Kop. It was a terrific goal, and City were in an unassailable 2-0 lead. Stuart McCall said, "Beni scored against Chelsea and we knew we had a special talent in him. He had the flicks and all, but he was also a hard-working kid." With his goal against Chelsea appeared to be the lift off of the club. Here comes a top half Premier League finish.

Alas, it was the cruellest of false dawns. City never came close to replicating that night. It was the high water mark of an incredible few years under Richmond. City were full of quality in their passing and attacking play, and Chelsea were blown away. "The huff and puff that just about kept Bradford in the Premiership last season has been replaced by a far superior style of football," roared a Daily Telegraph match report. And there, pulling the strings and making it happen, was Benito Carbone. This is what the future might have looked like, but it was all a mirage. As Mark Douglas summarised, "As a crowd we almost took the victory for granted a bit. It was like we felt we belonged here, which is a good attitude to have at the time. But unfortunately it was all built on sand. We didn't have anything below it, we didn't have the foundations."

After referee Mark Hasley blew for full time, Bradford City's twelve years of misery commenced.

The sharp decline

Although Chelsea were defeated on that balmy August evening, it wouldn't be until a wintry December afternoon before City won another Premier League match. Stuart McCall reflected, "We drew with Leicester 0-0 the Saturday after. At the end of the season before, when they won 3-0 against us, Neil Lennon had sat on the ball taking the mick. So in this game everyone wanted to kick him and we were lining up to have a go. In the end they had to take Lennon off! But soon after that day we started to lose some narrow games. We had a few nearlys. I remember we lost at home to Southampton with an own goal." Talk of Europe very quickly looked foolish, as a struggling City dropped into the relegation zone during September. A position they would never recover from.

After ten matches that read W1 D4 L5, Richmond elected to recruit another high-earner – the talented but notorious trouble-maker, Stan Collymore. A former England international, Collymore was a huge talent for sure but had largely squandered his gifts. He first burst onto the national stage by scoring a hatful for Nottingham Forest in 1994, but was so unpopular with his team mates that by the end they wouldn't celebrate his goals with him. A British transfer record £8.5 million took Stan to Liverpool, where he never really blossomed. Then came a doomed move to Aston Villa, a miserable loan spell at Fulham, and a brief flicker of life at Leicester, before he was sacked for fighting a team mate during a reserve team match. Collymore was real trouble, damaged goods, and not cheap either. In February 2000, and with Paul Jewell still in charge, City attempted to sign Collymore from Aston Villa and, in his autobiography, Stan claims he was offered £40,000 a week – double what he was on at the time – to move to Valley Parade. He turned it down and moved to Leicester instead, but with that transfer having turned sour, a desperate Richmond eyed up the out-of-work Collymore, and again judged he was worth gambling on, even though no one else seemed to agree.

McCall recalled to me just how little influence he and Chris Hutchings had on the decision to sign Collymore – and how misplaced the optimism of the board continued to be regarding City's prospects, "Chris Hutchings had rung me up and said 'the chairmen's on about bringing in Collymore' and I said 'you're joking aren't you?' We've got one out-and-out individual in Carbone, and unless you are a top five Premier League side you can't have two. Stan had also just left Leicester after an altercation, and hadn't played much football. So I remember saying to Chris 'what sort of shape is he in?' and Chris wasn't sure. He added that he had agreed with the chairman that the two would meet up with Collymore at a service station, so I said 'have a look at what shape he is in, ask him about his state of mind and ambition, ask him if he still has that hunger'. We didn't want a player who would disrupt the team spirit.

"I didn't hear anything else and the next morning I was driving to Bradford and speaking to Chris on the phone. I said 'I never heard again from you last night, what happened with Stan?' Chris replied that he hadn't met him, so I said 'oh, so the deal is off then?' and he replied 'no, the chairman has signed him, we just have to go on and get the best out of him'. We had Ashley Ward, Dean Saunders, Dean Windass and Carbone – where would he fit in? It was nothing personal, but I just didn't think we needed him. It was tough for Chris, because we weren't scoring a lot of goals and, when the chairman had lined up a move for a striker who was proven to score goals; it was tough for him to turn that down.

"Stan scored against Leeds on his debut with a wonderful bicycle kick. The place erupted, and it was live on TV. And I remember coming off the pitch at the end, and the chairman's son was stood near the manager's office. He knew that I hadn't been keen on Stan, and as I walked past he said to me 'Europe here we come'. I just rolled my eyes and thought 'if only you knew'."

Hutchings was sacked just two matches later, and McCall was asked to be caretaker manager for a couple of games – which proved to be a real eye-opener for him, in terms of realising the scale of City's financial commitment to the likes of Carbone and Collymore. "I remember a lower league manager rang up asking about taking one of our young players on loan. He asked me how much his wages were, to see if they could afford him. So I said I would find out and ring him back, and I asked the secretary for the details. He explained there was a book inside the bottom draw of my desk, listing every player's wage. So I opened it up and saw what money everybody was on – it was the worst thing I could have done!

"I realised that it was true how much Carbone was rumoured to be on. At the time David Beckham and Roy Keane at Manchester United weren't on wages as high as that – I think they might have used Carbone's wage to strengthen their own negotiations! I didn't have the forward vision to question how a Premier League club could afford those wages. You could argue it was a case of ambition. I have nothing against Carbone. There was no resentment from any players towards him. He was offered the money and would have been stupid to turn it down."

Jim Jefferies was brought in to replace Chris Hutchings, after a successful spell at Hearts in Scotland. By January and with just three wins all season, the white flag was hoisted up. City were rock bottom and clearly going down, and so the clearing of the decks began. Talented players like Andy O'Brien and Dean Windass were sold on to other Premier League clubs, whilst David Hopkin, Dan Petrescu and Collymore were shipped out – Collymore's incredible debut goal against Leeds aside, he had contributed next to nothing. Richmond and Jefferies tried to get rid of Carbone too, but his wage package frightened away suitors. The four-year deal that City agreed with the Italian would prove a millstone around the club's neck.

It was a strange period to come in and cover the club, which is exactly what Simon Parker did after joining the Telegraph & Argus in early autumn of the 2000/01, to become the newspaper's new Bradford City reporter – a position that he still holds. A South Coast native, Simon is a Portsmouth supporter and spent years covering their fierce rivals, Southampton, for the Portsmouth News. An established Premier League club, defying the odds each year at their creaking Dell stadium, Parker's move from covering the Saints to the Bantams offered him an interesting perspective on the growing problems at Valley Parade.

Simon explained to me, "When I took the job I thought Bradford City were basically a Division One club in the Premier League. I didn't think there was a lot of longevity about it. The ironic thing was that I was covering the Southampton-Wimbledon game, the day that City beat Liverpool to stay up, so I saw the other half of it. At the time you thought it was brilliant Bradford City were staying up, looking from afar. But you wondered if the second season would be too much, even though they started it well. The bubble burst very quickly. By the time I started the job, they were second bottom. They had drawn at West Ham 1-1. My first win took nearly three months, Coventry in December. By then the writing was on the wall."

In April, City were officially relegated. The attempts to upgrade from 'boring Bradford' had gone terribly wrong. The club had lost sight of its values, and what had made them successful. It was like a mid-life crisis, with the purchase of Carbone representing a splurge on a Ferrari that looks good but is impractical for your lifestyle, and far too expensive to maintain. It would be easy to paint Carbone as the bad guy, but really he wasn't. Of all the signings made during that ill-fated summer of 2000, the Italian was the only one who delivered exceptional performances week in week out. And his work rate could rival even Stuart McCall and Jamie Lawrence. The problem was that the expectations were too high. Rather than net 20 goals, he managed only five – typical of his seasonal average over his career. And the players around Carbone weren't good enough to bring out the best in him. He was a luxury player who the rest of the team couldn't carry. Stuart McCall said on the club's over-ambition, "It was crazy what they did. What had kept us up had been the spirit and scrapping. There was nothing wrong with looking for more quality, but we were always going to be battling against the odds that season."

And besides, Carbone would ultimately play a big part in saving the club. Back in the Football League, money was evidently tight, with no new signings made during the close season. But the retention of McCall for one more year, and Carbone (who no one was willing to buy from City) meant expectations of a promotion push were high. City started well but faded away, Carbone was loaned out to Premier League Derby County to get him off the wage bill for a time, and later on to Middlesbrough. Jefferies walked out, with City in mid-table, at Christmas, having had a training ground bust up with Stuart McCall, who left himself in the summer of 2002. "Jim Jefferies had said to me 'your legs have gone'," McCall revealed. "After I left Bradford in 2002 I ended up playing around 80 times for Sheffield United and was involved in one of their most successful seasons; and after every game I always used to think back to that dig and think 'well there's another game you've done'." Nicky Law came in as manager and steadied the ship, but a final position of fifteenth was a major disappointment. Geoffrey Richmond was in no doubt where the blame for the club's under-performance lay. After March saw dismal back-to-back defeats against Sheffield Wednesday and bottom of the table Stockport, Richmond used his programme notes for the next game, against Man City, to launch a stinging attack on his players. He wrote, "The exit door is open for the vast majority of our overpaid, underachieving footballers. Many of them will get the shock of their lives when their present contracts end and they see that the world of football will value them at a fraction of the value of their present inflated salaries."

With City's debts mounting, and Carbone's talks with Middlesbrough about a permanent deal breaking down due to his wage demands, City were left in big trouble. And then the Football League's TV deal with ITV Digital collapsed, meaning the 72 clubs – and particularly those in Division One – faced a major shortfall in their expected revenue. The game was up, and City were forced to go into administration.

Julian Rhodes told me, "I got a lot more involved after we got relegated in 2001. To be honest, we would have been better going into administration the day we got relegated from the Premier League. We tried to keep going, but the situation was completely unworkable. You try to delay it in the hope that things will happen, like selling Carbone. But in reality it would have cost a fortune to get rid of him. Even then, it was still a shock when we had to put the club in administration. I think some people thought it was some kind of wheeze but it wasn't. The final straw was I saw some cash flows that showed the club was going to be haemorrhaging £1 million a month. But when I looked more closely, that assumed that we were receiving all of the ITV Digital money, which we weren't, and it also assumed we were getting rid of Mr Carbone, which we weren't. So it was more like we were haemorrhaging £1.5 million a month. And it would get worse than this ten months after that. So the game was up.

"I think the other problem we had was that we were one of the first ex-Premiership sides to go into administration. A lot of our creditors were common to other football clubs. And the other clubs were out to make a stance. We put together a CVA agreement that was difficult to say the least [where the club agree to pay a percentage of what it is owed, and the creditors agree to write off the rest], which was why we ended up back in administration a year later."

The disclosure of the mess that City had fallen into was truly shocking. Rather than signing players outright, Richmond had used a financing company to borrow £12 million to purchase players like

David Wetherall (£7 million was still owed to this company). The mortgage taken out to fund the extension to the Main Stand stood at over £7 million. Player contracts were huge and had to be honoured or settled. City owed Carbone £3.5 million. Ward was due £1.2 million for the remainder of his contract and Wetherall £734k. The Bantams were £4.5 million overdrawn at the bank, and owed the Inland Revenue close to £1 million.

The club had barely any assets of their own. The floodlights, furniture, equipment – even the paint on the wall, apparently – was leased rather than owned. Much of the money and profit made by City had fallen into the pockets of shareholders, by way of sizeable dividends payments over the previous two years. The Rhodes family and Richmond were the chief beneficiaries of these payments, which according to David Conn's superb 2004 book, The Beautiful Game?, totalled some £8.125 million, plus VAT, between April 1999 and August 2000. Richmond also paid himself six-figure consultancy fees. Whilst some reward was clearly merited for the way the owners had funded the rise to the Premier League, it was shocking that not only had Richmond recklessly gambled the future, but paid a huge portion of the Premier League windfall to himself through dividend payments. In the summer of 2002, Richmond told the Rhodes family that he couldn't put in any more capital to help the club, in its hour of need. A couple of years later the reason why would become clear – he was made bankrupt over an unpaid tax bill when he sold his business, Ronson Lighters – the very business deal that had funded his purchase of 58% of Bradford City. The Rhodes, to their credit, would pay all of their dividend windfall back, and then some, over the following years, as they took on true ownership of the club and its huge debts.

Hundreds of smaller creditors were owed money as well; most shamefully of all, the St. John's Ambulance charity – which did so much to help the club during its darkest hour on 11 May, 1985 – was owed almost £6,000. The CVA document, which was sent to all creditors, was a horrifying list of badly managed debts and a statement of the club's terrible excess. The bonanza of the Premier League money should have set City up for years to come, but instead it was frittered away wastefully, with barely anything concrete left to show for it.

Julian Rhodes added, "It was horrendous. What you have also got to consider at that time was that all our wealth was in Filtronic shares [the company Julian's dad, Professor David, had founded]. They were put up as collateral for everything we owed. The peak of Filtronic shares was £25. In October 2002 they were down to 27p. We were lucky that the bank didn't pull the plug on us. We had nowhere near enough coverage for what the debts were. Really, they should have bankrupted us and bankrupted the club. Luckily they didn't. The bank manager at the time, who has now retired, still comes down here to watch games. If he hadn't given us such leeway at the time, we wouldn't have a club.

"It was a really difficult time for us. I remember being really concerned about my dad. I thought he was either going to have a heart attack, a nervous breakdown, or both. In the end I told him to stay away, get back to what he was good at and I'd sort the mess out."

For supporters the legacy of Richmond would be forever tainted by his terrible decisions over the summer of 2000, as Mark Douglas reflected, "There was a definitely a feeling that we had gone for it in the summer of 2000 in order to establish ourselves in the Premier League. And if they had have stayed up that year, they would probably still be a Premier League club now. They'd have gone onto the gravy train at the right time; they would have avoided the problems with ITV Digital that happened a year later. I think Richmond's reasoning was that we were overstretching ourselves a little to stay in the Premier League, but I think he got carried away with himself.

"Richmond said 'nobody was complaining when we signed the players' [in 2000], but I think that's a rubbish argument really. He was the man who knew what the finances were, the rest of us didn't. He'd always said all along that he'd never put this football club in any kind of financial danger, he had been so outright about that, and I think we'd all taken him at his word. He had earned that trust from us. I don't think anybody was questioning him back then."

In desperation, the administrators made an unprecedented move – they sacked 19 players. They announced this decision on the City website, with the players finding out in this way too. Jamie Lawrence recalled to me, "I remember exactly where I was when I heard I'd been sacked. I was on holiday in Ayia Napa with Barry Hayles and Kevin Betsy. I was watching Sky Sports, drinking a Guinness, and looked at the TV and saw the announcement that my contract had been terminated. I thought, 'what's going on there? I'd better tighten the purse strings for the rest of my holiday!'

"I didn't know where the next wage was coming from, and a few clubs rung me about signing. But we were told that the club couldn't sack us, so we came back for pre-season even though we weren't being paid. There were the likes of Wayne Jacobs, Aidan Davison, Andy Myers, Ashley Ward – we all mucked in together and moved on. We forgot about the fact we weren't being paid, and I think we became a closer bunch through that adversity."

Mark Bower was a young defender who had emerged through the City youth ranks, and became a regular over the 2001/02 campaign. In total, Bower played more than two hundred times for the club over a twelve -year period, and he has later enjoyed notable success as manager of Guiseley, steering the club into the Football Conference. Back in the summer of 2002, Bower was one of only a few players who weren't sacked. He explained to me, "Geoffrey Richmond had been keen to tie me down on a new contract, although I thought it strange that he was getting involved. So I signed a three year contract and with that I thought, oh, I will treat myself to a new car. Nothing too flash, a BMW. I went on holiday and received a text message from Nicky Law saying there's an announcement going to be made today, don't worry it doesn't affect you.

"Then I read in the paper the next day that Bradford City had sacked all their players. Like I said, Nicky had stated don't worry it doesn't affect you. The club had not sacked myself, Michael Standing, Lewis Emanuel and Tom Kearney. So we went back for pre-season training and eventually all the sacked players came back to train as well. But of course I had this new car. And I thought the players are going to give me loads of stick: they've not been paid for over two months, and I'm turning up in a new car! I hid it around the corner for a few weeks, but in the end I got found out and I got some real stick off the old pros.

"It was a horrible time. I remember a pre-season friendly at Hull with just the lads that were signed and a couple of trialists. And on the bus there was this feeling was that this was going to be the last game that Bradford City was going to play. It was a strange, strange game to play in and a strange, strange feeling coming back. But the club going under was genuinely what people thought was going to happen."

The Professional Footballers Association fought back and the administrators were forced to honour all player contracts. Eventually, a CVA agreement was reached by the administrators, Kroll Buchler Phillips, where City would pay 17.5p of every £1 they owed to creditors, meaning the club could go on. Which is how Carbone left Bradford City as a hero. The CVA deal hinged on whether Carbone would waiver the £3.5 million he was due over the final two years of his contract, as there was no way the Bantams could afford to keep him. Carbone agreed to write off this vast sum of money off and left the club.

In January 2013 Carbone reflected on this decision in the Daily Mail by saying, "I agreed to walk away, but it was some sacrifice. I don't know if other players would have done that. I hadn't earned anything like the amounts on offer in the Premier League today, and I had a young family. But when I thought about it, there was only one choice I could make.

"I couldn't be the person who put Bradford City out of business."

When the news broke that Bradford City could continue to exist, it was a moment to celebrate for supporters after so much stress. It really did seem as though City were going to go under, and each of us had to contemplate the very real possibility of losing something that was so important to us. Our way of life. It was of little consolation to any City supporter, of course, but the Bantams were trailblazers in this respect. Within a matter of years, more than 30 Football League clubs – many ex-Premier League – had also endured spells in administration. It was an English football modern phenomenon. As the rich became everyone richer, everyone else attempted to keep up and many failed miserably. Just as the game was pumped full of unprecedented levels of wealth, the uneven distribution of the TV windfalls had a devastating effect on the have-nots.

Gordon Gibb, the Flamingo Land owner, emerged as a saviour for Bradford City by investing money into the club; and he and Julian Rhodes took City out of administration. Geoffrey Richmond exited the club, because he did not have the funds – or the support of fans – to continue. Six years of magnificent management of the club by Richmond, forever blotted by six weeks of madness. To this day, opinion is mixed over whether we can ever call him a hero, and if the good times were worth the painful legacy that was left behind.

The-then Telegraph & Argus journalist, David Markham, summarised, "Geoffrey Richmond was a controversial character with good points and bad points like the rest of us. He was an impatient, ambitious man who was determined to bring success to the football club. You could say he was ruthless in his pursuit of success; but whatever his faults, supporters will remember him for bringing two seasons of Premier League football to Bradford City, who have spent much of their long history in the bottom two divisions of the Football League.

"His lucky break was the win at Blackpool and play off victory over Notts County which took the club into the second tier of English football. Supporters should always be grateful to him for having the drive and vision to extend the ground – the Midland Road stand opened in 1997 by the Queen and the extension of the Spion Kop and main stand, ironically completed just before the club were relegated. His downsides were that he tended to interfere with his managers – the Chris Kamara sacking didn't make sense and the falling out with Paul Jewell a month after he led City to Premier League survival had dreadful consequences for the club. His overspending in the so-called summer of madness – 2000 – had even worse consequences for the club and threatened its survival and, in some ways, is still being felt today some fifteen years later."

Julian Rhodes added on Richmond, "Don't get me wrong I was bitter at the time. We fell out during that summer, but we did have to work together to get things through. There was no way he could have stayed, so off he went. But I have spoken to him since. Let's be fair, he didn't deliberately set out to ruin the club. But he was a gambler, and like many gamblers he didn't think about the downside of the risks he was taking.

"If you speak to the Football League, they still say that Bradford City was in the worst position out of all clubs who went into administration. Even though Leeds United had bigger debts, they was a much bigger company underlying those debts; whereas Bradford City, traditionally, has been a much smaller football club."

Simon Parker has fond memories of working with Richmond, and was actually in the process of writing a book with him about his time at Valley Parade, before the crisis at the club put the project on hold indefinitely. "Richmond was brilliant from a press point of view. He'd give you everything first. I remember he rang me and at quarter past seven one morning and said 'I've got a back page story for you, and I think it's a front page story too!' Turned out he'd just signed Stan Collymore and the player was due in his office in ten minutes. Geoffrey invited me to join them.

"The other side of Geoffrey was if you got on his wrong side, and then you'd get a call with a different tone, and you knew straightaway that you were in trouble. You'd get hauled before him. But he was never dull. He was a great character. In hindsight, the way he ran it was car crash to be honest. But he's not the first and he won't be the last to do that."

And the book production? "We'd got three quarters of the way through it, and it was edgy stuff, but then he sorted of disappeared. He went off the radar. He was a lot more withdrawn and you could see, for whatever reason, whether it was guilt, embarrassment or stress, he went into himself a lot more, rather than the big, overbearing character of before. I think by the end of administration that summer, he admitted that he had nothing left. Looking at him you could see that he had run out of steam. I don't think there was any way he could have stayed on. Or, even if he had have stayed on, I don't think there was any way he could have rebuilt it the way that he would have liked to."

Having looked as though it would go out of business, City's continuing existence as a club was a source of major celebration, and the first game of the 2002/03 season – a 0-0 draw with Wolves – was a special moment. Simon Parker added, "The Wolves home game seemed quite emotional. There was a genuine fear that that team wasn't going to be there. But there they were still together, playing a fancied team like Wolves and scrapped for a 0-0 draw. It was a real against-the-odds moment."

But still, it had been a spectacular fall from grace for the club over a two-year period. From the bright new dawn against Chelsea, with the most expensively assembled Bradford City team in history, putting the fashionable West London club to the sword, to scraping a draw at home to Wolves, largely relying on a group of players that the club had attempted to sack. On that hazy August evening against Chelsea, there had been so much promise about the future, but at the time no one knew that City had effectively doomed itself to a bleak existence; and that the rise and rise of the club between 1996 and 2000 was to come to a shuddering halt. Bradford City looked invincible that night against Chelsea, but their world was about to cave in.

Some fans ruefully argue that it would have been better if City had lost to Liverpool in May 2000 and been relegated at the end of their first season in the Premier League. Others claim that if Jewell had been given the respect he deserved by Richmond, he would have stayed and with it the club would have remained grounded; building upwards in a sensible, measured way. Either way, if City had have continued to understand its limitations, accept its place in the modern football world, the future could have been so different. If City had gone down in 2000, or even if they had survived, spent sensibly and been relegated in 2001, they would have been in a strong position to challenge back for promotion again. For the Premier League parachute money they received would have given them a big advantage over their Football League rivals. Instead, that parachute money went towards bills the club had no hope of fully repaying. Their hopes of being competitive undermined for years to come. Six weeks of madness almost underplays the seriousness of the mistakes Richmond made during the summer of 2000. At what should have been the club's greatest position of strength in decades, Richmond – the gambler – chucked everything on black, and it landed on red. As red as the club's accounts would quickly become.

Mark Douglas reflected of the Premier League adventure, "Looking back I still think the Premier League was not really who we are. I don't think Bradford will ever be a kind of Swansea City, I don't think that really happens anymore. But that almost makes the memory of that first season at least all the more special. I don't think the second season soured it. You've got to bank that experience, as I don't think you'll ever see it happen again for City."

And however painful the episode proved to be, however bittersweet it is that we supporters saw someone as talented but expensive as Benito Carbone in claret and amber, at least we did have that one wonderful, mesmerising evening against Chelsea to savour. That all too brief moment, where the masterplan looked inspired. It's just a shame that the one moment ended all too quickly; that the dark clouds were already gathering. And that, ultimately, it would take twelve years for the storm to clear, and for Bradford City to be able to go back to doing things The Bradford City Way.

City (vs Chelsea): Matt Clarke, Dan Petrescu (Ashley Ward 76), Peter Atherton, Ian Nolan, David Wetherall, Andrew O'Brien, David Hopkin, Stuart McCall, Lee Sharpe (Gareth Whalley 79), Benito Carbone (Andy Myers 89), Dean Windass

Not used: Aidan Davison, Peter Beagrie

Intensive care

Bradford City vs Wimbledon

Division One, Saturday 17 April, 2004

For this home game against Wimbledon, my friends and I took a break from the usual pre-match routine of going to the pub, and instead headed to Bradford's Centenary Square. We joined a crowd totalling a couple of hundred, all wearing Bradford City colours. We listened intently to a couple of speeches. We looked suitably downbeat, as a fake coffin was carried back and forth through the middle of the gathering, a local photographer taking pictures. And then we headed off to Valley Parade to see our team be relegated to the third tier of English football.

The bitter irony of the 2003/04 campaign was that it was supposed to be a season of celebration. It was the club's centenary year; but efforts to mark this occasion were undermined by the huge worries that emanated over the club's present day struggles, and with it major question marks about its future existence. It was the worst season that I have ever experienced supporting the Bantams. They won just six games in front of their own fans, were badly lacking in quality and looked doomed to relegation as early as January. They set a record for most single goal defeats in a season, which meant most matches were closely-fought but undermined by one defensive error. They were never going to win this fight, and went down with three games still to play. But relegation wasn't even the worst of it all: for in February, financial problems once again engulfed the club and threatened to kill it off. City returned into administration for a second time. They remained saddled with debt and were failing to come even remotely close to realising their original cash flow projections. They were on course to celebrate a hundred years of life by dying. This was an utterly, utterly miserable period for everyone connected with the club.

And so on that April afternoon, before the Bantams hosted bottom club Wimbledon, the Bradford City Supporters Trust organised a meeting at Centenary Square to raise awareness about the increasingly desperate plight. And to hand over to the council a petition with more than 2,000 signatures, urging them to provide the stricken club with support. It was a strange and colourless atmosphere. You wanted to be there to show your support and dedication, but it wasn't entirely clear what we could achieve by doing it, other than for the event to get a nice write-up in the Telegraph & Argus. The level of the debts to tackle seemed completely beyond us regular supporters, unlike in 1983 when City had faced a financial crisis and the sums needed to save the club were more tangible to the ordinary person. We could pass around collection tins, but we would need to gather a heck of a lot of coins in order to acquire the millions that the club required to stay afloat.

Living on the breadline

It was only in 2002, of course, that City had first fallen into administration – taking the unwanted tag of trailblazers. Before the summer of 2002, your average football fan would not have known what the term 'administration' meant. Yet over the next decade and longer, around a third of the 92 Premier League and Football League clubs would subsequently follow the dark path first trodden by City. The legacy of the club's six weeks of madness in 2000 had been near-financial implosion, with the Bantams only surviving that troubled summer of 2002 because of the injection of significant funds and guarantees by the Rhodes family, alongside a new investor, Gordon Gibb. In order to continue to operate as a business, City had to reach a CVA agreement with its long-list of non-footballing creditors: a deal that was supposed to work out as the club repaying 17.5p of every £1 it owed. There are very few instances in everyday life when debts will ever be agreed to be written off like that – imagine a home owner asking their bank if they could reduce their mortgage repayments by more than 80%? Yet despite creditors accepting this less than desirable offer, the truth was that City were not even going to be able to fulfil those incredibly favourable terms. The mess they were in was not sorted in July 2002. It was only the beginning.

Whilst these financial issues would have been keeping the new partnership of Gibb and the Rhodeses wide awake at night with worry, for us supporters – largely in the dark – there was genuine optimism that the headaches were behind the club, and that it could start to move forwards again. The 2002/03 season that followed the first spell in administration was a challenging one that featured long losing streaks, a revolving door of disinterested loanees, and the unwelcome ongoing presence of the highly-paid but under-performing striker in Ashley Ward (just three goals all season), but it ended with mission accomplished. City survived relegation from Division One with relative ease, confirming their divisional status on Easter Saturday with four games left to play. And the summer of 2003 offered manager Nicky Law – who had taken over at Valley Parade just months before Administration One – the chance to move on under-achieving high earners (including Ward) and bring in his own players. With the T&A positivity machine in full action, no one really looked upon it as a negative that Gibb imposed an incoming player salary ceiling of just £750 per week. Law probably did, as he attempted to persuade Division One-standard players to join one of the lowest-paying clubs in Division One. To put £750 per week into perspective, the players brought in that summer earned less in a year than what City had been paying Benito Carbone on a weekly basis, only twelve months earlier.

In what in hindsight looks like a very cruel joke, on the eve of the 2003/04 season Gibb publically pledged a £1.5 million bonus, to be shared amongst the revamped squad, should they achieve promotion to the Premier League that season. He may as well have promised to pay them £1.5 billion each. There was simply no way that they were ever going to be good enough to be knocking on the door of the Premier League. There was only one way in which these players would be exiting the division, as would very quickly become painfully evident: relegation.

In 2001/02 – City's first year back in the Football League after relegation from the Premier League, and before Administration One – the players' wage bill was £9.0 million. Post-admin, and with Benito Carbone and others moved on, the payroll was almost halved to £4.8 million in 2002/03. Now in 2003/04 it had been halved again, to £2.3 million. There was only one team in Division One with a lower wage bill – basket case outfit Wimbledon, who were in administration and embarking on their highly controversial relocation to Milton Keynes. Midway through this season the once-proud Crazy Gang would move from South London to the National Hockey Stadium in Milton Keynes, as all right-minded football fans looked on aghast. In such turmoil, the Dons' own relegation was obvious from the outset. In effect, Division One in 2003/04 was a 23-team league.

Reflecting on what would prove to be an utterly dismal campaign, Simon Parker of the Telegraph & Argus stated that the warning signs were there from day one, "It started off with this terrible pre-season tournament at Valley Parade [a competition to celebrate Bradford City's centenary that featured teams from Scotland, Wales and Northern Ireland]. I think there were only a thousand people there on both days, and they lost both central defenders to bad injuries. If ever there was a sign there was a curse that was it.

"The recruitment that summer was dreadful. The likes of Luke Cornwall and Robert Wolleaston; players who were never going to pull up any trees. I remember a pre-season tour at Scotland and City were dreadful. They looked awful and I thought then 'it's going to be a long season'. So it proved. They started okay. Then they got into this losing run and it seemed to slide away."

Richard Wardell began the 2003/04 season like any other Bradford City supporter: hopeful for a good campaign. He would end it as a board member for the Bradford City Supporters Trust, as the crisis around the club grew extremely serious. Of the football itself, he recalled to me, "The beginning of the season started in bright sunshine and on a positive note with us gaining a well-earned point against Norwich City, who would be promoted to England's top division by the end of the season. Michael Branch [one of the £750 per week summer signings] scored in that opening game and I thought that we might have a good season. Little did I know how the next nine months would pan out."

The tone for a difficult campaign was set within days of the season's kick off. After the Norwich City draw, the Bantams suffered a midweek League Cup exit at home to fourth tier side Darlington on penalties. Gibb – who would, no doubt, have been seething over the missed opportunity to raise much-needed revenue through a good cup run, and noting Darlington's reward was a trip to Premier League Wolves – publically criticised Law regarding his tactics. Despite taking four points from the first two games, three straight league defeats followed which included a truly appalling 4-0 reverse at home to Sunderland. Cue more public criticism from Gibb and supporter panic. The team looked well short of the required standard.

The next two games were won, but twelve winless matches followed that ensured the Bantams were firmly marooned in the relegation zone. Law's team were desperately unlucky at times, as the record tally of single goal defeats began to be chalked up; but playing well and still getting beaten didn't bode well at all. In the middle of November, Law was sacked barely an hour after a 1-1 draw at home to Walsall. Simon Parker revealed, "I think Shaun Harvey [then-City chief executive] had made his mind up a week before that if they didn't win the Walsall game Nicky Law was gone. The awkward one about that was I actually knew Nicky Law had been sacked before he did. He went into the press conference not knowing. Nicky spent the press conference talking about the upcoming international break and the training he would do, and I ended up stopping taking notes because I knew there was actually no point. As we came out, Jon Pollard the secretary came down and said to Nicky 'Shaun Harvey wants to see you in the boardroom', and I think he realised at that point what was going to happen."

It was a harsh sacking in some respects, but the club had to try something to reverse the slide as there were few positives about the season so far. Richard Wardell added, "On the plus side, we saw the emergence of Simon Francis, whilst Paul Heckingbottom established himself at left back playing the most number of league games in the squad. However, Wayne Jacobs was coming to the end of his playing career and too many players, including Jason Gavin [a notoriously poor summer signing], didn't seem to give 100% whilst playing for the team that season."

There was no doubt that the hunt for Law's replacement was commercially-driven as much as it was about football. Crowds had dipped to under 11,000, when just three years earlier in the Premier League there had been more than 18,000 every other week. Gate receipts had fallen significantly too, from more than £4 million annually in 2000 and 2001, to around £1 million in 2003. Commercial revenue had also been hit hard by the effects of Administration One, with Bradford's business community turning their backs on the club. So if a manager could be recruited who could provide a buzz amongst supporters and sponsors, these alarming trends might be reversed.

Former City manager Chris Kamara was interviewed for the position and his return would certainly have captured the imagination of the Bradford public. However, Kamara opted to stay on in his high profile, well-paid job at Sky Sports where he had become one of the broadcaster's biggest stars. Instead, City turned to a former Manchester United and England legend: one Bryan Robson. Robson had being out of managerial work since leaving Middlesbrough two years earlier, but in a mixed time at the Teesside club he had delivered two promotions and attracted a wealth of big names to the Riverside stadium. Colin Todd – who also interviewed for the position – accepted the consolation prize of the role of Robson's assistant. Gibb and the Rhodeses loosened the purse strings a little, allowing Robson to bring in more high calibre players via the loan market.

Yet despite a sensational start – City beat Millwall 3-2 at home in front of Sky Sports' cameras, having trailed 2-0 at half time – there was no magic wand. The Bantams lost eleven of Robson's next thirteen games in charge, to remain rooted at the bottom of the league with only Wimbledon beneath them. After a 1-0 loss at Gillingham at the end of January, Gills boss Andy Hessenthaler declared that the battle to avoid relegation had simply become a matter of who would take the third spot and join City and Wimbledon in going down to the third tier. It was hard to disagree with his bleak assessment of the Bantams' survival prospects. That 24-team division, which had become 23 due to Wimbledon's problems, was now in effect a 22-team league. On 14 February, City made it an unhappy Valentine's Day by enduring that eleventh defeat in thirteen, at the hands of Ipswich Town. It was such a depressing time to be a supporter and so unrewarding attending matches.

But just when it seemed as though things couldn't possibly get worse, they did. By a long, long way.

The sequel

"CITY BACK ON THE BRINK" screamed the front page of the Telegraph & Argus on Wednesday 18 February, 2004. The accompanying story, written by the paper's then-business editor, Andrew Hebden, confirmed every City fan's worst nightmare. "Bradford City's directors today warned that the football club could be forced back into administration within the next seven days," it began, before providing details of the grim financial situation. The money injected by the owners would run out the following week and, if City's creditors refused to reach an agreement over the outstanding debt, the club could be forced to file for administration. In other words, those people who were still owed money, and who were only getting 17.5p of every £1 they were owed, were about to be asked to accept even less.

This news came as a major shock to City supporters, but there was at least one fan who was fully clued up on the crisis facing the club. In the November before, John Dewhirst – a lifelong supporter, co-founder of the City Gent and author of several Bradford City books – found that his work and personal life would cross-over, when his own accountancy firm was asked to undertake a review of the club's financial position. Dewhirst was a member of the creditors' committee that had been set up in 2002 to oversee the terms of the Creditors Voluntary Agreement (CVA) made during Administration One. Following his November 2004 review, he was required to submit a report of his findings to the major creditors. It did not make good reading.

Speaking to The Independent in February 2004, Dewhirst admitted, "It was a strange situation. As a professional, I had to assess that this business is simply not viable. As a fan, I desperately wanted the Rhodes family to put more money in. The hardest thing was wondering what I'd tell my five-year-old daughter if we no longer had a Bradford City to support."

In summary, the club was no longer able to meet its requirements under the CVA. The club needed an injection of £3 million to continue operating until the end of the season. Gate receipts and commercial revenue were well down on forecasts, and following the difficulties caused by ITV Digital's demise the player transfer market was no longer a viable way to raise income. City continued to have high-earning players, including Ashley Ward, who still had to be paid despite leaving the club during the previous summer. Ward was on a basic salary of £880,000 a year – which was more than City's entire season ticket income for the 2003/04 season. They also owed huge sums to the likes of the Inland Revenue and Gerling (a player lease company used by Geoffrey Richmond to fund the purchase of players during the Premier League years). Despite these debts having being reduced under the CVA terms, the club still couldn't generate the money to meet these obligations and operate as a business.

Making the situation even more complicated was that, by this stage, Gordon Gibb and the Rhodes family had fallen out; with Gibb resigning from his position of chairman over the Christmas period. One of City's biggest financial hurdles had been repaying the mortgage taken out with Lombards to fund – in hindsight – the completely unnecessary building of a second tier on the main stand. (Unnecessary given it took the ground's capacity to 25,106, when post-Premier League they couldn't even fill half of the stadium.) On the eve of 2003/04 campaign a solution had seemingly being reached through taking the drastic step of selling Valley Parade to Gordon Gibb's family pension fund, called the 'Flamingo Land Self Administered Pension Scheme', for £2.5 million. Meanwhile, the stadium's adjoining shop and office blocks were sold to Development Securities for £2.55 million (a company which later became part of a new venture called Prupim). The £5 million raised helped to pay off the Lombards debt. When it was announced in July 2003, it was hailed as the last financial stumbling block for the club to overcome. Under the terms of the deal, City would play at Valley Parade free for a year, and then begin paying annual rent to the Flamingo Land Self Administered Pension Scheme.

Julian Rhodes told me of Gordon Gibb, "I was amazed that he came in in the first place, but obviously very grateful. I think perhaps that if he had his time again he would have found a different football club to invest in, with perhaps not so many problems. From Gordon's point of view he was young, he'd put a lot of his family's wealth into the club, and yet we were still after more.

"We got through that first season by hook or by crook, and I was very surprised that he offered to do the property deals at the end of 2002/03. Football League rules are very clear that football creditors have to be paid in full, so we had to find a big lump of cash to continue paying the wages. We had the option to sell the office block and club shop or the stadium, but really we needed to do both. Gordon offered to buy the stadium, which I was surprised at given only a year before he had parted with a lot of money to buy half the club, but I suppose he saw it as offering a bit more security. Still, to be fair to him, it was a very brave thing to do."

Yet as Dewhirst's findings confirmed, even these steps would not clear the financial black hole. In 2002, the Rhodeses' reportedly put £4 million into City to keep it going, which included guaranteeing a £2 million loan from the Professional Footballers Association (PFA) to cover players' contracts, with the Rhodes family home put up as a guarantee (in other words, if City failed to repay this loan, the family home would be repossessed). Gibb paid £1.875 million to acquire 49% of the club in 2002, but more money was still needed. Hence the £5 million raised from selling Valley Parade and the adjoining land, followed by the Rhodeses pumping in a further £1 million. Dewhirst concluded that £3 million more was needed to keep City going until the end of the season, which the Rhodeses were prepared to provide. But this is where the fall out occurred.

For in return for injecting a further £3 million into the business, the Rhodes family asked for Gibb to hand over his shares. Incensed by this request, Gibb quit as chairman and the impasse began. The Rhodeses were not prepared to put in the extra money unless they owned more of the club in return; pointing out that Gibb's £2.5 million injection to buy Valley Parade left him with the stadium as an asset that would generate him an income. Gibb didn't believe that he should hand over shares for nothing in return. The road to Administration Two seemed to begin as an exercise in brinksmanship – who would blink first?

At the next home game, against Crewe, Gibb dramatically turned up unexpectedly at Valley Parade, and went onto the pitch with a microphone before kick off to tell fans of his efforts to keep the club going.

He also protested that he had been let down by the Rhodeses, who weren't at the game themselves. This prompted professor David Rhodes into issuing a statement to supporters, via the club's website, on the Monday after, painting a full picture of the financial mess that Bradford City were in.

The fall out between the Gibb and Rhodes families continued in public, with Gibb telling the Yorkshire Post, "I do not think it is necessary to seek an administration order; the club can progress in its current state. They simply want my shares – and I am not interested in giving them up." A few days later a compromise was agreed where the Rhodes family would make regular payments to Gibb to rent the ground, over a five-year period, and gradually Gibb's shares and Valley Parade would be owned by the Rhodeses. Looking back on the fall out with Gibb, Julian Rhodes stated, "I was a bit upset when he went on the pitch and slagged me off when I wasn't even there. Perhaps he could have reacted differently. But I will always be grateful for the fact that he came in when he did when there was no one else willing to do it."

And of going back in administration? "It was completely necessary. We were trying to find a way to get around administration, but part of the reason we did go into administration was because we couldn't agree a deal with Gordon. We were looking to put some more money in to pay the bills. All I will say is thank god we did go back into admin when we did. Had we not, we would have ended up going back in at some point in the future having blown a load more money and the club would probably have been in a much weaker position."

By the time of City's next game, at Notts Forest, City were indeed back in administration. Most of the clubs who had loaned Bryan Robson their players hastily recalled them, and with it the struggling team was virtually doomed to relegation. The administrators – desperate to find money to keep the club going – sold on the club's remaining prize assets for what seemed like peanuts. Andy Gray and Simon Francis went to Sheffield United for bargain fees, as the Blades manager, Neil Warnock, sensed the opportunity to prey on City's weak bargaining position. The pair cost Warnock a quarter of a million – both players would later play in the Premier League, demonstrating their true value. Andy Gray would be sold for a £1.1 million – more than 20 times what Warnock had paid Bradford City for him.

Just as administration first hit, on the field Robson was starting to deliver some positive results – they went on a run of three wins and a draw from five games that offered a chink of hope that they could pull off the greatest of escapes. Yet by late March and with the squad having been ripped apart, Robson had to turn to players who, a few months earlier, had been informed by the manager that they should find new clubs, because they weren't good enough. A cruel 2-1 home defeat to Burnley at the end of March pretty much ended hopes. In April, Bryan Robson was quoted in the Guardian saying, "I thought we'd turned the corner, we'd gone on a good run, but then you go into administration and the goalposts change."

It was now a matter of when, not if, City would be relegated. Simon Parker summed up how hopes of relegation had been all but ended by the financial mess, "They still had half a chance. But once admin hit, that was it." On Easter Monday City lost 3-2 at Derby meaning they were fifteen points off survival with five games remaining. And on top of that, City remained in administration; with deadlines to agree a new CVA continuing to be pushed back, after the Inland Revenue filed an objection to the proposals put forward.

Still, with a home game against already relegated Wimbledon next, the inevitable would surely be delayed for at least once more week.

The last stand

History hasn't been kind to Bryan Robson's time at Valley Parade. Brought in to save the club from relegation, he achieved just seven wins from 28 games as the Bantams went down. There are few City supporters with positive things to say about his tenure. Yet there was no doubt he inherited a bleak situation, and that after the return to administration it became an impossible task to stay up. He had to manage with both hands tied behind his back, and yet he still ensured that the team fought hard and displayed passion. They lacked quality, but not effort, and looked set to battle until the very end.

But then, against Wimbledon, that fight mysteriously disappeared. Wimbledon, who spent the entire season in administration themselves, had been relegated a fortnight earlier and Robson's opposite number, Stuart Murdoch, was forced to mainly play youngsters. Whether the pressure being off Wimbledon gave them greater freedom to express themselves, or City simply underestimated their ability, is unclear; but right from kick off the visitors were first to every ball and quickly began to win every 50-50 challenge. The tone for a dreadful Bradford City performance was set after just three minutes. Young striker Malvin Kamara was played clean through on goal, with the back four nowhere in sight, and he was easily able to slot the ball past goalkeeper Mark Paston and into the goal at the Kop end.

The reaction from the City players was poor and they continued to flounder. If such a desperate season surprisingly hadn't featured too many pathetic performances, this was quickly proving to be one. In the first 45 minutes of the match they achieved just one shot on target. This despite a three-man attack made up of the experienced and wily Dean Windass, Danny Cadamarteri and Michael Branch – who had all played Premier League football. The three midfielders behind them were make-shift to say the least. Nicky Summerbee had quality, but alongside him Robert Wolleaston and Gareth Edds were part of that group of back-up players told they were free to find another club last January, only to remain on the books due to no takers. Collectively, the eleven players couldn't match the work-rate and enterprising running of their youthful opponents. This was a team lying down and accepting its fate too feebly.

Boos followed the second goal, which had inevitably arrived following a period of strong Wimbledon pressure. Wade Small crossed the ball from the Midland Road side of the stadium and it somehow evaded a clutch of City players in the box. Eventually it fell to Gary Smith, who had all the time in the world to tee up the shot and finish low past Paston. There were more boos at the half time whistle.

Any possibility of a second half comeback was all but ended five minutes into it, with the worst goal of the lot. A free kick was swung in deep from in front of the Main Stand, and Paston came out to complete what should have been a simple catch. Yet perhaps slightly distracted by his own defender, David Wetherall, Paston somehow let the ball slip through his fingers. It presented Wayne Gray with an empty net and bags of time to roll the ball home. Bradford City 0 Wimbledon 3. There was some booing, but more worryingly there was a mass exodus of City fans too. In a season of so many low points, the team had sunk to new depths. They were going to get relegated by losing at home to the division's bottom team, badly. Simon Parker said, "It was a terrible match between two terrible teams, one a lot worse than the other. The way they went down was probably as poor as you can get."

Watching these dismal proceedings from the back of the Kop, and by now with my feet stretched out onto the empty chair in front of me, I will always remember a steward coming up to me at that point and telling me to move my feet, or he would throw me out of the ground. 3-0 down, about to be relegated after a rotten season – and the club's future in grave doubt – and here was a steward threatening to eject me from the stadium for putting my feet on a chair. I snapped back at him following his warning "you'd be doing me a favour". He just walked off without saying a word. My feet stayed where they were.

Robson seemingly lost patience with his players at that point. On a humiliating afternoon for the man who used to captain his country with such courage and passion, the manager responded to his team's abject showing by withdrawing three first teamers and throwing on some youngsters: Danny Forrest, Kevin Sanasy and Tom Penford. The trio brought with them enthusiasm and a bravery that had been sorely lacking from claret and amber shirts all afternoon. Penford in particular began to dominate possession and spear-head regular attacks. With eighteen minutes on the clock, Paston rolled out the ball to Sanasy, who charged forward with pace and purpose. He then passed it to Penford in the centre, who sprayed the ball out wide to Cadamarteri. The forward crossed the ball into the box, and there was Sanasy free and able to strike an excellent-flicked half volley that whizzed into the net, the ball slightly behind him when he had come to make contact.

Rarely has a consolation goal being met with such glee by its scorer. A first senior goal, and for his hometown team, Sanasy raced over to the Kop with unconfined joy and offered us a ray of light that suggested the future might not be so dark after all. And, amazingly, it was 3-2 just three minutes later. Summerbee passed the ball to Cadamarteri outside the box, and he struck a powerful, speculative effort that arrowed into the bottom corner. The most improbable of comebacks was on. Those of us who had remained in the ground roared on the team with renewed hope. They still had to win the game to delay the inevitable for another week, but even coming back for a 3-3 draw would at this point feel like a minor victory.

There was no such ending, and in truth Wimbledon saw out the closing stages with relative ease. There was no doubt that they deserved the victory, and that it was an appalling afternoon for the Bantams; but there was a slight lift in the mood thanks to the endeavours of Forrest, Sanasy and Penford. At full time there was an eerie silence around Valley Parade as the players came over to thank the fans. There were no tears from fans, no shock at the club's relegation. Richard Wardell recalled of the day, "In the end a point would have been of little significance. In fact, Bradford City failed to score in their remaining three league games and were eventually relegated on 36 points. The relegation seemed irrelevant when compared to the on-going problems surrounding the football club's administration."

There were still three meaningless games to endure. Simon Parker reflected, "The last game of the season was the lowest point of covering them. They'd already been relegated, it was a Sunday lunchtime at Millwall. One of the players had told me that they hadn't been paid the week before, so the players didn't want to be there. They lost 1-0 and after it Bryan Robson was moaning about the ref. And we were saying to him 'Well what about your future?' but all he was bothered about was the ref. He was guarded about the questions on the future."

City's Division One status had endured a slow and painful death, but in truth there were much bigger concerns that had taken over everybody's focus. Now to somehow ensure that City were actually playing in the third tier next season. It was far from a given.

City fans to the rescue

The meeting between Bradford City's administrators, Kroll, and the club's creditors kept being pushed back. Friday 14 May 2004 was supposed to be the final, final D-Day, but once again the meeting was postponed. A deal had to be struck in order to ensure City's survival, but it was clear that what was on offer was a long way short of what already-frustrated creditors were willing to accept. The crisis had been deepening every week and, after this latest delay, the situation reached boiling point as club non-playing staff staged public demonstrations to highlight the club's plight. Then on Thursday 13 May, 800 supporters gathered outside Valley Parade to hold a vigil. The administrators' hosted a meeting after the demonstration, inside the Main Stand suite, where both the gravity of the situation and the way forwards were discussed.

In short, City faced a funding gap between then and the start of next season, and supporters were asked to raise the money needed to plug it. Having up until now faced talk of millions of pounds being required to rescue the club, which was way out of the grasp of regular fans, there was suddenly a tangible target to aim for. £100k was needed urgently and £500k over total – if City fans could raise £100k (quickly increased to £250k), the Rhodes family would match it. The Bradford City Supporters Trust took the lead. And the summer was filled with City supporters doing anything and everything they could to reach the overall target.

Richard Wardell takes up the story, "I think that my initial involvement with the Bradford City Supporters' Trust was in March 2004 when I attended a meeting in Bradford organised by the Trust. Shaun Harvey discussed the financial situation at our football club and answered questions from the audience. On the 19th anniversary of the Valley Parade fire, I remember attending another Trust meeting and it was at these meetings that I got to know Mark Boocock who was then the Chair, Phillip Marshall who was then Vice Chair and other passionate BCST Board members including Margaret Hainsworth, Mike Mason and Alan Flood. By this time I had become a member of the Trust, and like many other supporters, I wanted to help raise funds to keep my football club alive.

"On Wednesday 12 May, the Company Voluntary Agreement (CVA) meeting scheduled for the Friday was cancelled. At this point, I realised that the future of Bradford City was under serious threat. That evening, I met a few Trust Board members at Margaret Hainsworth's house and we made some banners using old bed sheets and paint. These were to highlight a hastily planned vigil and meeting which was to take place at Valley Parade the following day. In the late hours, Mike Mason and I drove along some of the key roads leading into Bradford to put the homemade banners up. I don't remember all of the spots where we placed them but I do remember putting one up at the end of the M606 and another on the A650 near to Drighlington. I got to bed in the early hours of 13 May and then I had to be up at 5am to catch a train to London for a work meeting. I managed to get to Valley Parade on the evening of Thursday 13 May, for the meeting organised by the Trust. I was pleased that so many people had turned up to discuss ways to save Bradford City from vanishing off the football map. At that point, the target was to raise £100,000 in five weeks."

It was an amazing reaction from the Bradford public and especially supporters, as all sorts of fundraising initiatives were spear-headed. Most notably, there was a special 'Save our City' celebrity match at Valley Parade, featuring legends of the previous seasons: Stuart McCall, Gary Walsh, Jamie Lawrence, Chris Waddle, John Hendrie, Wayne Jacobs, Darren Moore and more. So many heroes came back to do their bit, staging an entertaining match that attracted a near five-figure crowd (indeed, kick off had to be delayed due to the attendance exceeding all expectations). Fans did sponsored runs, auctioned off memorabilia and even organised for loose change to be brought by people to Valley Parade and left around the perimeter of the pitch. A claret and amber day was organised where people were encouraged to wear their shirts to raise money. Local businesses and club sponsors did their bit to. It was a very special period. It was a measure of the dedication of supporters and the Bradford community through adversity.

Richard Wardell continued, "During the fundraising efforts, it was heart-warming to hear people who weren't Bradford City supporters provide words of support. Bradford Council had pledged some financial support and just over a week after the meeting at Valley Parade, a large proportion of the £100,000 had been raised. Michael Wood from the Boy from Brazil website was very supportive and published an article that I wrote on his website to spread the message about saving the football club. I remember asking family and friends to become members of Trust.

"On 30 May, 9,167 supporters turned out at a wet Valley Parade to watch the Pro-Celebrity game which was to raise further funds to save the football club. John Dreyer, who typified the commitment on the pitch which Bradford City supporters appreciate, signed my programme and my brother had his England top (the one worn at the 1990 World Cup finals) signed by Chris Waddle which made his day. The day reminded people how important our football club is to the district of Bradford.

"Further Trust meetings took place and Michael Wood suggested to me that I should become a Trust Board member, which I did in 2005. On 11 June, I met with a Telegraph & Argus photographer/reporter who took some photographs of me stood outside Valley Parade to promote the sponsored ground hop event which my Bradford City supporting friend, Andrew Ashcroft, had proposed. The fundraising continued two days later with a collection at The Goldsborough pub during the Euro 2004 game between England and France. England conceded two late goals to lose the game but I wasn't too disheartened as more money had been raised to support the fundraising campaign."

In the end, the £250k target was not only reached but comfortably exceeded – to this day it remains the biggest fundraising effort by fans of a UK football club. The money that was raised bought the administrator time to try and find a buyer for the club, and a deal with those creditors. Yet those discussions continued to drag on. Julian Rhodes was waiting in the wings to buy back the club (there was no other party interested), but he still needed to strike an agreement with the creditors in order to take control and move the club forwards. There was a settlement needed with Ashley Ward, who despite playing for Sheffield United (he was another player that Warnock had snapped up on the cheap from the City wreckage) was still being paid £46k a month by the club in what were staggered payments for the remainder of his contract. There was still £500k owed to Lombards, despite the sale of the ground to the Gibb family pension fund; there was £1.5 million owed to lease creditors for the carpets and fittings inside Valley Parade; and there was the Inland Revenue, who around this time lost a similar case against Wimbledon which meant they were to be paid only a fraction of what they were owed.

The liabilities totalled some £10 million in all. After extensive talks, Gerling and the Inland Revenue agreed to the proposals; but there was the added complication for the Rhodes family of dealing with Gibb about the ground/shareholding situation, which was proving a stumbling block. Eventually Kroll issued a 1 July 2004 deadline of 10am for someone to come forward with a viable plan to take the club forward that would meet the creditors' approval, otherwise they would pull the plug on the club. It was an incredibly upsetting time for City supporters, and on that morning hundreds gathered outside the stadium, praying for good news or else they would be left mourning the death of the club. Rhodes needed creditors representing at least 75% of the club's debt to agree a deal, prompting last minute negotiations and pleas with the likes of Ashley Ward and Gibb. After finishing his training session over in Sheffield, Ward agreed to write off some of what he was owed by City, and a way forwards looked viable. Gibb voted against the CVA proposal, but the deals struck with Ward, Gerling and Lombards, plus the Inland Revenue reluctantly agreeing to accept £100,000 when they were owed £2.8 million, meant the CVA could go through.

A key reason for the creditors agreeing terms was the intervention of a group of five businessmen, led by Jim Brown, who rocked up at Valley Parade that morning without warning and got involved with the negotiations. Brown later told the Telegraph & Argus, "I remember the administrator running round like a lunatic that morning and it didn't look good. He was getting a bit nervous wondering where we were heading. When you think about the masses of problems we had in all areas, it was an absolutely dreadful time."

Richard Wardell was also heavily involved with the drama, "On 29 June, I received a text message from Andrew Ashcroft saying that unless Gordon Gibb would let us play at Valley Parade rent free for the next season, the football club would be liquidated. All of a sudden, all of the fundraising efforts seemed to be for nothing."

Yet 1 July 2004 was not, after all, the death of the club, but the start of its rebirth. Many of these creditor negotiations continued up until the 19 August CVA meeting, but a majority agreement was made. The new CVA was based upon much more realistic club income forecasts, such as average gates of 8,000 next season, commercial income falling by 20% following relegation, and increased repayments to the PFA for the loan it provided in 2002. The Flamingo Land Self Administered Pension Scheme eventually dropped its legal challenge. Finally, in December of that year, City moved out of administration. The most important point was that the club would continue to exist beyond its centenary season.

Reflecting back on a turbulent period, Julian Rhodes told me, "I know for supporters the summer of 2004 was a difficult time, but I actually felt a bit more in control of what was going on compared to the first time. I was always relatively confident that a positive outcome could be achieved. I know that the administrators set that deadline to shut us down, but I knew they wouldn't do it before I had chance to get a deal done with the creditors.

"We didn't actually come out of administration until December that year. One of the reasons it took so long was because we had some money set aside to pay stadium rent. We'd had a twelve-month rent free period, but by the time the rent was due we were in administration. So the rent owed had built up. Gordon Gibb took an injunction or something out against us. It got to the stage where they were actually stopping us from paying the rent. I remember speaking to their solicitor and assuring him that, if we got out of administration, we had a great chance of surviving and paying the rent. That we did and we have done ever since. Apart from one month where we were a week late in 2011."

And of that high noon deadline day of 1 July? Rhodes played down its significance. "I couldn't figure out what was going on then. I remember that day. I had organised to meet Mike Moore, who was the administrator, to go through the deal in the afternoon. So there was no way he going to shut it down at 10am like it was suggested. I got the feeling Mike was trying to push the council to see if they would do anything to help. But they didn't help. I could have told him that!"

Exiting administration for a second time didn't mean all the debt issues were settled, but it was a major step forward and Rhodes was able to turn it around. There can be little doubt that the Gibb pension fund rent commitments to play at Valley Parade, and the deal with Prupim to use the office block and club shop building, was detrimental to efforts to move forwards on the pitch. The club has subsequently attempted to buy back Valley Parade but have been dissuaded by the asking price. They tried to renegotiate the rent levels but negotiations proved futile. Still in 2012, they were able to buy the office block back from Prupim, thus eliminating half the rent liabilities. Rhodes added, "It has been getting easier and easier, slowly, since 2002. When you have a monumental problem and you keep chipping away at it, it gets easier. But it does take up all your focus, and you do sometimes think 'there's other things I could be doing'.

"I was lucky really. I had put my last bit of money into a start-up company in North Yorkshire, based at a pig farm. That has been going along nicely and in 2013 I sold it. But before that it was something that gave me a regular income at the time when all the club's difficulties had been going on. That was important, because I wasn't getting any money out of here!"

With all of this going on, the playing side of things took a backwards seat. The club were in limbo over whether Robson would opt to stay on as manager – he ultimately decided not to – and the entire squad were told they should look for another club. Mark Bower was one such player and remembers it well, telling me, "I could have gone, I had a few offers from lower down. Bristol Rovers were dead keen and they put an offer on the table which I rejected. Because I didn't want to leave, I had a contract for another year and there were still some good players that were left. The Bristol Rovers manager thought I was mad turning it down and staying, he kept saying how Bradford was going bust. But I just couldn't bring myself to leave at that point."

Colin Todd was promoted from assistant to manager following Robson's exit, and he spent pre-season waiting patiently to see if he would be allowed to sign up the promising trialists he had brought in for training. Once the club's financial position was clear and their future assured, Todd set about agreeing contracts with those players. Despite a difficult situation, he steadied the ship and City's first season in the newly-rebadged League One proved much better than expectations, the club finishing eleventh and not a million miles short of the play offs. It was great simply to still have a club to support, and it meant that expectations were for a time reined in.

"I think it's hard when you are going down the leagues, because people think 'we used to be in the Premier League' but potentially ignore the fact we were in the Premier League with a £36 million debt," added Julian Rhodes, on the club's frugal existence in League One. "So you get people expecting us to get back up there. But I knew with the budgets we had, that was a difficult challenge. I used to have regular meetings with the Bradford City Supporters Trust, and I remember telling them 'you do realise we are far more likely to be relegated from League One than we are promoted?'

"In the end, Colin was a victim of his own success. That first year he was in charge, at the end of October we were second. And because we missed out on promotion, people said it was narrow failure. But it wasn't. We were in admin when that season started, with just five players under contract, so he actually did quite well."

The legacy

For City, this dismal 2003/04 season and traumatic summer saw a line finally drawn in the sand over significant money problems. They were still hampered for many years by the foolish over-spending of the Premier League days, and the scars of 2002 and 2004 did not heal quickly; but there has been no serious suggestion that Administration Three would occur and, eventually league-wise, the club bottomed out before moving back upwards. They didn't achieve this by going with the kids – of the three youngsters who impressed against Wimbledon that day, only Tom Penford threatened to have a meaningful professional career – but the future has at least proven brighter than it worryingly appeared to be on that dark afternoon when they were relegated.

Indeed for all the sleepless nights and stress, Richard Wardell has fond memories of the fundraising efforts, and has built lasting friendships on the back of what he went through with others. He explained, "I remember three pairs of people including Andrew Ashcroft and myself completed a twelve-hour ground hop with the aim of visiting as many football grounds as possible, to raise money. The starting and finishing point was of course Valley Parade. I can't remember which pair visited the most grounds but I do know that between us we raised about £400 and it was also the day that Andrew and I commenced our friendship with Stephen Onions who participated in the ground hop. To this day, Andrew, Stephen and I still attend Bradford City games together.

"The 2004/05 season finally commenced on 7 August. I travelled with a Cath Tomlinson, who had become heavily involved in the fundraising efforts of the Trust, to Victoria Park home of Hartlepool United, where we met Andrew Ashcroft. Although we lost the game 2-1, after the summer months of fundraising, it was a relief to see Bradford City playing a league fixture."

A relief, and a chance to move on from an utterly wretched period for Bradford City. The lessons of 2000-2004 were brutal ones to take on board. The over-spending by Geoffrey Richmond was designed to secure a lasting place at the top table, yet instead it almost brought the club to its knees. Only a year out the Premier League City went into Administration One and yet, after seemingly surviving that ordeal, the dream of a return to the top flight lingered on for some, as exampled by Gordon Gibb's £1.5 million promotion bonus pledge. Administration Two was to put such wild fantasises firmly to bed, like a blast of water to the face that was designed to wake you up from a blissful day dream. City were still in a mess, City were still paying for their past mistakes.

The legacy is that, at Valley Parade, speculate to accumulate is an unwelcome mantra. 30 plus other clubs went the way of City going into administration (and all, after the Bantams' Administration Two, faced the extra punishment of league point deductions, after the Football League tightened up the rules in a bid to discourage clubs from attempting to live beyond their means), yet the club have largely remained in the black ever since. They have overspent on the playing budget sometimes, but only in a calculated manner – always with back up options if needed. On seasons they have gone for it with the budget, they have recouped the deficits later – occasionally through some tough measures. The point is that financial prudence has remained the order of the day. There were more falls to be had on the field after 2004 – as we will get to – but the subsequent rise back up has been done on a sensible and sound footing. No leasing of players, or carpets for that matter. No six weeks of madness. And although this greater level of sanity has not been enough to prevent the odd financial headache, it has been a much gentler ride, relative to the traumas of 2002 and 2004.

It's easy to pay lip service to the approach of living within your own means when there is no other option on offer; but in 2015 City fans were presented with an alternative vision and the reaction was mixed. Gianni Paladini – who was chairman at QPR during their 2011 rise to the Premier League – held advanced talks over buying the club. Due diligence took place, and all manner of speculation reigned over which of Paladini's rich friends were backing him; but when push came to shove he couldn't raise the funds he promised and the deal fell through. The talk was that City would have a £10 million transfer budget and a further £15 million would be set aside for wages. One well-known director told a friend of mine at the time "it's going to be a really exciting ride for you". The objective would be to climb the leagues, possibly replicating QPR's ascent to the top. It sounded enticing, but a large section of supporters held deep reservations over the prospect.

At QPR under Paladini, it looked like madness. Managers were hired and fired in quick succession; the turnover of players was considerable. Big wages were paid out to bring talented players to Loftus Road, but QPR supporters had to contend with huge hikes in ticket prices to pay for some of it, as Paladini and co attempted to rebrand the West London outfit as 'The Boutique Club'. Even with eye-watering tickets, QPR ran up huge debts. Without the Malaysian entrepreneur, Tony Fernandes – who bought the club after they reached the Premier League in 2011 – to prop up the losses, they would have been in significant financial trouble. Whilst some people welcomed the prospect of Paladini and his backers, others rejected the idea of the risks that might be involved pumping money into City in an unprofitable manner. When the deal fell through, not too many fans were upset.

Perhaps that's because many of us spent much of 2002 and 2004 considering the unthinkable – that City were going to fold, and what that might have been like. Their opponents on the day of relegation in April 2004 offer some indication of such a reality. Wimbledon joined City in League One in 2004/05; but with their feet under the table at Milton Keynes, they completed the rebrand by changing their name to MK Dons. Overwhelming evidence that a club's identity had been stolen; but for fans of the old Wimbledon, there was a stark choice: accept it and keep watching them in their new surroundings (some did), turn your back on football, or go and build your own club. Most Dons supporters chose the latter, and AFC Wimbledon were formed. They started at the bottom of the pyramid and in 2011 reached the Football League. But whilst this is an outstanding achievement, AFC Wimbledon are not the Wimbledon FC of old (nor, either, are MK Dons). Their Football League status is their ceiling. They are unlikely to ever recapture the glory days of top flight football and winning the FA Cup. And whilst Dons fans have had to come to terms with the way they were shafted and accept their new reality, it must still rankle and depress them at times.

Had Bradford City folded in 2004 there is little doubt that an AFC Bradford City would have been formed, starting in a similar position to AFC Wimbledon (the idea was floated amongst fans). They would not have played at Valley Parade of course (probably Keighley Cougars' Cougar Park, at first at least); but with strong support relative to their new rivals, they would have climbed the divisions quickly. They may have returned to the Football League, but again they would have been weaker compared to the one that reached the League Cup Final in 2013. But then AFC Wimbledon are the exception to the trend of clubs that have gone bust and being reformed by their supporters. The likes of Scarborough, Halifax, Chester and Darlington have not gone straight back up. And of course, on City's own doorstep is Bradford (Park Avenue), the first professional football club that Bradford lost.

The point is that it wouldn't have been the same. The story of Administration One was that of reckless over-spending on players. Administration Two, it can be argued, was about Valley Parade. For so many reasons that include May 11 1985, Valley Parade is such an intrinsic part of the Bradford City experience and the idea of a replacement club having to be reformed in its place, playing elsewhere, is difficult to fathom. Sure, many of us would have supported it and enjoyed non-league life, but it would have been no one's ideal scenario. Keeping Bradford City – our Bradford City – alive in 2004 was a remarkable achievement. Julian Rhodes was the savour, but so too were the fans. Without those fundraising efforts, there would be no club. The bond between us supporters and the club is so much stronger for it.

For City fans, every subsequent close season has been spent fretting about summer signings, rather than over the club's ongoing existence. The ups and downs of the club have almost entirely taken place in the right place – on the field. But no matter what the frustration of the day – such as a poor home defeat, an unpopular manager, or a failed promotion bid – a true sense of perspective has been maintained by just about every supporter. Amongst those fans who rallied behind the club during the summer of 2004, during its darkest hour of need, one truism has always remained since.

At least we still have a football club to support.

City (vs Wimbledon): Mark Paston, Peter Atherton (Tom Penford 58), Jason Gavin, David Wetherall, Paul Heckingbottom, Gareth Edds, Robert Wolleaston, Nicky Summerbee, Dean Windass (Kevin Sanasy 68), Michael Branch (Danny Forrest 58), Danny Cadamarteri

Subs not used: Alan Combe, Mark Bower

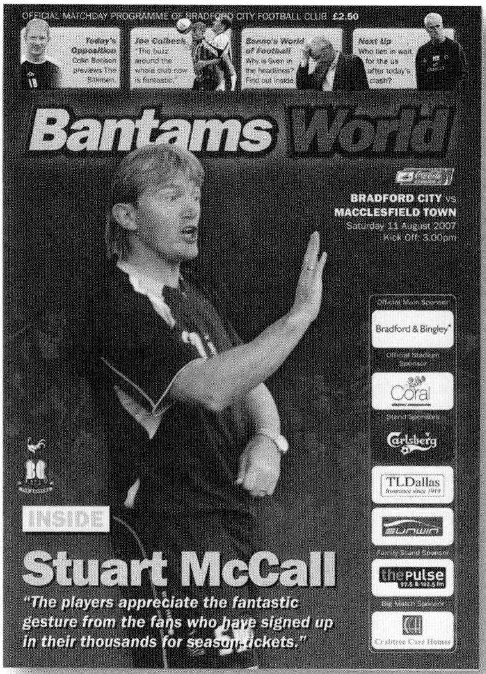

The (slow) rebirth of Bradford City

Bradford City vs Macclesfield Town

League Two, Saturday 11 August, 2007

Few people know Valley Parade as well as Stuart McCall. 395 appearances for the club, over two separate spells that collectively added up to ten years, means that this corner of West Yorkshire has become a home from home for arguably Bradford City's all-time most popular player. And yet as he made the very familiar walk from the dressing room to Valley Parade pitch on Saturday 11 August, 2007, everything was very different.

With thousands of eyes trained upon his every step, McCall slowly walked along the touchline and to the dugout, with loud applause ringing in his ears. He went to shake the hands of a couple of supporters immediately behind the City bench, before moving to the edge of the technical area so that everybody could see him. And then, he waved both of his arms in an upwards motion, before turning to face the main stand, the Kop and then the Midland Road stand. The message was clear to everyone of a claret and amber persuasion – he's back, and now he wants you to roar louder than ever.

Stuart McCall was home again. Not, this time, as a player – but as the Bradford City manager. This was his first job as a number one, and it was highly fitting for him to begin the next stage of his career at the same club where he started out as a player. After making his debut in 1982, McCall became a hero and legend over six years of Bantam progressivism. He left in 1988 to pursue his ambitions of playing in the top flight, only to return in 1998 and lead Bradford City to the Premier League. He departed City again in 2002 just before his 38th birthday, with the club – on the verge of going into administration the first time around – unable to afford to offer him another contract. But he was far from finished as a player, moving to Sheffield United and playing an integral part in the Blades reaching two major cup semi finals and the play off final in the same season. McCall finally retired in 2004 – fittingly his last game was at Valley Parade in a reserve team match – and stayed on at Bramall Lane as coach, learning from the vastly experienced Neil Warnock.

Now feeling ready to become a manager in his own right, the emotional pull of the job vacancy at Valley Parade was too much. Even though McCall had ended the previous season as a Premier League assistant manager (to Warnock), he was prepared to drop right down to the bottom tier to cut his teeth. The third coming of Stuart McCall was about to begin on that baking hot August afternoon, as the Bantams prepared to launch the 2007/08 season with a visit from Macclesfield Town.

The SOS call

And how badly McCall's presence and inspiration was needed. It had been a hugely difficult few years for Bradford City, as the rebuilding of the club following the second spell of administration in 2004 proved to be slow and far from plain sailing. After the Bantams were relegated in 2003/04, their time in the third tier proved tough, as stagnation threatened to take hold of the club. For two-and-a-half years in League One, City didn't move backwards but yet couldn't move forwards either. They appeared to be stuck in a state of League One mid-table flux. Good enough to avoid relegation, but not good enough to push for the play offs. Crowds dwindled, and excitement was in short supply. After the horrors of 2002 and 2004 we supporters were, of course, grateful to still have a football club to support. But, eventually, ambition returned, prompting a growing sense of dissatisfaction about the status quo. We hadn't survived from drowning in a sea of debt, merely to tread water forever.

This prompted mixed views on the manager who had taken over from Bryan Robson, after the former England and Manchester United star turned down the opportunity to continue in the hotseat following relegation to League One in 2004. Colin Todd – Robson's assistant – took the reins, and initially did a commendable job applying the brakes to City's fall down the leagues and in steadying the ship. Todd was unable to build upon that – vastly undermined by the lack of resources available – and it didn't take long for some to argue that stability wasn't exactly sexy.

At the start of 2006/07 – Todd's third in charge – City started well and raised hopes of a promotion push. By autumn, form collapsed and, once again, a mid-table finish looked the most likely scenario. The money problems hadn't gone away either; and in January Julian Rhodes had to take the very difficult decision of selling City's biggest asset – Jamaican winger Jermaine Johnson – to raise much-needed money, and to loan out top scorer Dean Windass to his hometown club Hull in return for a substantial loan fee. Not for the first time, Todd had to resort to the loan market to replace his two best players. But with form slipping and with City having fallen from fourth in October to sixteenth in February, Rhodes decided to take action and sack his manager. A 1-0 defeat to Gillingham was Todd's last game in charge.

Julian Rhodes explained to me, "Colin was a victim of his own success. That first year he was in charge, at the end of October we were second. And because we missed out on promotion, people said it was narrow failure. But it wasn't. We were in admin when that season started, with just five players under contract, so he actually did quite well. After that, I think expectations were much higher. Colin did well to keep us in the top half of the division for quite a while, but he wasn't popular with a section of supporters and ultimately they are the people who pay the money. I think Colin would have preferred it if I had kept him in charge until the end of the third season and then we made the change, and to be fair I had just sold his two best players; but I felt that we needed some kind of change of impetus. We had only won something like three from the past 20 games. People say we were only mid-table [when Todd was sacked], but at the end of September we had been fourth and then went on a horrendous run."

David Wetherall – the club's captain and a hugely influential player – was appointed caretaker manager. As gambles go it failed miserably. City's form nosedived. Wetherall was faced with the dual challenge of managing and playing, and found he was unable to focus on his own performances. Without him, the back four struggled badly. Within weeks of Todd's departure, City had fallen into the relegation zone. It looked within their hands to get out of it, and Wetherall did deliver the occasional good result, but a failure to win a home game from December onwards was largely their undoing. Two of their final three games were against relegation rivals Leyton Orient (home) and Chesterfield (away). They toiled well against Orient but missed chance-after-chance, ultimately going down 2-0. At Chesterfield the players didn't turn up, and were swept aside 3-0 by a team who simply wanted it more. It meant the Bantams were demoted to the bottom tier of English football for the first time in 25 years. It was also a third relegation in the space of seven seasons. Never before had the club fallen so quickly.

Mark Bower reflected on this difficult period for the dressing room, and in particular coping without Windass and Johnson. "It's just football and you've got to deal with it, but unfortunately as a group of players we didn't deal with it well enough at the time. But I don't think relegation that season was down solely to one player leaving or the manager going, I just think that as players we played really poorly. That was certainly the case with me, and unfortunately that carried on into next season."

I was part of the sell out away crowd at Saltergate, Chesterfield on the day of City's relegation. It was such a painful and wretched afternoon, as you watched your players fold so meekly. The Telegraph & Argus' Simon Parker was scathing of the players, telling me, "That Chesterfield game was a disgrace. They just rolled over. There were a few games like that towards the end of that season, but at Chesterfield they never turned up."

All season long, almost half the team had been made up of loan players and it had been difficult to identify with the team. During the summer before, the club had seemingly been boosted by the prospect of significant investment from Peter Etherington – father of former West Ham and Stoke player Matthew – but a delay in finalising the finances prevented Todd from making signings. The Etherington deal fell through just one week before the season began, and it was again left to Julian Rhodes to solely fund the club. Todd did end up with a decent budget, but at such a late stage of pre-season the loan market was over utilised. The January loss of Jermaine Johnson and Dean Windass couldn't be compensated for by the rest of the team, and some of City's own players suffered dips in form at the worst possible time. At Chesterfield, Steven Schumacher left the field in tears as he was showered with boos from City fans, who felt the young midfielder had let the club down with his performances during the run-in. Wetherall was also crying as he walked off, but received a much more positive reception. Eventually we headed out of the wooden away stand and into the housing estate around the ground. It was a sunny April afternoon, and there was an eerie silence (Chesterfield, despite their victory, had been relegated too, due to other results). From the highs of Premier League survival in 2000 to yet another low point. Two administrations and now three relegations. When would the misery come to an end? How much further could the club sink? Not for the first time in recent years, I worried over the future of Bradford City Football Club.

It was against this backdrop that the SOS call to Stuart grew even louder. Earlier in the 2006/07 campaign, McCall had announced his desire to take the first step into management at the end of the season. Such words were music to the ears of many City fans, who longed for his return as manager. The criticism of Todd – and his teams – was that there was a lack of passion. And as the grumbles over his tenure grew during the 2005/06 season, calls for McCall or Peter Beagrie to be installed as manager increased. At the end of 2006/07, as we watched our club be relegated on a whimper, the passion and never-say-attitude that Stuart McCall personified as a player was achingly desired. All we wanted was a team of Stuart McCalls; and logically he was surely the right man to build it. To unite an increasingly disunited football club. To reverse the tide.

Stuart McCall told me, "I was assistant manager at Sheffield United. We had an up and down time in the Premier League, and then with about half a dozen games to go I got a call from Julian Rhodes. We had been on a team building day at Cheltenham and were travelling back on the coach when the call came. It was on an evening when Bradford had won 3-2 at Bristol City and I was so over the moon for them when I had checked my phone, as it meant there was hope for them. Julian asked me what my situation was going to be at the end of the season and if I might be interested in the job. I said to him it is something I would think about as it is about time I started thinking about becoming a manager."

Michael Wood, editor of the long-running City website boyfrombrazil.co.uk, told me just how much McCall was wanted at the time. "The key message the club was attempting to give out in that summer was that Bradford City were moving away from a coldness that was associated with Colin Todd's time at Valley Parade and towards something new. With that in mind it is not a huge leap to imagine 2007 starting with Peter Jackson or John Hendrie as manager in much the same way it did McCall. Of course McCall occupies the highest rung in the Pantheon at the club but the same campaigns to bring people back could have – and I think would have – carried on without McCall."

Two weeks after the Bantams' relegation was sealed at Saltergate – on the day of which McCall recalled driving past City fans on their way to Derbyshire, and stopping to wish them luck – Sheffield United themselves were relegated on the final day of the Premier League campaign. Neil Warnock stepped down as manager, throwing up the possibility that McCall might take over at Bramall Lane. But instead Sheffield United opted to bring in Bryan Robson of all people. McCall was let go, and quickly agreed to take over at Valley Parade. A two-year contract was signed by McCall in-between two lorries at the Hartshead Moor service station, just outside Bradford, on the M62, where he and Rhodes met to seal the deal.

McCall explained, "At Sheffield United on the last day of the season we get robbed! Everything that could go wrong went us against us. Neil was sacked. I had been groomed to become Neil's replacement. When at one point it looked like he was going to leave Sheffield United for Portsmouth, it looked like I might take over. Neil left in unhappy circumstances, and they ended up with Bryan Robson. They wanted me to go for an interview for the job, but I sensed that I wasn't going to get it.

"Julian convinced me that so many teams who go down to League Two had come straight back up. I looked at the fanbase and the fact it was a club I wanted to be part of, so I said yes to the chance. I remember I was due to go on holiday, and I gave Julian my word that I would become the manager. But he was worried and said 'what if you change your mind on holiday?' I assured him I wouldn't, but in the end we arranged to meet up at a service station on the M62 and I signed a contract in-between some lorries. I went on holiday and somehow the news broke. In the end I didn't have a holiday."

Simon Parker had the inside track on the developments and highlighted the key role that Neil Warnock played in shaping McCall's future, "Julian had been hinting about getting McCall in. He kept hinting at it and so I asked him how he would react if I ran stories about it and he said 'well I'm not going to come out and say you are wrong'. So I started to run stories about it. At the time we thought he would get the Sheffield United job and that Neil Warnock would step aside. But Warnock did City a massive favour by basically shafting Stuart. When he stepped down, instead of recommending Stuart I think he basically told their chairman that he wasn't sure if Stuart was ready. No one could have blamed Stuart if he had turned down City for Sheffield United because at the time they were two divisions apart. Once it became obvious he wouldn't get that job, he took the one at City.

"As far as Julian was concerned, Stuart was the only person he wanted, to lift the place. There was no other candidate. I remember driving home one day and Julian rang me. I missed his call but he left an answerphone message and it was just one word long. 'Yes!' So I went home and put it on the website that Stuart McCall would be taking over."

The ticket revolution

As McCall swung his arms in front of the dugout prior to his first game in charge, gesturing for the crowd to roar, we all duly obliged and the noise was fantastic. Bradford City might have been relegated the season before, but here to mark the start of the season was a crowd that was six thousand higher than the previous campaign's average. 13,401 people had made their way through the Valley Parade turnstiles for the visit of little old Macclesfield Town – it was by some distance the biggest crowd in League Two that day. And it was to be no flash in the pan either. The trend of dwindling Valley Parade crowds, over the previous seven years, was being reversed.

Back in January – and with Todd still as the manager – Julian Rhodes had caused a major stir. The traditional announcement of season ticket prices for the following campaign was very different from before. No price increase, no price freeze – instead, a commitment to cut the cost of watching Bradford City in half. Rhodes offered the Bradford public a special deal. If 10,000 people pledged to buy a season ticket, they would be priced at just £138 – a massive difference to the £276 cost of the season before.

It was an imaginative and bold step by Rhodes, one that would change the club in the long-term. In Bradford, a city with economic and social struggle, watching professional football would become more affordable to its population. £6 a game, the deal would work out at. With crowds averaging between 6,000-8,000 over the three years of League One, but Valley Parade's capacity 25,000, the atmosphere had been poor for years. And the rows and rows of empty seats added to the impression that this club was not only badly under-achieving, but ultimately likely to die. It seemed so implausible to believe that anyone, beyond hardcore fans of many years, would want to come to Valley Parade to watch the team struggle on. Not with £276 season tickets or matchday tickets priced at £20.

There were no guarantees that a 10,000 pledge could be achieved, especially against the backdrop of Todd's dismissal, Wetherall's struggles to juggle two roles and a doomed battle against relegation, but Rhodes went ahead with the offer anyway. The trump card up his sleeve was Stuart McCall. Securing Bradford City's greatest modern-day player captured the imagination of the sporting public, just as McCall's return as player in 1998 created a huge buzz around the city. As it was, the 10,000 target was well and truly smashed – more than 12,000 people ended up buying a season ticket. There was a real sense of achievement in the fact the club had gambled their trust in the area's appetite to watch professional football. In the immediate aftermath of the season ticket offer announcement, there were plenty of people quick to claim Rhodes had got it wrong, but he was proven right. With many League Two clubs averaging three thousand crowds or less, such big attendances were sure to be a major advantage during the battles ahead.

The third and final source of close season good news was belated investment in the shape of long-standing supporter and successful businessman, Mark Lawn. The co-creator of the Driver Hire franchise business, Lawn had initially expressed an interest in investing into City when Peter Etherington was in advanced talks to buy half the club from Rhodes. On that occasion Lawn stepped back, but a year on and with Rhodes still flying solo, Lawn bought 49% of the club. This meant that City finally had the resources to compete with their rivals, and wouldn't have to be so over-reliant on the loan market.

Rhodes reflected of Lawn's arrival, "It was massive. You look at major things that have happened over the last fourteen years – that was up there. We were down in the bottom division. At this point, most of the debts were sorted. But we still had a lack of money and we needed more. We still had the shop and office building rent, which was a drain. Mark came in May and some of his money paid the wages of the players about two hours later. His investment gave us a platform of being able to set bigger break-even player budgets. Mark, the cheap season tickets, and Stuart's arrival that summer all gave us a new lease of life. From a personal selfish point of view, Mark helped me out no end. It was someone else to share the burden. I'm not sure he thanks me for it! I think he thought running a football club would be a lot easier than it was. But I think he enjoys it!"

Along with Lawn came David Baldwin – another City fan who had enjoyed success in the world of business, who Lawn coaxed out of early retirement to take a look at City's commercial activities and instigate improvements. Baldwin assumed the role of head of operations, and he would become a hugely influential figure, right up until leaving Valley Parade for a similar job at Burnley in 2014. He told me of his 2007 arrival, "I sold a company in 2001 and moved to Spain full time to retire. It had been a stressful few years before that. I've been a City fan all of my life, and I was on the books as a schoolboy. One of my friends is Mark Ellis, and while I was in Spain I did a charity fundraiser for some boys from one of the inner city colleges in Leeds, where they came out to Malaga and trained on the pitches there. I played in a charity match against the college team with Mark Ellis, John Hendrie, Stuart McCall, Terry Dolan and Mark Lawn.

"And it came about that Mark Lawn was a mutual friend of Mark Ellis, and they had known each other for many years. I got chatting to Mark Lawn and said to him 'I'm in a position where I've got time on my hands in Spain, if the club ever needed assistance I'm always happy to help because I'm from Bradford'. And basically Mark Lawn flew out to Spain, prior to taking up the reins at Bradford City, and we went for a coffee. He told that he was looking to buy into Bradford, he knew a bit about my background and felt that I could apply my skill set at the club. He asked me to come over for six weeks in order to provide a fresh overview of the commercial side of things."

Reflecting on the state of the club, off the field, when he came in, David continued, "I think it was still recovering from the aftermath of the first spell of administration. There was very few operational staff in the building. It was a very reactive environment in terms of dealing with enquiries and issues. The key was to turn it into a proactive environment in the first place. I made a joke that, with regards to the commercial and marketing desk, we first had to polish the dust away!" He added of the relationship between the two chairmen, "They are chalk and cheese as characters. The one thing I would say is that each takes their areas of responsibility and understands the strengths of the other. For example Julian is a relatively private man, and so he is happy to let Mark do the front of house. On the other side of things Julian is very knowledgeable on the finances and on the player contract element side of things. If Julian recommends something Mark will always support his view on it, and that's a good thing."

McCall, Lawn, Baldwin and – after luring him from Halifax to become the assistant manager – Wayne Jacobs. The mantra became that Bradford City was now being run by Bradford City fans and people who held the club dearly to their hearts. With all of these factors added together, it was easy to be swept up into believing that the home game with Macclesfield Town was the beginning of a bright new dawn. That promotion would occur instantly, and that a season in League Two would be a minor blip – the final chapter of a dreadfully difficult period in the club's history.

That this was going to be the start of something very special.

Reality bites

In so many ways, the outcome of McCall's first match in charge would set the tone for his full tenure as manager. There were big, big expectations – but the reality was that the bar was set too high, and it was something that his teams struggled to live up to. Promotion to League One was the be all and end all, but in two-and-a-half years at the helm, McCall was unable to even get City into the play offs. From day one he made no attempt to play down the pressure to deliver instant success, telling the Telegraph & Argus in June 2007, "I will see myself as a failure if I don't get the club up at the first attempt, and I've got the strongest desire anyone could possibly have to achieve that. I know I'm there to be shot at but that's how I feel."

Looking back on it years later, McCall told me, "A lot of people told me when I took the job: don't let your heart rule your head. But I remember thinking that the club had sunk as low as it could and the only way was upwards. Yet I came in after my holiday and found that I had only eight players on the books – but that those eight players took up half the budget." Many of McCall's predecessors would smile at that statement. Ever since the six weeks of madness in 2000 [chapter six], Bradford City managers have had to contend with the issue of inheriting players who were on relatively high wages that took up a huge percentage of the overall budget. When it came to making new signings, they would be forced to rummage through bargain buckets and bring in players that, all too often, weren't up the job. Yet the public perception from the crowd would often be that the manager had the overall resources to do better than they were, rather than acknowledging the unevenness of the budget. It was a seemingly never-ending spiral.

Beyond the budget issues, the problem for McCall was two-fold: not only was he a rookie in the job, learning about the role as he went along, he simply didn't know the division that City had fallen into. Not since starting out with City in the early 1980s had McCall played at this level, and the previous few years coaching and assisting Neil Warnock at Sheffield United meant he was focusing on players and teams of a much different standard. It wasn't that McCall underestimated the challenge at hand – he also told the Telegraph & Argus that June, "I don't know the division, I'm going to have to quickly to get to know the players and what we are going to be up against" – but he was facing a steep learning curve. Not only in terms of figuring out how to beat opposition teams at this level, but in bringing in the right players to succeed.

A look at McCall's summer transfer activity and starting line up against Macclesfield was a case in point. McCall did well in the striker stakes, bringing in Peter Thorne from Norwich City and journeyman forward Barry Conlon. Thorne – injured on the opening day – was City's top scorer for two seasons in a row. In total he netted 32 goals from 84 appearances, and was an all-round class act. Conlon had his critics and was ultimately frozen out by McCall eighteen months later, but when his mind was right he produced some strong performances and netted important goals. McCall recalled, "I brought in Peter Thorne and Barry Conlon as strikers. I didn't know Peter but I knew how much he was on at Norwich. He had been thinking of retiring. He was probably the best signing I made. Everyone told me that we needed a big centre forward at this level. I looked at a few people and in the end I settled on Barry Conlon. It didn't always work for him but he did well at times. He had his moments."

Elsewhere, McCall brought back former City players Paul Heckingbottom and Paul Evans – who endured dreadfully disappointing campaigns. Alongside Evans in midfield, McCall entrusted Scott Phelan (an Everton reject who looked well short at this level), Eddie Johnson (a Colin Todd signing who struggled for consistency), Joe Colbeck (a youngster emerging through the ranks) and Alex Rhodes (an erratic winger). Despite the aforementioned issue of their relatively high wages, McCall was fortunate to inherit David Wetherall, Mark Bower, Donovan Ricketts and Omar Daley, but overall quality was in limited supply. Of the XI that started against Macclesfield, only Daley and Conlon would either still be playing for the club, or in the first team, by the following season.

Macclesfield Town were also a perfect embodiment of the considerable strength of League Two. The season before, they had looked completely doomed to relegation, only to recruit Paul Ince as manager and narrowly survive the drop. Ince departed for MK Dons and Ian Brightwell came in as his replacement. The bookies had Macclesfield Town as one of the favourites to be relegated, and their starting line up at Valley Parade contained just one player that most of City's bumper crowd would have heard of. Yet only nine minutes into McCall's welcome home party, it was the Silkmen who opened the scoring. Full back Carl Regan picked up the ball on the half way line and charged through a City midfield that had committed too many bodies forward. Paul Evans lunged in to tackle Regan, but missed the ball – a worrying sign of the season that was in store for the Welsh midfielder – and striker Francis Green was given too much space to expertly fire the ball into the bottom corner, right in front of Macclesfield's tiny away following in the Bradford End. The 13,000 City fans were silent and the players struggled to get going. So early into the new era, that positive mood had been punctured.

Indeed it was a strange afternoon, which I spent sat in the Midland Road stand. It was an amazing sight to see Valley Parade so full after years of being largely empty on a match day; but the atmosphere didn't initially take off. A lot of new people, or lapsed supporters, were seemingly getting used to the experience of going. Long-standing fans, who had endured years of struggle and in particular year-on-year appalling home records, continued to be quick in getting on the players' backs. This wasn't a united and coherent crowd just yet, even though it was to have a telling influence on the game's outcome.

Four minutes before half time, a scramble in the Macclesfield Town penalty area saw the ball fall to

City's on-loan Congolese frontman Guylain Ndumbu-Nsungu, who went down very easily under the challenge of Kevin McIntyre. Three sides of the ground screamed for a penalty and referee Graham Horwood – making his Football League debut – blew for a spot kick. Macclesfield Town protested vigorously with Ian Brightwell later claiming Horwood was "bullied the whole game" by the crowd. Even McCall would later admit it wasn't a penalty, but he wasn't complaining about the help that City had received from their own fans in pressurising the official. As Simon Parker wrote in his Telegraph & Argus match report, "Take a bow, supporters. If that's the effect that boasting an attendance figure far too big for League Two will have on some officials, let's have more of it."

Barry Conlon took the penalty kick, only for his tame effort to be tipped away by Keighley-born Macclesfield stopper, Tommy Lee. It didn't matter, as Ndumbu-Nsungu was on hand to tap home the rebound. And with that, the McCall era had lift off. In the second half City produced a much improved display. Alex Rhodes – who won the man of the match award – tormented his full back on the left wing, with Omar Daley a menace on the right. In total, City had 21 shots on goal over the 90 minutes. Conlon spurned two further good opportunities – local lad Lee was in excellent form to deny him. Late on Daley was played through one-on-one by Conlon. The Jamaican's low effort flew past Lee, but bounced back off the outside of the post. Paul Evans also struck a couple of free kicks that narrowly missed the target. The inflated crowd responded well to the pressure City exerted, and continued to cheer them on to the end, but there was to be no late winner. The game finished 1-1.

I remember a feeling of anti-climax leaving the ground at full time. After the misery of relegation and fearing for the club's existence, it had been such an exciting summer and everyone was so anxious to get started. But whilst the large crowd and McCall's big entrance were memorable moments, the day didn't quite live up to the hype, or take off in the way that we had all assumed it would. Macclesfield were left to defend for large periods, but they weren't a bad side. Perhaps after the previous two relegations we should have learned not to assume that City would steamroller the weaker opposition of the league below. As for the huge crowds and big stadium scaring the visiting team, Macclesfield wouldn't be the last team to look inspired to play on such a grand stage.

Nevertheless Stuart McCall was not downhearted, stating in the Telegraph & Argus after the match, "Overall I was reasonably happy with the performance and we tried to entertain the fans. Chances-wise we deserved it but because of the penalty decision it was probably a fair result." 'Bradford regain feelgood factor' was The Observer headline of the game and that was certainly how Julian Rhodes saw it, as he told the Telegraph & Argus, "The atmosphere made the hairs on the back of the neck stand up. When we started the season ticket scheme, I never imagined it would be as good as this."

Michael Wood recalled, "Perhaps I was out of step because I doubted the season would be an easy one, but the bullish nature of the talk coming out of Valley Parade seemed to suggest that many people did. The club seemed to badly underestimate how difficult League Two would be to the extent where collectively they seemed to believe that City were favoured in the division. Perhaps we can put this down to seats sold or the recent stay in the Premier League but there seemed to be a sense that City had only to turn up to win. This is never true." Indeed, McCall was the first and not the last City manager to realise that playing in the division's largest stadium could be a hindrance, given it inspired opposition players to put in their best performances. Simon Parker said, "Every team who came to Valley Parade raised their game. Teams like Dagenham used to play like Barcelona. They'd come up on the train the morning of the match, have a Burger King after the match back at Leeds station, and then go back home again with the three points. It was ridiculous."

Stuart McCall added, "I remember one time going to watch Barnet at Chester on a Tuesday night. It was a dreadful game and Barnet were terrible. They came to Valley Parade on the Saturday and I remember walking past them as they come up some steps and they were going on about how wonderful the stadium was. It was their Wembley. And although we drew the game with them, I remember they played really well and it was a totally different performance to the one they had given at Chester a few days earlier.

"Instead of inspiring our players, Valley Parade used to inspire the opposition."

Third time unlucky

No one wanted to succeed as a Bradford City manager more than Stuart McCall. His intensity and passion for the job was evident to everyone. He kicked and headed every ball on the touchline, and was known to spend hours upon hours scouring over match videos, opposition and tactics. He made a point of learning the name of every single youngster in the academy, right down to the lowest age group. As fans, we were desperate to see him deliver success too. It would have meant so much more to achieve things with McCall at the helm. For that reason he was granted a longer honeymoon period than other City managers have enjoyed – from both supporters and the board. There was always a fear of how painful it would prove if this didn't work; no one really wanted to contemplate a Stuart McCall managerial failure.

But ultimately it wasn't to be. In McCall's first season in charge, it quickly became apparent that the team he had constructed was not good enough to challenge for promotion, and that he needed to be given leeway to make and learn from his mistakes. In September and into October, McCall's City lost five games in a row to fall to fourth bottom of the league. This run included the truly appalling 3-0 home defeat to League Two minnows Accrington Stanley. The East Lancashire team were magnificent at Valley Parade, but shambolic defending and goalkeeping contributed to their easy victory. Gallows humour emanated from the crowd that evening, as the Kop resorted to chanting "Let's pretend we've scored a goal" and jokingly celebrated fake Bradford City goals. Suddenly, even £6-per-game season tickets weren't looking quite such a bargain.

McCall turned it around and brought in players on loan who made a positive difference, but they still weren't good enough to seriously threaten the play off places, finishing the season tenth. He admitted, "In the first season I remember getting beaten 3-0 by Accrington – that was a low point. We had a run in the middle of the season but we were never close enough to the play offs." McCall's sense of disappointment was obvious at the time, as he clearly struggled to cope with losing. Simon Parker added, "Stuart really took defeat personally and some days he looked haggard. Every manager when they lose says they go home and have a bad weekend and I'm sure they do, but he seemed to take it so personally."

The year after, the feeling was that McCall now had the experience and League Two know-how to deliver promotion, and Mark Lawn elected to loan the club a further £1 million that was used to expand the transfer budget. With the cheap season ticket initiative continued – albeit with a slightly reduced uptake – the big crowds continued. McCall said, "In the second season, I had built a list of targets: Graeme Lee, Paul McLaren and Michael Boulding – and I got them all. They cost a bit of money and I remember in pre-season thinking 'we've got a chance here'. It was a top five budget. I think the worst thing that happened that season was we got off to such a good start. We were top of the league for a bit, and in the top three. We played some really good football, and there was a buzz. It was going great. I remember we won at Gillingham and their chairman said we were the best team they had seen by a mile."

This time, until the middle of March at least, City looked the real deal – fighting at the top end of the table and in contention to take one of the three automatic promotion places. At the very least, they looked destined to make the play offs. Alas, form deserted them at the worst possible time. McCall continued, "We lost Omar Daley and Joe Colbeck for spells through injury which hurt us. We went to Notts County and lost 3-1 and some of our fans chanted at the players 'you're not fit to wear the shirt'. And I think that affected some of our players – even the experienced ones. When you look at City's promotions in 1996 and 2013, the team made strong ends to the season and had everyone behind them. We went the other way in this season. I remember feeling sick after the Notts County game. We were poor, but we were still in the play offs."

But not for long. McCall and City won the next two matches, but then went nine games without a win, dropping from automatic promotion contention to outside the play offs. A key factor in the sudden collapse of form was an off-the-field issue involving Barry Conlon and defender Matt Clarke. City had faced three away games in a row and lost the first, 3-0, to promotion rivals Rochdale. Next up was a double header down South, yet the day after the Rochdale defeat Conlon and Clarke went on an all-day drinking session, taking along the young Joe Colbeck with them. Conlon and Clarke were left out of the first of those two Southern games, at Exeter, as punishment. Exeter won the game. Simon Parker recalled that McCall took this indiscipline very badly, "The club were desperately trying to hush it up, but you knew that it had a massive effect. I think it hit Stuart particularly hard as I don't think he could believe how people could be so unprofessional at such a crucial stage in the season. They have a chance of promotion and then the players go and do that. I think he took it very personally."

After the Exeter defeat Conlon and Clarke were brought back into the fold but the crisis grew deeper, with a 4-1 loss at Bournemouth on the Tuesday night. McCall – who had signed a new contract in February, but who was now under pressure from a small section of supporters – told BBC Radio Leeds after the game, "If we don't finish in the play offs I don't deserve to be here, I will walk". Parker continued, "They were absolutely dreadful. There was a slanging match on the pitch after the game between Conlon and Rhys Evans. At that point Stuart first threatened to walk away. It was all heat of the moment but a manager wanting to walk away. They were still in there, but you realised it was really getting to him."

A dismal 3-0 loss at Dagenham in April, with three games to go, all but confirmed City couldn't make the play offs. I was stood in the away end that day and at full time a devastated McCall walked over to the supporters to apologise – he looked a broken man. He then went to the press box and told the Telegraph & Argus, "I just feel I've let everyone down; the club, the fans, my own family – even my little lad, who thought it was nailed on that we were going to Wembley." It could have been different that day, had Peter Thorne not had a perfectly good goal for the Bantams ruled out when the score was 0-0. McCall added to me, "At Dagenham the referee came afterwards and apologised to me – I could have ripped his head off. That was the defeat that killed it off for us, and he said 'I believe I have made a mistake. I've seen it again and it's a mistake. I'm sorry'. I was nearly in tears at the time."

Having answered City's SOS call two years earlier, it was time for City fans to return the favour. Rather than allow him to walk away as he had promised, supporters held up signs at the final home game that read 'S.O.S - Save our Stuart', begging him to stay on. Overwhelmed by the support, McCall agreed to continue and even took a pay cut. It was his heart ruling his head, "I didn't think I was going to come back as manager. I thought it was the right time to go. I'd had my two years and we should have reached the play offs that season. Not getting into the play offs cost us £250k, because we would have had a home game and TV money. The budget then got slashed. And I knew that next year's budget wasn't going to match the year before.

"At the last game of the season there were banners of support asking me to stay. I didn't want to walk away and have people thinking I'd spent the money and just left. I felt it was the coward's way out. So although I knew next year was going to be tough I stayed on. I took a 20% wage deduction because I knew that other people's jobs were getting cut. So I voluntarily took a cut to save other people. But then they asked others like Wayne Jacobs to do the same."

Michael Wood stated, "Stuart McCall got a great number of things right as manager as evidenced by the arrest in the club's decline while he was manager. More than anything Stuart McCall got the question of if he should stay beyond his second season – and promised resignation – absolutely right. The mind struggles to recall the hasty Save Our Stuart appeal to the manager who had declared that he would leave the club following a failure to win promotion in his second season, but that moment was a significant display of the Bradford City community's belief in the direction the club should take.

"That the fans spoke at the end of the second season and requested McCall stay at the club – not in unison but with a common voice – was the community going against – so it seemed – the wishes of members of the boardroom. There was a desire to get rid of McCall after two seasons which supporters did not share. Those members of the boardroom were not allowed to get what they wanted over the will of the community of Bradford City supporters. It was right that McCall listened to the will of the Bradford City community rather than malcontents in the boardroom."

David Baldwin refutes this suggestion that the board wanted McCall to leave at the end of the second season, "My recollection was that there was no doubt that we wanted him to stay. Stuart initially offered his resignation at Bournemouth, where he went over to supporters after the game. He was bitterly disappointed about the way the team had started to perform. He wore his heart on his sleeve and had so much passion for the club. It was a tough task going into the third season, but there was certainly no desire from the board to accept that resignation."

With a reduced budget for 2009/10, McCall dipped into the local non-league scene for new recruits, most notably bringing in a Guiseley forward named James Hanson following a strong recommendation by former City winger and ex-Stuart team-mate Mark Ellis. As a kid, Hanson had been on the books at Huddersfield Town but was released and later had a trial at Bradford City that led to similar rejection – his chances of impressing were not helped by both clubs trying out the big striker as a left back. Hanson retreated into the non-league scene and took up a job in Idle Co-op. Yet he would make a notable impact at first Bolton Woods and then Eccleshill United, where he would catch the eye of Terry Dolan and Ellis.

Hanson explained to me, "When I was at Huddersfield as a youngster I was playing left back, which is totally not my position, so I wasn't enjoying it really anyway. It was a sigh of relief when they released me, because it enabled me to go and enjoy my football again. I played with my mates and played in the position that I wanted to play, the one that I had been scouted for. I felt like I never got a chance to play in my position at Huddersfield, so I went back to Sunday League and started enjoying it. Luckily the team that I was playing for on a Sunday had a Saturday side as well, so they came and watched me, put me on the bench a few times when I was sixteen, and I started to work my way up from that really."

Eccleshill were drawn to play Guiseley – at the time managed by Dolan and Ellis – in a West Riding Cup game. Dolan and Ellis were impressed by what they saw of the striker, and took Hanson to Nethermoor and, eventually, to another trial at Bradford City in the summer of 2009. Hanson continued, "It was down to Terry that I got a chance to play at a higher level than Eccleshill. Once I found my feet at Guiseley I was scoring quite regularly. Mark Ellis always said that, with the situation that Bradford City were in at the time, there could be a chance for me to have a trial with them during the summer. It depended on which route they wanted to go down. I think they had splashed out the money that season but failed to get promoted. So Mark said they might be cutting the budget and that there could be a chance for a couple of non-league players to get a trial there.

"All summer I was getting told I was going to go on trial there, but I had a summer holiday booked. It was bad timing because I think I missed the first four or five days of pre-season training. So I had to make sure I had a good level of fitness to build on. I came in and then a couple of days later I was playing in a friendly against Burnley, so it was a massive shock really."

Hanson impressed Stuart McCall during that game against Burnley, he played in other friendlies, eventually earning a contract offer from the manager. Yet despite the opportunity of playing professional football, Hanson – still working at the Co-op – admitted he was very hesitant about taking it up. "It sounds a bit silly now, but I wasn't sure about it at the time because the money they offered was significantly lower than what I was earning at the time. They also had Peter Thorne, Michael Boulding and a couple of strikers. But I spoke to my dad and he said 'you've just got to back yourself; it's not about the money, you have a chance to have a career doing something you love doing'. So I took the gamble and thankfully it paid off."

Indeed Hanson was a huge success story of the 2009/10 season, ultimately winning the player of the season award. "Stuart McCall was a massive influence. He was a great man-manager, and he would keep giving me confidence boosts. I felt confident playing under him." Yet it was a short-lived player-manager relationship. For despite lower resources, the expectation to get promoted remained and – with that prospect looking increasingly remote – McCall continue to harbour thoughts about leaving. He explained, "I set about trying to build a young side in the third season, and we got in players like James Hanson and Steve Williams. We had a terrible start and hadn't scored in four games, and then we went to Cheltenham and were 4-2 up. But they got it back to 5-4 and in the last minute had a great chance to make it 5-5. And I said to Martin Allen [the then-Cheltenham manager] after the game 'if you'd have equalised I would have packed up'."

That win helped City to go on a run, and they were in the promotion shake-up early doors. McCall said, "We went ten games unbeaten although drew too many. But there were positive signs and big James Hanson was doing well." Sadly, it fell away over December and January, and McCall's third spell at the club was heading towards a sad end. He said, "The season began unravelling. We tried to stick together and there was no pressure from the club, but in early January I said that if we didn't win three of our next four games I would go. The first of those games was at Lincoln and we lost. And then next week we went to Torquay United. We were absolutely rotten in that game and went 1-0 down, and I questioned whether the players were playing for me. But then Gareth Evans scored two late goals to win it. And after the 90th minute winner, every player ran to me and jumped on me. In the dressing room after the game I remember I had to go and hide in the toilets because I was crying. I was that emotional. I then walked back into the changing room with the players gathered round and said 'ssh a minute'. I pointed to Evans and said 'you! You think you've done well today – well you've just put me and my family through another week of hell!' We got the players a lot of beer for the bus journey home that day, as I knew it was probably going to my last away journey."

And it proved to be the case. The next week saw a 1-0 home defeat to Bury that left City sixteenth and twelve points off the play offs – "They had one shot on goal and scored; we battered them and Thorne missed chances he used to put away from breakfast". At full time McCall went on an unexpected walk around the pitch applauding fans in the stands. Everyone knew what was happening, and that one of the most popular names in Bradford City's history was saying goodbye. Two days later the club announced that a settlement had been reached on his contract. There would be no managerial glory for Stuart at City. McCall admitted, "I had come to the stage where it was really affected me. I remember we were supposed to have a home game and it got postponed, and I remember feeling a sigh of relief, because it meant I had not spoiled anyone's weekend."

A year later, I interviewed Mark Lawn for boyfrombrazil.co.uk and he told me, "When Stuart left he was an ill man. But still in my mind he is a legend. It wasn't nice seeing what Stuart had to go through. And I think if anything Stuart was too near to the job and it hurt him too much, if that's possible."

Julian Rhodes added, "Of course I was disappointed with how it turned out. But we shouldn't forget that in the 2008/09 season Stuart was desperately unlucky. Up until Omar Daley got injured, we were flying. The number of fans who didn't like Omar Daley, but when he got injured we didn't pick up another win for ages. I think even his most ardent non-supporters realised at that point that Omar was integral to our success. I think that Stuart was really unlucky. After that season it became more difficult for Stuart as we had to cut back. He was getting really frustrated. It was getting to him.

"I thought the way Stuart handled himself at Bradford was incredible. When we appointed him as manager, he was the biggest legend the club has ever had – and we know that all managers get the sack eventually! So it did concern me that, at some point, we might have to be parting company. But I thought the way he handled it was brilliant. He left in such a dignified way that he is still loved here. He has been to a few games since, sat with me in the box, and everybody comes up to him and people still love him. He will always be a legend here."

David Baldwin was similarly positive about working with Stuart McCall, "When I was a young kid and came to the club on the YTS scheme, Stuart was playing in the first team and he was someone I had great respect for. To go full circle and work alongside him was very good, as Stuart was absolutely Bradford City through and through.

"My only wish was I wish I had worked with him after I had been in the job a few years, rather than day one. My role was very different when I left to the one that I had first come in to do. If Stuart's tenure at the club had been when I had been there for five or six years, I feel from my point of view I could have helped him more behind the scenes, when I had more experience under my belt. But unfortunately we were both in day one of our roles at the club."

Speaking to the Telegraph & Argus on the day he quit City, McCall declared, "I don't regret coming back for a second. I'd have regretted it more if I hadn't taken the job. It has been fantastic in one way but ultra-hard in another because you're carrying the hopes of everyone...The pressure I've put on myself because I want to succeed here has been immense at times. I've loved being manager of this club but it's a results-based business and the results have not been good enough."

McCall reflected back to me on his time in the Valley Parade dugout with mixed feelings, "Although there were highs and lows I loved running and representing the club. I have so many special memories. There were a lot of good performances. We had spirit, we had some memorable comebacks. On the day I left every single player came to my office to say goodbye. It was such an emotional day.

"I remember going to Accrington and we were 2-0 down [during his second season in charge]. There were more City fans than Accrington fans there, and at half time I said to Wayne Jacobs 'this is my last game in charge' because we were letting too many people down. We went out and made two subs, scoring three times late on to win it. I remember going to Lincoln in my first season on a Friday night and winning 2-1 in front of one thousand City fans. As much as I look back and remember disappointments, I have some great memories as well.

"If I had my time again, I wish I had come into this job at a different time. I wish it had happened at a different time. But it was what it was."

There was undoubtedly a major split amongst supporters over McCall's departure. Many wanted him to go as success was not forthcoming, whilst others were prepared to give him as long as it took. The fact that City continued to struggle over the subsequent two-and-a-half seasons – finishing lower down the league, in fact – would suggest that McCall did a better job than he was credited for at the time.

Michael Wood added, "Stuart McCall's teams were subject to greater variances in mental strength than any other City manager. They had the capacity to be excellent, and excellent over periods of weeks where winning became habitual, but they had the same tendency to dipping into losing form. These fluctuations happened for small reasons, and too often. During his time at City McCall never got the hang of arresting the declines in form, his team could turn upset over an offside decision into a three-game losing run. But perhaps to do so would have meant that they no longer enjoyed form booms. That aside McCall's greatest failure was that he did not get outrageous slices of good fortune which went for other managers. There is an adage about the more one practices, the luckier one gets and there would be some truth in this applied to McCall's teams. Certainly they lacked the spirit of Phil Parkinson's sides who can be said to make their own luck, but often one got the sense that McCall's sides were more at the whim of bad fortune than most."

McCall has subsequently enjoyed notable success as manager with Motherwell in Scotland, and in 2014/15 was even given the chance to manage his other love, Glasgow Rangers. For the 2015/16 season, McCall is part of the Scotland coaching staff, where they came agonisingly close to reaching the play offs for Euro 2016.

The future is sown

Yet although the Macclesfield Town game in August 2007 proved in one way to be another false dawn, there is no doubt that it was the start of the turning point in the rebirth of the club. The first game of the cheap season ticket era: a policy that has since been continued by the club. The prices were initially increased slightly year-on-year, and uptake did dip a little, but success from 2012 has fuelled greater supporter numbers and the price was once again slashed in 2015 – City charging just £149 for a season ticket.

They have also taken steps to help fans who can't go to every game, but who still want to be able to afford to attend when they can. In 2012 David Baldwin launched the Flexi-Card idea, where fans pay £50 for a guaranteed seat and then only have to pay £10 to attend games. The result of this consistently cheap ticket policy has been a generation of new City supporters, and a home atmosphere that is the envy of clubs up and down the country. When City defeated Sunderland in the FA Cup in 2015, referee Kevin Friend commented that he had not heard an atmosphere like it all season – and the Premier League official was usually in charge of games at Anfield, Old Trafford and the like.

When City climbed up the divisions in the 1990s, they did so with season ticket prices frozen for five years. It is partly coincidence, but the decline began when prices suddenly shot up and people began to be priced out. And then, during the immediate post-administration years, City were not only an unappealing team to watch but an expensive one too.

Michael Wood stated, "The club made promises at the start of the scheme – talking about promotion to The Championship within two years was not uncommon – rather than putting forward the scheme as being a reward to the Bradford City community for its support over the two periods of administration. The reason for this – I suspect – is that that support through administration had largely been forgotten and the scheme was a simple function of supply and demand. While bums were being put on seats with promises of winning football and promotion the reality was different, and that probably influenced the atmosphere."

Nevertheless, the cheap season ticket initiative has proven workable and sustainable. Bradford City might not receive the same level of revenue per season ticket holder as many of their divisional rivals, but they can certainly count on having many more fans. That will help them for years and years to come. We might not have enjoyed success under McCall, but we have enjoyed the rewards of a principled and wonderful financial stance on season tickets – one that goes against a football industry that generally cares little about pricing fans out of the game.

And none of this would probably have happened without Stuart McCall answering that SOS call.

City (vs Macclesfield): Donovan Ricketts, Darren Williams, David Wetherall, Mark Bower, Paul Heckingbottom, Omar Daley, Paul Evans, Eddie Johnson, Alex Rhodes (Nathan Joynes 89), Barry Conlon, Guylain Ndumbu-Nsungu (Joe Colbeck 77)

Not used: Ben Saynor, Simon Ainge, Scott Phelan

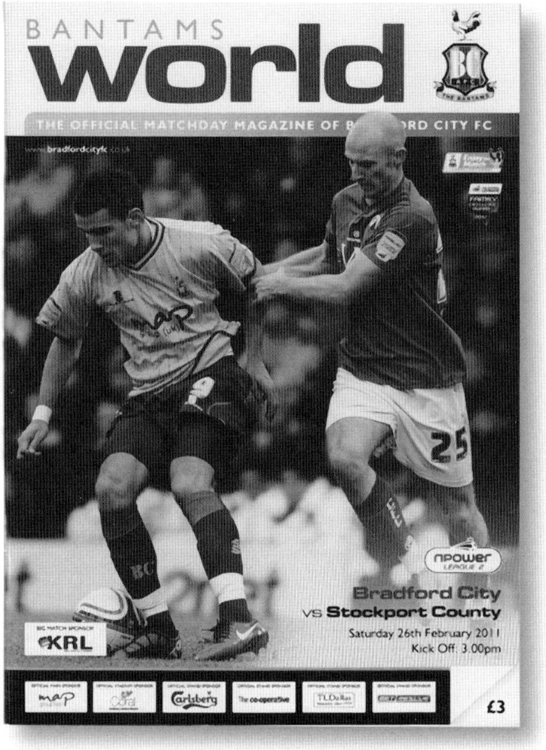

Living on the edge

Bradford City vs Stockport County

League Two, Saturday 26 February, 2011

At Valley Parade for this vital fixture against struggling Stockport County, the past, present and future of Bradford City management were all in attendance.

The past was Peter Taylor, who took his place in the Valley Parade dugout for a 50th league match in charge of the club, with everyone already knowing that it was also going to be his last. The present was Peter Jackson, who was sat in the Main Stand's 1911 Club section, watching a group of players that he was about to inherit, as Taylor's interim replacement. And there in the press box was the man who, ultimately, would prove to be the future. Phil Parkinson was doing some media work for BBC Radio Leeds and his long-time friend, Derm Tanner. He would apply for the vacancy caused by Taylor's immediate departure, but be overlooked – at least for now.

Taylor, Jackson and Parkinson each watched a dramatic afternoon unfold with the club teetering on the brink of a new low point in their decline from the Premier League days. Five goals, two sendings off and one missed penalty told only half the tale of a game filled by panic, anxiety and fear. Valley Parade's biggest crowd in just over three years – many of whom paid just £1 to attend – more than got their money's worth in the end. But City's habitual habit of making things hard for themselves was really on show during this one.

The past

Football as an industry can so often be brutal in its lack of sentiment. Up and down the country, managers and players who produced heroics can suddenly leave a club without supporters having a chance to say goodbye and thank you. Other, less successful gaffers and footballers will equally get the chop in clinical fashion.

And yet, here, a Bradford City manager was in the most unusual and unprecedented position of being offered a leaving party – in the shape of one final match in charge. And what made this situation even more unusual was that the Bradford City manager was unpopular and under pressure. Few people in the 15,332 crowd that came to Stockport game were here to wave the manager off and wish him good luck for the future; the majority were confused as to why he was being afforded this one final game. This leaving do.

Peter Taylor and Bradford City should have worked out gloriously. After the struggles of Stuart McCall to turn around the club and the painful parting of ways, the feeling at the time was that City had to look for a proven, experienced replacement to address the problems that stemmed from McCall's novice managerial status. That if we are not going to give McCall all the time that he needed to learn his craft, build up the club and ultimately achieve success, we should go for someone with the know-how and track record to deliver instant rewards. To get City out of League Two and back up the league ladder, no matter what it takes.

And this made Taylor the standout candidate, and the clear choice, from the many out-of-work managers who applied for the managerial vacancy that had arisen from McCall's departure, in February 2010. Less than twelve months earlier, Taylor had guided the unfashionable Wycombe Wanderers to League Two promotion on a budget inferior to the one McCall was working with. That promotion was Taylor's fifth over a managerial career that stretched back nearly 30 years. He had not been successful everywhere and had some notable, high profile failures, such as managing Leicester City in the Premier League. But his standing in the game was strong, and his record in the lower leagues was impressive. If there was one job that particularly made Taylor attractive to the City hierarchy, it was the one he performed at Hull City between 2002 and 2006, where he guided the Tigers – a big club – from the bottom tier to the Championship. The second tier was also where Bradford City saw their rightful home, and they wanted someone capable of delivering such a meteoric rise. If Taylor could do it at Hull, why not at Valley Parade too?

Mike Harrison has supported Bradford City for decades and has the proud distinction of being the longest-serving editor of the City Gent fanzine. He told me that Taylor's arrival provided the club's support with a much-needed morale boost, after the sadness over how McCall's time in charge had ended, "I think the initial reaction was positive. We had the disappointment of Stuart McCall not working out. And now here was a proven manager, certainly at League Two level. It was our third year of being in the basement division, and we were pretty desperate to get out of it anyway we could. The prospect of Peter Taylor, with all his experience and contacts, left most people feeling upbeat."

The only serious doubt was over his style of football. Taylor was well known as a football pragmatist and at former clubs there had been repeated complaints from fans over his dour approach. For City's board, this was an appointment that was solely about results. McCall had, after all, tried to play exciting, attacking football – and that hadn't worked out as well as hoped. Everyone connected with City was desperate for a winning team, and Taylor's managerial record suggested that, by appointing him, they would be getting just that.

So initially Taylor was handed the reins until the end of the 2009/10 campaign, with the proviso that both he and the board would decide later whether they wanted to continue working together. And Taylor did a decent job over this period, instilling greater grit to McCall's soft backline, and even producing some thrilling victories. It certainly wasn't always pretty – the arrival of towering centre back Luke Oliver on loan, only for him to deployed up front and the ball repeatedly hoofed towards him, was hardly progressive thinking – but the crowd warmed to Taylor. They tolerated his unwillingness to commit players forward, and his unusual tactic of bringing every single player back to defend corners. City became hard to beat, ending the campaign with four wins and two draws from the final six games. It seemed like a good fit, as Mike Harrison – who met and interviewed Taylor the City Gent – remembered, "Taylor seemed a very friendly guy. He loved the area and walking his dogs on Baildon Moor. He liked the club and the city. On the pitch we started off quite well under Taylor. We stayed up, and I don't think there was any real doubt that we would."

Telegraph & Argus journalist Simon Parker summed up the mood of cautious optimism that was around at the end of the season, as the board mulled over offering a more permanent contract for their caretaker manager, "There was a feeling that City could go up on a series of 1-0 wins, like Wycombe did under Taylor. That Wycombe team were dreadful to watch, and hardly scored any goals, but they got promoted. So you thought that you could put up with a season of dour wins just to get out of the division." Not that Taylor saw it that way, as Simon Parker explained, "For journalists he would have you up if you ever mentioned 'direct' or 'long ball football'. He would be straight on the phone, arguing how Arsenal play different types of football and that they play direct football too. How there's more than one way to win a game. He was a great interviewee. He would always front tough questions."

In January 2011 myself and my former writing partner, Michael Wood, interviewed joint chairman Mark Lawn for Boyfrombrazil.co.uk. During our conversation, Lawn admitted that, during Taylor's trial period, he held reservations about the caretaker manager's long-term suitability for the role. In particular, he compared a March victory over Aldershot Town, and the conservative manner it was achieved, with the gung-ho approach that McCall took against the same opposition, a year earlier. "Out of the whole board I was the last one to make my mind up. I watched the games and – after the Aldershot game which was 1-0, 2-0, and we had beaten them with Stuart (McCall) 5-0, it was a different type of football but I believed it was a type of football which would get us out of this league." Buoyed by the way Taylor had managed the club over this period, a one-year contract was eventually agreed. Optimism was high. City went into the 2010/11 season as promotion favourites with the bookies. With Taylor's vast experience and a decent budget to operate on, it finally looked like it would be City's year.

Michael Flynn was one of the squad's most important players around that time and a key part of Taylor's plans. A box-to-box midfielder with a rasping shot from distance, Flynn had been signed on the eve of McCall's final season in charge and very quickly became a fans' favourite for his passionate, committed approach. When Taylor took over from McCall later that season, Flynn became one of the new manager's most trusted players.

Flynn told me, "Peter Taylor was brilliant. He was a lot firmer than Stuart, but one thing I loved with Peter was you knew where you were with him. There was no airs or graces: if he didn't want you he was honest about it. I remember after the first game he took charge we played Accrington Stanley awa and we lost 2-0. And it was an absolute hammering to be honest. They battered us. They played us off the park from start to finish. And Peter came up to me after it and said 'Flynny, I might just get back down the M1 now!' He realised that it was a big job. I said to him that a positive was it can't get any worse!

"Peter was very tactical and I've taken a lot of things that I learned from him into coaching. In terms of tactics and preparations, he was spot on. In the summer that he was made permanent manager I had a chance to go back to League One with Leyton Orient, for more money. But I decided to stay and I signed a new two-year deal. I wanted to carry on playing under Peter, and we both genuinely thought we could do something that season. But it was just one of those things, it didn't happen."

Sliding doors

Right from the start of the 2010/11 campaign, the mood around Valley Parade wasn't right. The team made a mixed start, with a 3-1 opening day loss at Shrewsbury Town and 2-1 League Cup triumph over Championship side Notts Forest. And then the Taylor-inspired debate over whether it was better to watch winning football, or to be entertained, unexpectedly came to a head, following the first home league match of the season.

In that game, City defeated newly promoted Stevenage – one of Taylor's old clubs – 1-0 thanks to a first half penalty from Gareth Evans. But watching in the stands, it had been a dismal afternoon. Taylor's revamped City side were functional and organised, but dreadful to watch. They sat back and defended their early lead; inviting visitor pressure that deserved to be rewarded with an equaliser, if not a winner. It was a tad unfair on Taylor, who probably didn't want his team to play quite so conservatively; but at full time there was a damning verdict from many City fans – instead of cheers about the victory, they booed the team off.

Taylor was rattled, criticising fans in the local media, and from that point on a frosty supporter-manager relationship developed – one that eventually became untenable. After that victory, City lost three games in a row without scoring a single goal. This included a 2-0 Friday night defeat to Southend at Valley Parade, where the atmosphere was awful as fans quickly turned on the team. The tag of promotion favourites was already looking laughable, and September saw continued struggles. City won just two of their opening ten league matches, and found themselves second bottom of the entire Football League. The Yorkshire Post summed up the gravity of the situation, "No city or town has lost two clubs from the Football League – Bradford is in danger of becoming the first."

Simon Parker recalled the tough start to the season for Taylor, "He fell out pretty quickly with Mark Lawn. There was no love-lost in that relationship from quite early on, which made it a bit of a strain. It never got going that season, although I don't think he had that much budget to work from. It was more than the season before, but it still wasn't one of the most competitive." Mike Harrison added that the blend of new players just didn't sit right, "It was the usual City recruitment policy in the summer. We let go of a lot of players, perhaps because we didn't want them or couldn't afford to keep them, and then you look around to see who was out there who is out of contract, if we could afford them, and if they would want to come to Bradford City. I don't think the budget was really there for him to get who he wanted. He clearly used a lot of contacts from down south and also from other former clubs like Hull City; but I just don't think he got the right amount of players for what we wanted.

"That summer in the Yorkshire Post I had the temerity to suggest that we weren't one of the favourites for promotion, and I was taken to task by one of the joint chairmen. But I just couldn't see us doing well from the players we had recruited. It just wasn't the right mix of players. As it proved I was right to say we weren't one of the favourites."

The end of September was where it all came to a head. Firstly, green shoots of optimism emerged from a Tuesday night tussle with Rotherham at the Don Valley stadium. The Millers were going well and amongst the promotion pace-setters, so a heavy City defeat was expected. But instead, the visiting Bantams played well and had the better of the chances, drawing 0-0. Rotherham keeper Andy Warrington made a string of superb saves and earned the man of the match award. At the back, City were particularly outstanding. Zesh Rehman, Shane Duff, Steve Williams and Luke O'Brien kept only the third clean sheet of the season.

It seemed that a corner was being turned. But then the morning after, it was announced that Taylor had made a double loan signing from Manchester United. Reece Brown – younger brother of the then-United stalwart Wes – and Oliver Gill: whose father, David, was then the United chief executive. They were both defenders, and there was widespread bemusement amongst supporters. City were largely doing well defensively; the problems lied as the other end of the pitch where – in nine games played so far – the Bantams had notched a pathetic four goals. Why sign these young and completely unproven defenders? It got worse when – an hour before the next game, at home to Morecambe – the teams were announced and two of the stars from the Rotherham display had been dropped. No Rehman, and no O'Brien. In came Gill, a centre half, as left back, and in came Brown, as right back. The groans from the stands were audible. A club insider would later tell me just how badly Taylor's decision to omit his two established players, in favour of two kids on loan, went down in the dressing room – but in truth everyone could quickly see it for themselves.

For the subsequent 1-0 defeat to the Shrimpers ranks as one of the worst Bradford City performances of the 21st century. Forget how close the scoreline makes the game seem, the home side were utterly dreadful, devoid of any spark and creativity, lacking in passion and desire. "No City player created any chances or had the chance to miss any," reported Omar Eliwi for Boyfrombrazil.co.uk. "Something is not right. These players are not playing for this manager. We don't seem to have a clue how to score a goal. Confidence is at an all time low. The fans want Taylor out."

As City prepared to travel to Barnet the following week, the national media began to circulate reports that Taylor was just one defeat away from getting the sack – something Lawn later denied was ever the case when we interviewed him. "The Thursday before the game Peter came up to me and said that there were rumours in the press that Barnet was his last game, and I turned round to Peter and said 'Peter, you will be in charge for Cheltenham [the game after]. That is definite, you will be in charge'. So he knew. Never mind Barnet, you go concentrate on Barnet and Cheltenham – so he knew what he was doing."

I went to the Barnet game and it was a strange affair where City were dire for an hour and many of the visiting fans barracked Taylor. But in the end a vital victory was earned, courtesy of goals from Leon Osborne and Tom Adeyemi. Whatever the rumours at the time, Taylor's job was safe for the time being. Indeed, that Barnet win helped to turn around the season for Taylor and City, at least for a time. They won three of their next four games to amazingly climb to the edge of the play off positions, and over November and December kept ticking along reasonably well enough to suggest that – if they could really get their act together in the second half of the campaign – a play off place was within their grasp.

Yet it ultimately went completely the opposite way. First, Taylor was unexpectedly faced with a huge career dilemma in early January. A few weeks earlier, Newcastle United had appointed Alan Pardew as manager and Pardew decided to offer Taylor the role of his assistant. Newcastle made an approach to City for Taylor, and compensation was agreed, but amazingly Taylor turned down the move. The-then head of operations, David Baldwin, told me, "We had played Lincoln City on New Year's Day and then we had an approach from Newcastle for Peter to become the assistant manager. We agreed that he could speak to them and it looked as though he was leaving on a deal, but then it turned out he wasn't leaving. But then in less than a month we were thinking 'this isn't really working'. I think that's where the problem stems back to. Once the head had been turned for an alternative club and then when results weren't going as well."

Indeed, the decision to turn down Newcastle is one that probably Taylor regrets. The 1998 film Sliding Doors explores two parallel universes of Gwyneth Paltrow's future, based on the two paths the central character's life could take, depending on whether or not she makes it in time for a train. By catching the train she gets home early and discovers her boyfriend is cheating on her, and as a result her life falls apart. In the scenario where she misses the train she continues a blissful life unaware of what her partner is up to. The point of the film was to show how one single moment could trigger very different outcomes in someone's life. This Newcastle dilemma was Taylor's very own Sliding Doors moment. Had he moved to Newcastle, for a much bigger salary, history suggests he would have remained at St James Park until 2015, when Pardew eventually left. Instead, Taylor stayed at City, believing he could get them promoted, only for that to unravel spectacularly and his managerial career to suffer.

On the day Taylor turned down Newcastle, City had just beaten Bury 1-0 to go tenth in the league, just three points short of the play offs. It would prove to be one of Taylor's last wins as manager. The next nine games yielded just one point. They lost week after week, often in the most dismal fashion. Promotion hopes were extinguished. The pragmatic dour football continued. But without the victories to back it up, the whole thing was just wretched. All managers need to win matches, but others City bosses have been afforded more patience from the Bradford City crowd because at least they were playing entertaining football, even when results weren't great. Taylor simply didn't offer that consolation. David Baldwin added, "After Peter turned Newcastle down, I remember we had seven games over a very short space of time and I thought 'after these games we could either be in the play offs or languishing in mid-table'. Unfortunately it was the latter scenario. I can't really put my finger on why he didn't succeed at Bradford City. The budget we were operating on was the same budget he had got Wycombe promoted out of League Two, a couple of years before. So I don't think it was fiscal. I think in sport you need a bit of luck and I don't think he had that when it was needed."

A lack of luck was certainly an issue, but Mark Lawn also felt the players were to blame, and especially the ones brought in by Taylor the summer before. In that January interview we asked Lawn why the season wasn't going to plan, and he replied, "Well, it's the players isn't it? Does anyone think that the players we did bring in, we should not have brought in? Jake Speight for example. We paid £25,000 for Jake, you look at what he did at Mansfield, you look at his background and you think 'what a great player to bring in' and he has not done it for us. [Tommy] Doherty has done it at every single club he has been at, he's come in, and he has not done it for us at Bradford City has he? He's not performed to his best. I'm sure the players would all turn around and say that. Some of the players we have brought in have not performed to their best and don't think that they are not capable of it…We look on paper a very good squad but sometimes when we play we don't look as if we have congealed at all.

"We are all looking at a certain standard of where we have to be. Where we are at present is not good enough, Peter knows that, I don't need to tell him he is an intelligent man."

Looking back at the season Michael Flynn said, "I think we were short up front, to be totally honest. We only really had James Hanson, and he had been playing in non-league only eighteen months before. He has done really well and come on leaps and bounds, but with just him I don't think we were good enough up front then."

James Hanson added, "Peter Taylor gave me a four-year deal and he obviously rated me highly. I think in the second season I got injured at the wrong times. I tried to do a bit in the gym over the summer and I got a bit too big and didn't balance my fitness right. And that led to a few injuries which was frustrating for me and for the club." And in terms of where it went wrong for Taylor? "I think he was a little bit unlucky if I'm honest. A lot of players seemed to get injured at the wrong time. Myself, and other key players were out too. I don't think we ever had a settled side that could play every week."

It came to a head at the end of February, when City lost 1-0 at home to runaway league leaders and future champions, Chesterfield. Despite the scoreline City were never in the game and the crowd was now firmly on Taylor's back. More worryingly, City had slumped from tenth to 21st – fourth bottom – and were just six points above the relegation zone. Third-bottom Burton had five games in hand on the Bantams too. And on the basis of this awful form, relegation really was looking like a possibility. Mike Harrison recalled with a shudder, "We were sinking fast. The fans were getting on his back. Results weren't going well. We weren't playing well."

Taylor held talks with the board the following day, and decided it was best that he step down, which Lawn and Julian Rhodes agreed with. But what Taylor didn't expect was an unusual request – he was asked to delay his departure until after Saturday's vital match against second-bottom side Stockport County, to prepare the team and lead them through the game. As Julian Rhodes told me, "The unusual thing with Peter, when we parted company, was we told him that he had to be in charge for one more game. 'oh and by the way we are only charging £1 admission so there's going to be a full house!'"

Simon Parker continues the story, "It was very odd. I got a call from one of the chairmen saying 'come in we've got quite a big story for you, regarding the manager'. I got there and they told me that Peter was stepping down, but that he was going to still take the team on Saturday. Initially they were suggesting that it wouldn't be announced until after the game. I said that no you've made a decision, everyone will soon know because this stuff gets out, you can't just carry on."

Julian Rhodes added that Taylor's reign was disappointing, "The season when he came in and replaced Stuart for the final three months, we finished it quite well. So we were all quite optimistic. But to be fair to him, the budget was coming down again. Peter had the worst budget that any Bradford City manager has had in League Two over that six-year period. So I think we were perhaps asking a bit too much of him. When he came in, the expectation that we had was that if anyone can pull it out of the bag maybe he can. But sadly it worked the other way and we found ourselves in a relegation battle."

Flynn was understandably disappointed by the news that Taylor would be leaving – and was generally frustrated about how the season itself had panned out. "For me it was a 'here we go again' type of thing. I was really gutted because in the January we beat Bury at home and were right by the play offs. I think if we had got another striker, and one or two other players, I think we could have actually reached the play offs.

"But instead things ended badly for Peter. It was something that I was absolutely gutted about; because I thought that with Peter we had a real chance of doing something. I really thought that with him in charge we had a real chance of getting promoted, and that would have been absolutely unbelievable. It would have been amazing to have been a part of it."

The present

In the days between Taylor's announced departure and the Stockport match, Peter Jackson hatched a plan. Out of work since being sacked by Lincoln City eighteen months earlier, one of Bradford City's greatest-ever players was desperate for an opportunity to manage his hometown club. But rather than take his place amongst over 40 applicants for the position, he cleverly gave himself a head start over others by picking up the phone to Julian Rhodes and making an unusual suggestion.

Jackson offered his services as interim manager on a week-by-week basis, to give Rhodes and Lawn time and space to search and appoint the right man for the job, whilst knowing that immediate matters were being taken care of. With only Wayne Jacobs an obvious candidate to be caretaker manager, Julian thought it was a good idea. "I persuaded Mark to let Peter come in for the rest of that season. I thought 'we can't strengthen the squad, what we need is a motivator. Peter is as good as anyone. Surely he can come in and do enough to keep us up this season'." That foot in the door meant Jackson had a live opportunity to impress in the role. If he could turnaround an under-performing squad's results, he would be firmly in the driving seat for the permanent job. Again, the club was veering between extremes in its choice of manager successors. After McCall's passion but inexperience, City went with the proven record of Taylor. But in doing they hired a man who took passion out of the performances and built a team that the crowd struggled to identify with. So in came Jackson to instil that enthusiasm. Passion was back in vogue.

His impending appointment was not made public to anyone, including the players, and so Jackson sat quietly in the stand with a notebook for the Stockport match on the Saturday, as he studied his new charges. Meanwhile Taylor went into an unexpected final game at the helm with the stakes high. Lose to a Stockport side already looking doomed to relegation, and he might need police protection getting out of the ground. Win and at least he could bow out on a high and with the prospect of City falling out of the Football League looking much less likely. Flynn added, "The situation with Peter about to leave didn't affect the preparations for the Stockport game. Peter is an absolute, 100% professional in anything he does. He spoke to me and made me aware of things before it came out.

"He wanted more than anybody to get promoted. Because at the end of the day, it's good for him as well, let's not be short-sighted about it. If he had got Bradford promoted, after the amount of people who tried, that would have further enhanced just what a good manager he was at that level.

"I don't think the younger players appreciated really what kind of experience he had and what kind of manager Taylor was, but that's football. That's not to say they didn't care, I just don't think they appreciated enough what sort of opportunity they had under such an experienced manager."

The increased Stockport crowd was either a burden or motivation. The offer of £1 entry was aimed at boosting attendances that were starting to dwindle, despite the continuation of the cheap season ticket prices. Many of the new or lapsed supporters – enticed by the rock bottom prices in 2007 – possessed limited patience over City's continued floundering in the bottom tier, and drifted away. This was a chance to win some of those people back, and to give the team extra backing for a monumentally important match. For James Hanson, the 15,332 people present was a big deal for the player, "It was a massive crowd, probably the biggest I had played in front of at that point. We knew what was at stake for the game because we were struggling at the time and there wasn't long to go. We were near the bottom two and we knew that we had to get a result." The atmosphere was even more emotionally charged when, just before kick off, news broke that former City defender Dean Richards – one of the greatest players produced by the Bantams' youth set up – had unexpectedly died aged just 36. He was a big favourite with supporters and a heavy sense of sadness spread around the ground.

Flynn believed that the expectation caused by the larger crowd was an issue for some of the players. "I think to be honest a few of the players would have felt that pressure before the game, because of the crowd. Not many of them would have played in front of that many people. At the time the club's wage bill was down. Okay you had certain players who were established League Two, League One players, but the majority hadn't been in this position very much.

"The pressure playing for Bradford for a lot of them was too much. You see people like Gareth Evans. He has since gone to Rotherham and Fleetwood and he's done well. I think he struggled a bit at Bradford. Even though he had some really good games, he had more ability than what he showed week in week out. But that's the reason why people are at that level because they are not consistent enough." James Hanson added of the mood pre-match, "We all looked to try and do it as a good send off to Peter Taylor. I thought he was a bit unlucky in losing his job."

The Stockport game itself started very well. Perhaps Taylor felt less inhibited now that he knew his future lied elsewhere, but he seemed to have taken the shackles off his players and they attacked in greater numbers, and with more frequency, than in recent weeks. The 4-3-3 formation that Taylor had played for most of the season was ditched for a more attack-minded 4-4-2, with Michael Flynn and James Hanson leading the line. Hanson had an early goal disallowed but then, after just fourteen minutes, the breakthrough came.

Fittingly, on the day of Richards' untimely death, it was a promising City centre half who got it. Steve Williams was on hand to head a free kick home and calm the nerves felt by the crowd. The Stockport marking was woeful, and they continued to struggle badly with balls into the box. Numerous goalmouth scrambles went unrewarded. If City could get a second goal, you sensed the floodgates would open. The early Williams header was the 74th that Stockport had conceded that season – this was only game number 33.

But then there was a major shock: Stockport equalised. Steve Williams was again, unfortunately, heavily involved, as he dallied too long on the ball in a dangerous area and was pick-pocketed by the excellent Paul Turnbull. Williams' mistake meant Turnbull was left one-on-one with Lenny Pidgley in front of the Kop, and he finished low past the City keeper. No matter, as City kept attacking and the club's player of the season, David Syers, smacked the crossbar with an effort. Williams also had another shot that was cleared off the line. Six minutes after Stockport's equaliser, another scramble in the box saw Kevin Ellison's shot blocked illegally by the arm of Adam Griffan. Penalty to City, and a red card for Stockport. Surely now the afternoon would go more swimmingly for an up-to-that-point excellent Bantams side?

Alas, Hanson's penalty was weak and saved by former City keeper Matt Glennon. And instead of going in at half time 2-1 in front, the home side amazingly trooped off 1-2 down. Five minutes before the interval, Williams was once again caught out. Ryan Doble would have been offside when he was played through on goal, but Williams stepped out a fraction later than the rest of the back four and the flag stayed down. Even so, Pidgley should have gathered the ball as he slid in to claim it on the edge of the box. Somehow it went through him and Doble was presented with an open goal. Bradford City 1 Stockport County 2. City had shot themselves in the foot very badly, and the half time interval felt like a long one as supporters began to ponder the growing possibility of City being relegated to non-league. Not only were second-bottom Stockport on course to close the gap between the two clubs to three points, bottom-placed Barnet were 2-0 up in their game and on track to end the day four points behind City. This was becoming really, really serious.

With 45 minutes left in the job, Taylor went even more for broke. At half time, he threw on strikers Gareth Evans and Jake Speight for midfielders Tom Adeyemi and Lee Bullock, pushing Flynn back into midfield alongside David Syers. This looked a more balanced approach, but for 20 minutes nothing much happened and the pressure on the players intensified. Yet at the same time the inflated size of crowd proved to be of huge benefit; as everyone in the stands put to one side their frustrations over Taylor and the way the season was unfolding, in order to get behind the team. Instead of getting on the backs of the players, fans roared them on. And the cause was further aided on 65 minutes, when Doble was sent off for elbowing Luke Oliver. Now Stockport had only nine men on the field, and City had 25 minutes to save the game and their season.

In the match report of the game that I wrote at the time for Boyfrombrazil.co.uk, I noted, "One last throw of the dice – Robbie Threlfall for the bloodied Oliver – and never before have City gone so gung ho under Taylor. It appeared the Bantams were playing 3-3-4 – hey, it might even have been 3-2-5. Evans and the outstanding Luke O'Brien were playing as widemen and enjoyed loads of space against an over-loaded Stockport side; Lewis Hunt was also getting forward well. Numerous corners, endless balls pumped into the box, plenty of throw ins too. Speight hit the post, the crowd roared the players on even louder. The clock must have been ticking down ever-slower to the Stockport blue shirts."

With sixteen minutes to go, City finally equalised. A corner wasn't defended very well, and Syers did an outstanding job of keeping the attack alive by heading the ball back across the penalty area. There at the backpost was that man again, Steve Williams, and his effort on goal hit a Stockport player before trickling over the line. Joy swept around Valley Parade, followed by a huge collective sigh of relief. That said, a draw would still feel like a poor result given City's two-man advantage over their struggling opponents. Speight, O'Brien and Ellison went close as the Bantams continued to pile forwards, and then in the fourth minute of five that were added on for injuries, a jinking run and low drive by O'Brien saw the ball cannon off a defender and fall invitingly into the path of Gareth Evans. Everyone held their breath, and Evans drilled a perfect low shot goalwards. It flew past Glennon and into the back of the net. 3-2 to Bradford City.

After a season of underachievement and frustration, after weeks of dismal defeat following dismal defeat – and after worries had increased hugely over the prospect of relegation – this moment was a huge release. Valley Parade erupted. Everyone apart from the small band of Stockport fans in the Midland Road corner went wild in celebration. I wrote at the time about this moment, "We've just gone through 90 minutes of utter torture, all of which can now be forgotten as I jump up and down like a five-year-old, only pausing to hug those around me. The players have chosen to run directly to the front of my block in the Midland Road stand to celebrate their euphoric moment. Eventually the cheering subsides, but I'm feeling so good and shaking all over too much to be able to sit down. In no time at all we're punching the air as the final whistle is blown.

"This is why we love Bradford City. This is what makes all the other crap worthwhile."

The celebrations contributed to this game going down as one of the most dramatic and memorable in the club's modern history. Julian Rhodes even admitted that it was amongst his all-time favourite ever Bradford City games. "Just because the atmosphere was fantastic and to come back and win from 2-1 down was fantastic. It sticks in my memory as the best, because I was seriously concerned we were going out of the league and that win turned it round."

Flynn recalled of the match, "It was a strange day because we won 3-2, but they had two players sent off. No disrespect to Stockport but they were a bad team, and in the end we were lucky to beat them. It was just really frustrating. We made hard work of what could have been an easier day – looking back that was the story of the season!"

On the feelings triggered by the last minute winner, Flynn added, "I'll be honest, it was a mixture of a few things. It was big relief, because we knew that we weren't very good that day, and any winner in the last minute is always a really good feeling. When you get a last minute winner, it's brilliant. It's massive for the crowd, it's massive for everyone. But it was such a big relief. We wanted to get a result for Peter. Because he worked really hard and he was really professional." Mike Harrison stated, "The game was madness. Stockport had had a dreadful season and were sliding down the league. And yet we still managed to almost not beat them. I think to be honest Stockport deserved something from the game. I thought they played well and, for a team that was in a mess, produced some decent football. It just showed how bad we were."

At full time the players hugged each other and saluted the crowd, whilst Peter Taylor wandered off the pitch and out of the Valley Parade spotlight to a reasonably warm reception. Rhodes recalled, "He left a hero. Gareth Evans scored that 90th minute winner and Taylor left the pitch with everyone clapping him." Flynn continued, "He came into the dressing room and thanked everyone for their efforts. He was straight, he thought players could have done better and told them. But I wouldn't expect anything else from him. He was always straight with you.

"It was sad because I thought that season we could have done something. He was unlucky with injuries. Big players he brought in like Tom Doherty. Tom was an unbelievable player but he didn't get to show his best at Bradford. Things like that are really frustrating because he was a really talented footballer. From January when we were around the play offs and the transfer window was open – if we'd have got a push for two or three more players, then I really believe we would have been in the play offs. And I think the Bradford fans would have accepted that. It would have been another big improvement on previous years."

Taylor's final duty as manager was to speak to the press, and Parker recalls him being in a relaxed mood, making jokes about Steve Williams' mixed afternoon. "Taylor said 'if I was marking Steve Williams for you, I'd give him naught. I'd give him eight out of ten going that way, and minus eight going the other way!'" Taylor's next job would be to manage the Bahrain national team, before returning to England with Gillingham and getting a warm reception on two subsequent returns to Valley Parade with his Gills side.

The future

2010/11 was the first season in which supporters Dominic Newton-Collinge and Tom Fletcher produced their award-winning Bantams Banter podcast show. On their recording of the Stockport game, the pair shared their incredulity that Phil Parkinson was sat in the press box, a few rows in front of them. "Why is he here?" Parkinson had lost his job at Charlton two months earlier and was looking for a route back into the game, combining some media work with scouting for Arsenal. Parkinson applied to take over from Taylor, but was overlooked on this occasion. He would very soon be the King of Valley Parade, but for now that opportunity eluded him.

Instead, the focus instantly turned to Peter Jackson. He was spotted at the Stockport game by several fans, and less than 24 hours later it was announced that he was to be Taylor's replacement on a week-by-basis. Jackson told the Telegraph & Argus, "When you are born in Bradford and have captained the team, you want to be manager as well. It's a really big honour...Saturday's result [against Stockport] was a major boost. It was a must-win game and to come back like they did in the second half showed tremendous spirit...We're not out of the relegation situation yet but hopefully we can rise to the challenge."

Flynn holds a sense of disappointment about Jackson's reign – not so much regarding the man himself, but more about what his appointment said about the ambition of the club. "I thought Peter was the cheaper option. I think basically what the club thought was 'we can't do any worse this season, let's save money on wages'. You can't blame them for that, but it kind of said that maybe the club had given up already, but I hadn't and that was the frustrating part for me.

"That's no disrespect to Peter, because Peter was brilliant. He raised everybody; he is a very good man manager. But with all the names you had banded around at the time, people like Martin Allen – I think someone like him, who had a more impressive recent record than Jackson, would have been a statement of intent."

Jackson quickly instilled an improved playing style and achieved two wins from his first three games in charge. Soon after, his interim position was confirmed until the end of the season at least. It wasn't always pretty and in truth some of the performances under Jackson were far worse than what Taylor achieved, but with a game to spare City's Football League status was preserved after they drew 1-1 at Hereford. Mike Harrison reflected on the end of that campaign, "It was another peculiar situation. Peter Jackson got in touch with the two chairmen asking to help out. I still think whoever would have taken charge would have probably kept us up. We were too good to go down, especially with Stockport struggling. I think by the end we were just relived to see the back of that season. It could have been worse but it could have been a lot better."

For Jackson, a combination of preserving City's Football League status and the club's financial struggles meant he was given an extended opportunity to manage City with a permanent contract, although it wouldn't be one that he saw out. Five games into the 2011/12 season, and after a truly awful start, Jackson resigned, citing unwelcome interference from the club's summer-appointed chief scout and head of player recruitment, Archie Christie. Before Jackson was appointed, City had interviewed Dagenham's long-standing manager John Still for the vacancy, and he brought his long-time colleague Christie along. Still was reluctant to take his initial interest in the City job further and withdrew from contention, meaning Jackson got the job he was so desperate for. But Rhodes and Lawn persuaded Christie to join the club anyway. Christie was asked to write a sixteen-page plan for the future and given his own budget to sign development squad players. It didn't take off, despite the development squad leading to City signing the highly talented Nahki Wells. Jackson did not appreciate Christie's presence and influence in the boardroom. Christie was equally no fan of Jackson, believing that he didn't work hard enough.

In truth, Julian Rhodes had been far from convinced about keeping Jackson on that summer anyway, and was less than enamoured by the squad he and Christie built over the summer. "We felt we should reward him [Jackson] by making him manager for the following season. Now, unfortunately, I think perhaps he had spent a bit too much time away from the game and he wasn't as up-to-date on player situations as he could have been. So that summer was a difficult one.

"I must admit I was horrified after watching our pre-season friendly defeat to Carlisle. I walked away thinking that we were really bad. The first home game of the season before [2010/11 under Taylor] that was against Stevenage, where we won 1-0 – I've no idea how! I went home and said to my wife 'this is the worst squad we have had for a long time'. One year on I went home after the Aldershot game [City lost 2-1 on the opening day of the 2011/12 campaign] and said to the wife 'you know what I said last year? Scrub that. This lot are even worse'.

"After the first four games we had just one point, and that was a very lucky point picked up at Oxford where they battered us and we were poor. So we approached Peter about what we were going to do – and to be honest we were quite prepared to continuing working with him – and he said that he wanted to leave."

It was at this point that the club finally turned to the future – Phil Parkinson – under the recommendation of Christie. "Archie was responsible for Phil Parkinson joining the club," confirmed Rhodes. "It was Archie who recommended him and introduced us to him. For some reason Archie doesn't get the credit for this, but it was down to him."

Jackson was hamstrung also by the club's plight off the field, where once again worries about the future surfaced. The legacy of the 2002 and 2004 administrations were still a burden, in that the club was paying around £700,000 a year on rent for both Valley Parade and the adjoining office blocks, to the Gordon Gibb family pension fund and Prupim respectively. This was hindering the club's ability to move forwards, and so Rhodes and Lawn approached both parties about doing a deal where the rent they pay would be reduced whilst City remained in League Two, and then increased if and when they climbed up the leagues. The Gibb family pension fund was unwilling to budge from their position – causing the club to publically threaten to break the lease agreement and move to Odsal, with Valley Parade's fixtures and fittings ripped out of the ground and taken with them. Gibb did not blink.

In the end, a deal was agreed with Prupim for Rhodes and Lawn to privately buy the office block, and therefore remove the associated £370,000 annual rent burden from the club. A year later the pair sold this land for a profit to the One in a Million charity co-managed by Wayne Jacobs, and this building is now used as a primary school.

City finished eighteenth in 2010/11 under Taylor/Jackson, and repeated that underachievement in 2011/12 – Parkinson's first season in charge. But although relegation concerns were prevalent during the 2011/12 campaign, they were not as serious as they had seemed the year before. And the removal of half of those rental commitments enabled the board to set increased budgets for the manager, and the club finally started to climb upwards again.

Which means the Stockport County game carries quite a legacy. It was the moment where, going into it – and at half time – you genuinely feared that relegation was on the cards. All the signs of the previous demotions were there; and if City had lost or even only drawn that day, the possibility of non-league football would have grown extremely serious. As Mark Lawn told the Telegraph & Argus on Saturday 14 May, 2011, "If we go into the Conference while we are here then we do not exist."

It might not have seemed much to have beaten nine-men Stockport County – or to have avoided relegation to the Conference for two seasons in a row – but the brakes were finally applied on City's dismal slide from the Premier League that had begun in 2001. People stood up to be counted when it really mattered. Supporters backed their team when they desperately needed it.

Stockport County is a reminder of some of the darkest times of Bradford City's modern day history, but it is also something to smile about in recognition of how far the club has since come.

City: Lenny Pidgley, Lewis Hunt, Steve Williams, Luke Oliver (Robbie Threlfall 71), Luke O'Brien, Tom Adeyemi (Jake Speight 46), Lee Bullock (Gareth Evans 46), David Syers, Kevin Ellison, Michael Flynn, James Hanson

Not used: Jon McLaughlin, Jon Worthington, Leon Osborne, Scott Dobie

The greatest cup run, ever

Aston Villa vs Bradford City

League Cup semi final second leg, Tuesday 22 January, 2013

The name Yoann Arquin means very little to English football fans. He is known to Notts County supporters as an unremarkable French striker who netted thirteen goals over two seasons at Meadow Lane. Arquin also played for Hereford and had mediocre spells at Ross County and St. Mirren, before returning to France. His name is destined to be recalled only in the most obscure pub quizzes.

Yet his impact on Bradford City's history is colossal.

It was August 2012 when Arquin – making his Notts County debut – wrote his name into infamy. A League Cup first round tie against the Bantams at Meadow Lane had reached the 90th minute with a 0-0 scoreline, when the home side – who at the time were playing in the division above – broke forward. The controversial striker Lee Hughes sent a low cross into the box, and a deflection deceived City goalkeeper Matt Duke. There at the far post, with an empty goal to aim for, was Arquin. A winning goal and a place in the second round of the competition surely beckoned. Yet he somehow managed to steer his shot over the bar and into the empty Meadow Lane Kop behind the goal.

And on such thin margins, Bradford City's destiny changed forever. Arquin's horrendous miss led to extra time, during which James Hanson found the breakthrough with a stunning effort from distance. League One Notts County 0, League Two Bradford City 1. The BBC website's match report described the result as a "giant killing".

Flash forward five months and those thin margins had continued to benefit Bradford City in spectacular

(*Above and below*) The modern day Valley Parade. City's home towers above the Manningham community that it is a part of. As Mark Ellis summarised of the ground, "It might be a bit lop-sided, but it's got character. I think it's a brilliant stadium." Images by Paul Thompson.

(*Above*) The long climb back up the leagues. Peter Taylor spent 12 months attempting to reverse the club's decline and earn promotion, but his style of football proved unpopular with many fans and he departed following a dramatic 3-2 victory over Stockport. Image by Paul Thompson.

(*Below left*) A home game against Gillingham on Saturday 18 September, 2010. Image by Paul Thompson.

(*Below right*) The rebirth of Bradford City can be largely attributed to Phil Parkinson, who took charge in September 2011 and has delivered year-on-year progress up the divisions. Image by Alex Dodd.

(*Above left*) The Bermudian striker Nahki Wells, who was recommended to the club by former City winger Mark Ellis, and who netted a prolific 53 goals from 76 (36) appearances. Image by Alex Dodd.

(*Above right*) Garry Thompson. Another key figure from the 2012/13 History Makers team, who scored the famous League Cup quarter final goal against Arsenal. Image by Alex Dodd.

(*Below*) Back where he first rose to prominence. City's long-serving forward James Hanson in pre-season action at Guiseley, who Stuart McCall signed him from in 2009 for a bargain £7,500. Image by Alex Dodd.

(*Above*) Wem-ber-lee. More than 30,000 City fans descend on the national stadium for the utterly insane occasion of reaching a major cup final, whilst playing in League Two. Image by Paul Thompson.

(*Below left and right*) Disbelieving supporters revel in the Wembley atmosphere and wave claret and amber fans. Images by Paul Thompson.

(*Left*) Gary Jones contests the ball with Nathan Dyer during the League Cup Final at Wembley. The veteran proved to be an inspired signing from Rochdale the summer before, and was the runaway winner of the 2012/13 player of the season award. Image by Paul Thompson.

(*Above*) A dejected looking City team, as Premier League Swansea City net again on their way to a 5-0 victory. Image by Paul Thompson.

(*Below*) The Sky TV cameraman takes in the incredible sight of 30,000 City fans standing, singing and waving their flags in recognition of their team's achievements, despite being hopelessly outclassed on the day. Image by Paul Thompson.

(*Above*) 12 years of misery, firmly over. The final whistle against Northampton at Wembley that means that players can celebrate promotion from League Two in May 2013. Image by Mike Holdsworth.

(*Below*) Putting ghosts to bed. Phil Parkinson admitted that the team used the painful experience of losing the League Cup Final to Swansea City as inspiration to get promoted at Wembley, just three months later. Image by Mike Holdsworth.

(*Above*) Let's do this. Bradford City prepare to play a Chelsea team with some £200 million worth of talent in the FA Cup fourth round, January 2015. Image by Mike Holdsworth.

(*Left*) Scenes of disbelief. Chelsea take a 2-0 lead in the first half, but the best team in the country are in for an almighty shock from the battling Bantams in the second half. Image by Alex Scott.

(Above and below) A capacity Valley Parade crowd cheers Bradford City to victory over Premier League Sunderland in the FA Cup fifth round. This includes the first ever Tifo display at Valley Parade. Images by Mike Holdsworth.

fashion. Of the 92 clubs who entered the League Cup, only four were left. Chelsea, Swansea City, Aston Villa of the Premier League – and also the bottom tier, and deeply unfashionable, outfit, Bradford City. On a bitterly cold and snow-filled 22 January 2013 evening, City travelled to Villa Park for the second leg of the semi final against Aston Villa. And what's more, they made the trip with a 3-1 first leg advantage. All they had to do was avoid a two-goal defeat, and they would become the first ever fourth-tier side to reach a major Wembley final.

It was an astonishing adventure, especially for a club that had until recently endured a desperately disappointing record in knock out competitions. Between October 2001 and August 2005, City slumped to nine consecutive cup defeats. In other words, for four years they exited every cup competition at the first stage. In truth, it didn't get much better after that hoodoo was finally ended with a 5-0 victory over Rochdale in the League Cup. In 2009 and 2011, City reached the last eight of the unloved Johnstone's Paint Trophy competition. Yet beyond that, the cup competitions were a constant source of disappointment and underachievement. Cup runs and giant killings were the preserve of other lower league clubs.

2012/13 changed all that in a big, big way. After Notts County were knocked out in round one, another three higher league clubs would be defeated during City's remarkable run to the semi finals. This included Championship Watford at Vicarage Road in round two at the end of August; where the Bantams responded superbly from going a goal down in the closing stages, to win the tie through late, late goals from Kyel Reid and Garry Thompson. It meant they had reached the third round of the competition for the first time in eleven years. The Telegraph & Argus' Simon Parker felt it was a pivotal night in City's season – the first true indication that something special was brewing. "They went 1-0 down with about 20 minutes to go, and you thought 'oh well they've done okay here against a Championship side, they can hold their heads high'," he recalled. "But then they came back to win and you thought 'blimey'. It had no resemblance to what you'd seen before for many years. And you thought 'wow they might be onto something here'."

The rise of the Bradford City special one

For the manager, Phil Parkinson, the early round League Cup successes were proof that he was successfully starting to turn around the mentality of the club. He had taken over at Valley Parade in September 2011 – a year earlier – after a poor start to the 2011/12 under Peter Jackson led to the former City captain quitting. For Parkinson – who had enjoyed success in charge of Colchester before spells at Hull City and Charlton – it was the right route back into management after a spell scouting for Arsenal. He explained to me, "I'd left Charlton January time and I had been fortunate to get a job working for Arsenal, which was brilliant for me. It gave me a great insight into their recruitment policy and I was really enjoying it. I had a couple of options to go back into management, but I didn't feel they were right. I then had the opportunity to speak to Mark [Lawn] and Julian [Rhodes].

"Like everyone else I was very aware of the potential at Bradford City, including the fanbase. I knew that it would be a very tough challenge, but I felt that we could get the club going. It's a fantastic football club. So when I was offered the job I didn't really hesitate. I thought it was a great opportunity."

Nevertheless the players that he inherited were a long way short of the standard required for a club with ambitions for promotion – Mark Lawn dubbed it the worst squad in Bradford City's history. Parkinson knew that big changes were needed, and that they would take time to come to fruition. "You'd quite often hear people say that it's difficult to play here [at Valley Parade], but I thought they were excuses really, to justify poor individual displays," he continued. "I felt that people were hiding behind that. And that a lot of people were just going through the motions.

"I quickly established a mantra that players had to put in the effort and commitment that you'd expect. It didn't happen overnight, but gradually we started to get a few results. That first season was a tough one because we had a poor side. We obviously had Nahki [Wells] who emerged during the season, but we didn't have the right mentality in the team. We didn't have the hunger and desire, and it needed changes."

Having survived relegation in his first season in charge, the summer of 2012 was the opportunity for Parkinson to really stamp his authority on the club and to bring in players who would raise the standards of those around them. "Character is one of the big things that me and Steve Parkin [Parkinson's assistant] check for when looking at players. It's such a big thing. Stephen Darby, Rory McArdle, Gary Jones, James Meredith – those type of people were brilliant for us, because they helped us to progress the club. They were winners. They want to give their best every week. And they set the tone for new players coming in for years after." Simon Parker stated of the new signings, "There were people who when you looked at them you thought 'they're clever signings'. Parkinson had been building a long time for it, he couldn't wait to offload many of the previous lot. It was such a turnaround."

A good start to the season in the league – City were fourth at the end of September – suggested that things were moving in the right direction. And the two early round cup wins over higher league Notts County and Watford were further proof that this team was made of the right stuff. Round three, against Burton, was to go down as another major night in Parkinson's revolution. Faced with the possibility of playing a Premier League big gun by being in the third round draw, there was understandable disappointment when fellow League Two side Burton were paired with City, with the tie to be played at Valley Parade. No matter, as sensible ticket pricing from the club – and a system where those who attended the game would receive a special ticket stub to put them first in the queue for a ticket for round four, should City progress – ensured a healthy home attendance. Burton rocked up on a monsoon-esqe September evening. The rain was bouncing off the ground and made for a zippy playing surface. The thin margins continued.

City were brilliant in the first half, and yet two defensive lapses meant they went in at the interval trailing 2-0 to Burton. Yet there was something incredibly special in the air that night, and the home support continued to back the team to the hilt rather than dispensing with boos or groans. The players had performed so well, and even at 2-0 down there was no need to feel despondent or to fear that the game was lost. Carry on in that vein in the second half, and a recovery would surely take place.

City continued to dominate as they attacked the Kop, but Burton held firm. Phil Parkinson – who had made some changes to the starting eleven – decided to throw on the big guns of substitutes Nahki Wells, James Hanson and Kyel Reid, and the tide finally turned. Just as the Kop found a new chant that seemed to happily shrug off the inevitable defeat – "it's only a cup, who gives a f**k? We're super City and we're going up" – Wells broke through and finished superbly. 2-1 with six minutes to go, and the volume increased further. "It's only a cup, who gives a f**k? We're super City and we're going up." In stoppage time, Wells pounced again following a scramble in the box for 2-2. It was a poacher's finish from two yards out, and Valley Parade erupted. The celebrations were special. Extra time beckoned, and over this additional 30-minute period Stephen Darby netted the winner from long range.

And it put the Bantams in the last sixteen of the competition, and once again into the hat for the possibility of a lucrative tie. There was again a sense of disappointment over the outcome of the draw – not Manchester United, not Arsenal, not Chelsea, but Wigan away were to be the opponents – but it would prove to be an even more special night. City took over 5,000 fans to the DW Stadium for the game with the Premier League Latics – it was a complete sell out in the away end. A loud and proud noise bellowed out from the first whistle to the last, with Parkinson later commenting on the look of shock that appeared on the face of his opposite number, Wigan manager Roberto Martinez, as he gazed over and took in the intensity of the City support.

It was October half term, and the 5,000 crowd was made up of an assortment of ages and experiences. For those too young to have seen City's Premier League adventure at the turn of the millennium, they had witnessed so little to cheer and certainly nothing on this scale. Everyone relished the occasion, and firmly got behind a City team that had suffered the pre-match blow of losing first choice centre backs,

Luke Oliver and Andrew Davies, to long-term injuries, after they had both been injured at Burton in the league the previous Saturday.

Yet the patched-up Bantams' rear-guard action was exceptional. The League Two side were forced to defend for long periods, as Martinez's well-drilled team attacked with purpose. But the back four of Stephen Darby, Rory McArdle, Carl McHugh and James Meredith were outstanding, backed up by the inspired Matt Duke in goal. City attacked when they could, but it was all about containing Wigan and taking the chance of winning it via a penalty shootout. 120 nail-biting minutes later, and the goalless game did indeed go to spot kicks. City won 4-2, with victory sealed by Duke saving from Jordi Gomez. The goalkeeper was mobbed by delirious team mates, whilst at the other end of the ground the sell out City crowd went crazy in celebration. After a difficult decade of struggle on and off the field, this huge cup upset felt like the night where the gloom began visibly shifting away.

Phil Parkinson is in no doubt that the Wigan game was one of the biggest moments of Bradford City's 2012/13 season, "We lost Davies and Oliver in the game at Burton the previous Saturday, and Carl McHugh and Rory McArdle played at the back against Wigan. We had a pretty much makeshift team out, but I think the result proved to the lads that if you have a gameplan and you stick to it, you can be very hard to beat.

"We were very disciplined in our approach that day. That result gave us huge belief. It showed that anyone in the squad was good enough to come in and play, which is obviously crucial. Carl McHugh emerged in that game, and put in a terrific performance. Players like Carl, who weren't in the team every week, their attitude was fantastic in and around the group. That was so important, and, when players like him get in the team, other players like McArdle and Meredith want them to do well, and will go that extra yard to make them look good at times, especially when Carl was still finding his feet at that level. It was a big game for us, and we kind of grew in confidence from that."

Amongst a DW Stadium press box that was packed full of national newspaper journalists were Bradford City fans Tom Fletcher and Dom Newton-Collinge. The pair had set up a dedicated podcast named Bantams Banter in 2010, and the downloadable shows – which are recorded live at games – have grown and grown in popularity amongst City fans. The League Cup adventure would give the pair a national audience beyond Bantams supporters, as football fans across the country rushed to listen to their less conventional, and highly emotional, take on the amazing events that a lower league club was experiencing.

Dom explained "We set up this show when Bradford City were in the doldrums, because we wanted to do something that was a bit more positive. Everything was negative back then. The City Gent could be very negative, because it was full of moaning old men. We wanted to do something that – although the form on the pitch wasn't great – would perk City fans up a bit. And it did work for those first few years. We got a lot of people listening to us, who said that we had been a positive during some really bad seasons." On the Wigan evening, Tom recalled, "Honestly, it was massive. It was the first game in maybe ten years against a remotely big club where we felt we stood a chance. The DW has never been as full when we rocked up. Looking back the game almost pales into insignificance compared to who we've played and beaten since, which says it all really."

Indeed, the quarter final draw produced that long-awaited money spinner for the Bantams, and it was such an exciting prospect the Wigan game was quickly forgotten. Bradford City would play Arsenal, at Valley Parade. One of the biggest clubs in the land. A full house was assured, plus there was the added financial benefit of Sky TV broadcasting the tie live. This was a throwback to the Premier League days – and, at last, an opportunity for the club to fully benefit from the expansion of the ground in 2001. The tie caught the imagination of the Bradford public, even though most expected the Bantams to be defeated by a second string Arsenal side.

For the club's then-head of operations, David Baldwin, the sell-out game brought a huge workload and plenty of logistical challenges. He explained, "There was no expectation before the game, it felt like we were putting an event on. So much work went on behind the scenes getting areas of the ground ready that hadn't been used for years – you were talking about 12,000 seats. It literally was clearing off the bird crap and washing the seats. We had to sort out the concourses and turnstiles that hadn't been used for so long. The ticket system had to be revamped. It was fantastic to see a full stadium, and it proved such a memorable night."

It was a bitterly cold December evening when Arsenal travelled to West Yorkshire, yet a real sense of occasion hung in the air. I was in town with friends and we caught a taxi to Manningham Lane before kick off. As we got closer to the ground we were surrounded by thousands of people making their way, with traffic on both sides of the road reduced to a snail's pace. There were vendors selling unofficial merchandise, and burger stands every few yards. Every takeaway and every pub nearby was packed out. And at the ground, there were lengthy queues to go through the turnstiles and into the concourses that were bursting with people. It certainly hadn't been like this a few days earlier, when League Two Torquay had been in town.

It had felt like a long time since a Bradford City game was such a big deal; but as we made our way to our seats the scale of the challenge facing the home team was suddenly heightened. Over the PA system, the line ups were read out. Far from an Arsenal team made up of youth players and reserves – which over the years was how Arsene Wenger had treated League Cup games – the Arsenal manager had picked virtually his strongest line up. In total, his starting eleven players had cost £70 million to bring to the club. James Hanson was the only home player who cost a fee – and that was a modest £7,500.

Yet City were not daunted or overwhelmed, nor did they lack a game plan. Parkinson had them superbly organised in a 4-4-2 set up, with two banks of four squeezing the space and pushing out at speed. Sixteen minutes into the match, and the League Two side took a sensational lead. Nahki Wells had earned a free kick close to the corner flag, which Gary Jones swung into the box. Will Atkinson got in front of his marker to flick the ball on at the near post, and there on the opposite side was an unguarded Garry Thompson, ready to smash the ball into the roof of the net. Cue bedlam and epic scenes. Almost 20,000 City fans celebrated the shock goal with gusto and verve. It was said that the roar could be heard over a mile away from Valley Parade.

City continued to attack, with Hanson and Wells causing all manner of problems to an experienced Arsenal backline. Arsenal pushed forward too in search of an equaliser, with the Brazilian Gervinho somehow missing an open goal – his effort was so feeble that it rivalled Notts County's Yoann Arquin's dreadful miss in round one. Inevitably Arsenal dominated more and more during the second half, yet it wasn't until the 70th minute that they actually managed a shot on goal. Did the Arsenal players truly fancy it on a bitterly cold night up North? The rumour going around was they had got changed at the hotel before the game, rather than roughing it by using the Valley Parade changing rooms.

With just three minutes left on the clock, a major cup shock looked set to come to fruition. Alas for City, an Arsenal corner was swung over and Thomas Vermaelen got free of his marker to head home the equaliser. It was heartache for Bradford City; and it was relief for Arsenal, Wenger and the 4,500 visiting supporters, who were celebrating the Belgian's goal in the Midland Road stand. Yet still, despite the visitors almost snatching a late winner, City at least held on for extra time. Drawing 1-1 with a Premier League team was a great achievement, if slightly spoiled by conceding the equaliser so late. A nervy 30 minutes of extra time followed with no further goals – despite Arsenal hitting the woodwork – and the final whistle was greeted with a huge cheer from the fervent City crowd.

You could say that we knew what was coming next.

World record holders

It wasn't just the confidence gleaned from defeating Wigan on penalties in the previous round that meant home fans were expectant going into the shootout – there had been eight other spot kick successes before. Three years and two months earlier, a much smaller City crowd were in attendance for a Johnstone's Paint Trophy tie with Notts County. Apart from the presence of former England manager Sven Goran Eriksson – a short-lived and doomed Magpies experiment – there was little glamour about the evening. Yet after a pulsating 2-2 draw led to a penalty shootout, County keeper Kasper Schmeichel missed the decisive spot kick which meant City went through.

And so began what unofficially became a world record number of successive shootout victories. After Notts County, Port Vale in the JPT went the same way a month later. Then Sheffield Wednesday, Huddersfield Town and Sheffield United in the JPT during the 2011/12 season. Hartlepool in the JPT earlier in this 2012/13 campaign; then the aforementioned Wigan in the League Cup and Northampton in the FA Cup in November 2013. Eight penalty shootout wins in a row, and next up: Arsenal. Be afraid if you're a Gunner. Be very afraid.

So it was that nine in a row was reached. Nathan Doyle and Gary Jones scored for City, and Santi Cazorla and Marouane Chamakh missed for Arsenal (Duke saving Cazorla's). Stephen Darby had the chance to put City 3-0 up, but his effort was tame and easily saved. Jack Wilshire scored for 2-1, Alan Connell made it 3-1 City and Alex Oxlade-Chamberlain was successful for 3-2. All Ritchie Jones had to do was score City's fifth spot kick and they were through, he missed. But no matter, Vermaleen fired Arsenal's fifth onto the post and City were through.

"Cue the celebrations, the like of which they have not seen for many a year" bellowed Sky Sports commentator Bill Leslie. He was talking over pictures of the players charging towards the Bradford End and piling on top of Duke; Nathan Doyle memorably turning to the camera, jumping in the air and roaring. I was in the Kop at the other end of the ground, lost in my own sea of emotions; jumping up and down frantically, hugging everyone near me and screaming at the top of my head. When I started to come to, there were some supporters on the pitch hugging the players and – after they were cleared back into the stands – Parkinson led his troops on a lap of appreciation around the ground. It has been an incredible night of non-stop singing, and the noise wasn't going to subside anytime soon. BBC Radio 5Live commentator Alan Green told listeners around the country of how "unconfined joy was dripping from the stands at Valley Parade".

Sitting near to Green inside the Valley Parade press box, a surreal evening for Tom Fletcher and Dom Newton-Collinge became even more memorable. It was surreal because they had been jointly podcasting on the events alongside the Arsenal podcast show 'The Tuesday Club'; which was headed up by the well-known TV actor and comedian, Alan Davies. Tom explained, "Either Alan was the nicest man on the planet agreeing to it or he thought we were The Chuckle Brothers. He was such a good sport, and the rest of the Tuesday Club Podcast gang were as equally friendly. It kind of put our podcast on the map and, without their support we probably wouldn't be in such a fortunate position now.

"It was a cold, misty and drab evening in Yorkshire; perfect conditions for a giant killing. I must have spoken to about 50 City fans who all thought we would beat them. I don't think that's quinky dink, there was definitely something in the air that night! My main memory was Garry Thompson's goal, amazing finish at the back post and trying really hard not to celebrate too much in front of Jonathan Creek himself!" David Baldwin added, "We assumed that we would earn a few hundred grand in gate receipts, and then that would be our adventure in the cup over for the season. To actually go on and get a result from the game was mind-blowing."

What a night to be a Bradford City supporter, one that put them in the semi finals of the League Cup for the first time in their history. The achievement was even more colossal given their status as a fourth tier outfit. Arsene Wenger woke up the following morning to headlines around the world of his team's embarrassing cup exit. City captain Gary Jones did his bit to pile on the shame by describing the game as easier for his team than the previous Saturday's hard-fought victory over Torquay in the League. "I think Torquay gave us a tougher game… No disrespect to us and our lads but they (Arsenal) should be beating Bradford City. But team spirit means a lot and it can take a team a long way. We have a massive team spirit and we showed it." Arsenal's chief executive, Ivan Gazidis, took the step of apologising to this own supporters. "Last night was not good enough and it made us all upset and angry. I would like to apologise to all of you, especially the fans who travelled up there. It was unbelievable support as ever and you deserved better."

Whilst the footballing world chuckled at Arsenal's humiliation, there was also wholesome praise bestowed on their conquerors too. Bradford City were massive news everywhere. And they weren't yet finished.

"I'd take a draw, just to keep the tie alive"

There was a whole week to wait for the semi final draw, but eventually City found out that they would face Aston Villa over two legs, with the first game at Valley Parade just after Christmas. Whilst they increasingly struggled to concentrate on the bread and butter existence of League Two, there was a licking of the lips over their Premier League opponents' dreadful festive experience – Villa were thrashed 8-0 at Chelsea and lost 4-0 at home to Tottenham – that made them look ripe to be on the end of a giant killing.

Although the attendance didn't quite hit the heights of Arsenal, it was another packed out Valley Parade that welcomed Aston Villa, on what was once again a freezing West Yorkshire evening. This time there were far greater nerves amongst supporters. Whilst, similarly to Arsenal, the expectation was that City would bow out, there was a fear that a bad home defeat in the home leg would render the second game at Villa Park academic. The mission, it seemed to us supporters, was to end the first 90 minutes with the tie still alive.

Phil Parkinson clearly thought on similar lines, admitting before the match that he would be more than happy with a draw. In the event, he and we City supporters got much, much more than that. After another thrilling 90 minutes, played in front of a red hot atmosphere, City eventually headed home with one foot firmly in the League Cup Final. In the run-up City's chief executive David Baldwin had told me that officials from the club had been asked to attend meetings at Wembley for the final – along with the other three semi finalists – to discuss ticket arrangements. It seemed a waste of City's time, surely they wouldn't be reaching the final? But after the first leg, every City fan was keeping Sunday 24 February date clear in their diary. We might just be taking that implausible trip to Wembley.

For City did not scrape a victory that night, they took a two-goal winning margin to defend at Villa Park. Despite a strong start from Aston Villa that should have seen them three goals up in the first ten minutes, the League Two side's defence once again looked resolute and Matt Duke was at the beginnings of surely the best game of his career. City then broke forward, Nahki Wells won a corner for his team, and after the ball pinged about the box it fell loose to the Bermudian – in an onside position – and the highly rated striker put the Bantams in front. It was a brilliant start, but just that – a start. Nevertheless the expected Villa onslaught never materialised. The visitors' confidence, which had been ravaged by the eight-goal thrashing at Stamford Bridge, was in tatters. Villa's travelling support – much louder than Arsenal's – fell silent after making lots of noise during the opening stages. At half time they booed off their players, whilst City fans cheered their heroes and sensed another glory night was in the offing, one to rival the Arsenal victory.

After Villa manager Paul Lambert tore into his charges, the visitors began the second half in more determined fashion and for fifteen minutes pushed the Bantams back. Duke once again stood up to everything chucked at him. Other players threw themselves into tackles and blocks, demonstrating incredible work-rate. Lambert sent on Darren Bent from the bench, but the miss of the season competition, spearheaded by Notts County's Arquin and Arsenal's Gervinho, continued. Bent, an England international, headed a great chance over the bar with Duke lying on the floor. And with that costly wastage, Villa's threat receded.

Incredibly, in the 77th minute City went 2-0 up. A corner was half cleared but kept alive by Wells, who fed the ball back to Gary Jones, who crossed perfectly for Rory McArdle to glance home. The Valley Parade volume reached another new high, with the celebrations more than surpassing Garry Thompson's Arsenal goal and Wells' first half strike. For the first time since the semi final draw was made we could actually start to believe we might reach the League Cup Final. A minute after McArdle's goal, James Hanson hit the bar with a powerful diving header. Villa were on the ropes and close to receiving the knock out blow.

Yet the Premier League team awoke us from our Wembley dreams with a near instant response from Andreas Weimann. 2-1 and – crucially – an away goal for the visitors, which might prove huge in the final reckoning. Yet despite the obvious urge to drop back and make sure that they completed a famous win, City counter-attacked well and substitute winger Blair Turgott won a corner. Jones swung it into the box, and there was the young 19-year-old centre half Carl McHugh to plant the ball past Shay Given. 3-1 to Bradford City, and even more astonishing scenes of celebration. The sheer absurdity of the moment was summed up perfectly by Sky Sports commentator Martin Tyler – "You just can't write stories like this!"

The full time celebrations were lively but not over the top. There was still a second leg to play and, as joint chairman Mark Lawn stated in the Telegraph & Argus, "We've got to remember that Villa are a Premier League side and they can easily score three goals at home." But still, we enjoyed an amazing night and astonishing achievement – one that was greater even than the Wigan and Arsenal wins. This time, League Two Bradford City had beaten a Premier League side over 90 minutes. It wasn't a penalty shootout win, that some could argue is lucky. There was no question they had been the better team on the night, and that the scoreline was a true reflection of the game. "To get that result at home gave us so much belief", reflected David Baldwin.

There were two weeks until the second leg at Villa Park. They passed by painfully slowly.

The snow effect

Checking the weather forecast for Birmingham became just as crucial as the team news during the build up to the second leg. It had snowed for days, bringing with it the usual Met Office warnings of how we should all limit our travel plans to only those journeys that are necessary. Bradford City had sold their full 6,500 away allocation at Villa Park. And with the Premier League side's undersoil heating and fact the game was being shown live on Sky TV, there appeared to be no chance the game would be called off – no matter how hazardous the driving conditions might be on the M6. This was necessary travel.

In the event, the snow was to be a positive for Bradford City's preparations. It led to a rejig in training that meant the Bantams used the state-of-the-art facilities at the new National Football Centre in Burton, St George's Park, rather than their own less-than-perfect training ground. Phil Parkinson explained, "On the Monday before the game, the snow was so bad that we had nowhere to train. I quickly had to ring St. George's Park. We diverted the coach and we went down to St. George's Park. We trained on the pitch there which was very similar to the Aston Villa pitch. The surface was so slick. Premier League pitches are different, and I remember thinking after the training session 'that was a stroke of luck that we were able to do that'."

Yet whilst the team were all set up in the Midlands, for supporters a hazardous drive lay ahead. I had a ticket for the game – and a car full of City fans – and we set off to Birmingham early, allowing plenty of time for hold-ups along the way, without missing kick off. Others would not be so lucky; getting stuck in supporters' coaches that came to a halt in the snow, a mile or so away from Villa Park. They had to do the final leg of the journey on foot, only arriving at the ground midway through the first half.

The snow was thick in the streets that surrounded Villa Park. We arrived at 4pm and yet it was already getting dark. The chill of January was biting. Walking to the nearby Witton Arms was a challenge due the freshly laid coat of snow on the ground. We paid a couple of quid to be allowed in, walked around to the back of the building, and discovered hundreds of City fans drinking, singing and building up a raucous pre-match atmosphere. Clearly we weren't the only ones to plan well in terms of getting down to the game early. In no time at all, we made the two-minute walk to the turnstiles of Villa Park. The nerves had been temporarily put to one side as we enjoyed the chanting in the Witton Arms; but now they returned and felt more powerful than ever.

90 minutes away from Wembley. The impossible dream was in our grasp, and so the prospect of it being snatched away felt even more painful. Simon Parker had similar feelings pre-match, "It was the first time I felt nervous before a cup tie in that run. Up until then it was more of a novelty. But after the first leg against Villa where they played so well, you just thought 'hang on a minute, they've got one foot at Wembley here'. I remember driving down to Villa in the snow, thinking 'how horrible will this be if they lose 3-0 tonight?' Because they were that close and you could almost touch Wembley. And it was never going to happen again. I don't think there would ever have been a lower moment than going out then. It was our one and only chance."

This could be a long night.

Plastic flags

Villa sold out the home stands, and a crowd of 40,193 built up nicely before kick off. Just as the teams were about to come out, the home side unleashed their secret weapon – every Aston Villa fan had found a claret and blue flag on their chair when they got inside the ground. In unison, they all suddenly began to wave them, and at the same time let out an almighty roar. It was an amazing sight, one that demonstrated the scale of the challenge ahead. This is a big, big club with big, big tradition. And they meant business.

Phil Parkinson recalled, "Walking out at Villa Park that night with the flags waving from the Aston Villa fans, it was awesome really. You could see how much they were up for the game. And it was a huge game for Aston Villa, and for Paul Lambert." But the City manager and players couldn't allow it to distract them from the task at hand, as James Hanson added, "Taking a 3-1 lead into the second leg against a Premier League side meant we thought we had a great chance of getting through. It was the biggest game any of us had played in our careers."

The opening 45 minutes were the near-total realisation of our worst nightmares. Villa attacked with gusto and determination from the very first whistle. City were caught between trying to implement their usual game plan and worrying about defending their precious first leg advantage. Stephen Ireland – a fine midfielder who has never realised his full potential – enjoyed a strong night, playing in a free role behind the front two of Christian Benteke and Gabriel Agbonlahor. Charles Zgobia – a powerful and direct winger who had been signed for £9.5 million in 2011 – looked like he really fancied it. 35,000 Villa supporters roared, sang, and waved their flags. Somehow City had to quieten this storm, or they would be blown away.

David Baldwin remembers feeling so nervous during those opening exchanges that he literally threw up, "The surreal thing was I had been to a convention in America a few days before, and I got in to Manchester airport that day and caught the train to Birmingham in the afternoon, with the jet lag. I got to the ground and I felt quite calm and relaxed, had something to eat before the game, but then I walked out into the seats just as the game was approaching kick off, and my heart went into overdrive. I sat there for the first 20 minutes and just felt sick with nerves, and in the end I literally dashed from my seat and to the toilet and I was physically sick. The anxiety of the game and what was at stake was so huge."

24 minutes in, Aston Villa found the breakthrough. Joe Bennett was given too much room by City's

stand-in left back, Curtis Good, and he crossed for Benteke to strike the opening goal of the night. The noise from the Villa fans was incredible. In the away sections, we slumped to our seats. The two-goal cushion has been halved; and as Villa continued to pour forward it seemed a matter of when, not if, they would wipe out the deficit out completely and book their place at Wembley. Benteke missed a brilliant chance to make it 2-0, but there still seemed a sense of inevitability that a second goal was coming. Finally just before half time, Nahki Wells struck an effort from distance that went wide of the post. It was City's first attack of any note, and suggested they could still gain some joy tonight. Still, the half time whistle was greeted with relief from the City fans and, no doubt, the players too. It had been a torrid first half, with the only comfort being that the Bantams were somehow still leading the tie 3-2 on aggregate.

There was no doubt that it was a big half time team talk for Phil Parkinson. He reflected back, "I felt in the first half that we didn't play as well as we could. And I said to the players at half time 'we've come a long way in this competition. If we're going to go out, we've got to go out playing the way that we can'."

James Hanson said, "In the first half they showed how good they really were. Dukey kept us in it with some great saves. We went in at half time 1-0 down, probably lucky really that we were still in the tie. The gaffer calmed us all down because a lot of people felt nervous. He said 'look lads you've got 45 minutes, who'd have thought we'd still be ahead in the tie overall? You've got to keep plugging away and one goal could change the tie'." Parkinson added, "We played with more belief in the second half. We believed in ourselves. And the rest is history really."

Yet to the fans, it didn't look like much changed after the interval. Villa continued to attack with poise and composure, whilst City continued to struggle to get out their own half. There was a moment that – to me – firmly changed the tie; a moment where City finally got a grip of themselves, and brought the fight back to Aston Villa. It occurred after a low cross from Villa should have been simple for Curtis Good to deal with – yet rather than put the ball out for a corner or boot it up the pitch, the Australian sliced a clearance that fortuitously fell into Matt Duke's hands. That panicky mistake was the moment the players seemed to collectively shake themselves up and down and say to each other, "right, no more of this".

And they duly went down the other end and scored.

"Flying in the face of all football logic"

Set pieces had been the feature of the Arsenal and Aston Villa first leg goals, and once again it proved to be the route to success for City. Winger Zavon Hines pressurised young home full back Bennett into conceding a corner, and the first attempt from Gary Jones was cleared for a second set piece. This time, Jones' delivery was bang on the money. James Hanson got free of his marker, the Dutch defender Ron Vlaar. Benteke could not react in time, and City's number nine was free to plant a bullet header into the back of the net.

Of all the people to get this historic goal, it was fitting that it was Hanson. The club's then-longest serving outfield player had been present for some of City's darkest recent hours, and he'd endured his own difficulties winning over a doubting crowd. In fact, he was in the midst of a goal drought that stretched back nine games. But here he was – the ultimate Bradford City working class hero. The man who used to stack the shelves of the Idle Co-op, scoring the goal that put his local team on the brink of a major cup final. It had to be Hanson. He recalled to me with a smile, "I think it's the best goal of my career. I've been fortunate over the last few years to play in some really important games and score goals in them, but I think that that one was the one."

The celebrations amongst the travelling supporters were something else. There was a momentary pause of disbelief, before 6,500 people went wild jumping up and down on top of each other, hugging strangers. Tears were shed. The snow was falling down once more, but no one of a claret and amber persuasion was bothered by the plummeting temperatures. The Bantams Banter pair of Tom Fletcher and Dom Newton-Collinge were in the Villa Park press box to cover the game. Dom recalled, "When that goal went in, I felt my eyeballs move forwards – and that's not supposed to happen to your eyeballs! The two of us cuddled. I have never cuddled anyone as tightly as we did then. I nearly started a fight with Talksport. They weren't happy with us!" Tom added, "It was just surreal as we had a view of the fans and the sheer volume with the atmosphere that they created was just barbaric – in a good way! It was also our best podcast as it was one of those episodes where we just totally forgot we were recording and the end product was special." Simon Parker too struggled to remain professional, "When they got that corner, and then when Hanson got in there, it was just incredible. It was one of those moments where you were trying to type, but I just froze. I was just staring at the pitch."

Villa's brittle confidence once again got the better of them, and they struggled to muster a response to City's equaliser. It was the Bantams in the ascendency, and Hanson should have made it 2-1 but missed a headed chance at the far post. Soon after the superb Stephen Darby charged down the wing and crossed the ball for the substitute Garry Thompson, who with his first touch fired a half volley that rattled against the crossbar. James Hanson added, "I think you could see in the second half we played with a different mentality. We got the goal and it knocked the stuffing out of them. Thommo hit the bar so we could have won the game."

Yet there was to be a late, late scare, as Aston Villa retook the lead with a minute of normal time remaining. Substitute Blair Turgott had the ball for City down by the corner flag, but rather than hold onto possession the young West Ham loanee opted to cross when there was no one in the box. Shay Given booted the ball downfield, and Andreas Weimann was able to run through and around Duke for a goal that made it 4-3 on aggregate.

Suddenly the nerves returned. The fourth official signalled four minutes of injury time, and every player on the field bar Shay Given spent it inside City's half. One more Villa goal would have forced extra time, and would have been such a body blow that it would have been hard to see City recovering from it. It felt like a lifetime, but finally referee Phil Dowd blew his whistle for full time. Martin Tyler's reaction on Sky Sports summed it all up. "Bradford City go to Wembley, Bradford City go to Wembley…flying in the face of all football logic". Tom Fletcher reflected on his feelings at full time, "Jubilation, hysteria, pure adrenalin and the fact we had just reached a major cup final, not the JPT, an actual cup final! We drove home and the M6 was a sea of claret and amber beeping all the way back to Bradford." Phil Parkinson added, "It was a memorable night for us, getting to Wembley. The atmosphere with 6,500 Bradford City fans, it still makes the hairs on the back of my neck stand up and I'm sure it does for supporters. All my family were there. It was just a brilliant night."

Simon Parker added, "The final whistle was one of those moments where you could feel yourself welling up. I remember thinking to myself 'well you're not a supporter, you're not from Bradford, but you've covered this lot for years and years. You've covered some of the biggest dross ever. You've seen some terrible games at terrible grounds, and now here you are at Villa Park, you've knocked Villa out the cup and you're going to Wembley'. It was one of those moments where in terms of your career it felt fantastic. I interviewed many of the players after, they all gave me a hug. Matt Duke and Gary Jones had tears appearing underneath their eyes."

The celebrations seemed to go on for hours. The players and coaching staff charged over to the corner where the two visiting supporter sections were based; and on the pitch and in the stands there was mutual punching of the air, hugging and cheering. Oh and tears too, especially from me. I couldn't believe what I had just witnessed. Only being at Wolves in 1999 comes anywhere near as close to the feeling of joy and delirium that I experienced at Villa Park.

Dom Newton Collinge said, "The away game against Aston Villa was my favourite ever moment as a Bradford City fan. The home leg was pretty special, but being at that away leg was just something else. We felt very fortunate being in the Villa press box because it gave us a unique vantage point where we were watching all of our fans enjoying the moment. We had the benefit of being able to see their reaction as well as watch the game. So from a broadcaster's point of view, it was so amazing." Up in the Villa boardroom there was equally unconfined joy, as David Baldwin remembers, "It was disbelief. My most abiding memory was Phil Parkinson's young lad George was up in the boardroom with us, at the time he was only nine or ten-years-old, and I said to him 'do you want to go down and see your dad?' He said yes so we headed to the dressing room and there is a fantastic picture that Phil has of him and George with three of the players. Those memories will be priceless for George, and it was a pleasure to be able to do that for him."

It was the first time in English football history that a fourth tier side had reached a major Wembley final. And this, during an era where the financial imbalance between the haves and have nots had never been greater. The difference between the budgets that Wigan, Arsenal and Aston Villa operated on – compared to City – were colossal. Yet the Bantams downed all three Premier League sides, producing sensational performances that were out of this world.

On Wednesday 23 January, the footballing world woke up to headlines about Bradford City's heroics the previous evening. The embarrassment of Aston Villa was a big story, but the incredible achievements of a bunch of unknown and unheralded footballers over-shadowed everything. And with James Hanson, the Co-op shelf stacker, at the forefront of the aggregate victory, the angle was assured. The day after Villa Park, the branch of the Co-op in Idle suddenly found it was inundated with TV cameras and journalists. Former workmates of Hanson were interviewed about what he was like to work with, and what they made of their former colleague's achievements. The hero himself added, "It was an unbelievable night. To get a team to a cup final was a great achievement."

Living the dream

The media hype didn't die down for weeks. There was a month before the League Cup Final with Swansea City, and TV stations from around the world flocked to Bradford to cover this incredible story. The Bantams Banter lads found themselves right in the middle of this storm, fronting up the competition's main sponsor, Capital One's publicity, and even recording a song that was played on Sky Sports News and BBC Radio 5 Live. Tom reflected, "The most surreal moment was pulling up outside Valley Parade in our campervan to do a piece for Football Focus, and just as were about to get out these Norwegian guys came up with cameras and said 'Can you do a quick interview with us for Norwegian TV?' They stuck the camera in the window before we had chance to get out! That was surreal.

"We also ending up dancing on the Valley Parade pitch to sing our Wembley song 'Let's get ready for Wembley' for Al-Jazeera TV. I'd love to see that footage!" Dom added, "There were so many amazing moments. One of the best was the BBC Radio 5Live evening at Valley Parade, where we were asked to sing 'Let's get ready for Wembley'. When the fans in the room started singing our song back to us, I felt like Billy-Ray Cyrus!"

And how did it feel to become celebrities? "We'd argue that we didn't become celebrities!" continued Tom. "Maybe we became mildly famous around certain areas of Bradford – but it was good fun. It was just something stupid we felt would suit the mood of the fans. We never thought it would go 'viral' and the biggest memory has to be signing autographs for kids outside Wembley. The nearest we had ever come to that was writing cheques and I'm pretty sure I was just doing my signature every time!"

Simon Parker said of the day, "It was just a case of enjoying it. I remember wandering around Wembley Way the day before with posters of Rory McArdle and Garry Thompson on lampposts, it was crazy. The atmosphere was superb, but unfortunately the game never lived up to it. It was great just watching them warming up and thinking 'they're the players who you normally see playing at Barnet and Dagenham'. The closest they normally get to Wembley is Brentford! It was one of those Playstation moments. Bradford City in a cup final – even to this day it doesn't sound right!"

The Wembley Final was one of the biggest occasions in the club's history. They had won the FA Cup in 1911, but that was 102 years ago and occurred at a time when City were amongst the biggest clubs in the country. The 33,000 ticket allocation for the Swansea game was gleefully snapped up, and Parkinson claimed they could have sold more than three times that amount. On the weekend of February 23/24, 2013, London was invaded by Bradford.

Alas, the final itself did not contain the fairytale ending. Swansea were not the ideal opponents, given they themselves had never reached a major final before and would therefore be guaranteed to take the occasion extremely seriously. When a week before the match, Swansea rested players for a Premier League match at Liverpool, the writing was arguably on the wall. Swansea were 5-0 victors against the Bantams, aided along the way by the unfortunate and heart-breaking sending off of Matt Duke. It wasn't until the 86th minute that City managed a shot on goal. Swansea were magnificent and ruthless; for City it was a game too far. The best memory of the day was the reaction of the 33,000 City fans, at 4-0 down, as every man, woman and child rose to their feet, waved flags and out-sung their victorious opponents. It was an amazing moment to be losing 4-0 and yet still feeling incredibly proud of the players.

Dom from Bantams Banter reminisced, "The cup final was brilliant. I mean forget about the result, because I think most City fans expected us to lose in the cup final. Getting there, being at Wembley and to see 30,000+ City fans singing proudly during the closing stages. Again we got to see that from a broadcast position. It was unreal. I've never experienced anything like it. It was just spectacular."

Tom concluded, "Yeah we lost 5-0, but so what? The whole day was just one big Bradford City carnival and the achievement of a League Two side making it to a final after playing three Premier League teams on the way will always go down in history. Being a part of that history is what makes it even sweeter."

The cup run was incredible from start to finish. It put Bradford City back onto the map, and gave everyone connected with the club a massive confidence boost – especially the players. It was the catalyst for the club's rise back up the Football League. It was a moment City burst back into the national spotlight and it will be recalled for decades to come. Andrew Davies told me, "It was massive. It gave everyone confidence beating teams like Arsenal and Aston Villa. I think that people didn't quite realise just how good we were, but I thought our team then was fantastic."

It was the cup run of our lives. Six rounds were successfully negotiated, major clubs, players and managers were toppled. The club punched above their weight in a manner they never had before, and in doing so captured the imagination not only of the Bradford public but of the footballing world. Michael Laudrup, the winning Swansea manager, sportingly summed up the legacy as he celebrated his team's victory on the pitch at full time. "What they [Bradford City] have done this season is absolutely outstanding and I think this final this year will remain in history, a small part because of us and a large part because of Bradford."

And a small part, also, because of Yoann Arquin.

City (vs Aston Villa): Matt Duke, Stephen Darby, Rory McArdle, Carl McHugh, Curtis Good, Zavon Hines (Garry Thompson 71), Gary Jones, Nathan Doyle, Will Atkinson, James Hanson, Nahki Wells (Blair Turgott 87)

Not used: Jon McLaughlin, Michael Nelson, Ricky Ravenhill, Kyel Reid, Alan Connell

One fine day

Northampton Town vs Bradford City

League Two play off final, Saturday 18 May, 2013

For Bradford City, the road back to Wembley following the Swansea City League Cup Final defeat proved to be a short one. It was a return journey that began just 14.8 miles away from the national stadium, on an evening when the players and management were still licking their wounds from the Swansea hammering. And it was a route that ended less than three months later, as the Bantams staged a remarkable late rally – twice – to reach the play off final at the national stadium.

The Hilton Hotel in Watford was the scene where that first step that was taken. The club used it as their base for cup final weekend; and on that Sunday evening after the match a disco and food was laid on for the players, coaching staff and their families. It could have proven a celebratory party, but Swansea had not been in the mood to lie down and go the way of Wigan, Arsenal and Aston Villa. So instead there was a more muted atmosphere, as disappointment sunk in over the heavy defeat, and of the amazing cup adventure coming to an end. But Phil Parkinson used the downbeat occasion as an opportunity to lift sagging spirits and to ensure that the club focused on moving forwards, rather than feel sorry for themselves. Back in the bread and butter of League Two, the cup heroics had cost them a strong play off position and they were slumped in mid-table. But there was still time to make a late promotion push, provided they got their act together quickly.

So Parkinson got onto the microphone in front of everyone to deliver a speech. He reflected on each round of the League Cup and the memories they provided, and he paid tribute to the players and Bradford City supporters. And then he made a pledge. A pledge that his players were told to take on board. A pledge that they ultimately followed to the letter. It came right at the end of the six-and-a-half-minute speech – filmed by City supporter John Boyle and uploaded to YouTube for the world to see.

"I'd just like to say that we've got fifteen games left. And we are going to have a major charge at these last fifteen games. Major. Everyone. We have got a squad capable of getting on a good run and we are going to have a real go at it. Every single game we are going to play it like it is our last game. We are going to run harder. We are going to tackle harder than the opposition. We are going to play in a positive manner every single game. And if at the end of those fifteen games, we haven't got where we want to be, we will hold our hands up. But it's really important, and I want all the lads to listen to this, that we are on it. We can have a few beers tonight, but on Tuesday morning when you come into training, forget this cup run, it's been great, but we are on it against Dagenham & Redbridge at home on Wednesday night and they better be ready for us."

They were strong words and big promises. But that is exactly what Phil Parkinson and his players delivered over those final fifteen games. They never gave up, even though everybody else appeared to give up on them. And they would be rewarded handsomely for fighting until the very end.

The right character

For on May 18, 2013, Bradford City made only their third-ever visit to Wembley Stadium. Not only looking to banish the ghosts of Swansea City, but to seal a first Bradford City promotion for fourteen years and to bring six, mainly difficult, years in the bottom tier of English football to an end. It was an amazing achievement to be back at Wembley, simply because of how much ground they had to make up over such little time. With the clock ticking and the season petering out, the team found its second wind to deliver the best run of results all campaign. They did, indeed, as Parkinson promised, run harder and tackle harder than the opposition – and they also played positive attacking football, with their big players finding their best form at the right time.

There was no doubt that the League Cup heroics had taken their toll on City's promotion push. A promising first half to the season saw the Bantams climb up to fourth in the league in early December – the edge of the three automatic promotion places. They'd defeated Torquay United 1-0 to earn that promising league position, and three days later welcomed Arsenal to Valley Parade for that League Cup quarter final. After that amazing night against the Gunners, and with the excitement of Aston Villa in the semi finals to come, league form started to suffer. They defeated Accrington 2-1 on Boxing Day, but then went on a dismal run of just one win in eight matches, taking them up to the Swansea cup final. There was an absurdity to the fact that – three days before beating Aston Villa 3-1 in the first leg of the semi final – the Bantams were defeated 2-0 by struggling Barnet, and then the Saturday after that they lost 2-1 at home to a mid-table Oxford United. Minds had been turned by the glamour of the cup adventures, and it was hard to begrudge the players of that. But the collapse in league form pushed City well away from automatic promotion contention and outside of the play off spots, too.

The week before Swansea at Wembley, City carelessly lost 2-1 at bottom club AFC Wimbledon. Their next game against Rotherham United was postponed due to the Bantams' Wembley date with the Swans, but results from the other eleven League Two fixtures that weekend pushed them down to twelfth in the division. The League Cup miracle was amazing fun, but there was a very real risk that it had badly damaged the promotion push to the point that it would soon be over.

And that would have been difficult to take, given the quality of the squad. In the summer of 2012 – Phil Parkinson's first close season after he took charge the September before – the squad was revamped with spectacular results. Having struggled with the finances over the previous couple of seasons – and with the team having recorded consecutive eighteenth-place finishes – joint chairmen Mark Lawn and Julian Rhodes opted to push the boat out, and to try a new approach for providing the manager with adequate resources to mount a promotion push. Despite only being able to afford a £1.3 million playing budget, in order for the club to break even, they gave Parkinson £1.8 million, with variants in place to cover the £500k deficit over the course of the campaign. Those variants included any extra revenue generated from a good cup run – Lawn and Rhodes budgeted to go out in the first round of each competition – all the way through to the last resort of selling a player. It was, as David Baldwin told me, a "calculated gamble".

"It was all about getting to July, the end of the year for spending, and making sure we have protected the club and not over-spent the budget, so that we are not going into the following season with a deficit to make up. Generally we set ourselves the objective of breaking even every year, and if we don't break-even, it's usually because we know there is a certain piece of income coming into the club shortly." Julian Rhodes added, "It was a bit similar to the strategy of the 1998/99 season [the year City were promoted to the Premier League, see chapter five]. We thought the league was there for the taking. Phil had done well: let's give him a decent budget and let's have a go."

With the enhanced resources, Phil Parkinson set to work that summer shaping the squad in his mould. I first got to meet Phil the September before, just three weeks after he had taken over in the job, and on a sunny morning at the club's training ground he talked me through his philosophy towards team building. He wanted character above all else, and had quickly identified just how important the right character was at Valley Parade especially; with the club floundering in a league that it should be too big for, and with a relatively large crowd short on patience and understanding. He shared an example of a striker who he had got rid of when manager of Colchester United. The striker subsequently had a good career elsewhere, and wasn't short of ability, but Parkinson judged him to not be of the right character for his dressing room, and felt Colchester were able to move forwards as a team because of getting him out the door. Character mattered greatly to Parkinson.

Looking back on the 2012/13 squad building activity when I interviewed Phil for this book, he told me, "We recruited a group of players who had real hunger to do well. They really bought into everything that myself and Steve Parkin wanted to do. They had an incredible work ethic. No one liked playing against us. Every manager you'd speak to would say 'it's really difficult playing against Bradford'. We put teams under pressure. We made their back four defend. I think there was real character and a never-say-die attitude instilled into the players that they've always got to keep going to the end. I think there were lots of examples of that over that year."

Parkinson was supported closely by David Baldwin, whose role had grown from head of operations into the club's chief executive. David explained, "From a personal perspective, Phil was the trigger point where I defined the completeness of my role. I originally came in to help for six weeks and ended up being there for a few years, focusing on the commercial side of things. It then progressed during the Peter Taylor era to dealing with the football problem elements. And then by the time Phil came in, it was me and him working together on all aspects. I became the support mechanism for Phil very early on. I was the go-to person for him, and then going straight to the chairmen, whereas Peter and Stuart [McCall] had been dealing directly with the chairmen first and foremost. It meant that I was at the sharp end of knowing what was needed to improve the environment that Phil and the team operated in."

David was also hugely instrumental in making sure that Phil – unlike his predecessors – had training ground facilities that were fit for purpose. For decades Bradford City had trained at Apperley Bridge, 3.8 miles away from Valley Parade in the south side of the city. This included the strange arrangement of the players having to meet at Valley Parade to get changed before driving down in their own cars to Apperley Bridge, completing a training session and then driving back, often muddy, to get changed again. It was outdated in modern football and the story goes that, back during City's Premier League days, they avoided showing prospective new signings the training ground as they knew it would put them off joining the club.

With City floundering in League Two, there had been increasing attention and pressure on the club to do something about the situation – Peter Taylor was especially vocal on the matter. In the summer of 2011, just before Phil Parkinson joined, the club finally acted and set up a partnership with Woodhouse Grove school – which is located next to Apperley Bridge – where City have onsite changing facilities, offices and a place to eat, which David Baldwin is especially proud to have overseen.

"I always say that my biggest achievement at Bradford City, for me as an individual, was the redevelopment of the training ground and the environment that the team operate in. When I was there as a kid in 1987 playing football, and compared to when I came back in 2007, the facilities were worse! When I left in 2014 they were equal to a good Championship facility.

"Phil ran a more regimented process and had the tools to do it as well. He had an office down there, the coaching staff and medical team had offices down there full time. It created a really cohesive environment for football, and Phil made good use of those tools. He utilised the sports science side of things and brought Bradford City into the 21st century – and he had the facilities do that. That was my contribution to the club. It's my biggest feeling of pride. The people who you work with in your life can make a big difference. So now the players were able to come in together in the morning, have some breakfast and play some pool or watch Sky Sports. They'd all get changed together, go out together and train, and then have lunch together around the same table, before going home in the afternoon.

"All of a sudden these players were spending a lot of time together, and that adds to that cohesion. If we hadn't have made those decisions about Woodhouse Grove – which were brave decisions to make at the time – we wouldn't have had the tools to give Phil the environment to create that cohesion and spirit. During the summer of 2012 we had eleven players out and eleven players in and we worked really closely together. I did most of the contracts. And with the training ground we had an environment where you were proud to show to prospective signings. It allowed us to be more ambitious about the players we targeted."

Back in September 2011 and two weeks after taking over as manager, City had lost 2-1 at home to Wimbledon in feeble circumstances, and in the post-match press interview Parkinson spoke of the club having a "losing culture" that he wanted to put right. It wasn't a quick win, and the 2011/12 season was a difficult one to turn around, with relegation concerns lingering into late April. But in the summer of 2012, he had the time and the resources to truly stamp his imprint on the club. And so in came the likes of Rory McArdle, Nathan Doyle, Stephen Darby, James Meredith, Garry Thompson, Zavon Hines and Will Atkinson; players who would prove their mettle over the course of the season, and play huge roles in what proved to be a memorable campaign.

Another key player brought in was Andrew Davies. A central defender, who had been signed by Parkinson on loan during the season before, who was playing for Premier League Stoke City. Davies was the perfect embodiment of the character mantra Parkinson instilled. Davies replaced club captain Guy Branston – signed by Peter Jackson the summer before, and clearly someone who Parkinson did not rate – and he proved to be the bedrock at the back for four seasons.

On first signing for City on loan in September 2011, Davies told me, "I was at Stoke City and I was having quite a few problems with injuries and stuff, my wife was working at home [in the North East] and it was one of them where I was just desperate to come home and I just said to my agent 'look just find me a club near home, who would take me now'. Luckily Bradford City came in. The manager rang me and said 'look we've been interested in you for a while. Now you've mentioned you'd like to come home would you be interested?' and I said yes straightaway. It was one of those decisions where you thought 'this will be great'. It's a big club, and hopefully things will be good."

Having had a taste of life at Valley Parade that season, in the summer of 2012 Davies was happy to turn down interest from other clubs and make the loan move a permanent one, signing a one-year deal. "A couple of Championship clubs wanted to take me. But I thought if I go to one of them I might be sitting on the bench, playing now and again and stuff, whereas at Bradford I could carry on playing at a club where I had settled in. I wouldn't say money wasn't a problem, because you want to earn a good amount throughout your career, but it was one of those decisions where I did it because I was enjoying my football, and money wasn't a massive deal to me."

It was evident also just how much Andrew Davies enjoyed playing for Parkinson. "He was very good. What you see if what you get. If you go out and give 100% he will like you. It's as simple as that. You can see in players who left the club where he thought they weren't giving their all, he was a ruthless manager and he would just get rid of you. Any player that came in he would say the exact same thing to them. I think if you have a manager like that, they are very easy to work for."

Davies proved to be a huge player, even though several injuries disrupted his time at Valley Parade. But arguably Parkinson's most important and successful signing that summer was not even amongst his initial summer targets, and he came onto the radar in unconventional fashion.

His name was Gary Jones, a veteran lower league midfielder of advancing years. The story goes that Parkinson – at the time assessing whether to sign Liverpool right back Stephen Darby – watched a video of one of the young defender's performances whilst on loan at Rochdale the season before. Jones was playing in this particular game too, and Parkinson noted, with increasing enthusiasm, just how involved and instrumental the Rochdale captain was in proceedings. He was everywhere, running the game. Parkinson picked up the phone and called his assistant manager, Steve Parkin – who managed Jones at Rochdale and Barnsley – to ask for his views on the player. Parkin's response was everything that Parkinson wanted to hear in his pursuit of character. "The best thing I can say about Gary Jones is the only time he is ever happy is at 5pm on a Saturday when his team have won."

Parkinson pounced quickly. Jones – who was a loyal servant at Spotland and Rochdale's record appearance holder – had endured a fall out with manager John Coleman, and he was ready for a new challenge. He snapped up the chance to move to Valley Parade, and Parkinson had his talisman. Jones was 35-years-old when he signed for City, and it was a move that raised eyebrows amongst supporters and the rest of the division. I must admit I was unconvinced, but it took just 45 minutes of watching Gary in a City shirt to realise just how big a player he could be. It was a pre-season friendly at Guiseley, and Jones ran the game with incredible levels of work-rate and dedication. Not since Stuart McCall had I seen a City player look like such a leader, and play in a manner that so evidently lifted the standards of everybody around him.

Katie Whyatt, a teenage Bradford City supporter who in 2012/13 was sitting her GCSEs, and who is the deputy editor of Widthofapost.com, reflected on the qualities of Gary Jones. "In my opinion, he was the most important player in that squad. Everything about that team, that season, was Gary Jones: that refusal to be denied; that energy and desire to run an inch further to push themselves to victory; that need to produce when the chips were down. He was the pulse of the side, the lifeblood behind the things that endeared them to us."

There weren't too many players from the old regimes who could live up to the raised standards, but James Hanson was one of them. He reflected, "Phil has been a main factor in why I keep improving year on year. He and Steve Parkin have got a great bond, especially with Nick Allamby [the club's sports scientist] as well. Under Phil Parkinson I definitely got fitter as well, which helped me get round the pitch and to pick up fewer injuries. I still get the odd injury, but looking back over the two or three years before he came in I picked up a lot more injuries. And looking back on the promotion season I ended up playing 60 odd games. That just shows how fit Nick got me.

"The gaffer, Steve Parkin and Nick would do so much stuff for the players at the training ground that the fans don't see. They're constantly pulling players to the side and working on different bits. That's definitely improved me as well."

The tackle

And so the team was constructed, and it quickly ran out of the blocks. City lost the opening League Two game of the season at Gillingham, but followed it up with a 1-0 victory over newly promoted Fleetwood at Valley Parade. And there was a moment, at 0-0, which showed the players just what was needed to win over the demanding Bradford City crowd. It came with Fleetwood on top and threatening to score, only for a thunderous sliding tackle by James Meredith to halt the attack and prompt huge roars of approval from the home fans. This is what we asked of them: hard work, commitment and dedication. Not too many crowds in the country would cheer a tackle so loudly. The players took on board the message and ran with it.

A few days later they were 5-1 up by half time to Wimbledon, and over the coming weeks they continued to record memorable victories. The team had balance, marrying up grit with skill. The back four looked solid, the midfield led superbly by Gary Jones and Nathan Doyle. And there, up front, was the little and large combination of James Hanson and Nahki Wells. The pair formed the best strike partnership seen at Valley Parade since the 1999 promotion-winning side was led by Lee Mills and Robbie Blake.

In Wells, Hanson had the perfect partner to run onto his flicks and to link up with, to deadly effect. Wells had joined City on the recommendation of former Bantams winger Mark Ellis, after the Bermudian was signed up by the RIASA academy that Ellis had launched with David Baldwin. RIASA offers a college degree, combined with playing football, for overseas players. The aim, similar to colleges in America, is to help talented footballers break into the professional game, whilst having a degree education to fall back upon if needed. Wells was the brightest star of RIASA and Ellis – with his City contacts – tried to persuade his old club to take a look at him. But then-manager Peter Taylor wasn't interested, and Wells ended up at Carlisle. Having being given little opportunity at Brunton Park, Wells was released and once again Ellis banged loudly on the City door. This time, Archie Christie – recently appointed chief scout – took a look and was impressed enough to sign him up for his development squad. Wells made the breakthrough in 2011/12, impressing greatly. 2012/13 would be his coming-of-age season.

Between them, Hanson and Wells netted over 40 goals over the season. They were such a talented partnership who seemed capable of reading each other's minds. Wells would finish the season as the division's fourth highest goalscorer with eighteen goals, but that told only part of the story of his amazing campaign – with a further nine strikes coming in the cup competitions. Andrew Davies enthused, "We had a front two who on their day you couldn't play against. They would have scared any centre half pairing whether in the Championship or the Premier League." James Hanson was full of praise for his former strike partner – who in January 2014 moved to Huddersfield Town – and the way they linked up, "It's was frustrating the amount of strike partners I had before Nahki. I didn't seem to find the right one that would complement me. But I suppose, whilst at the time I was improving, in the first couple of years there were a lot of times I was just flicking things on. If I had gone and played with those partners again it might have been different.

"Nahki was just so alive. There were a lot of times I could just flick the ball onto him knowing he would finish it off. And although I'm getting the credit for the assist, he's done all the hard work. That's what he was so good at: reading flicks and anticipating stuff. So many goals came from when defenders made mistakes, but he was the one chasing them down and sensing that opportunity. I'm delighted for him that he got his move and that he is now proving himself in the Championship."

Despite a hugely encouraging first half to the campaign, the effects and the distractions of the League Cup endeavours took their toll during January and February. In addition to the tussles with Arsenal, Villa and co, City made decent progress in the FA Cup and Johnstone's Paint Trophy. Managing the resultant fixture pile up was a real challenge given the size of the squad wasn't especially vast. It became a real marathon, and – if promotion was to be achieved – it was clear that City would have to go the whole nine yards.

And you questioned whether they had any stamina left, in the wake of the Swansea cup final defeat. They'd been playing two games a week for months, but they still faced another fifteen regular season games in order to make the play offs – and then a further three matches would be required if promotion was to be achieved. That's at least another 1,350 minutes on top of the 4,320 completed so far. It would mean playing an amazing 64 games over the season. Chelsea were the only club in the country on course to play more matches, but they had a much bigger squad from which to choose from.

Fortunately City had an off-the-field weapon who could steer them through such a gruelling schedule – the aforementioned Nick Allamby, who James Hanson rates so highly. Brought in during the summer of 2011 by the then-manager Peter Jackson's assistant, Colin Cooper, Allamby's sports science approach gave City a real advantage over many of their promotion rivals. In the summer of 2013, Width of a Post writer Nick Beanland interviewed Allamby for the website, and he explained, "We know we have to get them ready to play every game at full speed, so it's a question of short duration drills in training but they have to be at game tempo. You can't say 'we've had loads of games so we won't train very much'. If you do that they'd just go into games and not be able to cope with it."

Allamby added on the uniqueness of his role at a League Two club, "There are still some managers who are not as convinced of sports science as Phil is, so my appointment was still quite an unusual one for League Two level. The integrated approach we have here is one I believe in so I'm really lucky to have a manager who thinks the same way."

Reflecting on how he got the players buy in to his fitness approach, Allamby recalled the very first game of the 2012/13 season, "After pre-season we started at Notts County in cup – it had been a tight game until extra time, but then we ran all over them. The players came into the dressing room after that and were delighted at how fit they felt. At that point I think they were convinced by the work we were doing. They're a good bunch of lads. Phil's hired decent characters and they don't mind working hard."

In the immediate aftermath of the Swansea game, squad rotation was also the key in keeping things ticking over. Some players, such as Nahki Wells, had endured a dip in form and needed some time out. Others like Nathan Doyle looked fatigued and in need of a rest. Parkinson turned to some of the squad players, who hadn't figured so much, to come in and do a job – and most delivered. City drew a lot of games post-Swansea, but crucially would lose only twice over those final fifteen games. Nevertheless, it still felt like they had too much to do to make up the lost ground on the play off chasers. And that they didn't have a sprint finish within them to win the marathon.

Run harder, tackle harder

I'll admit that I gave up on promotion somewhere in the middle of March. I had travelled down to Plymouth with some friends to watch a Tuesday evening encounter with an Argyle side who, at the time, were stuck at the bottom. City laboured to get going all evening, before staging a late rally that had the air of too little, too late. The match finished 0-0, and it felt like a summary of how the season was surely going to turn out. We'd left it too late, and we didn't have the capacity or energy to do more.

That game had been City's fifth since the Swansea cup final defeat, of which they had only won once. In my match report of the Plymouth game I wrote, "What we needed post-Wembley was to hit the ground running. Instead of finding top gear, we're still chugging along in the slow lane, with the front runners dauntingly far away on the horizon. And recent results, performances and tactics would be okay if we were in the play off positions, looking to consolidate a top seven or top three finish. But we are not. We remain frustratingly not even close." I gave up the ghost that night, and when a few days later City were thrashed 4-1 at Exeter – who were in the final play off spot – I wasn't surprised or too downhearted. City were eleventh. Promotion hopes were surely over, so all we could do was accept it and move on.

Katie Whyatt reflected on the mood of supporters at that point, "I think there was widespread doubt, given the deficit and congestion of teams at the top of the table, and the amount of time it took for the team to find their rhythm again after the cup final. We were understanding, as supporters, and almost forgave them before their time was up, accepting promotion was the price we'd paid for the hedonism of January; but the very fact the cup exploits had become a key part of defining the way we saw that team meant there was always a quiet hope they'd do what they set out to do. I think the scepticism peaked after Exeter, but when Parkinson began his rotation policy and publically implored his players and supporters to trust him, something clicked, and that triggered a clinical run to cement a place in the play offs."

Indeed, the players and management never gave up. They upheld Parkinson's pledge to run harder and tackle harder, right to the end. They finally found that top gear, and embarked on a scintillating run. As Exeter's form collapsed from that point on, and no one else could take advantage, City edged nearer and nearer to the play off positions – even threatening to sneak into the automatic promotion spots. Andrew Davies admitted that, following the Exeter defeat, the reduced expectations of promotion meant the pressure eased on their shoulders, which helps to explain how they pushed themselves back into contention. "We got beat at Exeter but we all felt that the pressure was now off us a bit, as no one expected us to go up, so let's just go and enjoy it. It wasn't through lack of effort that we got beaten by Exeter, it just wasn't our day. But I think it gave everyone a kick up the backside and we all thought 'let's just enjoy this' and that was the big factor."

Phil Parkinson was certainly not prepared to throw in the towel after the Exeter loss, and the day after the heavy defeat – a Sunday – he hauled the players in for a special meeting. He explained, "The Exeter game was a particularly poor day for us, but it was probably the day that kicked us off really. We got them all in on the Sunday morning, had a training session and then sat them down to watch the video again. We weren't going to leave that room until we were happy that we were going to get what we wanted from the team. In that game we were second best, but from there on in, it didn't happen again.

"If you look at Sir Alex and Manchester United, the way they always kept going in certain games. We tried to instil that in the team. After we lost the Capital One Cup Final there were fifteen games to go and a lot of people would have written us off. But I think that period showed what that group of people and the staff were all about." Julian Rhodes said of the late surge after the Swansea cup final loss, "We drew the next few games and the result that seemingly killed it was Exeter away. I thought, after that, forget it. If someone had said at that time 'you'll get into the play offs with a game to spare' we'd have rightly thought they were stupid. But we went on a great run. We actually had a great run at the start of the season and a great run to end the season."

Andrew Davies continued, "We did think that promotion might be out of our reach. But football can change really quickly. And it was one of them where when we started to get on a run of games, winning games, all the lads were thinking 'we can do it this year'. And that's how it panned out."

It all began with an unassuming 1-0 home win over Wycombe, where Garry Thompson netted six minutes in and not much else happened. Then a 2-2 draw at home to Southend – during which City had been 2-0 down after eleven minutes – and 3-1 Easter Monday victory over Torquay meant that, coupled with results elsewhere, new hope was flickered back into the season. City then beat play off chasing rivals Northampton 1-0 at home – Nahki Wells netting his first goal in three months – and amazingly ended the day inside the top seven, a position they strengthened with a 4-1 thumping of Bristol Rovers at Valley Parade three days later. Wells got two that night, with Andrew Davies and Thompson also on target. Valley Parade hummed in satisfaction over a fourth victory in five.

The atmosphere was really special in the next game, at Chesterfield. City brought a huge away following who made an almighty racket all afternoon, and goals from Wells and club captain Ricky Ravenhill put City 2-1 ahead to spark scenes of delirium. There were just seconds left on the clock and there would only be three games to go after the final whistle was sounded in Derbyshire. Incredibly, the top three was suddenly in sight. Alas, a late Chesterfield equaliser badly damaged those late hopes as two points were dropped. A midweek 2-0 home defeat to fellow promotion contenders Rotherham further dampened the mood. It was now all about holding their nerve and finishing inside the top seven.

A 1-0 home win over Burton, coupled with results elsewhere, sealed a play off spot with a game to spare. They could afford to relax in the final game at Cheltenham (a 0-0 draw). From going nowhere slowly, City had stolen a march and went into the play offs as one of the form teams. The parallels of 1995/96 and the late run to the play offs under Chris Kamara were strong [chapter four]. After five seasons of barely going close to the play offs, there was a sense of triumph that the club was finally moving in the right direction. Davies recalled, "We did great at the end of the season, and it just bred confidence." Simon Parker said, "One minute they were miles away and then suddenly they were there with a game to spare."

And during that run-in, the class of 2013 really were at their best. It was an enthralling sight to watch the way Phil Parkinson organised his team, and the way they mixed grit with flair. They were outstanding for most of the season at the back, with Andrew Davies the leader and Rory McArdle excelling alongside him. In the full back positions, Stephen Darby flourished after a slow start and James Meredith's worth was emphasised when the Australian was out for three months and results tailed off, only for an instant improvement to coincide with his return. That low-key Wycombe victory had been Meredith's first game back. In goal Matt Duke and Jon McLaughlin battled for the number one spot all season, and in the final run-in McLaughlin firmly made it his own.

But it was going forward where the excitement really lay for fans. With Hanson and Wells now back at their best, watching the way in which they were supplied with ammunition – and the damage they caused from it – had you on the edge of your seat. On the wings, Garry Thompson and Kyel Reid were in superb form. Reid, who Parkinson signed on the same day he was confirmed as manager back in September 2011, had proven himself to fit the Parkinson character blueprint. Reid possessed direct pace and excellent dribbling ability, backed up by a strong work ethic. In midfield, Jones continued to be hugely influential and possessed energy levels to match anyone else in the team. City could go direct for sure, with Rory McArdle adept at picking out Hanson with accuracy. They could play through the middle with Jones and Doyle/Ravenhill, and they could get opposition teams from the flanks through Thompson and Reid. They were not a gung-ho side, and would often start games conservatively; but they inevitably stepped it up during the second half, with their superior fitness levels proving to be a key factor.

"The squad was good, we had depth" stated Andrew Davies. "People got injured. I was injured and Carl McHugh came in and did really well. I think that was the biggest thing. We had pace, we had experience. You obviously had Nahki and Hanson on fire up front. We had Doyley and Jonah who were fantastic in the middle and had a good understanding. Me and Rozza. The full backs Darbs and Mezza bombing on. We had a massive understanding all over the pitch. We played a lot together. Everyone knew each other's game. We were a hard team to beat and that showed."

James Hanson added, "It was brilliant to play in that team. The gaffer drilled us to play a certain way. He says to us that as long as you give your passion for the club and you run yourself into the ground, that's all that fans want to see. They want commitment. And the players they have brought in have all bought into that. We had a great team spirit, and the way that we played was effective and ultimately got us promoted." Simon Parker agreed that the team embodied their manager, "The squad was very much in his way and his mould. As a player he was very disciplined. He admits he wasn't the best player, but he ended up playing a lot of games. He put a lot of effort in. He pushed himself hard and never let himself go. He made the most of his ability. And he's always tried to bring in players like that. You look at the likes of Stephen Darby and Rory McArdle, who give everything."

Katie Whyatt continued the theme, "That team was everything we've ever wanted a football team to be: fearless, invincible, battling until the very end. They seemed like superheroes, capable of achieving the impossible because of the bond that existed between them. Parkinson fostered such a strong sense of belief and duty within the core of that squad, and seeing a team that cared, really cared, after all the faceless strangers of campaigns prior, defined the season. It was the awareness that existed between the players and the fans, the knowledge that it meant as much to them as it did to us."

The Burton Albion comeback

Within the play offs, City were pitted against Burton once more. The striking similarities to 1995/96, and the club's last play off semi final experience, against Blackpool in 1996, continued.

At one stage in the Burton tie, City were two goals behind, and they lost the first leg at Valley Parade. On a warm May evening, Burton caught City cold with a blistering first half display. Calvin Zola – who always seemed to save his best form for games at Valley Parade – struck two excellent goals. The pacy winger Jacques Maghoma gave Stephen Darby a torrid night. City pulled a goal back through Wells from the spot, but Burton went 3-1 in front before half time. Crucially, Burton sat back too much in the second half and City at least reduced the arrears with fifteen minutes to go, through a stunning Garry Thompson strike that deflected in off Gary Jones. They walked off the park defeated 3-2, but the momentum was firmly with them going down to the Midlands three days later.

Andrew Davies revealed that Thompson's goal had been vital in keeping the players believing. "It was a massive goal and that changed the mood. We knew that Burton were a good team, but we went to their ground knowing that they were only one goal ahead, and that if we could nick a goal early they might start to panic." James Hanson agreed, "We went into the semi finals as the form side and everyone was backing us to go up, especially after the big games we had played. But to be fair to Burton they came to Valley Parade and Calvin Zola scored two excellent goals. It knocked the stuffing out of us. We hung in there and at 3-1 down Thommo got us the goal to keep us in the tie. It helped us that there weren't away goals in the play offs, and we knew that we could go to Burton and cause problems." Simon Parker added that he could detect a sense of deflation in the Burton camp because they should have been out of sight, "There was a feeling that Burton had missed their chance a bit, because they had been so much on top. I remember Gary Rowett [the Burton manager] said as much in the press conference at Valley Parade. He was a bit downbeat and you could tell he thought 'we've let them off the hook here'."

The second leg at the Pirelli Stadium was one of those truly great days supporting Bradford City. Fans queued overnight at Valley Parade for tickets, and the visiting allocation of 1,600 was sold out. Burton – who had been outstanding at home, winning twelve of their last thirteen games – were caught in the dilemma of whether to attack or contain City, and a magnificent Bantams display resulted in a 3-1 victory that placed them in the play off final with a 5-4 aggregate victory. Wells opened the scoring in the first half, and then just after the break Hanson struck a powerful second with a low shot from distance on his weaker right foot. Maghoma pulled one back from the spot, but 60 seconds later Wells grabbed his second and City stood firm.

James Hanson said, "On the day me and Nahki formed a good partnership and got the goals between us to take us back to Wembley." "It was pure joy," reflected Andrew Davies, who had crucially missed the first leg home loss through suspension, but played a vital role in turning around the tie. "We all had to dig in very deep. Winning away from home is never easy and Burton were a good team. But to go away and play as we did, and win how we did. The team were fantastic. To come back from a goal down from the first leg, the way we played was fantastic."

The celebrations at full time were memorable, as the players, management and chairmen Mark Lawn danced about on the pitch. No one wanted to go home. We squeezed dry every moment of joy from that day. One chant in particular stood out: "We're proud of you". I wrote in my match report, "As fans we've spent years booing and jeering, singing 'you're not fit to wear the shirt' and, once, 'love the club, hate the team'. 'We're proud of you' is praise indeed and the players and management deserve every bit of credit coming to them and more."

David Baldwin admitted that he and Phil had dreamily chatted about this amazing scenario months earlier, and he couldn't believe it had come about, "I remember at Christmas time having a conversation with Phil on the telephone, and at the end of it we said to each other 'could you imagine the experience if we could get to Wembley and then get promoted in the same season? How unbelievable would that be!' It was literally a pie-in-the-sky conversation, but to think that we achieved it five months later was surreal."

Twelve years of hurt

It had been such a bumpy ride for City fans. From the high point of beating Chelsea 2-0 in the Premier League in August 2000 to the relegations and the administrations and the managerial merry-go-rounds and the changes in the boardroom and the endless stream of under-performing players and the never-ending home defeats. Twelve years of utter misery, until the 2012/13 season came along and gave us the League Cup miracle and two trips to Wembley in three months. Now an incredible season came down to one massive game. Beat Northampton Town at Wembley, and promotion would be ours. Twelve years of hurt was on the verge of coming to an end.

The importance of the play off final was massive, as Julian Rhodes reflected, "Going into that game at Wembley, the outcome of that game would determine whether we had a fantastic season or not. Because if we had lost, we'd still have been playing Dagenham & Redbridge in League Two. So I was very nervous before the Northampton game. I wasn't nervous at all for the Swansea game. I didn't really think we'd win it. It was just fantastic to have got there." Katie Whyatt was similar in her views when comparing the two, "There was definitely more of a business-like approach to the return visit. We had a job to do. There was a quiet confidence, being back for a second time, but it was edged with a tinge of grizzly nervousness.

"The stakes were so much higher – standing atop Wembley Way, surveying the arch and the ocean of claret and amber, there was an awareness that this was the culmination of what we'd actually set out to do in August – that this was the one that really mattered. But having seen everything this team had done, and lived the journey to dreamland with them, you were imbued with belief, rather than hope." Simon Parker added, "The first Wembley was all about the occasion and glory of being there, the game was immaterial. The play off final was all about one thing. It was either black or white. It was either the greatest day ever or the worst day ever."

There were undoubtedly huge nerves going back to Wembley. Just short of 30,000 City fans made the trip back to the national stadium, sat in the same end as they had been for the Swansea game. We hoped it would be the only similarity to that afternoon. Surely this time at least we wouldn't have to wait until the 86th minute to register a shot on target?

Parkinson and the players were utterly professional. The novelty of Wembley was enjoyed in February, but this time they rolled up to do a job and they remained fully focused on that. After the game Northampton manager Aidy Boothroyd admitted that he had hoped the scars of the Swansea experience would have prompted a negative psychological effect on City's players, but the opposite proved to be true. They were ready and determined to exorcise those demons, and to leave their mark on Wembley stadium. "I think the Swansea defeat was a motivation," admitted Andrew Davies. "I think we were used to the surroundings of Wembley and had played in front of 90,000 against Swansea. It was one of them where we were determined not to let it happen again."

Phil Parkinson explained, "We used the Swansea experience to get us promoted, simple as that. The lads were just so calm, cool and collected on the day. And I was looking at the Northampton players and their staff and they were almost looking starry-eyed at the Wembley surroundings. We'd been there and we'd done it. We were in a good place."

City played with a swagger and determination straight from kick off. The early stages saw a flurry of tackles from both sides, but Northampton – noted that season for their physical style – could not bully or intimidate their opponents. City were up for the challenge and bettered the Cobblers in every department. It was only a matter of time before they made the breakthrough. It came from James Hanson with fifteen minutes on the clock. It was a wonderful looping header at the backpost. An initial ball into the box had evaded everyone, but Thompson kept the attack alive by whipping a cross straight back into the danger area and onto the head of his team mate. Hanson revealed, "To score the first goal was an unbelievable feeling. As soon as Thommo put the ball across I knew I could get there with the header and that I just had to direct it over the keeper." Hanson was unplayable in this game, and after the match his Northampton marker – Clarke Carlisle – admitted that the Bradford City striker had "owned" him and was a "nightmare to mark".

Amazingly, just four minutes later it was 2-0 and virtually game over. Again Northampton thought they had repelled the danger and switched off for the second phase of a City attack. Nathan Doyle was alive to the opportunity and crossed the ball towards the near post. There was Rory McArdle, free from his man, to plant a header into the net. At the opposite end of the stadium, we City fans celebrated both goals with unbridled joy and delirium. The outpouring of emotions was a sight to behold. People around me burst into tears. Others couldn't stop jumping on top of everyone in sight.

And before the game had reached the half hour mark, it really was game over. Thompson flicked the ball on, and there was Wells the predator to fire it into the goal. The game clock read 27 minutes 14 seconds. Wells had caused some pre-match tremors by predicting he would score in the final and upsetting Boothroyd; but the Bermudian lived up to his promise and in the process gave Northampton a colossal mountain to climb. Lee Nicholls in the Northampton goal made an excellent save from Reid that would have made it 4-0. He and his team were desperate for the half time whistle and a chance to find their composure. Bradford City 3 Northampton Town 0 at the break. Game over.

Phil Parkinson recalled with pride, "Let's be fair, which teams have produced their best 45 minutes of football of the season on such a big stage? To do that is enormous credit to the lads and all the staff." James Hanson added, "It was a bit surreal to be honest. I never thought we would have been so comfortable. We started the game so well and I think we caught them by surprise. To score three goals in the first half was an unbelievable feeling but I think that it was a weird one, as we knew we still had a job to do in the second half to see out the game." Simon Parker said, "It was awesome. It was as one-sided as the League Cup final had been. It was an almost total role-reversal. The bullied became the bully. They didn't just beat them they totally dominated. Everyone turned up. They used the width of the pitch well. All the big game players turned up. The Northampton reporter said to me at half time 'I just want to go home'."

The second half was a non-event in truth. City remained professional to the end, but were limited in their ambition to attack. They contained Northampton and never offered them a sniff of a comeback. As Simon Parker said, City did to Northampton what Swansea had done to them. Even down to the fact Northampton's only shot on target did not come until the closing stages of the game. "We battered them for the whole game," stated Andrew Davies. "We looked a lot stronger. We were the better team. We had more experienced players. It did feel like men against boys at times. It was a breeze really!"

In no time at all the final whistle went and the celebrations began. The players took time out to commiserate their opponents, before converging in front of the City fans and spraying champagne all over each other. Gary Jones and Ricky Ravenhill jointly lifted the play off final trophy from the Wembley balcony, to huge cheers from everyone of a claret and amber persuasion. It was a truly emotional moment when they did raise the trophy. It felt like a dark chapter in the club's history was finally over, and that the good times had well and truly returned.

An afternoon to savour

It was a beautifully sunny day in London – it had to be. A moment as wonderful as this could only be decked out in sunshine. Davies commented with pride, "On a personal note I was proud because we had been through a lot. I had made big sacrifices to come to the club and to get rewarded. Some players never get to go to Wembley, so to go there twice and finish the way we did was a very proud moment for myself and for the whole team."

Katie Whyatt reflected, "As soon as that whistle went, I burst into tears. I was so proud of this team, so proud of us, my club, of this journey we'd been on together. That we were out of the basement, that we'd done it in our way, that the players were linking hands and racing to the throng of City supporters that filled the Wembley half-moon. That elation was mind-blowing, incomprehensible, indescribable. You wanted to bottle it up and carry it in a hip flask, savouring every swig and sip and morsel. It was so overwhelming that it felt like a mirage. It was such a perfect, fitting end to that season. You couldn't have written it any better. There was finality to it, like it was written in the stars. We'd seen them fall in love with each other, then fall in love with us, and it came to the most beautiful end atop the Wembley staircase." David Baldwin was equally full of pride, "This club was too big a club and the passion of this football club was too important for it to be languishing in League Two indefinitely. The club is worth more than that."

Writing the Width of a Post match report, Alex Scott stated, "There isn't anything I can say about Phil Parkinson's job this year that would do him justice. He has been vindicated in every decision he has made. He has been the catalyst that brought this club from the bottom of the Football League, to these magical heights in a matter of eighteen months. Today will go down on the short list of our club's greatest days, a short list within which he is already a frequent character.

"As time passes and we look back, these players will go down in history amongst our pantheon of our greatest. To a man, they've all made a critical contribution at one point or another. But that isn't really relevant today. What is relevant is that the club is now in place to keep its core, its young core, together and this wonderful story, this wonderful ending, may only be a beginning. The present is perfect; the future could be anything."

The return to League One football was a huge moment in Bradford City's modern history. For all the joys of the run to the League Cup Final, climbing back up the leagues was always far more important. Unlike when City were relegated to League One in 2004, there was a feel-good factor about going back into the third tier, nine years on. Whenever any club is relegated to a division below, there is disappointment and a sense of urgency to climb back up as quickly as possible. It means you struggle to enjoy your new surroundings, and the opposition sides that you face. For City, going back into League One and swapping regular trips to Dagenham, Barnet and Accrington with Wolves, Sheffield United and Bristol City meant that at last they looked comfortable in their own skin again. As a fanbase we still consider ourselves a club big enough to ultimately find a home in the Championship, but League One has felt like a step up and more a place that can be enjoyed. And the wonderful way that City were promoted to Wembley meant that the prize of third tier football was relished that bit more.

Julian Rhodes summed it up, "To be 3-0 up against Northampton after half an hour, I still felt this was too good to be true and waited for it to go wrong! So I was just relieved at the end. It was great for all supporters and particularly for the players, who were rewarded for all the hard work they'd put in over the season.

"Was it the best season in the club's history? Probably."

City (vs Northampton): Jon McLaughlin, Stephen Darby, Rory McArdle, Andrew Davies, James Meredith, Garry Thompson, Gary Jones, Nathan Doyle (Ricky Ravenhill 87), Kyel Reid (Will Atkinson 78), James Hanson, Nahki Wells (Alan Connell 85)

Not used: Matt Duke, Carl McHugh, Michael Nelson, Zavon Hines

Truly shocking

Chelsea vs Bradford City

FA Cup fourth round, Saturday 24 January, 2015

Chelsea Football Club were without question the dominant team in English football over the 2014/15 season. They defeated Tottenham Hotspur 2-0 at Wembley to lift the League Cup, and set the pace in the Premier League right from the start. Having left all rivals trailing in their wake, by early May it was obvious Chelsea were going to be crowned Champions of England. All they had to do was beat Crystal Palace at home to seal the title. Sky Sports were there to cover the game, and in the studio beforehand pundit Graeme Souness was asked about the dangers of Chelsea underestimating their mid-table opponents. "To guard against complacency, Chelsea just need to remember one word," began Souness.

"Bradford."

The day that the earth shook

Rewind fourteen weeks, and to 24 January, 2015. It is an afternoon that no one connected with Chelsea or Bradford City will forget for a long, long time. What was supposed to be a routine FA Cup match ended up sparking worldwide headlines. What should have been a comfortable afternoon for the Premier League giants instead proved to be utterly humiliating. What should have been nothing more than a nice day out in London's West End for the League One club turned out to be one of their greatest hours. This was massive. This was colossal. This was earth-shattering.

Three days before hosting Bradford City in the fourth round of the FA Cup, Blues' goalkeeper Thibaut

Courtois claimed that Chelsea had a squad good enough to win the quadruple – that is the Premier League, Champions League, League Cup and FA Cup. His manager, the great Jose Mourinho, played down such talk in his press conference ahead of the tie against the Bantams; but did make it clear that he would consider it a "disgrace" if Chelsea lost to their lower league opponents.

At that stage of the season, Chelsea had been defeated only twice in all competitions and were unbeaten at their Stamford Bridge home. In fact, over two spells as manager of Chelsea, Jose Mourinho had only ever lost once on his own patch to English opposition. And though Mourinho rested some of his biggest players for the game against the Bantams, the team selected by the Portuguese still cost more than £200 million to assemble.

But what the Special One hadn't appreciated was that he was up against Bradford City's very own Special One.

The (second) greatest cup run, ever

The glitz and glamour of Stamford Bridge could not have been further from Phil Parkinson's thoughts three months earlier, as the half time whistle at the Shay was sounded.

It was the FA Cup first round, and Bradford City were trailing 1-0 away to non-league neighbours Halifax Town, live on BT Sport. The visitors had been awful, conceding a dreadful goal after just three minutes and subsequently struggling to match Halifax's work-rate. The Shaymen wanted it more, and were unlucky not to be further ahead. City were staring at a defeat that would have been their fifth in six games; they looked set to extend a recent run of poor results to just two wins in fourteen games. And amongst the 3,429 visiting supporters who had packed out two of the stands, dark murmurings were uttered over the interval. Coming up next was a big 45 minutes for Phil Parkinson; 45 minutes that may even prove to be his last at the helm.

If that sounded sensationalist in view of the amazing feats of 2012/13, it reflected what had been a difficult twelve-month period for the City boss. Initially after promotion from League Two, City adapted to the higher league impressively and, ten games into the 2013/14 season, they were sat fourth in the league. But just as fanciful talk of back-to-back promotions began to take on credibility, form evaporated in worrying fashion and the club embarked on a mid-season slump of one victory in 21 matches. Forget promotion, suddenly an instant return to League Two couldn't be ruled out. Eventually Parkinson and City rediscovered their winning habit and saw out the season in a mid-table position. But behind the encouragement of ultimately achieving a top half finish, there was an uncomfortable feeling: without such a blistering start to 2013/14, City would probably have been relegated.

All of this was played out during a period of transition. The 2012/13 history makers had performed wonders and started life in League One well; but slowly it began to become clear that some of them had reached their ceiling point, and that the club would need wholesale changes in order to continue its progress. And they lost star striker Nahki Wells in controversial circumstances. His exploits at Valley Parade meant he was firmly in the shop window for nearly a year; but rather than making a big money move to the Premier League, Wells ended up joining fierce local rivals Huddersfield Town for a rumoured, and underwhelming, £1.2 million initial fee. The deal was full of add ons that, in time, would recoup City plenty of extra money, but it was of little consolation to supporters as they faced up to seeing a player they loved so dearly suddenly decked out in Huddersfield blue and white.

The issue was exacerbated by Wells' replacement, Aaron Mclean. A player of some pedigree and who was on the books at Premier League Hull City, Mclean's move to Valley Parade proved to be a massive disappointment. That it took him eleven games to break his goalscoring duck set the tone for a difficult spell. It was no secret that Mclean was commanding a relatively high salary, but his style of play was too different to Wells and City just couldn't get the best out of him.

Over the summer of 2014, Parkinson rang the changes and released many of the promotion heroes of a year earlier. Garry Thompson, Jon McLaughlin, Carl McHugh, Nathan Doyle and – most upsetting of all – Gary Jones left Valley Parade. A new-look squad began to take shape, with the likes of Billy Knott, Billy Clarke, Gary Liddle and Alan Sheehan arriving. Although 2014/15 started well – including a long-awaited victory over Leeds United in the League Cup – September and October saw several poor results. A week before the Halifax game, City lost at home to Doncaster despite playing very well. Doncaster looked an average side, yet had still won comfortably in the end. It didn't bode well. Parkinson took the decision to cut his losses with the still under-performing Mclean (three goals all season). He dropped the striker from the squad, and sent him out on loan to Peterborough United. It was the right move by Parkinson, but Mclean's exit only added to the feeling that things had gone wrong over the past year. City fans themselves were, for the most part, firmly behind Parkinson, but these had become worrying times.

Alex Scott, one of the chief writers for Widthofapost.com, reflected on the mood around the club in November 2014, "It was spiralling for sure, amongst the fans at least. City had recovered slightly towards the end of the previous season – after a truly wretched run – and carried the momentum into the early part of the new campaign, energised by the League Cup victory over Leeds. Unfortunately, with only one home win between that night in August and the Halifax tie in mid-November, and a run of one point in five games in the immediate build-up, the atmosphere had definitely turned. It's hard to believe now in hindsight, but Parkinson's grace period was just about up." Simon Parker also felt that the manager was in a less than ideal position going into the cup match, "There was a bit of pressure on him. I got the impression that if they had lost against Halifax his position would have come under quite a bit of scrutiny. It would have really put the spotlight on him for the next couple of games. It was a really testing moment for him.

"They started the Halifax game badly and Sheehan gave away a ridiculous corner from which they scored. Robbie Savage [a pundit for BT Sport, covering the game live] was behind us punching the air and getting all excited." Going in 1-0 down at half time that day offered up the very real prospect that it could be one of Parkinson's final games. If the afternoon ended in a humiliating defeat, it would almost certainly have resulted in a section of fans turning on the manager. And as so many of Parkinson's predecessors in the Valley Parade dug out could have told him, once you reach that point where the City crowd starts to turn on you, it is extremely difficult to turn it around.

At half time at the Shay, it felt like the beginning of the end.

The Parkinson intensity

But the second half saw a complete reversal of the way that the opening 45 minutes had unfolded. What was said in the visitors' dressing room by Parkinson worked quickly and emphatically. Inspired also by the half time introduction of Billy Clarke, City shook off the first half shackles of fear and dominated the second 45 from start to finish. Within five minutes of the restart Jon Stead – signed on loan from Huddersfield three weeks earlier, and given permission by his parent club to play in the FA Cup – netted the equaliser when he rounded former City keeper Matt Glennon and tapped the ball into the net. Three minutes after that, Filipe Morais ran onto Clarke's intelligent through ball and finished emphatically. It became a stroll in the park for City, much to everyone's relief.

Phil Parkinson recalled, "It was a big game. It panned out exactly how we'd expected. They were a big strong team, good on set plays. I watched them play a number of times, and I'd seen teams pass the ball and cut them open with good football. We were poor early on, gave a corner away and conceded from a set piece. But even in the first half we had moments of good football where we switched the play quickly. We got in some good positions.

"In the second half we said to the lads 'look you've got to keep doing what we set out to do in training. Switch the play, pass it, move the ball quickly, and they will fatigue'. Because they were a non-league side and only trained twice a week. I'd seen that happen in games they'd played before, so I was confident that if we remained calm we'd get chances against them. It was great that we took the chances. They were two moments of real quality."

The Halifax game was some first week in the job for the club's new chief operating officer, James Mason. A City fan in his youth, Mason harboured strong ambitions of becoming a sports journalist and had worked his way up the BBC to become one of its Premier League reporters on Final Score – his regular workplaces including the likes of Old Trafford and Stamford Bridge. Mason, who combined sports journalism with building up a major joinery business, was appointed by City as David Baldwin's replacement, after the latter accepted a lucrative offer to join then-Premier League side Burnley. Mason's first game at City was this tricky FA Cup game at Halifax.

"Everything wasn't rosy in the garden," Mason reflected to me. "The league form was stuttering to some extent. We'd got Halifax Town in the first round of the FA Cup, which immediately was a televised game. That was great for the finances of the club, but equally it brought its own pressure on Phil. It was always a game that could have been a potential upset.

"At 1-0 down at half time, fans naturally were disgruntled. And there was disharmony. Had Bradford City lost that game, who knows how that season might have panned out? I'd like to think there would have been no knee-jerk reaction and I'm pretty sure that within the club that wouldn't have happened, because that's not what our legacy is built on. But it was such a pivotal half time team talk."

Despite the apparent nerves felt by City fans, the players had remained calm going into the tricky Shaymen cup tie and were rewarded. Andrew Davies stated, "It was one of them where it was another cup, and we were always confident in the cups. It was just a game where you thought 'if we could get through this we could eventually get drawn against a bigger team'. That was the way we went about it."

It might be an exaggeration to say that the FA Cup saved Phil Parkinson, but in James Mason's view it was a vital moment. "Thankfully those two second half goals changed not just that game but the season, and perhaps the modern history of Bradford City." Alex Scott agreed, "In hindsight, the half time of the Halifax tie, staring an embarrassing defeat in the face, was certainly the turning point of the season. If things had gone another way in those 45 minutes, who knows what might have happened."

And from that afternoon, they never looked back. The Halifax victory was the first of seven wins and two draws in the nine remaining matches of 2014. From languishing in the depths of sixteenth place in the league following the Doncaster game, they ended the year in fifth and with a great chance of grabbing a play off place. Along the way they won impressively at Preston, Chesterfield and Fleetwood, whilst at Valley Parade they defeated Leyton Orient and a Notts County side featuring Gary Jones and Garry Thompson. The crowd were right behind the team and falling in love with the new recruits. The History Makers were now history. Simon Parker added, "Before the Halifax game Phil had said 'this could be our kick start, if we win this'. I alluded to it in the match report, and it turned out to be exactly that. That afternoon at the Shay turned around a season that was drifting nowhere."

And as part of that run of seven wins from nine, City cruised past another non-league team in the FA Cup second round. East London side Dartford were handed a trip to West Yorkshire, and the Blue Square Premier League side were easily brushed aside 4-1 by a City side limited only by their attacking ambition. James Mason said, "We pulled Dartford out of that hat, which was another banana skin. We knew it was Dartford's day in the sun and they were going to bring numbers. But it was a great performance, a very professional performance."

City were in the hat for the glamorous third round for only the second time since being relegated back to the lower leagues in 2004 (meaning they began from the first round rather than third). The draw itself was conducted at The Deep in Hull, and there was disappointment when the Bantams were handed an away tie with Millwall. "Before the draw, both Mark Lawn and Julian Rhodes accurately said to me 'James, forget this enthusiastic pie-in-the-sky idea that we are going to get a Premier League club, we'll get a middle-to-average Championship club away from home'," stated Mason. "When we pulled Millwall out, it couldn't have been a less attractive tie. A long trip on a Saturday, not particularly glamorous, losable – we could have lost that and again the season would have taken a very different turn."

But still, the Lions were struggling at the bottom of the Championship and beatable. Confidence sky high from the upsurge in form, City matched their higher league opponents and forced a replay back in West Yorkshire following a pulsating 3-3 draw. City were excellent, as Phil Parkinson recalled, "We were a bit disappointed to be honest that we didn't win it. We played really well, as supporters who went down there will know. I thought the support at Millwall that day was incredible. We didn't really expect so many supporters when we came out, but it was brilliant." With City still in the competition it meant they had a huge interest in the fourth round draw that took place two days later at AFC Wimbledon's Kingsmeadow stadium. And there was great excitement when their name was pulled out the hat to face the mighty Chelsea at Stamford Bridge. If they could beat Millwall in a Valley Parade replay, the glamour tie would be theirs to look forward to with relish. James Mason recalled, "I remember watching the draw on the Monday night. I'd just got in from work and I was playing around with the kids with the TV on. When Chelsea came out first I thought 'goodness me, surely not?' and then 'Millwall/Bradford' came out after, and I just jumped around the room. I went absolutely crazy.

"We've got a chance to play Chelsea, there can't be a bigger tie. Previous Premier League champions, recent Champions League winners, at Stamford Bridge. This is just absolutely phenomenal. But then reality dawned – we've still got to beat Millwall! A tough task in itself."

The Millwall replay might not be up there amongst the all-time great Bradford City games, but it was still some occasion. It was a game boosted by a surprise five-figure crowd, as City fans really got behind a clever marketing initiative around the hashtag #bethedifference that played into supporter emotions about the Chelsea prize that was at stake. Mason added, "We immediately switched to thinking 'what can we do as a football club to help the players?' We spoke to Phil and the players, and they all said 'get as many people in the ground as possible. A bigger crowd under the floodlights at Valley Parade will give us the extra help that we need. We need the crowd to be the difference'. From that phrase came the hashtag: #bethedifference – I'd like to think it will stick for my time at the club.

"As a Bradford City fan, everything about the three sides of the ground that we all sing from, everything about being a Bradford City fan, is about being the twelfth man. We've got wonderful support. We've always had wonderful support. Always vocal. #bethedifference was all about getting people in, singing from the first minute to the last minute."

Andrew Davies reflected on the replay, "We approached the game with the motivation that if we won we were going to play Chelsea. That's enough motivation to make you go out there and run through brick walls for each other. We ended up blowing away a team, who were in the Championship, with ease really. Our ground has never been easy to come to, especially when we play well. I think everything went for us that night. We played really well, and the goals kept flying in. It must have been a nightmare game for their team."

Indeed, that replay against Millwall showcased everything special about Phil Parkinson's Bradford City. There may no longer be Gary Jones fist-pumping in the centre of the park, or Nahki Wells scaring defenders with his soaring pace, but the class of 2014/15 embodied the ethos of 2012/13. What made that team so special – and how they beat the likes of Arsenal – was the incredible intensity and focus they demonstrated in big games, feeding off their passionate crowd. And now the new broom were at it too, approaching and playing the match in exactly the same way. With Stephen Darby, James Meredith, Rory McArdle, Andrew Davies and James Hanson surviving from 2012/13, that spirit had lived on. The awkward transitional period was complete.

Millwall never stood a chance. They were in freefall form-wise, and a complete shambles at Valley Parade. Their central defender, Mark Beevers, was sent off just six minutes in for hauling down James Hanson when he was clean through on goal. Two minutes later Hanson headed City into the lead from a corner, and by the 39th minute it was 3-0 after Jon Stead and Andy Halliday scored easily. Billy Knott added a fourth early in the second half, and the trip to Stamford Bridge was firmly booked. "Bring on the Chelsea" roared a delighted home crowd. Phil Parkinson recalled, "The Chelsea fixture on the horizon added a bit of extra pressure for the replay, for both teams. It would have been massive for Millwall to have played Chelsea, with the rivalry. But we were so focused and we knew what we had to do. We knew their weaknesses, and we felt we could exploit them. We started with an intensity which they couldn't handle, and very quickly the game was over." Goalscoring hero James Hanson added, "To get the first goal to get us going that night was unbelievable. I thought we played some of our best football of the season that night. We thoroughly deserved to thump them 4-0."

A proud James Mason remembered from that night, "I guarantee that Millwall did not have a clue what was coming to them. It was one of the loudest, coldest nights I have seen at Valley Parade. The most emotionally charged atmosphere. The carrot at the end of the stick was this huge money-spinner, and a great away day for fans. The 4-0 defeat was never in doubt. It was one of the best performances of a home team I have ever seen. It was just a brilliant, brilliant, memorable night. It was absolutely wonderful. We can talk about Wolves away, Chelsea at home, and Villa – I concur that those were some of the greatest nights in our Bradford City supporting careers – but goodness me, to beat Millwall so comprehensively, with what was at stake, was just brilliant. I remember having a good long drink into the night!"

City hadn't been in the fourth round of the FA Cup since 1999, when they were defeated 3-0 by Newcastle United. They'd also made the fourth round two seasons earlier where they faced Everton at Goodison Park. The Bantams pulled off a shock 3-2 victory that day which generated plenty of headlines, but at the time Everton were a struggling Premier League outfit and City were plying their trade just one division below them. Chelsea away in 2015, as a League One club, was an altogether different proposition.

Lowly expectations

Even accepting that the League Cup heroics of two years earlier showed that anything is possible, no Bradford City supporter seriously expected much from the trip to Chelsea. The Saturday before the tie, Chelsea had brutally dismantled Swansea City 5-0 at the Liberty Stadium, and the quality and depth of their squad was one that City simply couldn't match. Sure, Chelsea would rest players, but they'd done something similar in the third round against Championship pace-setters Watford, and still easily won 3-0.

6,000 City supporters made the journey South looking forward to a grand day out, a raucous sing-song in the Shed End and – if we were really lucky – a Bradford City goal to cheer. It was a pay day for the club; an afternoon in the national spotlight, before we quickly returned to the bread and butter existence of entertaining Colchester United the week after. Alex Scott reflected, "It was one of those 'event days', for sure. I remember being sat with family and friends in The White Horse on Parsons Green at lunchtime – this had evolved into something of an away pub of sorts – and you could feel that buzz." Over in the spacious Stamford Bridge press room, the mood was equally jovial. Simon Parker stated, "We were all tourists at the beginning. We made the most of the banquet in the press room and treated it as a day to enjoy."

Andrew Davies admitted that the players had a similar outlook going into the match. "I think we were realistic in that you just wanted to go there and enjoy the day. You don't want it to be a mauling, for it to go down in history as a mauling. Go there, put on a good show, and even if we don't win it will have been a great day. I think that was everyone's thinking before the game." This realism was shared in the boardroom, as James Mason stated, "No one ever thought that we would beat Chelsea. There were a few fans with rose-tinted glasses who maybe thought 'why not? We could get a draw'. But in truth it was all about the occasion, all about enjoying a day out. Seeing what Chelsea was like. Seeing what hundreds and hundreds of millions of pounds of talent was like. Seeing a glimpse of Jose Mourinho. We all bought into the fact that it was just a day out."

Yet although not making any bold claims, Parkinson seemed to have a quiet confidence about his team during the build-up. He made it clear that he would not attempt to shut up shop, park the bus in front of goal and hope for the best. His game plan – which would not be known in public until afterwards – was similar to the Arsenal and Aston Villa approaches. Let Chelsea have as much of the ball as they like in their own half, but as soon as they cross the half way line press, press, press. And when City have possession, attack and get bodies forward. Looking back, Parkinson told me, "We set out a game plan of what we needed to do in order to play well. Having the experience of playing Premier League teams before obviously helped, as we still had a core of players who were involved two years before. We stressed the importance of sticking to the game plan and playing with belief. Not building up expectations too much. However, we weren't going to go down there and just make up the numbers."

The other part of Parkinson's big plan was to target what the manager had identified as being the weakest part of the Chelsea backline. Andreas Christensen, an eighteen-year-old Danish right back who had only ever started one game in English football. Parkinson felt that his limited experience certainly wouldn't have included coming up against a big, physical striker like James Hanson. And so he moved his target man to the left wing and instructed players to get the ball up to him. Hanson won everything all afternoon, and his efforts would even earn praise from the Chelsea captain – sat on the bench for the game – John Terry. James Hanson was more than happy to try the role, "The gaffer says one of my qualities is athleticism and that there aren't many big men that can work as hard as I do. He had a feeling of what the Chelsea team was going to be that day, so he gambled on the young Danish lad playing right back. He didn't want to go with two strikers at Stamford Bridge, so gave me a wide left role and said to other players to use the diagonal ball up to me as an outball if we are struggling."

Yet even with a gameplan that would have surprised Jose Mourinho, a Chelsea side featuring the legendary Didier Drogba, Loic Remy (a £10.5 million signing), Mohamed Salah (£11 million), John Mikel Obi (£16 million), Oscar (£25 million), Ramires (£17 million), Cesar Azpilicueta (£7 million), Gary Cahill (£7 million), Kurt Zouma (£12 million) and goalkeeper Peter Cech (£9 million) should have had too much for a City side made up of free transfers and the £7,500 Hanson. Many of the players in the Chelsea team had won Champions Leagues, Premier Leagues and played in World Cups, after all.

And that seemed to be the case initially at least. Despite Andrew Davies forcing a world class save from Cech early doors, it appeared as though a bright start for City would be a mere footnote to a straightforward afternoon for Chelsea. After 21 minutes a home corner was swung over and Cahill got free of his marker to flick the ball into the roof of the net. When shortly afterwards Filipe Morais lost the ball in a bad position and Ramires finished off a flowing Chelsea move, to make it 2-0, it seemed as though the afternoon would become one of damage limitation for the visitors. Yet Phil Parkinson believed City had been unlucky and that his side could still come back, "I felt we were playing alright and that the 2-0 scoreline was an injustice." In the away end too there was a firm defiance and the noise never stopped.

Alex Scott had a different perspective over just how loud the supporter backing for the City players proved, "Unable to source a ticket in the sold out away end, I was reduced to scrambling around for anything I could get my hands on. In the end, I gladly settled for a spare in the home end, surrounded by tourists wanting to take in Stamford Bridge. I have always found it difficult to work out how loud you actually are as fans when you are sat amongst them; and never being in the 'wrong' end before, I'd never really had a point of reference outside of television appearances. As it turned out, the City fans dominated throughout; they were exceptionally loud. I've not really heard an away crowd dominate like that. Watching the game unfold live, I don't think you can undersell how important that crowd was."

Just three minutes after going 2-0 down, the game turned and – just like that day at lowly Halifax – Jon Stead was in the thick of it. He picked up possession on the edge of the box, manoeuvred space for a shot and smashed home a stunning drive past the outstretched arm of Cech. 2-1, and major celebrations in the away section at the opposite end of the pitch. Alex Scott continued, "The Jon Stead goal changed the game, no doubt about it. If City had gone into half time 2-0 down, they would have been too far gone to get anything out of the game. Pulling it back to 2-1 almost instantly stopped the players' – and fans – heads dropping, and what's more, the finish was so sensational, it actually felt like City belonged on this stage for the first time. City weren't just a backs-to-the-wall, long ball and corners outfit like a couple of years before, they were here to play. They could compete. They belonged."

James Mason added, "At 2-0 down, we just thought as long as it doesn't go to three, four or five-nil, we'll take that. I was lucky to be in the directors' box with Mark Lawn and Julian Rhodes and the other directors. It was as posh as it comes, like a nightclub almost. A very posh gentleman's club. At 2-0 down there were a few Chelsea directors that said to us 'unlucky Bradford, we'll try and keep it to 4-0, keep it respectable'. When Jon Stead scored just before half time, we couldn't control ourselves, we went nuts. A couple of burly security guards came up to us and said 'excuse me, this is Chelsea, that's not how we behave'. So we quickly apologised.

"It was great to see the Bradford City fans keep up this constant wall of sound, from the minute they got into the ground. And once we scored it was great to have something to cheer."

With Stead's goal some hope was restored as the teams went in at half time. At the very least we supporters had got our wish of a consolation goal to cheer. The day had something positive that we could treasure. And with 45 minutes to go, who knows?

Cue one of the most incredible second halves in the histories of both Chelsea and Bradford City.

Together, fearless

Bradford City has always looked more comfortable in its own skin when it is fighting against the odds. They are not the biggest club in England, yet a long way from being the smallest. They revel in the role of underdogs and in proving people wrong. And nowhere did it seem more unlikely that they could upset the odds than at 2-0 down to the English Champions-elect Chelsea, just before half time.

Buoyed by Stead's goal, everyone truly came together during the second half. The away crowd behind the goal that City were attacking were astonishing in their level of noise, and the consistency of their chanting. The players responded in purposeful fashion. It wasn't a matter of going into the second half feeling there was nothing to lose; there was genuine belief that they could come back and stun the best club in the country. They attacked right from kick off, and for the next 25 minutes placed the home side under a level of concerted pressure that – during almost every single Premier League game that they took part in that season – Chelsea never experienced. City were, as Alex Scott wrote in the Width of a Post match report, "fearless". And the knocking on the door for an equaliser never faded. Chelsea found that the storm was not disappearing, even after bringing on the rested Cesc Fabregas (a £30 million summer buy) and Willian (£32 million) from the bench in an attempt to bring about some composure.

Alex Scott stated, "City were playing well, and were for the most part untroubled. Looking up to see Stamford Bridge around you as this was happening was just bizarre. The tension was rising throughout the home fans, and after not seeing Jose Mourinho at any point during the first half, he was a fixture on the edge of his technical area. What's more, City were getting more and more on top as the half wore on. After Jon Obi Mikel picked up a head injury, I remember Jose looking to Cesc Fabregas on the bench with this sort of controlled rage, telling him to go and sort this out. Chelsea were genuinely rattled."

On the touchline too Parkinson could sense that his opposite number was growing more and more worried as City continued to attack with purpose, "There was an obvious air of complacency about them. Jose Mourinho stood up, and you could see in his eyes that he was worried. Even at that level of football, if you switch off, it's very hard to switch it back on again within a half. We really were the dominant team." Simon Parker too had a close up view of Mourinho's growing discomfort, "That second half they just came out and you thought 'wow, they're really having a go here'. The dugouts were just in front of us and you could see Mourinho was getting really twitchy. He was sat down for the first half but now he was stood up, very animated. It was almost more fun watching him. You could see that he could sense it was going away from them."

Despite the visitors' dominance, Chelsea could and should have put the game to bed when Drogba had a free header that he planted straight at Ben Williams. 40 seconds later, the ball was in the back of the net at the opposite end of the pitch. James Meredith's long throw made it into the box and to the feet of Billy Knott, who got a shot away that was superbly blocked by Cech at his near post. The ball ran free, with the goal unguarded. The first man on the scene wore claret and amber. Filipe Morais couldn't miss. 2-2, and pandemonium amongst the players and the visiting supporters directly behind the goal.

It had to be Morais, whose early career had included time in Stamford Bridge's youth ranks. The story goes that Morais was rated by Jose Mourinho – then in his first spell in charge – but with youngsters rarely given an opportunity in the first team, the player turned down a contract and opted to move into the lower leagues. Morais' subsequent career was spent at several English and Scottish clubs without any great distinction, and he was only initially brought in by Parkinson that summer on a non-contract basis to cover the first team. Morais got his head down, began to thrive at Valley Parade and his blistering form had recently being rewarded with a three-and-a-half-year Bradford City contract. His career back on track, he returned to his Stamford Bridge beginnings and netted that priceless equaliser.

Suddenly there was hope that City could force a lucrative Valley Parade replay. There were just fifteen minutes left on the clock. Mourinho clearly wanted the tie, which he had thought was already won by his Chelsea team, settled there and then, and summoned the future PFA and FWA Player of the Year for 2014/15, Eden Hazard (another £32 million player). But City's players were in no mood to settle for a draw either, and continued to attack with incredible purpose and courage.

With eight minutes left, the impossible happened. Jon Stead – who was having the game of his life, completely bullying his England international marker, Gary Cahill – received the ball with his back to goal in the area and laid it into the path of the onrushing Andy Halliday. The former Middlesbrough midfielder demonstrated amazing composure to pick his spot superbly, almost passing the ball into the top corner, past the despairing arm of Cech. 3-2 to Bradford City. An explosion of delirium at one end of Stamford Bridge; and utter dejection and disbelief everywhere else inside the stadium.

On a day of amazing stories Andy Halliday had one his own. He'd arrived on loan the previous October and his deal had run out earlier that week. Talks about a permanent contract at Valley Parade had gone swimmingly, but then there was a last minute delay and it looked as though City would miss the Friday midday deadline to register the deal. The consequences would be that Halliday could not have played against Chelsea. It went right to the wire, but City just made it – 11.58am was the time that the deal was completed. Phil Parkinson decided not to tell Halliday that there was at one point a serious doubt over whether he could play in the game, admitting to the Telegraph & Argus the Monday after, "We kept it from Andy. Julian [Rhodes] was saying we can't let him know. So I was trying to organise a team and go through the structure of how we were going to play and I wasn't sure that one of the players was going to be available."

Halliday's wonderfully-struck goal meant that City were on the verge of a historic victory, all they had to do was see out the final eight minutes – not that their delirious supporters could quite believe it. Alex Scott said of the goal, "I think this was the best moment I've had supporting City. Firstly, it was an incredible finish from Andy Halliday. Even now, I don't think that finish gets the credit it deserves.

But secondly, we had just taken the lead at Stamford Bridge after being 2-0 down! But it still didn't feel real. Even at this stage, with only eight minutes on the clock, I still didn't realistically think we could win, Chelsea were obviously going to make it 3-3, so I didn't feel any nerves."

Indeed, for the first time since the interval, City naturally began to sit back as the minutes ticked by. Mark Yeates had been brought on for Knott just before Halliday's goal, and Parkinson sent on Chris Routis and Billy Clarke during the final few minutes, to run down the clock some more. When the board went up for seven minutes of injury time, however, it was easy to fear the worst and that Chelsea would snatch a heart-breaking last-gasp equaliser. But although they poured forward in numbers, they failed to test Ben Williams. There was to be one more goal in the game – in the 96th minute – and it once again went to the League One side.

Yeates had brought the ball forward on the counter attack. In this situation, teams would usually race for the corner flag and waste time. But Yeates had other, more positive ideas. He initially headed wide, before flicking the ball into Stead's feet and continued his run into the area. Stead held off Cahill once again and timed the release of his lay off to perfection. The ball was played right into Yeates' path. He took one touch to steady himself, before casually placing the ball past a stunned Cech. A goal of supreme quality, from a team 49 places below their opponents on the football ladder.

Yeates charged to the corner flag and team mates raced over to jump on top of him. After the Morais equaliser, and after Halliday's 3-2 strike, it was hard to believe that the City fans could celebrate any more feverishly – but they managed to find another level. As Alex Scott wrote for Width of a Post in summary of the scale of what the players had just achieved, "Two nil down after 40 minutes; four two up at 96. Away from home. At Stamford Bridge. With European Cup winners, World Cup winners, Premier League winners, the Special One looking on helpless, and beaten. Clearly beaten. Embarrassingly beaten." Looking back on the Yeates goal now, Alex added, "I was just delirious. As the ball was played into Stead in the box, and I saw the wheeling run of Mark Yeates, I vividly remember grabbing my Dad's arm next to me, like I was eight-years-old again, and time stood still. My body was still recovering from the harrowing previous five minutes, but now had frozen taut again. It felt like an age passed between everything opening up, and the ball being slotted in the corner. The delirium didn't really wear off after this, but the disbelief did. There was no way back for them, there was no time. This was actually happening."

Andrew Davies added, "What happened was just surreal. Not just to beat them but beat them like we did. It was a dream come true for everyone. When the last goal went in, we finally felt 'we could win this' but even then you're thinking they could still come back. They could score in a second. We never took our foot off the gas, even when there were only 30 seconds to go. I was so tired after that game, I had never concentrated so hard in my life!

"It was pure emotion. To beat a team of such world class players, you just hope it could happen. But then to win against all odds; and you knew then that we were going to get the publicity that I think the club and the players deserved."

James Mason smiled, "When we got the equaliser, the whole place erupted. The Chelsea directors looked round at us saying 'we didn't expect this'. A security guard came over and again said 'listen, that's not how we behave, I know you're excited but you don't do that at Chelsea'. When we got the third goal we were telling him where to go! When we got the fourth he came up to us and basically high-fived us, saying 'it's your day, your name's on this game, enjoy it'. Most of the Chelsea directors were very gracious too."

The Special One himself attempted to shake Parkinson's hand just after City went 4-2 up. The Bantams boss refused, feeling that even though there was barely a minute left on the clock, it was still not right to assume the job was done. But in no time at all Andre Marriner brought an astonishing game to a close, sparking a major party in the Shed End amongst the City fans. The players, management and other staff all joined them in celebrating the achievement. When they finally headed off the pitch, the rest of Stamford Bridge was long empty – save for City fans who had hidden in the home stands, unable to get a ticket in the away section, and who could finally expose their true allegiance. Jose Mourinho made a point of going into the City dressing room and shaking the hand of every single Bradford City player, memorably stating that they had "big balls".

James Mason takes up the story, "Jose came into the dressing room after the game, and by all accounts it was like a headmaster walking into a rowdy classroom, where all the kids are throwing paper aeroplanes and dancing around on the desks. As soon as he walked in, they all stopped and looked at him. Jose went around every single player and shook their hands, and he said 'you deserved it. Bobby Robson taught me how to lose. He said that for every losing side, there is always a winning side, so well done and enjoy it'." Simon Parker recalled interviewing a disbelieving Andy Halliday, "We grabbed him after, still in his full kit, and he gave me a big bear hug. He couldn't believe it. I remember looking at his face and I don't think he blinked once. He was wide-eyed like a kid at Disneyland, he just couldn't believe it. It summed it up."

Parkinson reflected on the astonishing second half, "I can remember us kicking towards our supporters and producing wave after wave of attack. We were playing so well. The goals were great. It really was a surreal feeling at the end, because you were left thinking 'has that really just happened?' Because Chelsea don't get beat at home and don't concede four goals under Mourinho very often. It was just a fantastic day. Everyone associated with Bradford City will always remember that day."

The biggest FA Cup shock ever?

This was massive, massive news. An FA Cup weekend that had begun the night before with League Two Cambridge United holding Manchester United to a 0-0 draw suddenly had one of its biggest stories for years. Up in Manchester, Championship side Middlesbrough had also produced a cup upset by defeating Manchester City 2-0 at the Etihad. But there was no doubt who the headlines belonged to. News of Bradford City's astonishing win was shared around the world, with newspapers as far away as in Australia reporting on the extraordinary news.

There was only going to be one choice for the lead game on that evening's edition of Match of the Day. Highlights of City's remarkable comeback were seen by a national TV audience that was one million people higher than the number who regularly tuned into the show. Match of the Day ran a poll asking if this was the biggest shock in the FA Cup's history – 77% replied yes, it was. Viewers also got to enjoy a stunned-looking Mourinho stating, "It's a disgrace for a big team to lose to a small team from a lower league. Me and the players must feel ashamed." Mark Lawn was also interviewed, praising the quality of City's football and exclaiming "We've just beaten Barcelona!"

James Mason summarised, "It was just a great day. It was a day for the ages. It was an FA Cup game for the ages. I firmly believe it will go down as one of the greatest FA Cup upsets, and certainly one of the greatest comebacks, in the history of the competition. Yes you've got your Ronnie Radfords and Hereford, but we were at Chelsea. We were at the kings of the Kings Road. Home of that season's Premier League champions and who brought on £300 million worth of talent from the bench. We started with a team built for £7,500, and we came back from 2-0 down. We didn't get a lucky goal in the last minute; we scored four of the best FA Cup goals you will ever see. It was just phenomenal. It is a day for the ages and one to savour forever.

"I spoke to football fans up and down the country about how they watched it unravel; it was just great to hear their stories. Over the years it will get better and better. And poor old Ronnie Radford won't get wheeled out anymore, it will be the likes of Mark Yeates, Andy Halliday, Filipe Morais and Jon Stead getting wheeled out on Match of the Day and to pull out the balls for the third round!"

Alex Scott rates the game as his best supporting Bradford City, and he had extra reason to leave Stamford

Bridge feeling euphoric, "Before the game in the pub I got to hear one of my favourite City stories, from my Dad, and his trip to Goodison Park eighteen years earlier in the equivalent round of the FA Cup and a famous 3-2 City win. My favourite part of this story is how he, and the group of City fans he was with, pooled their money and lumped it on a 3-1 City away win before kick-off. As the game entered stoppage time with City 3-1 up, and after already planning their entire night out in Liverpool, as well as how to approach their significant others to explain not to wait up, their hopes were dashed in the 91st minute by a Gary Speed cross that floated into City's far corner for 3-2. Adamant not to follow in my Dad's footsteps, I stuck a fiver on City to win 3-2 as we set off across the park to Stamford Bridge.

"Just after the initial delirium of going 3-2 up at Stamford Bridge, the relevance of the voice in the back of my head screaming 'Three Two, Alex! THREE!!! TWO!!!' dawned on me. I then spent the next five minutes furiously attempting to 'cash out' my bet on my phone [claiming the money now, for less than you would win if you had waited until the final whistle, to guarantee the bet comes in even if the score was to subsequently change]. I was battling a failing battery, and the spotty phone signal typical of busy sporting events. Looking back, I imagine this is what the "red wire, blue wire" bomb disposal unit guys feel like. As Kurt Zouma ballooned a first time shot over the bar, I cut the wire and the clock stopped ticking. So this Chelsea win has given my Dad a new coda to his Everton story, 'if only they'd have had in-play betting back then…'"

Unsurprisingly, the Sunday papers were full of praise for City and what their players had achieved. For supporters – who would remain on cloud nine for weeks to come – the debate was over whether this was the greatest moment in the club's history, with long-standing fan John Wade in no doubt, "In 65 years supporting City, this is the best, better than Arsenal, Wembley, Liverpool, Wolves. How truly wonderful." Parkinson's popularity – which had been in doubt back on the day of the Halifax game – reached new heights. During the game City fans had sung "Parkinson is the Special One" – a ditty that would be repeated week in, week out for the rest of the season.

Andrew Davies – who had played for many years in the top flight – puts the achievement above everything else. "I think personally it was the best result of my career. I've played Roma and Stuttgart in the UEFA Cup for my hometown club, but I still feel that they are no Chelsea. For them to get beat on their own patch after being 2-0 up, I don't think that will happen ever again for a League One club. That's why it was so big. So I put that as the best memory of my career so far."

Bring on the fifth round!

Making more history

Sunderland were City's next opponents. There was plenty of controversy about the BBC and BT Sport overlooking the tie for live TV coverage, which festered for weeks; but what mattered most of all was the way that the game captured the imagination of the Bradford sporting public. Valley Parade hosted a capacity crowd for the Sunday afternoon kick off. The city was buzzing before the game; with every pub and takeaway around Valley Parade packed out, and the roads leading to the ground gridlocked.

James Mason continued to harness the rising power of social media to encourage ticket sales and also build up the positive mood amongst fans. This included making a play of the outrage that many people felt over the TV snub, and creating a siege mentality, "When we weren't on the BBC it really stuck in the throat. We were ignored by the BBC and yet we had helped to revive a struggling competition. That they didn't think we were relevant enough to be on TV hurt. But having worked for the BBC for most of my life I understood how these things work."

Mason also helped City break new ground, by spearheading a first ever Tifo visual display before kick off, as fans in the Kop held up claret and amber cards. "We did the big wall of sound in the Kop, the Tifo display with the placards. I don't think it had been done at Valley Parade before. It was all about inclusion and getting the fans on side to be the difference."

Sunderland were in the Premier League, but going through a tough period. They badly needed a win for morale and Gus Poyet fielded his strongest side, but they didn't turn up on the day. To the delight of over 20,000 City fans who made an incredible racket, Billy Clarke fired the home side in front after just two minutes with a shot that deflected in off John O'Shea. Sunderland just weren't up for the fight, as was illustrated by the timid reaction of their striker, Steven Fletcher, when Rory McArdle went in strongly for a tackle that left the Scot floundering on the floor. Although Sunderland had a strong penalty appeal turned down, they failed to register a single shot on target during a wretched first half. Valley Parade was bouncing.

Midway through the second 45 minutes, Adam Johnson was caught dallying with the ball in his own half near the corner flag. City pressed their opponents all afternoon in a way Sunderland clearly weren't used to, and on this occasion left back James Meredith was the most forward player, putting the pressure on Johnson. Eventually the former England international cleared his lines but his attempt was woeful. James Hanson was able to head the ball into Jon Stead's path, and the former Black Cats' striker dribbled the ball past a defender and struck a low shot that somehow squeezed under goalkeeper Vito Mannone's body and bounced slowly over the line. 2-0 to City, in front of the Kop. Three sides of Valley Parade went wild, jumping up and down and hugging each other. For the first time in nearly four decades, Bradford City were going to reach the quarter finals of the FA Cup.

The Sunderland match was another amazing afternoon, one that I personally rank amongst the best I have experienced at Valley Parade. The pattern of the game helped drive the positive home atmosphere. In contrast the Sunderland fans in the Midland Road stand turned on their manager, and at full time were full of rage towards their under-performing players. In truth they were never in the game, and City could have easily added another goal to make the scoreline more emphatic. James Hanson stated, "I can remember coming out against Sunderland and the fans were unbelievable. It just shows that if we can improve and get to the Championship that's what it could be like every week at home."

The quarter final draw threw up the possibility of facing Manchester United, Liverpool, Arsenal, Aston Villa or West Brom. But in the end City – the lowest-ranked team left in the competition – were handed a tie against the second lowest-ranked team, Reading, again at home. It offered a realistic chance of progress – Reading were mid-table in the Championship and had enjoyed a relatively untested passage to the sixth round – but it brought worries too that the game would mean a great deal to them, and that they would match the Bantams for effort and determination.

Valley Parade was a sell out, in controversial circumstances it must be said. A liberal policy that enabled season ticket holders to purchase unlimited tickets at one stage resulted in the home sections selling out before many season ticket holders had been able to buy a ticket. It was an awful PR gaffe by the club, who had to go to extreme measures to accommodate some of their most loyal supporters. This included purchasing new seats so that they could re-open sections of the ground unused for years and which were no longer fit for purpose. There's no doubt that it tainted the build up to the tie and disrupted the atmosphere. But on the day of the game – a Saturday lunchtime kick off shown live on BT Sport – all of that was forgotten as City's biggest crowd since 1960 gathered for the occasion. There was no Tifo display, but something greater – a carefully orchestrated scarf parade where fans in all three home stands help up their scarves before kick off. James Mason explained, "For the Reading game it was all about scarf parade. It was all about now that we are on TV, now BT Sport have backed us, we're going to give them a spectacle like no other. We wanted to create a real visual spectacle that basically said to all the fans and the public, this is what we're about now. We're now the stars of the show, and we're not here just to make up numbers."

If there was sign that Reading were made of sterner stuff than Sunderland and Chelsea, it came early doors. Just like against Sunderland, City produced some strong challenges from the off. But rather than such measures rattling Reading, they responded in kind with some equally heavy stuff. This lot couldn't be bullied. And the 4-5-1 approach undertaken by manager Steve Clarke nullified City's attacking threat. Stalemate ensued. The game fell a long way short of expectations, and the final score of 0-0 meant a replay in Berkshire. Mason added, "Reading wasn't the most glamorous of ties but it was a tie we would have chosen. A winnable game that could have got us to the semi finals. It didn't pan out like that."

Indeed, the replay is where the FA Cup dream came to a sad ending. Due to heavy-handed UEFA rules around their precious Champions League TV deal, a game between a Championship and League One club had to be played on a Monday evening so that it didn't clash with Arsenal's European game against Monaco. Both City and Reading had regular league fixtures on the Saturday before, which wasn't the ideal preparation for such an important replay. Reading, with nothing to play for league-wise, rested their entire first team for their game at Watford (they lost 4-1). But City, still fighting for the play offs, couldn't afford such luxury. Parkinson made six changes for the trip to Notts County (a 1-1 draw) but the Bantams had also played a league fixture at Coventry the Tuesday before that. A small squad was weighed down by a fixture pile-up. Reading won the replay 3-0 with some ease. It was a sad and disappointing way for City's amazing FA Cup adventure to come to an end.

Parkinson recalled with frustration, "I felt that it was unfair the fact the replay was on Monday, and the fact that Reading rested their entire team. You could just see the freshness of Reading on the day, and it proved a game too far for us. It was such a shame. After what we had done, for the FA to make us play it on a Monday, because it is a big difference those extra 24 hours. We didn't play well on the day, but the memories we've got from the FA Cup run will stay with us."

Unlike two seasons earlier, when the League Cup final defeat to Swansea acted as a catalyst for a late promotion charge, there was no fairytale ending in the league. City were on the edge of the play offs between January and March, but a bruising schedule of Saturday-Tuesday games, which lasted for more than two months, ultimately proved too much to cope with. Fast-fading play off hopes were finally extinguished by a dreadful 6-0 home thrashing by League One Champions Bristol City in April. Andrew Davies admitted, "I think we had a few injuries. The squad was a bit thin and, with the players who came in, I think the manager would have wanted them to do a bit better. We just didn't have that strength in depth when people filled in for injuries."

The Bantams ended the season unbeaten in four games and with a final league position of seventh – just one place and four points shy of the play offs. The summer was spent contemplating all of the what-might-have-beens, whilst Parkinson set about making sizeable squad changes that quickly meant three of the four Chelsea scorers – Jon Stead, Andy Halliday and Mark Yeates – were no longer at the club. And there was another surprise departure: one Andrew Davies. He took up an offer to join Ross County after City were too slow in offering him a new contract.

"I just thought it was going to be a simple solution, and it just didn't pan out the way I had expected it to," admitted Davies. "I had a few clubs interested in me from League Two and League One, but I just felt I couldn't really go to them. Then Ross County rang and said 'look we will chuck the kitchen sink at you. We want you to come and be captain. We will give you what you want and you can lead us forward'.

"I felt like what it felt like when Bradford did that to me four years ago. I sat there and I thought that a contract at Bradford hasn't really been offered until five or six weeks (into the summer). There was no serious offer. I thought the manager believed I was one of the main players, but the offer just didn't happen and I thought, 'I've got a young family, I can't wait around forever'.

"Their manager showed more that he wanted me, and as a player you think 'after everything we've been through at the club'. I was quite surprised with it. So after that I thought it was time for a change.

"You sat there and you're thinking 'my phone isn't ringing' and the lads are going back into pre-season in a week, and if I was like maybe eighteen, nineteen-years-old then maybe I'd have been thinking 'you've got to be patient'. But when you've been at the club for a long time and you're the club captain, you think they'd have wanted to sort things out as soon as possible."

The legacy

But despite the disappointment of a failed promotion bid, no City fan would have swapped a top six place for that glorious afternoon against Chelsea. It was a victory that has continued to be talked about at every opportunity; the players involved in it are destined to go down as some of the most celebrated in the club's history. From 2-0 down to the best team in the country, on their patch, to 4-2 up; triggering admiration from up and down the country. The club made a tidy profit from the cup run that further strengthened their finances. Parkinson was able to go into the summer with an increased playing budget, and his standing amongst supporters was higher than ever.

Alex Scott reflected, "This cup solidified Parkinson's legacy as the greatest City manager. He's built two incredibly, absurdly successful teams with two completely different styles and approaches. His pragmatic approach in prioritising whatever will give his team the best chance to win over anything else is admirable. Fans of big clubs, and high profile journalists, belittle the FA Cup, as it doesn't resonate with them any longer, but the narrative has always been misguided. This is the FA Cup, and City were the story of it. City will now always be woven into the modern retellings of the FA Cup story. That is an incredible legacy for everyone involved."

And yet the true legacy of the FA Cup run was the impact it had on Bradford itself. It captured the imagination of the city, and ensured the population got behind it in a way that overtook even the League Cup run to Wembley in 2013. And when season tickets went on sale in the summer of 2015 – at a reduced price of £149 – the uptake surpassed all expectations. More than 18,000 people snapped them up. The club went into 2015/16, still in League One, with more season ticket holders than it had enjoyed during the Premier League days.

City are traditionally an unfashionable club, ignored too often by its local community and kept going by a passionate few thousand. But by beating Chelsea – the mighty Chelsea – the club struck a right hook on the noses of the elite. And that achievement connected with people from across the local area. Interest in Bradford City has reached new heights. The club had a true legacy of new supporters that, if managed properly, can take it a long, long way.

None of which would have been possible, at least to the same level, without Jon Stead's blistering strike at Stamford Bridge, just before half time. Without Filipe Morais being in the right place at the right time to equalise. Without Andy Halliday's brilliantly executed finish for 3-2. Without Mark Yeates' positivity to go for a fourth goal and claim it during the final moments.

And none of it would have been possible without Bradford City's very own Special One.

Bradford City (vs Chelsea): Ben Williams, Stephen Darby, Rory McArdle, Andrew Davies, James Meredith, Filipe Morais (Billy Clarke 89) Andy Halliday (Chris Routis 87), Gary Liddle, Billy Knott (Mark Yeates 70), James Hanson, Jon Stead

Not used: Matt Urwin, Alan Sheehan, Jason Kennedy, Francois Zoko

Post script – the never-ending story

Bradford City vs Oldham Athletic

League One, Saturday 16 January, 2016

Match day, and the Sparrow Bier Cafe on North Parade street is packed out. It is a relatively small pub, distinctive from the outside by its green livery frontage, and its logo featuring a drawing of a Sparrow enjoying a hearty drink from a wine glass. Inside, there is plain wood decking and basic, no-frill tables and chairs that remind you of being back at school. The walls are painted a light shade of green, and decorated by iconic music-themed images of concert promotional posters and album covers, plus other pieces of art. To the left of the bar that stands at the far side from the entrance, a giant blackboard lists the vast range of beers, wines and spirits that are available. There is a clear European theme. Your bog standard English lager offerings, like Carling, will not be found here.

The Sparrow is modest in size, yet its impact on Bradford has been considerable. It opened in the summer of 2011 and very quickly grew in popularity. It was a trendy place to visit. The sort of bar you would see in Leeds and other, more fashionable cities. The people of Bradford embraced it, and its magnetic appeal caught the attention of other entrepreneurs. At the end of North Parade, the old Yorkshire Penny Bank – an iconic building that was built in 1895, with the outside covered in fine stone carvings – was re-opened as The City Gent pub in the summer of 2013. It was soon followed by the launch of Al's Dime Bar, an American-themed bar, a few doors down from the Sparrow. More and more pubs and bars have opened on the street, including well-known City supporter Keith Wildman's Record Café, which sells records, ham and beer.

The result is that North Parade has been transformed from a run-down street, only really used by people to access the city centre, into a happening place. An area you can go for a nice beer or a full night out. In the evenings, and especially at the weekends, the place is heavily populated with people hopping in and out of the bars. I took some friends to North Parade one Friday night – people who are used to going out around the trendy parts of Leeds – and they really enjoyed it. Bradford is cool again.

On match days, North Parade thrives. Today, it is standing room only inside the Sparrow, as City supporters occupy every table and every chair, both upstairs and downstairs in the somewhat dingy basement. The stereo system blasts out indie classics, such as The Verve's Bittersweet Symphony and The Specials' Ghost Town. Next to the bar, a sign advertises free pie and peas for people going to the match, and they are going down very well with customers. A big group of lads in their twenties push two tables together and engage in loud banter; half of them sporting claret and amber colours. Next to them, a couple in their sixties are talking quietly over a couple of drinks, looking nonplussed about Bradford City matters – perhaps they hadn't realised there was a game on. There are gatherings of people all over, and the collective sounds of their conversations drown out the music.

Business is good today for the owners. It is the same story inside bars a few doors down, and across the road. This area is set up for the weekend trade of people going out, given its close proximity to the city centre and to Forster Square train station; but much of the area's burgeoning success is down to the Bradford City match day trade, too.

Prior to the Sparrow's arrival, there were very few pubs anywhere near the ground, and especially not of this quality. I've long thought that very few opposition fans would consider 'Bradford City away' to be one of their favourite trips. Sure, Valley Parade is a fine stadium, but we put the away fans in the worst part of the ground, and there was little nearby for them to visit pre-match. When in 2011 Brighton opened up their impressive Amex stadium, the chief executive, Martin Perry, explained how they made sure the facilities for away fans were top-notch. Their away concourse is changed match by match, into the colours of the visiting team, with posters of their past and present heroes displayed on the otherwise featureless concrete walls. Once you leave the concourse and go out into the arena itself, away fans find that their seats are cushioned. Perry told the BBC, "Why not be welcoming to your visiting club? Why not make it a fantastic experience for them? Because actually what happens is, they look for the Brighton fixture and they say 'I'm going to that one' and we get a full house."

Bradford City don't do anything themselves of a similar standard for visiting supporters, and sometimes we are indignant when an opposition team brings an away following lower than you would have otherwise assumed from them, without questioning if there is more we could do to entice them to visit this part of the world in support of their team. But with the bustling North Parade scene growing in reputation, there is greater reason for away fans to pick a visit to Bradford City over other away games. Get the train into one of the two stations, take a short walk to North Parade, visit lots of great bars, and then it's just a 10-minute hop to Valley Parade. A great day out and, perhaps, a few misconceptions that some outsiders hold towards the city of Bradford smashed.

It is nothing more than sheer coincidence, but the launch of The Sparrow and the arrival of Phil Parkinson at Valley Parade occurred within a few weeks of each other. In their own fields, and in their own ways, both have had a dramatic effect on those around them, and both have altered the landscape for the better. By any measure, Phil Parkinson has done an exceptional job at Bradford City. His list of achievements is considerable; the glory moments under his watch are both plentiful and amongst the greatest the club has ever known.

Phil Parkinson has changed the culture at Bradford City, stamped out the "losing mentality" that he so accurately identified early into his reign, and raised the standards. He had succeeded a long line of Bradford City managers who – if it's unfair on some to say they underachieved – failed to live up to expectations. The value of Parkinson is not only evident in the amazing cup runs, the glorious victories over Arsenal, Chelsea and Aston Villa, the long-awaited promotion in 2013, the lengthy list of inspired signings, and the year-on-year improvement in league position – but by remembering what it was like before he came in. To recall the relegations, the dismal promotion bids, the endless defeats, the turnover of under-achieving players, and the constant feeling of disappointment and dissatisfaction. It has been this way for too long. The end of Parkinson's Bradford City story is yet to be written, but even if he is one day sacked, with people having called for him to go, we will roll out the highlights of the good times he delivered, revel in the incredible memories he provided, and be forever thankful to him. You will never be able to dismiss Parkinson's achievements. He will leave behind a massive legacy.

Mark Douglas, the Newcastle United editor of the Sunday Sun, Newcastle Evening Chronicle and Journal, and passionate City supporter, told me, "I think we are actually now in a better position as a football club now than back in the Premier League, because we now have the right mentality, and the way that the fans and the players are. Now, you know what you're going to get from Bradford City. We've had some bad times with Parkinson, it does happen. But what is great about City under Parkinson is that even if we lose a few games we bounce back. We go through bad runs, but it's very rare that we get into trouble. And it's because he's got this hard-working mentality. That's Bradford City for me, and it should define what they always are for the rest of their days."

Today, for the visit of Oldham Athletic, at the exact half way point of the 2015/16 season, Parkinson continues to be king. It seemed as though he might have left Valley Parade last summer, when Sheffield United came calling for his services. The Bradford City board recognised what an asset they had, and declined to give the Blades permission to speak to their manager. In September, Parkinson agreed a new three-year contract, with strong words of praise from the joint-chairmen, Julian Rhodes, who told the Telegraph & Argus of his desire to keep hold of Phil for a long time to come, "I've got to be honest, I think he'll be here beyond the next three years. I think we'll be talking about extending it two years down the line, hopefully in the Championship. Will he be here for ten years? Why not? The only problem would be if he attracts attention from a bigger club and he gets an offer that he can't refuse.

We would all understand that. Other than that, I can see Phil being here for a very long time."

It is said, from those who are better placed than me to know, that Parkinson and the two chairmen argue from time-to-time; that they challenge each other, and can be very forceful in their views. Other, recent City managers, evidently found Mark Lawn a difficult man to work under, and there were fall outs. Whatever is said behind the scenes between Lawn, Rhodes and Parkinson, there is almost always a united front. It all works as a partnership; and though football's volatile nature means you can never predict that a manager will last forever, Parkinson currently has one of the most secure jobs in the Football League.

And the question, as we enjoy a pint in the Sparrow ahead of this Oldham clash, is whether the club can take the next step and go to another level. Get back to the Championship, which they were last promoted into 20 years earlier, via that crazy night at Blackpool. Reclaim a place in the second tier; a place that they lost in 2004, with relegation confirmed during that awful home defeat to Wimbledon. Establish themselves in the top half of the 92-club ladder, just like they managed to do after 1985, despite all the turmoil and emotion of the Valley Parade fire, and the short-term move to Odsal.

So far, they are thirteenth in League One; but with games in hand on others that mean the play off places are still very reachable. They made a poor start to the season, losing three of their first four games, but over September, October and November came roaring back. Despite a lengthy injury list and an increasingly pragmatic style of football, the functional Bradford City have been effective. Over the Christmas period they endured a couple of defeats to promotion rivals, which have dampened the mood going into this game; but prior to that City had only lost one in thirteen. If they could only start finding the net more often, they would have a real chance of finishing in the top six.

It's not only a question of whether City can get back to the Championship – little old Yeovil Town achieved that feat in 2013, after all – but if they could then stay there. The Championship has moved on in the 12 years since City vacated it; the competition increasingly distorted by incredibly favourable parachute money that relegated Premier League clubs receive, totalling £60 million per club, over the space of four seasons. This gives them a big advantage over their new rivals, when it comes to players to sign and wages to pay; and the rest must either compete with that spending, or drop down into Leagues One and Two. The result is that even small Championship clubs operate on huge wage budgets, and have run up sizeable debts. In August 2015, the website Insider Football trawled through the accounts of every Championship club and found that, collectively, they have amassed more than £1.1bn worth of debt – averaging out at £48.5 million per club. Bolton Wanderers topped this table of shame with debts of £181.2 million – despite the fact they had been benefiting from parachute payments since their Premier League relegation in 2012. This is the economic backdrop of the clubs that City would be competing against if they were promoted to the Championship. This is the kind of borrowing that might be expected of them, if they want to compete. It is frightening stuff.

City are stable under Lawn and Rhodes, but not mighty. The club has operated in the black since 2009 – going against the modern trend of football clubs – but this current model would struggle to work in the Championship. Lawn admits that himself, telling Sky Sports in April 2015, "Julian and I can't afford to have this club in the Championship. We wouldn't be able to put the money in. When you look at the wage bills – £20 million at Leeds United, £35 million at Reading and they're not even competing at play-off level. Millwall – I've been talking to their chairman and he's been putting in £8 million for the last five years, every year, just to keep them in that league. I haven't got that sort of money and I've got to be honest about it." This statement was later amended by Lawn, when in May 2015 he told the Telegraph & Argus, "With Julian and I in control, the club can still compete at League One level and probably up to mid-table in the Championship".

All of this talk had come in April and May 2015, in the wake of news that Lawn and Rhodes were in talks over selling the club to the Italian Gianni Paladini [touched upon in chapter seven]. The former chairman of QPR, Paladini had some rich friends in the likes of Bernie Ecclestone, the owner of

Formula One, worth an estimated $3.8 billion, and Flavio Briatore, another Italian and also heavily involved with Formula One, and with a net worth of $150 million. These were some of the wealthiest men in the world, and said to be willing to provide Paladini with the capital to buy Bradford City, who claimed he was motivated to take over the Bantams because he was "bored". It didn't take long for credible stories to reach your ear of the millions of pounds' transfer chest Phil Parkinson would receive to fund a promotion push under Paladini. The Championship was the first aim, and who knew after that? The Premier League was suddenly talked up. Bradford City could finally dream big again.

Only, and perhaps to the surprise of even ourselves, most of us didn't want to dream big. The proposed Paladini deal was warmly welcomed by some supporters, but most gave it a muted reaction. There wasn't opposition as such, but many of us spoke about not really wanting it to happen. In a sense we were conflicted. Paladini's money could safeguard the future of the club for years to come, but we didn't want it in this way.

The takeover bid came just as City were finally experiencing success, finally moving forwards. And they had achieved it the Phil Parkinson way: through hard work, determination, character and courage. It gave it all greater credibility. We, as a club, had earned everything we have accomplished since 2012, and everybody has truly played a part in it. One particular fact about Paladini summed up why the prospect of his arrival at Valley Parade was a worrying one to many of us. Back in the day, Paladini had been the football agent to one Benito Carbone. He had history with Bradford City, sat on the opposite side of the negotiating table to Geoffrey Richmond in the summer of 2000, securing a contract that made his client one of the richest footballers in the land at the time. £40,000 a week was what the Italian signed up to, in agreement to play for little old Bradford City. You can't blame Paladini for the four-year contract that almost killed Bradford City – Richmond was the one who offered it – but his association with that excess, that mess of a transfer, and the dismal, long-lasting consequences that followed it, was nevertheless one that our prospective new owner was associated with. It was an unwelcome reminder of City's past mistakes, just at a point where they were finally moving on from them.

As it was, Paladini couldn't complete his takeover of Bradford City. His exclusivity period expired with him failing to secure the financial backing that he claimed to have. His rich friends were not prepared to indulge his boredom. Perhaps, they had been interested when Paladini first sounded them out, and agreed to look at the books, but then realised there was little profit to be had out of Bradford City. This was, after all, a third tier club, playing at a stadium they don't even own and have to pay annual rent to use, with the cheapest season tickets of the four divisions. It would have almost certainly taken a huge cash injection to have elevated the Bantams into a more lucrative division: namely the Championship or, optimistically, the Premier League. And their experience at QPR – which was clearly painful at times – would have taught them that none of this was cheap. Ultimately, when it came to buying Bradford City, the risk would have far outweighed the reward.

So the deal never happened, and the club continues to be owned by Lawn and Rhodes. Whilst some fans were disappointed, most were relieved. The fact the proposed takeover deadline occurred just as it seemed Phil Parkinson might depart to Sheffield United – he was rumoured to be unsettled by the takeover talk – heightened the sense that everything was on the line. We were talking about selling our values for something else: an alternative approach that might lead to greater success, but a very different type of success nonetheless. It would be stretching things to call Lawn and Rhodes universally popular, but there is a healthy level of respect for the way the pair had built up the club, following the difficult financial problems of the past. As one City supporter put it, when faced with the prospect of Lawn and Rhodes making way for Paladini: it is better the devil you know.

Nevertheless, Lawn and Rhodes do not have deep pockets, and the suspicion remains that City would struggle to take the next step – establishing themselves in the Championship – under this ownership set up. There is a question of whether the Bantams' current status of competing in the top half of League One is the club's ceiling under the current ownership. They could get City promoted to the Championship, but could they stay there?

The former Bradford City head of operations, David Baldwin, is uniquely placed to comment. In October 2014, Premier League Burnley came knocking for his services, and a decent compensation deal was agreed with City for Baldwin to move to the Lancashire club. Burnley had just been promoted to the top flight and – unwilling to take significant financial risks – would come straight back down, despite battling admirably. In the Championship for the 2015/16 campaign, Burnley are boosted by the Premier League parachute payments and spent a whopping £9 million signing the powerful Brentford striker, Andre Gray. They've brought in the notorious Joey Barton, too. A talented squad are fighting near the top of the league for a second promotion to the Premier League in three years (they are fourth, going into this weekend).

I asked David Baldwin, based on his Valley Parade background and new-found experience of the finances in the top two divisions, for his honest assessment on City's hopes of ultimately establishing themselves in the financial landscape of the Championship. "It is a very expensive league to be in. There are the people who have money and the people who don't have money in the league. A team like Rotherham United have a very different budget to a team like Burnley. Burnley's budget is built on the Premier League parachute money legacy. That money is a very powerful tool.

"But that won't stop the ambition of Bradford City in wanting to get promoted. Your revenues go up considerably. You are as a club at least five and a half million pounds better off just by being in the Championship, due to the central distribution funds. So if you work on the proviso that a club doesn't need to change its infrastructure to compete in the Championship, it just needs to change its wage budget, the revenue allows you to do that. There is also a sense of momentum that if a club goes up, the players have a lot to prove. It tends to be the second season that is the hardest. The changes you might need to make in the first season might be less dramatic than the changes you would need to make in the second season."

"The other unknown is that if you are promoted, you don't know what interest that might attract from other investors or potential new owners. Mark and Julian have always being very pragmatic in saying that if someone can come in and take the club to the next level, and it's in the interests of the club, they will step aside and allow that to happen. There is no better place to find out if there would be other interest than to get to the Championship in the first place, and see what interest it attracts."

City's current status – battling for the third tier play offs, with a hard-working squad – is not dissimilar to the situation that attracted Geoffrey Richmond to Valley Parade, 21 years earlier. Football is a team sport of course, but at its very essence are individuals and the influence they transmit. City's recent rise and rise from the depths of 2011 is down to many different people, but the manager Phil Parkinson is the one person that it couldn't have happened without. The club's even more spectacular rise, in the late nineties, was also largely attributable to one man's influence: Geoffrey Richmond. Despite what we believe or assumed at the time, it wasn't so much Richmond's financial support that made the difference – he never owned more than 58% of the club, and the 1998/99 promotion push was funded by the Rhodes family borrowing money – but his vision, energy and drive that drove City upwards. Richmond was an incredible marketer, and a true leader. But he tainted his legacy by taking too many risks, and by departing Valley Parade having made a profit out of the club via large dividends he paid himself. Albeit it was a profit he quickly lost, due to an unpaid tax bill from selling his Ronson lighters business (the windfall he used to invest into Bradford City in the first place). He left the Bantams in the lurch, with a mountain of debts that took years to fully tackle. He reinvented Bradford City, and then almost killed it.

The reinvention of Bradford City, over these past 30 years, is as much about expectation as it is the achievements and failures. Of what we wanted to become, and of who we thought we should be. Richmond left behind a rich collection of incredible memories, and taught us to value ourselves higher. But the crippling mess of the debts he ran up then made it impossible to create new memories, for a time. That only changed when Phil Parkinson came in, stamped out the losing mentality and found a way to move forwards again. The debate about Richmond will linger on for the rest of our days, but it is perhaps only because the twelve subsequent years of misery are now over, and the club has moved on, that we can look back at his time running the club and conclude that it was worth it. Sort of.

Nevertheless, as the modern day Bradford City wrestle with the long-term challenge of that next upwards step – a happy existence in the middle of the Championship – no one is demanding Geoffrey Richmond's triumphant return. These days, he is the chairman of the Leeds-based cricket team, New Rover Cricket club, keeping a distinctly low profile. City's current owners get criticised, but most fans acknowledge they are doing their best. They won't speculate to accumulate like Richmond. They won't make grand claims about the future, but they will keep the club on a sustainable footing, living within its means. They are making sure the Bantams can be passed onto the next set of owners one day, and that the club will still be around for the next generation of supporters.

After the Richmond days, Bradford City have been reinvented again – into a club that dream of better things, but who are comfortable in their own skin. Whilst supporters want to see City get back to the Championship, it isn't the be all and end all. In truth, we're all largely satisfied with where we are: competing at the top end of League One, winning more than we lose, appreciating our hard-working team, valuing the ongoing efforts of our inspirational manager. We moan, still, about poor performances and certain players (and, increasingly in early 2016, about the lack of goals); but that's normal, run-of-the-mill football supporting life. It's an enjoyable existence.

For now, on match day, the long-term future can wait. The focus of much of our pre-match discussion in the Sparrow is on the here and now. Loading up Twitter on our phones, we discuss the team news that has just been announced. There's a big game to be played in less than an hour. It's time to drink up and get outside into the biting January cold.

Down Manningham way

To walk from the Sparrow Café to Valley Parade requires you to cross over the dual carriageway Hamm Strasse – renamed in 2010, in tribute to the German city of Hamm, which Bradford is twinned with. Hamm dignitaries had been in attendance on the fateful day at Valley Parade on 11 May, 1985, and subsequently provided Bradford with a memorial stone, which is now erected on a corner by this road. After Hamm Strasse is Manningham Lane, which if you follow for ten minutes takes you to the road named Valley Parade and the stadium itself.

It is hardly one of the world's most beautiful roads, but going down Manningham Lane is one of my favourite walks. In my 2011 book, Paying on the Gate, I wrote about the first time I ever made the Manningham Lane walk, to watch Bradford City vs West Bromwich Albion on 1 November, 1997; instantly becoming a Bradford City supporter from the moment I gazed down from the back of the Kop, to the pitch below. This walk always acts as a happy memory of that special day.

Over the last eighteen years, not that much has changed about Manningham Lane. Businesses have come and gone; but with the exception of the recently built Tesco metro store, positioned almost opposite Valley Parade, the buildings largely remain the same. The old Town and Country nightclub, or Maestros, as it was called when I was growing up, remains abandoned half way along the route. Closed down some 10 years ago, it is an impressive building that has been left to ruin, its front windows plastered over by flyers for club nights in other towns that have long since come and gone. There are other businesses that have been established on Manningham Lane for decades, many with an Asian theme, serving the main population of the area. There has been so much talk about Bradford City failing to attract Asian fans, although you will find plenty in the stands on a match day. Whether they could do more is a matter of debate, but what cannot be disputed is how well the local Asian community, Bradford City, and its supporters live side by side. As massively inconvenient as it must sometimes be to have 18,000 people turn up on your doorstep every other week, the club and its community appear to view each other as good neighbours.

The closer you get to Valley Parade, the more indications there are that this is a match day. It's not just the growing throngs of people joining you in walking in the same direction, towards floodlights that are now increasingly visible over the houses that surround it; but the number of street vendors who have set up for an afternoon's business. People selling claret and amber scarves on a fold-out table, including those scarves linked – unofficially of course – with the hit Disney move, Frozen. There are sweet sellers, burger vans, and one man has simply rocked up with a car boot full of old programmes, inviting people to browse and buy. Just before you reach the turning for Valley Parade, a dutiful badge seller – who has been stationed here on match days for as long as I've been going – displays an impressive range of badges, priced at two pounds each or three for a fiver.

This committed seller aside, many of these street vendors are relatively recent additions to the match day scene. Just a few years ago, the roads around Valley Parade were absent of such entrepreneurs. Now, with the club enjoying success, and with crowds rising, there is money to be made, and these vendors are enjoying a decent trade today. It all adds to the sense of occasion that surrounds match days these days. These people could be somewhere else, at another sporting club or music event, but are earning a living here instead. Just like the Sparrow Café and North Parade, they are part of the community and the match day experience.

We stop off at the ticket office on the way, as my wife – on an infrequent trip to the game with me today, she doesn't go as often now we have a child – needs a ticket for the match. There is a healthy queue of people waiting to be served at the five window booths that are open. The person in front of us asks for "the cheapest student ticket you do". This student has seemingly never been before, as when asked by the staff member which of the stands he wants a ticket for, responds "wherever the nicest people sit". Our own extra ticket bought, we go through the turnstiles at the Kop and to the concourse that is already busy. A huge group of male teenagers stand by one of the walls, attempting to look tough. 90% of them are wearing baseball caps, 100% are sporting Adidas trainers. A teenage rebellion is still all about conforming.

We make our way to our season ticket seats on the front row of the top tier. It provides a great view of the pitch, and, indeed, of the city of Bradford itself behind. You can see trains come and go at Forster Square station; and on the horizon heavy traffic files up and down Manchester Road, leading to Odsal and Bradford City's temporary home of 30 years ago. But your eyes are drawn to looking around this wonderful stadium, our home, which is loved by so many people. The former City winger from the 1980s, Mark Ellis, said to me, "I think Valley Parade has got character. You go around to a lot of away grounds these days and they are just a bowl – some are bigger bowls than others, or they have different coloured seats, and that's the only real difference. Whereas Bradford City, it might be a bit lop-sided, but it's got character. I think it's a brilliant stadium."

Immediately opposite us lies the Bradford End stand. That basic, two-tier, pillar-dominated structure that was built in 1991, as the club was weighed down by mediocrity. Should the long-term sponsor of the stand, TL Dallas, ever decide to end that arrangement, and no alternative can be found, the club could do worse than rename it The John Docherty Stand, in tribute to the economical, low-expectation era that it was built in – and to keep reminding ourselves that we can always be better than what we are.

To the left is the Midland Road stand, a lasting memorial to positive ambition and aiming big. Its planned construction announced in February 1996, on an evening when the low attendance inside the whole ground could easily have fitted into it. Yet this stand would prove to be needed in order to house the swelling crowds of the nineties. The good side to Geoffrey Richmond's vision lives on in this side stand, whilst directly opposite it is the bad side. The main stand, with its second tier addition in 2000 that left behind a crippling mortgage, is a lasting monument to the folly of living beyond your means. For years, the building of this second tier proved wholly unnecessary. It is only of late, under Parkinson's inspirational management, that there have been occasions to prompt a genuine need for it. The 2015/16 season sees City have almost as many season ticket holders than the ground's capacity used to be, pre-2000. The second tier of the stand is now home to the board of directors, and to those fans who can afford to pay a few quid extra in order to enjoy the pre-match warmth and hospitality of the McCall and Hendrie Suites, or – on the floor above – the recently added 2013 Suite, in tribute to City's incredible double Wembley season.

The Kop feels like a home from home to me. The stand, built during City's 1998/99 Premier League promotion season, and opened just in time to welcome top flight football, has continued the mantle of the previous terrace in being home to the club's most vocal supporters. The chanting may spread around the ground, but it always begins from the back of the top tier. Just before the teams come out, the drumming begins, and the first songs of the day bellow out – "Bring out the Bantams". Someone has brought along a trumpet but, to the relief of most of us, clearly doesn't know how to play it and gives up after a few flat notes. There are four giant flags positioned across the length of the back of the stand, which are swung enthusiastically by supporters as the teams walk out. The top tier of the Kop feels full, and it's a similar sight around the ground. Oldham fans too have travelled in numbers – 922 are housed inside the Bradford End – although their own disappointing season means their crowd is down on what they have brought here in seasons gone by. Perhaps they've not yet heard about North Parade. Still, today's attendance is a whopping 18,522.

Michael Flynn, that combative midfielder, with no little skill, from the League Two era, and who played under Stuart McCall, Peter Taylor, Peter Jackson and Phil Parkinson, has fond memories of the Valley Parade atmosphere. He told me, "I'm lucky that I played in the Championship with three different clubs. But with Bradford, some of the games we played, you'd think we were playing in the Championship, the atmosphere was that brilliant. It made very appreciative of my career. I consider myself fortunate to have played for a big club like Bradford."

The Bantams' eventful modern history is in huge contrast to today's opponents, Oldham Athletic. Like City with Parkinson, they have enjoyed periods of success following an inspirational managerial appointment. In their case it was the former Everton and Man City player Joe Royle, who became Latics manager in June 1982 with the club in the Second Division. Royle took them to the First Division in 1990 – the same year that the Bantams were relegated to the Third Division, after the failure to get promoted in the 1987/88 season had left behind such a painful legacy. Oldham – who under Royle reached FA Cup semi finals and even the League Cup Final – were one of the founder members of the Premier League and must have thought they had made it when the new top division began in 1992. Alas they were relegated in 1994, Royle left, and three years later (1997) they went down again. Oldham have since remained in the third tier – not once getting promoted or relegated. That's nearly 20 years stuck in the same division – a truly unremarkable modern history to have. Boundary Park has endured far too many dull moments.

And in the 21 years that followed Royle's departure, an incredible 21 different people have held the title of Oldham manager. This long list even includes Royle, who returned on a temporary basis in 2009 for nine matches (only one of which was won). In the week leading up to this game, Oldham have sacked their second manager of the season – the former Blackburn Rovers player, David Dunn, got the bullet after just 20 games in charge. He had failed to win any of his last eight games, and has been replaced by former player and twice-manager, John Sheridan, who has been lured away from managing League Two strugglers Newport County. Today is his first game back in charge, with the Latics sat third from bottom of the league. Perhaps they won't make it 20 consecutive seasons in the third tier after all.

The opening to the game suggests this could be a classic, as Tony McMahon almost opens the scoring inside two minutes with a powerful volley that only just sails over the Oldham goal. But although City continue to dominate early proceedings, the tempo of the match drops all too quickly and the home side struggle to attack with any fluency. Oldham are set up to defend, and few blue shirts venture past the halfway line. John Sheridan might have only just re-taken charge, but he seems clued up about City's main attacking threat and ensures extra attention is paid towards Bantams winger Kyel Reid; one of the 2012/13 promotion heroes, who has returned to the club on loan for the season. The City crowd backs the team passionately, with a chant set to the Sex Pistols' classic, Anarchy in the UK, booming out. "I am a City fan, I am a Bradfordian, I know what I want and I know how to get it, I want to destroy Leeds and Town." The back of the Kop is the hub of the chanting, but people in other stands join in too. At the other end of the ground, the Oldham fans can barely be heard as they attempt to rally behind their struggling troops.

Yet although the home chanting continues from the hardcore at the back of the Kop, the volume starts to slide downwards elsewhere. By the 20th minute, a feeling of frustration is already starting to build up around the ground, as City fail to make any headway in breaking down the increasingly spirited Oldham side. Reid takes the brunt of the groans, as several times he is fed the ball in a promising area on the left flank, only to send over a series of dreadful crosses that either go above every City player in the box, or sail behind for a goal kick. Midfielder Chris Routis sends a long-range shot into the top tier of the Bradford End, to sarcastic cheers from visiting fans. Behind me one supporter cannot hide his despair – "Are we ever going to score a goal again?"

James Hanson, the club's longest-serving player, and goalscoring hero of the famous night against Aston Villa in the League Cup semi final three years earlier, is still leading the line. He has his critics in the stands, and they have been quick at times this season to get on his back, but his durability is admirable. James Hanson is the true Bradford City working class hero; plucked from stacking the shelves at the Idle Co-op, encouraged by his dad to give Bradford City a go – even though it meant taking a pay cut – and delivering so many wonderful memories to his Bradford public. He is currently the joint fourth highest scorer in the club's history, which is a remarkable achievement for someone of such humble beginnings – someone who, it seemed, had been forced to wave goodbye to his dreams of being a professional footballer.

Hanson has his critics, but thousands of others, like me, love him for what he has achieved, and will always root for him. Hanson told me, "I think my main strength is playing down the middle but whenever I put on a Bradford shirt I will play where the manager wants me to and give my all. Some games that might not be good enough, but on others it will be." Today, unfortunately, is proving to be a case of the former for Hanson. He has not scored a league goal for two months, and his confidence seems to be dented. Hanson is also getting nothing from a referee who ignores the somewhat over-physical way in which the Oldham backline are trying to stop the striker from winning flick ons.

The game finally has a talking point just before half time. A ball is played towards Reid, and Oldham substitute Connor Brown races over in an attempt to intercept it. Reid is not exactly the bravest in going in for the 50-50 challenge, and Brown wins the tackle. Unfortunately for the Oldham player, his lunge for the ball was two-footed and he ends up clattering into Reid, who falls straight to the ground. Brown got the ball, but you just can't tackle this way anymore. Referee Ben Toner races over and whips out a red card for Brown. The Oldham players protest vigorously, but it's all in vain. The tensions are still high when the half time whistle sounds shortly afterwards. The Oldham fans – who have started booing Reid's every touch – give Toner a torrid time as he heads towards the dressing room. There had been some boos, too, from home fans dissatisfied by their team's unconvincing first half display. Yet surely now, with a one man advantage and 45 minutes to make it count, City will score, win this game and put their recent mini-slump to bed.

It takes four minutes and 26 seconds of the second half to begin to do just that. With City now attacking the Kop end, the ball is worked to James Meredith on the touchline by the main stand, and the Aussie sends over a high hanging cross that is met at the far post by Tony McMahon. The summer signing from Blackpool – who has impressed over the first half of the season – sends a header towards goal that seems to loop up in the air in slow motion. No one – the Oldham stopper Joel Coleman included – seems to know where the ball will end up, but it finally drops down over the line for a City goal. McMahon is clearly ecstatic as he races over to supporters in the Midland Road stand to celebrate, his team mates racing behind him. After a lot of group hugging, McMahon emerges from the City huddle and salutes the Kop. A heavy sigh of relief is let out across three sides of Valley Parade.

Going 1-0 down springs Oldham into some response and they finally show some attacking intent, but its meat and drink for a City backline that has impressed all season. James Meredith, Stephen Darby and Rory McArdle – promotion heroes of 2013, and stars of the Chelsea win – are still doing the business. They embody Parkinson's philosophy. They instil and maintain the standards that all new arrivals are expected to live up to. Behind the back four, Ben Williams – another hero of the Chelsea victory – has very little to do. Phil Parkinson is clearly not satisfied with merely holding on for a 1-0 win and shuffles his pack by making two attack-minded substitutions. Hanson spurns two glorious chances in the final 20 minutes to double the advantage, and subs Josh Morris and Mark Marshall blaze presentable opportunities wide. 1-0 is how it finishes.

The game is a neat summary of City's strengths and problems this season. They look unlikely to concede, typically have the majority of possession (60% today), but simply don't pose enough of a threat in the final third. Today they achieve 15 shots on goal, but tellingly McMahon's goal is their only attempt on target. Still, a win is a win and City end the day tenth in the League One table. Four points behind the top six, with two games in hand. The play offs remain a realistic objective, even if the home crowd heads home unconvinced.

The in crowd

When speaking to me about the promotion to the Premier League in 1999, Stuart McCall wonderfully summarised, "Football is about players but it's for supporters". As the three home sides of Valley Parade loudly chant "Everywhere we go" during the second half of this game, I recall those words and smile with pride at my football club. Bradford City has put the fans at the heart of the club, when so many others pay nothing more than lip service to their local public. Most are happy to rip off their own fans by charging them a fortune, so they can pay footballers and, sometimes, themselves handsomely. Football used to be called "the people's game", but increasingly it has moved so far from reality that many people are turned off, repulsed and out of love with the sport. Others are simply priced out.

But not here, not at Bradford City. Affordable season tickets are not a gimmick, but a lasting stance. One that the club stuck to during the bleak years of Peter Taylor and fighting to stay in the Football League; one that has been continued as the club starts to rise back up the ladder. The Bradford public has embraced the idea, made it work, and packed out the place this season especially. The club has more season ticket holders to watch City play Shrewsbury, Fleetwood and Oldham than were here for Arsenal, Manchester United and Liverpool, in the Premier League days of 1999-2001. And they're paying only £149 for the privilege, and being rewarded with a play off-chasing team, this season at least.

Success will never last forever. Sooner or later City's progress will stop, and the lean times will return. The Bantams' modern history is full of examples of this happening: the post-1988 struggles, and the fall down the divisions after the Premier League. But when the next difficult spell inevitably occurs, City will be able to count on a bigger and more committed fanbase to help them through it. It might not remain 18,000-strong in number, but the days of 4,000 crowds appear to be behind the club forever.

The 1,249 people who attended Bradford City vs Hereford United in 1981 was a freakishly low league crowd that will never be repeated. That incarnation of Bradford City is completely unrecognisable to the one today, which has just completed its first home league match of 2016 with nearly fifteen times that amount of people present to see it.

The future is unwritten

Orson Welles, the legendary American actor, director, writer, and producer, once famously said "a happy ending depends on when you stop your story". I love that quote, and to me it sums up football beautifully. It doesn't have an ending; only new chapters. Great feats, like a club winning promotion, will always have the sequel of what happens next to them in the higher division, and then what happens after that. Even when a club has unfortunately folded, it has been reincarnated by supporters and reformed somewhere down the pyramid.

The story that I have told in this book is not an ending and could, indeed, be slightly dated, should City get promoted in 2015/16. But even though a return to the second tier would have a wonderful symmetry to how the club moved on from the Valley Parade fire 30 years ago, it wouldn't be the end to the story. Bradford City are destined to have ups and downs for decades to come. The last 30 years has shown just how plentiful they can prove. Perhaps, like Oldham, we are set to spend the best part of the next two decades sat in League One. But somehow I doubt it. It's rarely dull around here.

The modern history of the club is fuelled by the emotion – and coming together in the aftermath of – the Valley Parade fire. As Mark Lawn told Sky Sports in April 2015, "After the fire, Bradford as a football club is probably unique with its supporters and its fanbase." In March 2015 I interviewed long-standing Bradford City supporter, former City Gent editor and author of several Bradford City books, David Pendleton, who summarised, "The era of 'Bantam Progressivism', the solidarity, and sense of togetherness, in the wake of the fire meant that the club would never be quite the same again. And while the success of the club on the field has waxed and waned, Bradford City, and in particular its supporters, has never returned to being just another run of the mill club.

"In truth we may not be all that different from fans at a whole host of clubs, but the important thing is that WE think that we are different. It is the stories we tell to ourselves that can shape the culture of the football club."

The Sky Sports pundit, Gary Neville, once described Newcastle United as a "very emotional football club", where the extreme passions of their supporters play such a big part in defining their fortunes. On a smaller scale, I think Bradford City are very similar. We are a passionate bunch, and we deeply value hard work, character and commitment above all else. That emotion can lead to panic when things aren't going as well, and reactionary decisions that – in the cold light of day, and with the perspective of time – sometimes look foolish and rushed. Nowhere is there a better example of this than the six weeks of madness in the summer of 2000, and the deliberate attempts to abandon who we were, and to try and become something we weren't (and probably never wanted to be). To foolishly believe that our Premier League status should cause us to ape our new rivals, forgetting that what got us there in the first place was going about things differently to others. The recent rise under Phil Parkinson, stimulated by cheap season tickets and huge crowds, is a similar alternative approach. It must never be abandoned in haste. We must carefully manage our future emotions.

Bradford City has been through so much in these 30 years since the fire. Odsal, the nearly season, the Doc, Blackpool, Wolves, the Premier League, administration, administration again, relegations, hanging on the edge of the non-league cliff, reaching a major cup final, Wembley twice in three months, and Chelsea away. As we file out of the ground following the Oldham game, with the conversations of the day centred on whether our play off hopes are destined to be doomed by our lack of goals, the ongoing soap opera of following a football club remains as compelling as it has ever been.

The future is unwritten, and it is guaranteed to feature more plot twists, cliff hangers and unforgettable moments. We may not know when the next extraordinary match will occur, but we can be confident that these episodes will keep happening for the rest of our days, and then even beyond that.

The Reinventing of Bradford City continues, and it will never reach its conclusion.

SUBSC

Steve Abbott
Geoff Allan
Ben Appleyard
John R Armitage
Ben Ashcroft
Oliver Barrett
John Barker
Christopher Batley
Stephen Benson
Alan Martin Biggins
J & T Blanchfield - Idle
Denis Graham Blyth
Patrick Brady
John Brewis
Garry Brumfitt
Mark Brumfitt
Adrian Calam
Philip D Clarke
Tony Clegg
Chris Clements
John A W Clough
Paul G Collinge
Peter Collier
Stephen Connell
John Cook = Once a Bantam

Steve Cooper
Tom Coulson
Graham Coultous
Richard Cowling
Matthew Cox
Philip D Clarke
Robert K Cross
Brian Crowther
Karl Cunliffe
B Danylczuk
Garry Edward Davis
Alfie Dawes
Harry Dewhirst
Mary Dewhirst
Alex Dodd
Ken Dorrington
McCall Driver
Stanley Eibin
Paul E Farndale
David Fenton
Dominic Fitzgerald
Ben Firth
Andrew Flett
George Flyde
Richard Flyde
Robert Flyde

Jonathan Forrest
Stephen Forsythe
Arnie Fort
Malcolm Gardner
Peter Garford
Richard Garford
Ben Garford
Shirley Gavin
Frank Gee
Marcus Goldsbrough
Paul A Grace
Michael Grayson
Martin Greenwood
Adrian Greenwood
Susan Gross
Richard Gudgeon
Paul Martin Guest
Kevin Halligan
John Hancock
Roger W Hardaker
Mark Hassall
Chris Hawkridge
Ian Hemmens
Paul A Hodgson
Antony Hudson

RIBERS

Eric Hughes
Brian Hunt CH66
James R Isherwood
Philip Jackson
Mahesh Johal
Mark Jones
John C Kermode
Gary J Kerr
George Kowalczyk
David Knott
Mark Kristovic
Calvin Lawrence
Marc Lawrence
Michael C Leadbeater
Alexander Lee
Dale Lee
Eric Lee
Graham Leng
Rev Malcolm Lorimer
James Lovedale
Revd Nigel F Mason
Eric Markham
Joseph Marzec
Don McKeown
Catherine Mills
Max Milburn

Reetesh Mistry
David B Mitchell
David Moore
Paul Moreton
Andrew Muff
Andrew Norton
Andrew Padgett
Clive Alistair Palmer
Colin Parker
Chris Patterson
Finlay Pickles
Stephen Pickles
Steve Procter
Janet Rawnsley
Matthew Rishworth
Graham Rollinson
Ian Rostron
Mark Rymer
Mark Scully
Martyn Sharp
Neil F Shaw
John Simpson
Bill Simpson
Darran Stephen Slator
Mick Skelton
Graeme Smith

Paul R Smith
Adam Spolnik
Jeff Spolnik
Richard Stretton
Robert K Swithinbank
Ben Sykes
Joe Szalkiewicz
Mark R Thornton
Gareth James Walker
Paul Walker
Philip Walker
Andy Waller
Chris Walsh
Richard Wardell
Ian Webster
Benjamin Mark Welby
Sue Wellings
Katie Whyatt
In Memory of Richard Carl Wilby
Chris Wilkinson
Damien Wilkinson
Kieran J Wilkinson
Frankie Williams
Pete Williams
Paul Wood
Stephen Woodhouse

Bradford City vs Swansea City at Wembley Stadium, February 2013. Image by Paul Thompson.

BANTAMSPAST: HISTORY REVISITED

The History Revisited series of books published by BANTAMSPAST provides a fresh perspective on the history of football in Bradford. The series explains why things happened as they did rather than simply provide the chronological or statistical based narrative of events that is common to many sports histories. Between them the planned volumes will provide a definitive history, challenging existing accounts.

Produced in a consistent style in both hardback and softback editions, the books are likely to become future collectables and an authoritative reference.

The first volume in the series, **A HISTORY OF BRADFORD CITY AFC IN OBJECTS** by John Dewhirst was published in 2014 and met with critical acclaim as possibly the best book to have been published about the club's history. Hunter Davies described it as 'The best illustrated history of any club he had ever read'.

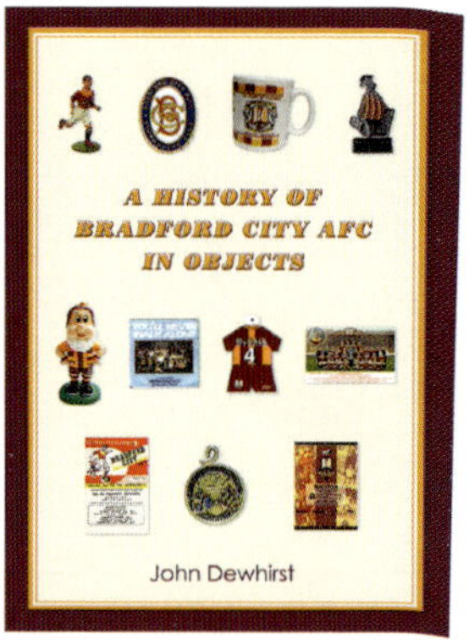

REINVENTING BRADFORD CITY is the second volume in the series.

The third volume, **ROOM AT THE TOP** by John Dewhirst (published in May, 2016) tells the origins of professional football in Bradford and the nineteenth century rivalry of Manningham FC and Bradford FC that shaped their twentieth century relationship as members of the Football League. It explains the formation of the two clubs, their secession from the rugby union and the background to their conversion to association football. It challenges existing explanations of how and why the Northern Union - precursor to the Rugby League - was formed in 1895. It is of equal interest to rugby and soccer fans and also provides a fresh perspective to the urban and social history of Victorian Bradford. At over 500 pages in size it is the largest book ever published about Bradford sport with coverage of the origins of activities as diverse as cricket, gymnastics, rowing and cycling. It also tells the long forgotten military heritage of Manningham FC and Bradford FC and the story of how Valley Parade and Park Avenue were developed.

Details can be found at https://johndewhirst.wordpress.com/

A fourth volume, **WOOL CITY RIVALS** (to be published in 2017/18) will examine the twentieth century rivalry of City and Park Avenue and include a variety of long forgotten artefacts and memorabilia relating to the two clubs.

Subscriber editions will be available by mail order for each volume and the books will be available from Amazon, Waterstones (Wool Exchange, Bradford) and Salts Mill Bookshop.

To get details of future releases, register your interest by contacting glorious1911@paraders.co.uk and follow tweets from @woolcityrivals as well as @bantamspast

The Bantamspast History Revisited series:

vol 1: 978-0-9566984-4-5 *A History of Bradford City AFC in Objects, by John Dewhirst Bantamspast 2014*

vol 2: 978-0-9566984-6-9 *Reinventing Bradford City: The Extraordinary Story of Bradford City's Modern History, 1985-2016, by Jason McKeown Bantamspast 2016*

vol 3: 978-0-9566984-5-2 *Room at the Top - The Origins of Professional Football in Bradford and the Rivalry of Bradford FC and Manningham FC, by John Dewhirst Bantamspast 2016*

vol 4: 978-0-9566984-7-6 *The Wool City Rivals - Bradford City AFC and Bradford (Park Avenue) AFC, by John Dewhirst Bantamspast 2018*